WITHDRAWN

ALLEGORICAL IMAGERY

809.031
T893a

ALLEGORICAL IMAGERY

Some Mediaeval Books and Their Posterity

BY ROSEMOND TUVE

1966

PRINCETON UNIVERSITY PRESS

PRINCETON, NEW JERSEY

Copyright © 1966 by Princeton University Press

ALL RIGHTS RESERVED

L.C. Card 65-14312

Printed in the United States of America

by Princeton University Press

Foreword

OUR present state is one of uncertainty as to what the sixteenth century meant by "allegorical reading," still more what they enjoyed in it. Granted the wide, and proper, variations in meanings of "allegory," the great difference between secular and religious use of the mode, the vast mediaeval development with its accompanying iconographical complexities, it seemed sensible to look for this meaning not among writings these readers could not know (those that were as yet unwritten, like Blake's and Coleridge's criticism, or the *Mariner*) but among writings upon which they were nourished. I therefore examined the uses, pleasures and apparent meaning of "allegory" in certain available mediaeval texts, famous even in the earlier centuries for their successful use of this figurative mode. All were of respectable size artistically, all caused the development of iconographical convention, all were "worth reading" quite aside from historical considerations, all would have been so regarded in the century concerned.

I tried in each case to "give the works their head," to follow where I was led rather than impose judgment or ask questions, to read works of art as if that were the one status that counted. Until the earlier work had freedom to make its own mark, I asked no question of influence or usefulness, and accounted literary pleasure, not serviceable usefulness in a literary-historical situation, to be the author's aim. But I have been adamant about the question of accessibility. If a work was not to hand for sixteenth-century use and reading, and in the form which we now can re-read, with the pictures we now can observe, I have paid no attention to it however interesting its use of allegory. Indeed, I have made no attempt to be complete, since the conclusions are not based on numbers of works but on kinds of response. Surprising and reliably disciplined and firm ideas result from such a procedure. I took sure evidence where I could find it, and where I could have no answer, asked no question.

In particular, both the practice of Spenser and the pleasures of reading him are affected. This is not a book on Spenser, but he is the author I should most wish to illumine the reading of. I unabashedly use examples from him for any purpose.

CA † Jan 4 '67

158820

ACKNOWLEDGMENTS

The AUTHOR acknowledges with great gratitude the generous permission of the following to reproduce illustrations, or quote, from early materials in their care: the Bodleian Library, Oxford, the British Museum, the Bibliothèque Nationale, and libraries of the Institut Mazarin and the Arsenal, Paris, the Bibliothèque Royale, Brussels, the municipal library of Rouen and the libraries of the universities of Harvard and Valencia; with gratitude for the same to the Fitzwilliam Museum, Cambridge University, The Master and Fellows of St. John's College, Cambridge, the Master and Fellows of Magdalene College, Cambridge. A particularly special debt is owed to the last-named and to the Pepysian Librarian for permission to reproduce with sufficient fullness from MS.Pepys 2258 to treat that manuscript's relations to the material of Book III; to the *Journal of Warburg and Courtauld Institutes* for permission to use similar illustrations and materials (quite differently presented) in Chapter Two; and to the entire staff, over the years, of Duke Humphrey's Library in the Bodleian.

The EDITOR has made minor stylistic changes in preparing the manuscript. Footnotes were standardized only when pertinent information was lacking. Quotations in the text and footnote citations have been checked for accuracy against those books available in the Princeton University Library. Changes have been made only where a definite error was found. Obsolete characters have been modernized and some punctuation has been added to Wright's text. Otherwise the text stands as Professor Tuve left it in manuscript. For the sake of clarity, the full manuscript pages on which the illustrations occur have usually not been reproduced.

PUBLISHER'S NOTE

PRINCETON UNIVERSITY PRESS wishes to add here our sincere gratitude to Thomas P. Roche, Jr. His expenditure of time since Professor Tuve's death has made it possible to produce her book in a form that will be true, we hope, to her intentions.

CONTENTS

ALLEGORICAL IMAGERY

CHAPTER ONE
Problems and Definitions

I T MAY be interesting and salutary at the outset to exemplify the kinds of relations Elizabethans had with early materials by following visible footsteps—those of some sixteenth-century writer who out-and-out borrowed from the materials and shows it indubitably. We also need a few distinctions and working definitions, merely to get started, although in general it is preferable for these to arise gradually from the materials. We are attempting, for instance, to discover, instead of impose, a definition of allegory (for literary pieces, of this time, and character). The number of words spent defining and delimiting allegory in this decade could never have been foretold two generations ago, and yet certain well-inculcated nineteenth-century assumptions about interpretation cloud the language of theory, and rebellions against them cloud the theory itself. It is well to let the mediaeval works do their own defining. Of the first trouble, the most persistent case is the Coleridgean definition of allegory (and symbol), born of nineteenth-century German critical theory, not mediaeval usage. Of the second trouble, the revolt, a leading instance is the faithful dependence upon the four senses, which in many modern writings are more dogmatically and perseveringly applied than we find them to be by mediaeval writers.

It is mere chance and luck, perhaps, but both clarification through an unquestionable case in point, and a few needful distinctions, can be achieved by a short look at a minor writer who made literary use—provable use—of almost every mediaeval "kind" here treated—Lodge. With his fondness for mediaeval materials (which we find duplicated in others but not so well attested by specific evidence), he will point to many kinds of questions and materials we will encounter; he will demonstrate connections without our needing to present evidence for the fact of dependence, for he flatly plunders mediaeval sources. Lodge is a quite sufficiently ordinary figure, and if he read and used the thirteenth-century *De oculi morali*, we need not worry over whether it was too recherché a book for ordinary sixteenth-century writers to read with interest. This simplifies the first presentation of questions.

The striking and well-known example, of course, is Lodge's remaking of the Middle English *Gamelyn* into that *Rosalynde* of 1590 to which we owe *As You Like It*. Manuscripts are generally so neglected as carriers of materials—textually and through illustrations—down into Elizabethan times, that it is right to remark that Lodge had to find *Gamelyn* in manuscript. However, since he probably thought it Chaucer's (the tale intended for the Cook), it would have an untypical eminence. This is scarcely true of some other mediaeval texts which Alice Walker showed Lodge to have used.[1] Both Thomas of Hibernia's fourteenth-century collection of sayings from the fathers, the *Manipulus florum*, and the thirteenth-century *De oculi morali* were common mediaeval books, but their commonness to a late sixteenth-century English author of no great pretensions to learning is not self-evident, and we would have hesitated to claim it as a likely thing. At any rate, Lodge used the *Manipulus* just as some mediaeval predecessor would have, or as Christine de Pisan did nearly two hundred years before him; and he makes neither a flourish nor a secret about using the *De oculi*. He found, or could find, both in print.

Miss Walker mentioned two other printed sources of large portions of Lodge's *Catharos* (1591), which, when we examine them, turn out also to have been mediaeval inheritances. The first is a *Somme des Pechez* by the French Franciscan Jean Benedicti; it is an elaboration of so common a type of mediaeval book, one so fruitful for figurative treatment of the virtues, that we shall have to give a whole chapter (Two) to pursuing some of the many and beautifully illustrated forms taken by such *sommes*. The second is the *Dialogues of creatures moralised* which Lodge read evidently in the printed sixteenth-century English version (STC 6815, 1535?).

---

[1] Other writers have not had the benefit of the kind of attention given to Lodge in A. Walker, "The Reading of an Elizabethan," *RES*, vol. 8 (1932), 264-81. On my ascription of the first to Thomas "Hibernicus" rather than "Palmer," see P. G. C. Campbell's study on the sources of Christine's *L'Épitre d'Othéa* (Paris, 1924), ch. 6. The article mentions numerous other mediaeval sources used by Lodge; for example, in *Wits Miserie* he evidently turned consistently for details on the sins to the fourteenth-century Holcot, but I choose rather the uninvestigated works; Holcot's popular pieces have been especially usefully described (for those interested in how images are transmitted) in B. Smalley, *English Friars and Antiquity* (Oxford, 1960), ch. 7.

Since our interest is not so much in later authors' attitudes toward mediaeval materials as in their continued use of them and pleasure in them, we do not care very much whether Lodge realized that the *Dialogues* are an early-to-middle fourteenth-century compilation; he surely did not know that they are probably by a Milanese physician Mayno de' Mayneri.[2] Like so many books which remained accessible, this one represents a whole genre and is but one exemplar of a long roster of similar mediaeval books. We shall see that Elizabethan dependence is upon mediaeval books that were eminently typical, not singular, and not "ahead of their time." The "kind" here exemplified is the collection of moralized exempla. Since the 1100's it had flourished rankly, and Welter's whole detailed volume is needed for mere description of these vastly numerous texts. One thing that astonishes us in his footnotes and data is the frequency with which collections achieved early printings; these books are often hidden in that corner still rather dark to us—sixteenth-century Latin books that were read but did not become famous classics. The example everyone knows is the *Gesta Romanorum*. But until there is more investigation of the unlighted bridges between manuscript and book publication, we shall not be able to judge how much effect *early* translation into vernaculars, and a manuscript tradition of illustration, had to do with a mediaeval book's chances for extended life into the Renaissance. The *Dialogues* had the latter of these advantages, but its translation into three vernaculars may not antedate printing.

[2] This ascription has seeped into a few catalogues since Rajna's work on this book in the 1880's; see *Giornale storico*, vols. 3, 4, 10, 11 (1884-88); also—depending on Rajna—J. T. Welter, *L'exemplum dans la litt.* (Paris, 1927), pp. 357-60. Rajna in his series of articles, whence we can build up a list of manuscripts, data on illustrations, etc., attributes the *Dialogues* to the mid-1300's physician and author of some note, Mayno de' Mayneri (so attributed in the Cremona Manuscript), and demonstrates various errors connected with attributions in B.Nat. MS.lat.8512 to a Nicholas Pergamenus, evidently nonexistent though become common in catalogues listing this item. The manuscript title is most often *Contemptus sublimitatis*, and many editions appear under the title *Destructorium vitiorum*, not to be confused with a different book of that title— a preachers' manual often reprinted in the Renaissance by Alexander Carpenter?, studied by G. R. Owst in *The Destructorium Viciorum of Alexander Carpenter* (London, 1932). Correction of these facts promoting errors in identification makes it likely that the list of known manuscripts will increase, and earlier forms of the several translations may be found.

A striking point is that Lodge finds it worth borrowing from for its most "mediaeval" element—he copies the moralizations of the fables. The plan of the *Catharos* (to overdignify that catchall pamphlet) shows that he snatched the stories, amusing as some are, largely because he had use for the morals that follow each. He thus differs from the nineteenth-century revivers and readers who busied themselves with these collections and characteristically omitted or telescoped the "dull allegories" in favour of including all daily-life interest and story motifs. To the sixteenth-century borrower, universality or a usefulness independent of epoch resides precisely in the significancies. I suspect that this is typical. Where we brush off the didacticism or the figurative reading of tales and stress their interest as straight recording or anecdotal narrative, the didacticism was, without any self-consciousness or sense of historical alienness, just as interesting, to a Renaissance reader of old books.

The 122 fables, conveyed as the title says in *Dialogues of creatures*, are often good stories, and occasionally clever, but that is not what makes this a gay book. The compiler has a turn for vigorous conversation and for the drama of a rhetorical situation, conveyed in tone, gesture and unobtrusive incongruities. The squabbles he invents are between such opponents as the Air and the Wind, the Seabanks and the Sea, the Carbuncle and the Glass, the Ass and the Wolf, the Dolphin and the Eel. The dialogue in each is followed by its "ditty," and this by its expectable, or more often its surprising, moral application or reading. Frequently, barefaced extravagances are presented with comical decorum. The quality most often felt is a serious-faced outrageousness, and one is convinced that the book had this from the beginning, the "morals" so-called being meanwhile intended as quite sensible, and readable by us as such. The book was, of course, to be read in snippets, mined for anecdotes, used or read orally. It was translated into Dutch and French as well as English; but some of the Latin editions are the most attractive as books. The collection was thought worth printing in Gouda, Antwerp, Köln, Stockholm (the first Stockholm-printed book), Geneva, Lyons, Paris, and more than once in four of these cities. The tradition in the woodcuts, as I have seen it, varies little as to plan or subject, but greatly in skill; some have much charm of design.[3]

⁋Of the Locke and the kaye.
Dialogo.yyiii

FIGURE 1*

Thus begins Fable 23, a dispute between the Lock and the Key: "A kaye there was som tyme. Which was verye goode/ and plesauntlye oppynde her locke/ and also made it faste/ in so moche that the patrone/ and ownar therof reioicyd greatly therin. Upon a tyme thys Locke fel in froward mynde and grutchyd agaynst the kay and sayde thus, O wykked creature why pursewyst thow me thus continually, dayly thow entrist into my bowellys and tournyst my stomake uppe and downe. Cece of thy greef and trowble me no more/ or ellys I shall caste the awaye or make the crokyd. To whom the kaye answerde & sayde. Sustyr thow spekyst evyll. By me thowe arte conservyd in pros-

---

* Please see the List of Illustrations and Sources following the text.

[3] Miss Walker's mention of at least eight Latin, three Dutch, and two French editions, before the end of the 1400's, can, for us, take the place of listed editions, since we do not have to support the undisputed fact of its availability; Lodge read it. I have used numerous Latin editions, the French, the Dutch and the English (that used by Lodge is STC 6815; the abridged Wyer translation [STC 6816] of the first seven is of little consequence); but I have seen only one MS., B.Nat. lat.8507, one of the mere five or six illustrated copies noted by Rajna (*op.cit.*, n. 2 above, see vol. II, p. 52n.). It is convenient to quote from an edition more likely to be owned by libraries—Haslewood's 1816 reprint *Dialogues of creatures moralised*, the translation of STC 6815, with cuts from the Gouda edition and not unlike the general series, though unbeautiful. It is worth noting that, if we did not know it to be a fact, the probability of an Elizabethan of the '90's making use of an Antwerp-printed English book *ca.* 1535 would seem like a hazardous guess; I shall indulge in none so shaky.

perite. . . ." But notwithstanding, the lock was not pleased; in a
fit of petulance it suddenly "stoppyd fast the hole/ and wolde
not suffre the kaye entyr into hym." Then came the owner, could
not open the door, and in sudden heat smote off the lock and
broke it. "And the kaye . . . sayde"—and here comes the ditty,
often not so concise and pert in the vernaculars as in the Latin.
And after it, the moralization proper, with quoted *auctores*, in
this case admonishing those "that desire to lyve peceablye with
ther neybowris" that they should "bere parte of ther charges, as
the Apostle wrytythe ad Galat. vi., Every one of yowe bere the
burdon of othir."

Or there is the Chayne (Fable 24) that has had quite enough
of carrying the Cawdron daily to the flame and never getting
even a share of some good morsel that the pot boils up. But he
receives the smart rebuke, "Thou servyst me to my hurte . . .
holdiste me uppe to the fyre . . . and cawsiste my sydes to be
brent and consumyd." The moral of this little encounter is no
other than: if you desire to do service to other men, serve them
to their pleasure. The Rosemary plant (Fable 25), which can
make ground fertile, is begged by the barren Field to come and
make it fruitful: "O pastor egregie et bone custos/ descende ad
me & protege me," says the Latin, echoing liturgical language.
She takes up residence there and all things flourish. To our surprise, the moralization of this fable is that commonwealths should
choose good and learned governors. The point of the similitude
with the fertility-bringing Rosemary is then repeated in the
timeworn advice of the Roman king to the French one, to edu-
cate his sons "in lyberall seyence" or he will have as successor on
his throne *asinus coronatus*. Part of our pleasure is evidently
expected to lie in seeing that a governor's learning is to a state
as the fertility-bringing rosemary is to a barren field.

Catching sight of a point of mere prudential alertness, of cunning in the true and Baconian sense, is quite as usual a meaning
of "moralize" as is the drawing of a moral in our sense. The collection is typical in that its author makes no such distinction, and
hands out the "wisdom" of intelligently practical hints through
just the same sort of figures as serve to uncover a deeper wisdom.
The "creatures" quietly witness to the sense and intelligent rationale of the universe as readily as to its moral laws; all phenomena
"discover" not only the probity of their Author, but also shadow

all the kinds of wisdom, lower and higher. Trivial as some examples seem, I am not overreading here, as the Prologue will presently show.

The Ass and the Wolf (Fable 107) are sawing together, with the humble Ass ready to work either at top or bottom of the saw, but the envious Wolf, at the bottom, steadily blows the dust into his fellow's eyes. It only hits the timber and falls back into his own eyes, and as we expect, this shows what happens to the malicious who dig pits for their neighbours. It is picked up by Lodge for the same use (under Envy). Yet the serious moral charge brought by the Silver against the Iron—that munitions make wars—and answered sharply with a long accusation that Silver has been behind centuries of evil deeds, from adultery to treachery, is moralized merely to warn that one should know when to hold one's peace or one may be out-argued.

Another oddity to our modern minds is the lameness of some of the story sections, those portions we have been taught to think were the focus of literary interest and the author's real concern, the "moral" being tacked on to satisfy public, church, the stuffy bourgeois—anyone, in short, but the composing author. But we read stories—and several are chosen by Lodge—which consist of how the black Crow, jealous of the whiteness of the Swan, blackens him while he sleeps; or of Laurus, a Bird, who being a shipman too, greedily overloaded the ships he captained so that they sank; or another in which the hawk Osmarillus and his partner, a goshawk, take a quail, to whom they give the seemingly pre-decided choice of being eaten on the spot or guiding them to her nest, where she and her young will be consumed in one multiple feast. There is no struggle between choices, no cunning twist, no revealed novel foible of personality. It is clear that we are expected to take our pleasure in the plain observation of similitude: in noting how clearly this Swan figures a human being taken, when not vigilant, by the devil, who cannot endure the cleanness and purity of God's servants; how covetousness can everywhere be seen meeting its ineluctable end; how the humble quail, deciding to die alone, can elect to set "the commune profite" above "syngler avayle."

Lodge extends the quail story to cover Divines, who if they were right-thinking fowl would die themselves and spare their flocks; in the "Laurus" he copies the original's application to greedy Merchants. He is engaged in the common mediaeval game of allocating vices-and-virtues class by class, estate by estate—a conventional design Chapman enjoyed using in *Bussy d'Ambois,* and fitfully present in Nashe and Dekker. Like the looser definition of "moralize," the pre-eminence of significance over an interesting story is typical of exempla collections. Hence, if they appear shorn of their moralizations by impatient nineteenth-century editors, or if we are too largely in search of the modern pleasure in provocative surface or local detail in narrative, the pleasure which is often the only one in such stories escapes us. It was clearly shared by mediaeval author and Renaissance imitator: the pleasure in pure seeing-of-similitude, taken in as immediately as an echo, while conceiving the literal story, as one sees a pebble under water with more significance than a pebble. Neither water nor pebble offers any great novelties; what pleases is merely to observe the nature of the world and correspondences one can see in it.

In Lodge's use of the Sea and the Seabanks, whose rambunctious quarrelings he copies outright, we see more of that comical pseudo-realism which is a special attraction of the *Dialogus creaturarum.* That it is a natural concomitant of the genre of fable, we are reminded by Spenser's example of this precise "kind"—the Oak and the Brier in *Februarie* of the *Shepheardes Calender.* Spenser had read this kind of mediaeval literature and had missed little it could teach him (as *Mother Hubbard's Tale* shows). The pleasure in mediaeval specificity and realism is more apparent in the Renaissance than is our typical interest in mediaeval detail which is "romantically" removed and strange—a connotation not yet in their word "romance"; we shall note this more especially in dealing with romances, where this pithy and matter-of-fact homeliness was a stronger influence on the fights and the conversations of the *Faerie Queene* than was any exotic unreality. It is barely worthwhile even to notice, as an analogue to *Februarie,* the Cedar (proverbially ambitious) left unprotected in the blast (Fable 35). Similarity in "kind," which produces similar conventions and relation to figurative meaning, had regularly produced the brash conversations, the minute, suddenly actualized details or tones of voice, the super-dramatic drama and super-weighty moralizations. The latter are often unexpectedly specialized: the Brier dies not for Pride but for scorning old age, such as Gods themselves have. The ditty of Fable 35, "Of the hyghe Cedre Tre," reads: "They that be rulers may nothinge avayle. If they that be undyr of helpe doth them fayle."

Just as in Spenser or in Lodge, we are expected to be sufficiently aware of how fables work—and sufficiently alert—to see the "moral" double meaning almost as soon as we embark on the description or tale, the later outright statement of moral point being deliberately heavy-footed. Thus our enjoyment of the doubleness involves tiny details and is subtler. It is typical that the near-irony does not corrode the serious sense of the "moral" ("extended signification" would be more precise), and we catch this habit if we read at length.[4] We, like earlier men, take amusement from the figurative sense long before its statement, and from the fact that fantasy is likely to be more striking in the literal story. For example, the overweening Cedar Tree who ". . . magnyfied hyr self inwardly and sayd within her self: I am gretly spokyn of/ and lawdid . . . for my beawte which is worthy to be lawdyd. But I trowe that if the smale plantis and treys that . . . growe rownde abowt me/ were cut down or pluckyd uppe I should apere most goodely and large withowte comparyson. [It were best and surest] to mayme them or fell them down betymes/ or they ascend so highe/ that they take not awaye my worshyppe . . . [hence she caused them all to be cut or pulled up by the root, wherefore] she aperyd nakyd and bare and within fewe dayes a great wynde blewe . . . & the prowd Cedre was Curvate and overthrowe. . . ."

Making exception for its greater variety and gaiety, the *Dialogus* can typify a considerable body of popular and accessible moralized exempla literature that was in its very nature allegorical. It is now time to look more closely at what precise kind of allegorical reading such books induced and the exact rhetorical character of their figures. The general points made about the character, popularity and uses of these books, their combination of narrative and signification and the types of relation made, exactly what they do when they "moralise" (the word which

---

[4] Any rustic raconteur has all these noted characteristics untaught, and of course, Renaissance tellers deliberately highlight the signs of the low style. One is wary of claims about how the Latin was felt by contemporary readers, but it is hard to believe that the pert conversations were not similarly responded to: the crisp interchanges between Sun and Moon, or the sharp talk of Stella transmontana and the other stars, or "De auro et plumbo" (Fable 19).

won out over others for allegorical figures), their way of applying figurative power, the assumed correspondences and serious
uncovering of universal meanings, the underlying particularity
that was simultaneously described and appreciated for its own
realistic sake—these various general points could be well exemplified from a Nicole Bozon or a *Gesta Romanorum*.[5]

Some stories or examples have a relation to their morals or
significances which even no known misdefinition could admit
under the figure of allegory. The Lead (Fable 19) goes to the
Gold, and says, "Why art thowe so prowde agayn me. Am not
I of the substaunce of metallys as welle as thowe." When, in the
suggested trial by fire of the virtue that is in them, the boastful
lead vanishes and the meek gold is purified, the notion we are
expected to see is that "much prowde people *be in that same case*
thinking they have vertewe/ which *is not in* them." Or a Topaz
(Fable 16), set in a cross in St. Peter's in Rome, was "infectte
with bad counsell" and said to himself, "What lyf is this, to con-
tinewe alway in the Chirche, I wyll for a season retourn to the
worlde that I may have a lytel recreacyn in it." Of course, the
monk out of his cloister, the topaz out of the cross, both lose the
worth they had in their fair setting, which they gave up so lightly.
The first of these stories is not figurative at all, save as inanimate
things speak—a prosopopoeia. Strength was not "in" the lead,
nor is it "in" the proud people. The second also is technically only
a comparison—if it is a figure at all; quite literally, the priest,
like the topaz, should have stayed in the place that gave him
value. It is interesting, and perhaps unfortunate, that it is apropos
of such parallels that editors or describers of texts most commonly remark sagely and with approval, "here the analogy is
not so strained." But this is not the kind of analogy that allegorical reading is exercised on. We apprehend a likeness, and from
it a moral point; but in several of these cases there is no metaphor to read, the comparison being based upon a property or

[5] The last-named collection limits its applications to a stricter allegorical reading. What assures us we are looking at common things is not the well-known
few titles but the great tribe of now-forgotten exempla collections which were
printed, usually after a long manuscript life; Welter's notes hold many such
surprises. The stories became proverbial, or were moralized because they were.
I have not separated off the beast fables and Aesopian materials and have kept
sub-kinds like miracle-collections and political-history exempla out of the foreground.

situation quite literally predicated of the creatures treated. Things talk or act; but only the topaz (and it only if given quite different elaboration) could start off a fiction to which we could give an allegorical reading.

We may recall, to point up the difference, the Rosemary planted in the field, thus figuring the good governor. I am not confusing the question by doubting the rosemary's power to make fields literally more fertile, but pointing out that Fertility has become metaphorical—in a commonwealth and as the result of learning. So too with the Crow-devil, who could not stand "whiteness" in the Swan-soul. So with the envious Wolf, whose blown dust comes back on himself; we immediately metaphorically translate "dust." Not so with Laurus the Shipman-bird, however; he greedily filled his ship too full; so do human captains. We could write about an allegorical ship, but the author has not told that story. The Lock that would not suffer its Key is fully capable of turning into a variety of allegorical forms of the notion that each must help suffer the cost of the other's duty. The difference is not in content, nor is it in the area whence the vehicle is chosen, the type or fancifulness of the tale or the a priori likeness or unlikeness of two objects held in a similitude. Strain has nothing to do with it; lead is not more like a boastful person than a crow is like a devil or a smooth lock like a loving neighbour. The difference comes in the logic of the relation made *in this use or story* between the two terms of the comparison. Lead and the weak talker are merely likened on the grounds of not having strength to withstand anything, and in truth they have not; but governors can bring fertility and devils hate whiteness of soul in the faithful only as these words are capable of metaphorical meaning. Thus what is said about farfetched analogies is beside the point. It simply does not matter where the parallels are fetched from in allegory; what counts is whether a metaphorically understood relation is used to take off into areas where a similitude can point to valuable human action, or to matters of spiritual import.

These last two phrases concerning human action and spiritual import describe, respectively, moral allegory and allegory strictly so-called; although this is a distinction new to our discussion, it can be observed and defined through the materials in hand. Lodge uses none but "moral allegories." He always uses quails, intelligent griffons, clever hare-lawyers and the rest to tell us what we ought to do, or what someone is doing but ought not to. We may illustrate the allegorical reading he does *not* ask of us (though others of the *Dialogues do*) by telling a story that is susceptible of a further reading than we are expected to give it; and we shall see that it is even possible to detect an author's wishes in such a matter.

⟨Of the Smaragde and the Rynge.
Dialogo.　　yiiij.

FIGURE 2

We may consider the fable of the Smaragdus (Fable 14), greenest of all stones, that was set in a ring of gold. And many came from far countries to see it. Upon a day, the Ring spoke uncourteously to the stone and said, "Thou haste long contynued/ and dwellyde in my stacyon/ and nevyr paydest me/ for thy standynge. Wherefore delyvre thy dewtye for thyn habitacyon/ and goe thy waye. Or I shall take from the all that thowe haste/ and putte thee owte of thy lodgynge." The Smaragdus, though maintaining that it is because of him that the Ring has been put on the King's finger, says, "Yf thow wylte nedis expell me," sell me then and from the proceeds "take thy dewtye for my howse-rent." But when the Ring had so done, behold he found himself but "bare and abject." But the moral has nothing to do with the obvious moral drift touching harsh methods toward debtors; it is: The servant of Christ is worshipful in like wise "as long as he retaynyth and kepith precyows vertewys within hym. And if he caste them from him he is to be cast awaye. . . ." The relation of the clear green stone to its significance is metaphorical rather than comparative, figuring virtue; and further, the image is turned aside from moral instruction to say something rather about the ultimate destiny of those who, asking that their virtue should pay off, find that they are become the empty rings whom the King of heaven casts away.

I have made one illegal extension of the figure, to demonstrate that that activity on our parts can be detected and refrained from; at the last I named the King. The text did not direct me thus to bring in the common image of Christ as the virtuous soul's Bridegroom, and I doubt if the author was thinking of it. We have, without it, true allegory. Not instead of, but in addition to, the moral of "it is vyle to be partyd from a worthy thinge," the story is so told as to reach into a signification touching our destiny as souls, to be cast away, or to be worn on the King's finger. This is an "allegorical reading" in the sense that long history and uncountable pages of interpreted texts had developed the meaning of that word; and this text of the fable itself demands it, or parts thereof are left idle.

The basic distinction lies in which particular realm of meaning the figure carries us into. We have only rediscovered the old commonplace, that moral allegory makes us read about how we should act, while allegory more strictly so-called brings us to the view of what we ought to believe. It seems to me unsafe to refer too easily to the traditional four senses in dealing with later allegory; but it is wise to make at least the present distinction, partly because the two sorts of figures operate differently artistically, and partly because the distinction (unnamed) is observed by writers.[6]

FIGURE 3

[6] It will be convenient later to quote the common mediaeval saying about quid credas which has done most to keep the commonplace common; see n. 20 below. We should not be rigid about the terms since the periods concerned were not; where the divisions are made with precision and care, there is generally some specific source (as in Harington's *Apology*; see II, 202 of the edition in Gregory Smith's *Elizabethan Critical Essays*, Oxford, 1904). The continued life of the distinction pursued in the text is obviously a part of one of our questions, whether allegory, as the usual Renaissance poet understood it, can be secular.

Another fable (No. 32) will demonstrate how the difference in the desired end governs minor artistic choices. "In a sertayne herbar" there grew a fair Rosier, and a Partridge desired to have some of the roses and said, "O thou beawtyfull flowre of all flowris graunt me of thy Rosys for I desyre to refresshe my self a while in these swete odowris." The Rosier answered, "Come to me moste interely belovyd sustyr . . ."; but when the Partridge had flown thither to gather the flowers, the sharp spines pricked its feet so sore it would gladly have departed without roses. "The Rosier," we are told, "betokenithe *the world*." The moral talks about riches, and, with the exception of one suggestion, this would be straight moral allegory about the unrealized pains that attend worldly desires. But to our surprise, by a quotation from Gregory, riches have thorns since they wound man's mind by the "prykkynge of their inordinate love." Though this underscores the wooing or seduction phraseology of the tale,[7] it is apparent that we must not press too far what could easily have been conventional religious allegory strictly so-called. For this careless sensualist does not wed saeculum; nor is he made a captive of that usurping lover who steals the soul from its real spouse. The image is a lesser one and keeps us within the narrower bounds of didactic warning anent the true nature of mixed evil-and-good (the beautiful, urging to excess). There is no indication that "pluck my roses" is truly symbolic, and this would disturb the narrative as told; in it there is no place for lost honor or for the significances of union and allegiance that made the marriage-image allegorically powerful.

One last fable in which the author fully extends the signification will perhaps make the formal difference which marks such figures quite clear. The reason why even indifferent authors can maintain this distinction lies in the fact that it is a difference in end and purport, not one in skill; a firm grasp of the distinguishing characteristic enables us to recognize a fully intended alle-

---

[7] There is no indication that the cant meaning of a Partridge as bawdy-house girl or harlot was to be taken, just as there is no warrant for obtruding the symbolical meaning of emeralds in Fable 14, or the fairly ordinary relation of the Carbuncle stone to the Virgin Mary, in Fable 17. When a traditional symbolical meaning is needed by the story and intended by the author, the manner of telling makes this apparent; I would propose that we should wait upon such indications.

gorical figure and will serve us well in reading masters of figurative language like Spenser. "There is a Fissh callyd Regina,"
says Fable 45, and she is so called "for she rulyth herself very
well" (*rego*). "A Water serpent callyd Idrus havynge many
hedes cam uppon a tyme to this Fissh and sayde. O Regina most
fayre to me before all othir fisshes, thow art . . . most interly
belovyd. And therefore I wyll be knytte unto thee . . . in holy
matrimony." To whom Regina answered, "That maye not be.
For it is not convenient." She means, of course, quoting *Eccles.*
xiii, that it is not fitting, and disregards the Lord's command that
every creature should seek out his own likeness or kind. The
serpent goes home "with confusyon," and the full purport of the
word is seen in the moral: "Every Crysten man shulde soo answer to the Devyl/ whan he temptith hym/ for *he is the olde
serpent* more subtyle than any thinge lyvynge. . . . And therefore
thus shulde every creature saye unto hym. Go thow fro me/ for
thowe arte not of my kynde. Nor thow arte noon of them that
shal be savyd. And if thou doo thus he cannotte abyde."

This is a fully developed allegorical image, and has to be so
read. Every likeness is metaphorical in nature: the old serpent
from the sea, the wooing, the non-kinship, the seven heads in
the illustrations showing that he was allegorically read, the magical strength of the refusal, which lies simply in recognizing and
stating the Adversary's identity. Of course, Regina is man, or
Anima. The marriage-image was best suited to draw in the desired ideas—of seduction, devouring, ravishment, pre-eminently
of full union and the giving away of the self. This idolatrous allegiance is resisted by Regina, but also the point about not marry-
ing out of her kind is important; Satan has lost his title to
heavenly sonship. This conception of man, as that creature whose
property it is to be salvationis capax, who belongs to the kind
that may be delivered from the ravishment of death and united
to the heavenly original whence it sprang, is a conception of man
which is of central importance to the question of allegorical reading. It is remarkable that it should have carried over into secular
writing, even into allegorized classical imagery, a sort of large
popular residue from more careful and precise understandings
of allegory in theological materials. For a figure to reach into
the area where it is read as speaking of man's metaphysical situation, it must use with clarity the translatio that defines metaphor

as a figure of speech—as here the "marriage" immediately conveys to us ideas touching the soul's captivation by evil. There may or may not be need of the systems of analogical correspondences between natural and spiritual reality so often spoken of, but what we do find is reference to man's ultimate destiny or meaning, perhaps his relations to supernatural Being—usually in some ancient similitude or element accustomed to bear this burden of reference.

If we turn to visual images, we find that it is easier to experience, in a way that does not admit of argument, the absence or presence of elements that make us respond to an image at this "allegorical" depth. Obviously we will now walk clumsily over ground that is daily flown over with competence and success both by art historians and readers.[8] Nevertheless, where there is opportunity for cooperation between the two fields of pictorial and literary art (and the use of evidence from iconography has entered English studies to stay), hurry and confusion on the very simplest mental steps and distinctions are the source of some grave difficulties. I shall therefore count no difference or distinction too elementary to mention. The numerous illustrators of the *Dialogues* have pictured the Lock and Key (Fig. 1); so also the Ring and the Stone (Fig. 2). It is obvious that it is not possible to detect the traits in either object which enabled the teller to give the Lock's actions or the Ring's emptiness a metaphorical point. Yet this is what enabled the fictions to constitute comment upon human self-importance or human weaknesses (moral allegory). With a simple comparatio like the Topaz set *in* the cross—

[8] No originality and no discoveries will be encountered in this attempt to observe when and how allegorical meaning, or even moral meaning, enters seen figures and read figures. I have purposely kept clear of similar attempts not focussed on the literary problems of this present book (like Panofsky's careful introduction to *Studies in Iconology*, New York, 1939, or Pächt's *Rise of Pictorial Narrative in Twelfth-Century England*, Oxford, 1962), which can be so much more sophisticated. For identical terminology is not possible, procurable evidence differs and overcomplication in the artistic problems would make the different complication of literary problems harder. Of course, one does not suppose this a chiefly modern question for speculation; Leonardo discussed it. Though its eighteenth-century developments were phenomenally rich, comparisons are not profitable here, given the different grounding of sixteenth-century notions of symbolizing meaning (e.g. the writers had not been nourished on eighteenth-century German classical scholarship).

if the other term (the priest *in* his church) were portrayed in juxtaposition—a cunning interpreter might conceivably see the naked comparison and jump to a moral point, from general notions about clerics "in" the church. Move to the Rosier story (Fig. 3), and not all the ingenuity in the world could extract the metaphorical significance of thorns as that which, in riches, pricks us with inordinate love of them. The sensuous experience of thorns which we share with St. Gregory would carry us as far as "prickly"—the logical base of comparison that allows the metaphor—but it becomes obvious that metaphor works through paralleling concepts that are too abstract or subtle to convey through the shared properties one can indicate visually.

We may observe also that the Rose-tree could be that of the *Roman de la rose,* or that of which Yeats wrote in the Easter Rising poems, or that in the nearest garden; further, we may try to think of any device by which the designer could unmistakably indicate that *this* Rose-tree is not these but mundus fraudulentus. Without another image, he cannot tell us to think well or ill of the roses, and even a worm in one would say something else; meanwhile, the metaphorical heart of the exemplum lay in an idea that would defy short statement, that the Rosier was saeculum, with all the burden that carries to New Testament readers.

FIGURE 4

Yet in this next picture, which illustrates Fable 38, "De syrenella," just such an evaluative distinction is conveyed (Fig. 4). We mistrust her and know why. The reader need not be told that when the boatman leapt into that sea he was destroyed. What the reader already knows is exactly the factor which enables this picture to evoke an evaluating response both sure and clear. I do not mean a "single" response, for even this simple image has the ambiguity of delightful-*and*-noxious, and we all allow the siren, without second thought, the beauty she has not to the eye (Fig. 5). The sole difference between this fable and that of the Rose-tree lies in what the auditor or spectator knows before-hand—some practically universally known story which has given an accepted conventional significance to sirens. This factor pro-vides many of the "moralizations" of fables such as those in the *Dialogus*; the conceptual or evaluative point that enables a figure to say something about quid agas (i.e. moral allegory) can even be communicated wordlessly if we already possess the notion which acts as a key. This is true for the unsaid significance of verbal images, too, and is a major objection to modern clichés about depending only on what is "in" the poem. Unstated moral-allegory meanings may be "in" a conventional image in one poem and not in it in another.

FIGURE 5

But it takes something the fable does not have for us to see this boatman's death as the death of the soul; the siren does not represent quintessential evil to most of us, and thus we do not read in it Adam's Fall or any other all-inclusive myth of the origin of man's woe or the meaning of his life. Yet we do read just that in the pictures alone, even, of the Regina fable (Fig. 6). The old Serpent from under the sea cannot possibly be a morally indifferent creature; more than that, he cannot, in our culture, be an allegorically silent one. We cannot catch the Regina-wooing image unaided, but we catch sight of the notions which caused that image to develop, for we realize from recognizing Leviathan, the Apocalyptic Beast, the Adversary, how meta-physically significant a rape or union is here threatened. If, like men of many earlier centuries, we are accustomed to seeing in the seven heads the seven sins that were the chief mode of the capture, and if we have much other knowledge of this "sea," we read still more of the whole complex of ideas and feelings the figure tries to speak of. It may not have power upon us, but it has profundity and subtlety in itself. Most images that undeniably require or allow allegorical reading convey in this manner, through public figures or symbols, the needed concepts which trigger thought. The thoughts are not only judgments or evaluations on moral matters, but are ideas concerning ultimate destiny, divine beings, supernatural forces. These seem to need a surer and richer language than any private or contrived symbolism, since the interpretation of the literal with the metaphysical, as well as the moral, meanings is an element we persistently find in mediaeval allegory.

FIGURE 6

I suppose it is not necessary to underline the fact that the images do not *equate with* the concepts spoken of (if this were so, no images would be needed). Equation is not quite the process even in late classical and Fulgentian allegories of pagan gods, before different and deeper Christian understandings changed the figure. "Bad allegory" may use a set of concretions to mean nothing more or less than some set of concepts we could write out, and to which they are "equal," but even this is so hard to work out in practice that it is far scarcer in literature than in critical interpretation. Some statable concept or nameable abstraction is generally a key and an indication; but so is the literal "thing." "Leviathan the sea-beast" and the word, "Evil" are, respectively, the closest men have come to the bodies of meaning they refer to. They represent two of the ways we have developed to refer to things too complex to state in full, though experienced by all of us. There are not very many such great public images (quest, pilgrimage, marriage, death, birth, purgation, for example) and not very many such metaphysical problems.

It might be useful to point up certain facts through a picture still more undeniably "allegorical." For example: the likelihood that illustrations will use an acquired language of metaphors (acquired by learning, and based often on developments taking place through some centuries, but taken for granted as commonplaces in their times); the firm relevance, nonetheless, of the literal meanings of things portrayed, or (in stories) of the plain narrated events; the conceptual solidity or continuity, so that a "continued metaphor" becomes a complex of several ideas symbolically stated; the greater richness and condensation of such symbolic statement, though a brief and general discursive statement is all we can manage if we are asked to say what the image means; the way in which such pictures (though static as always) can, like literature, reach backward and forward in time. These accomplishments are more complicated in their theoretical statement than in practice; we apprehend very readily such differences between Fig. 7 and the Rose-tree or the Lock and Key.

Figure 7 is a fifteenth-century drawing from a manuscript translation, in MS. Bodley 283, of the *Somme le roi*. This is the best known mediaeval text of the popular "kind" represented by the second of Lodge's sources (Benedetti's *Summa*), which we indicated as ultimately mediaeval. One has something of a key, recognizing Christ by his cruciform halo; had we used the parallel picture from the French tradition of late thirteenth-century illumination of this text, the key would not be there, for Christ appears as simply a larger central tree. The text at this point is describing a garden-image which is structurally important in later treatises of the compilation, which underlies many another treatment of virtues and their nourishment or roots, and which uses numerous basic Christian doctrines—Christ in the temple of the heart, the nature of grace, the meanings of "paradise." Mediaeval materials on the virtues and vices prove so important for allegory that they will need a chapter (Two) to themselves, but the quoted image will make the picture at least readable, if not mov-

FIGURE 7

ing and true as it seems in context.[9] "Holy writ likneth a good man
and a good womman to a fair garden ful of grene and of faire
trees. . . . The grete gardener, that is God the fadre . . . maketh the
herte nesche and swete . . . and good erthe al redy . . . to be . . .

[9] The manuscript apparently translates the *Miroir* redaction; for all such matters see below ch. 2. Nevertheless, since the texts are very similar just here, I

graffed with goode graffes. These graffes ben the vertues that the Holy Gost gyveth of grace. . . . [He makes the heart as a paradise right delitable, full of good trees and precious.] But rigt as God sett ertheli paradis ful of goode trees and fruygt, and in the myddel sett the tree of lif. . . . Rigt so doth *gostly* to the herte the goode gardyner . . . for he sett the tree of vertue and in the myddel the tree of lif, that is Ihesu Crist, for he seith in the gospel, 'Who-so eteth my flesch and drynketh my blod hath lif with-out ende.' This tree wexeth grene and fair bi vertue ouer al this paradis, and bi vertue of this tree wexen, blowen, and beren fruygt alle the othere trees." (Italics mine.)

Although any of us would probably correctly interpret the water in the foreground, possibly only an earlier audience would divine from the fact that there are seven trees the realization that "This welle is departed in sevene stremes, that ben the sevene giftes of the Holy Gost, that wateren al the garden." And perhaps only the position of the picture at the head of the Pater Noster treatise expected in this compilation would tell even a mediaeval observer that "The sevene peticiouns, that are askynges, ben as sevene rigt faire maidenes that leven not to helde evere-more water of thilke sevene stremes that wellen alwey, for to watere wel thes sevene trees of vertue, that beren the fruygt of lif with-outen ende."

This is an allegorical image by the definitions of its time and kind, before the entrance of the personification of the petitions. They are maidens that they may be pictured, or mentally imaged in tangible shape; seven fountains and conduits that the sinner could himself open would do as well. It teaches doctrine, "what to believe" (and is, in fact, more theologically careful than we have time to notice here); it conveys very little moral judgment or evaluative impulse and uses numerous ancient metaphors to read the literal facts of fruitful growth spiritualiter ("rigt so, gostly").

---

used a printed translation of the unrevised "Somme le roi," *The Book of Vices and Virtues*, ed. W. N. Francis, *EETS*, vol. 217 (1942), 92-97. Convenience is important, since allegorical imagery, of all kinds, most repays scrutiny of the whole context. Other illuminations portraying this image (and references to others reproduced elsewhere) will be found in the present author's double article in *JWCI*, vols. 26-27 (1963, 1964), "Notes on the Virtues and Vices," especially Part II.

"Personification of abstractions" is so often thought of as the very root of allegory that a quick consideration of some complications may be worth a moment. So much of language is just this—ossified—that the phrase is not very useful. The phrase cannot turn into allegory a figure that happens to occur before English developed the use of "it" to replace the personal pronoun, making it necessary for the Lock in the fable to say that he would not suffer the Key to enter into "him," the keyhole. The visual arts customarily personify to indicate the presence of allegorical meaning, but that element does not provide the meaning, as is obvious from the banderoles so often needed; and also something quite different may be indicated. In the illustrated manuscript of the *Dialogus* in Paris MS. B.Nat. 8507*, all the objects are provided with faces—seabanks and sea, topaz, the stick-like gold and lead ending in human faces, lock, key and all. Our way of understanding the figurative nature of the fables is unaffected by this, and it does not help us to distinguish between the simplest moral exemplum and a metaphorical image of ancient profundity.

¶ Of the ayre/ and the wynde.
Dailogo.   Vij.

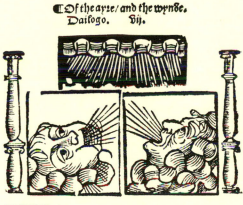

FIGURE 8

The illustrator was faced, in Fable 7, with differentiating pictorially "The Air" from "The Wind." In this fable the Air goes to the Creator and complains of being vexed and made "untemperate" by the Wind; "Therefore I saye to hym yf ever from hensforth he presume to blowe upon me/ I wyll choke hym and put hym from his lyfe." Figure 8 shows that the designer found the solution we might anticipate—but the Air is no less personified than is the creature we recognize as Aeolus. Nevertheless, the poets make the fullest use of such inheritances; Mammon is among other things a Pluto, and therefore some of the threatening and terrible meanings Mammon has will be conveyed without Spenser's mentioning them. What counts is less personification than the kinds of considerations drawn in by the recognized persons, what dramas they had elsewhere been *personae* in and have come to imply, like brief abstracts of much experience and feeling.

If personification of abstractions is not a defining or causative element in allegory, there is no doubt that it is a most natural form of it. But instead of personality giving the abstractions life, the figure often works the other way around; the excitement comes when we "conceive" the idea, the person suddenly then becoming charged with meanings of very great depth and extension. Everyone has had the experience of a genre-picture— or so he had thought it—turning into a symbol or allegory before his eyes, by something he learns (usually about the history and thence the deeper significance of the image). The curious inner revolution experienced, as *gestalt* replaced *gestalt*, came from moving out of the area of imitated literal life into an area where universals rather than particulars seem to be met, into an area where ideas themselves confront one or interact. Imagine an illustration of a rose-garden and an angelically beautiful youth which one suddenly saw put in its place at the head of a section of the *Roman de la rose.* Or suppose two pictures wherein a woman gives a garment to a naked man, and a woman sits by a sickbed—and that one finds the other five pictures and recognizes the Seven Acts of Mercy. The different experience that we move into is that of "seeing" all Love (not A Lover) in the God himself, all possible concrete cases of Mercy in the idea of her.

Moral allegory of some depth is possible as soon as we perceive that we can note the nature of universals in action—and this is often as true of genre-pictures as it is of naturalistic writing; bored people would probably stop looking and reading if it were not. But allegory in a stricter sense occurs so commonly that we ought to try to differentiate it; in a picture, it seems to depend on whether the action shows us, or whether an accompanying text or known significance makes us read in the images, something about the relations of Love or Mercy to the ultimate meaning of human life or about a divine source for them or their metaphys-

ical ground. If a picture could show us (as one like Fig. 6 might
if elaborated) Misericordia's place as the Fifth Gift of the Holy
Ghost, with her nature suggested, as so often, by the Works
of Mercy, or some of them—then that image would take on
before us the dimension we may as well call by its old name, allegorical.

These are not rules for allegories—with cards to be presented
at entrance, texts otherwise not admitted. I merely try to make
clear a distinction which is observed in the works written. Spenser
uses images which work in all these different ways, very close
together, as all literary works do, often indeed transforming one
kind into another as we look; but his choices of concretions to use,
associations to suggest, and so on, are unselfconsciously apt, and
we can damage "an allegory" markedly, for example, by asking
it to work like a moralization. Distinctions made in religious exegesis, and therefore familiar for centuries, were responsible for
calling this last kind of figure allegory, as some still did. The
term was not to hold on even partially for much longer, in spite
of the great Pauline passages that everyone knew. But the skill
that preserves such distinctions in practice stayed alive at least
long enough to show us why Milton's Sin and Death are conceptually and theologically two of the most accurate and fertile
images in his poem and to demonstrate a very particular relation between concrete detail and philosophical (not just ethical)
meaning. I do not know which we lost first—the terms or the distinctions. I do not think modern writing has a use for either.
Surely a differentiation between images based thus on difference
in function—whether we are brought to think about how to act
or how to believe—would be alien to us. Visual imagery may
have preserved it longest, for it was popularized along with the
use of certain truncated allegorical counters.

Poetic examples generally cover some compass, but perhaps
an unusually brief climax to one of Spenser's transformations of
one kind of image into another may illuminate the theoretical
remarks. If one recalls the whole complicated analysis of love
in Book III, and the story and characterizations which lead up
to the dinner-table scene in Malbecco's house, and the seemingly
quite realistic image of Paridell's lascivious use of erotic signs as
he spills his wine-cup toward Hellenore (to which she will respond by letting some of hers spill into her lap), one is egregiously

startled by Spenser's line: Hellenore read herein *A sacrament prophane in mistery of wine*. With a flash of comprehension we take in all that Spenser believed and might have said about the preservation of the nature of "love" (for example, that Love came down to make that nature clear forever in the sacrifice on the cross, and comes down persistently in the "wine" of the Eucharist); and we take in with shock the wild disproportion between the divine agape and this sensual use of others for self-indulgence. There is nothing but failure to be expected if one tries to explain something Spenser himself could only say by an image (Bk. iii.ix.30), but the agency through which the entire two cantos of the story now take on a new relation is unmistakable.

Poets have more varied and numerous ways of making us conceive ideas of such depth and extension than have artists, because of the inescapable conceptual dimension of their medium, words. This is dangerous ground, even if we try to keep close to a poetic example manifestly powerful by reason of its imagery. Two of the great images of Book II of the *Faerie Queene*—like the Rosier which is the world and the Sea Beast who tries to ravish and possess man's spirit—present two of the omnipresent concerns of allegory. Mammon images the first concern, Acrasia the second.[10] The far simpler fables also treated these same matters. We may thus toss ourselves in front of a danger always waiting for readers of allegory—that so many allegories "mean the same thing" that one is as good as another; "the idea" being in them, nothing intrinsic distinguishes a greater image, and bad poets cannot be told from good. This of course is untrue. Having voiced the protest we may leave it to each reader to supply the defense of poetry. We may court a second danger by noticing, in Spenser, the exact nature of some specific advantages which words have as conceptual instruments. The risk we run is that we may be understood to confuse allegory with "a discussion of ideas carried on by having some concrete equivalent stand for each one." This is a confusion met everywhere in commentary.[11] It describes

[10] There is in one sense only one allegorical theme—loss and salvation. Hence our feeling of starvation if literature's variety is boiled down to statement and re-statement of that theme. There is nothing monotonous about the shapes that body it forth. Mammon's difference from Acrasia is sufficient demonstration, even if both "mean" the same loss, to the same enemy.

[11] It creeps back under some disguise even among defenders of allegory, and

some allegory in English, but later than Spenser's.

One advantage of the conceptual medium, for both moral allegory and the stricter kind, is that comparisons or associations convey directly, without statement, a constant stream of responses —values placed on things, the tiny movements of attraction or repulsion which we share more in language than in sense experience. As we meet Mammon through description of his person and habitat, every detail awakens antipathy by virtue of something Spenser had only to name, not provide. The deserted unordered wilderness, the gloom, the sooty beard and coal-black hands carry evaluative notions about Mammon in themselves—and this is an ineradicable property of language. Words tip the scales of our affections, and we cannot call this rhetorical, but simply a linguistic fact; it has been provided by the long development of words as instruments of communication. Objects themselves are much more ambiguous in effect, as pictures of the wilderness and the beard would show. This semantic fact especially touches words that convey properties; they amplify or deprave (the technical Elizabethan words for *magnify* or *denigrate*) quite securely and almost without our realizing what is happening. This is a great strength when a poet wishes to convey through imagery some great abstraction from large areas of human experience toward which he expects to arouse attitudes of espousal or rejection. One result is that great allegories are usually the most concrete of all writings in texture. It is not only by temperament that Spenser became the painter of the poets.

Poets use this natural advantage (and frustrating disability) of the medium of words in every cunning way, often magnifying

of course denies the whole nature and point of the figure, which *embodies* ideas and thereby makes them manifest; if the critic who tells us what everything stands for were right, we could do very well without the allegory. This conception comes closer to the truth with allegories imposed afterward, as were late classical and Stoic interpretations. The insistence that the literal is true, and figures or means (rather than "stands for") the further spiritual reading is a legacy from centuries of habitual Biblical allegorizing. At any rate, the Elizabethans can still *write* so (the literal being the historical, i.e. the fiction standing up as narrative). Recent nervousness about conceptual elements in poetry make untendentious phrasing difficult. One is sure that modern touchiness about words similarly felt to be dangerous or obscurely associated with guilt is very temporary—words like "intention," "statement," "conceptual discourse," "static." They are used in this book as if they were not famous coterie-words.

in order to deprave or diminish—as the gold and brightness and artful richness (*FQ*, ii.vii.4; vii.28) are shown only to be negated by the coverings of "filthy" dust, jet-black clouds, webs of Arachne denominated "cunning," or subtile "nets." Two other plain advantages of the medium show up: first the ease with which a poet can interpolate abstract epithets or value-stating words whose only and proper function is to sway the judgment, and secondly, the natural operation of figures using comparison, which generally do this surreptitiously. Spiders' "nets" are no real danger to any but flies, but as with "nayles *like clawes*" or the "ravenous *pawes*" of the fiend who follows Guyon with "monstrous *stalke*," experiences are drawn in by way of the mere terms of comparisons which tacitly but inescapably press us to condemn or exalt. These are the simplest forms of a conceptual power which words have, from their history. It is shown more complicatedly when a poet loads a simile with some imported notion, one which frightens, for example, as the light in the cave is like that of the moon *to him that walkes in feare*, or is like that of a lamp "whose *life* does fade away" (as ours will, we half catch from this). Those who recall the canto stanza by stanza will remember that the crescendo—by which every kind of dark word (physical, moral, intellectual) turns the cave finally into a hell—includes many uses of dubious or terror-filled light, even that in the eyes of the laboring shapes.

These shapes brought their pain and terror with them when they entered, or rather, they brought their history, which is as important as their forms. In the Acrasia canto the analogue to these uses of darkness is the fearful sea. One remarks the crowd upon crowd of concretions that make the sea journey more fearsome than any experienced or pictured voyage; but they vary. There are mere "things" which in their verbal forms are simultaneously appearances and significances, in this case, of terror (the owls and bats and quicksands and sea-shouldering whales). There are ancient literary conventions with trains of associations (the mermaids and ivy and hell-mouth and squeezed potion, the magnet-rocks and wandering islands and the fée's Helpful Damsels). There are also inventions not seen but fully understood, like the carcasses stuck on the rock, but of *wanton* and *ruined* men only. All these sense experiences impregnated with meanings deepen the conviction that is usually the ground for reading a literal experience (verbal or lived) allegorically—that all things though fully present to the senses are meaningful beyond what sense reports. In the case of great numbers of the images, their meaning comes with them, carried by their history.

The images are based firmly on physical and psychological experience, often known individually, but chiefly known and made important by centuries of vicarious experience passed on to us through earlier literature; hence such images work at a deep associative level, and we are conscious of not being the first to whom they have reiterated their burden of more meant than is seen. That Spenser counts upon his images' history is provable from his text; and merely by their nature, some images themselves reach beyond considerations which belong (as do moral problems) to our life in the phenomenal world. Journeys into the otherworld expose, handle, discuss or pronounce upon just such matters of ultimate or metaphysical import as are the concern of allegory strictly defined (or the concern of so many actual allegories which otherwise fit very loosely with the definitions of Christian religious allegorizing). The graphic arts have difficulty matching this sure and concentrated deepening of "spiritual" significance except through literary aids like titles, or known conventions of imagery.

Although both cantos vii and xii of Book II of the *Faerie Queene*, are read as moral allegory, both undeniably talk about man saved or damned. Though Acrasia is a nameable vice, and the adventures of Mordant or Cymochles with her have a more limited moral meaning, Guyon in canto xii looks at the kind of complete seduction which means the final death of the soul; and there is firm evidence for this in Spenser's use of myths and figures which historically had been used thus. The Dantesque and Virgilian imagery and the mediaeval-and-Renaissance Circe figure are but single cases. Perhaps this is one of the reasons why he erects a "goodly frame of Temperance" instead of just forming a temperate person, and why Guyon is a man journeying rather than a tempted protagonist; poets who show us men conducted through hell do not picture them having fights there with their appetites, but discovering what hell is. If it could never *be* a paradise (to men like us), we should already know what Intemperance is, and would not need to have it proved upon our pulses in canto xii.

We add then to the advantages which literature's inescapably conceptual medium provides its good fortune in being able to go backward and forward in time—not only narratively but through images. Literature can mean something about future generations not in the story or communicate meanings found by past generations whose story is not being told, and all without deserting its subject. It is true that outright conceptual statement may be the way to make the extended meanings shine out in character and event most surely, as when we are shaken by Mammon's "God of the world and worldings I me call" (vii.8) or by the shocking completeness of "Here is the fountaine of the worldes good" (vii.38) or by the doctrinal accuracy of "See the mind of beastly man, That hath so soone forgot the excellence / Of his creation" (xii.87). But Spenser employs a poetic method almost as firm and sure when he makes the past uses of his images indicate to us that we are to read them with this reach into ultimate questions. We recognize them as instruments for the discussion of just such matters—but able to speak in the present of the timeless, and locally of the universal.[12]

I do not mean that images repeat the story they told in the past. It does not turn Guyon into a "Christ-figure" when in canto vii.9 Spenser directs us to see the parallels with Christ's three temptations. Rather, this indicates the amplitude of the issue and states a doctrine about the relation between all human temptations and Christ's.[13] Spenser uses classical images similarly, to

[12] I claim these extensions without in the least giving up what various studies have shown in these cantos: moral exposition more than usually indebted to Aristotle's *Ethics* (see Sirluck, "*FQ* II and the *Nicomachean Ethics*," *MP*, vol. 49, 1951-52); warnings to Elizabethan England to maintain a middle way; the evidences of the metaphor "British England: Fairyland" which Greenlaw brought out as long ago as 1918 in "Spenser's Fairy Mythology," *SP*, vol. 15. These largest images simply go farther.

[13] The point about the triple temptation was made in an interesting context in R. Durling's "Bower of Bliss and Armida's Palace," *Comp.Lit.*, vol. 6 (1954), 335-47. A recent comparison is Kermode's in "The Cave of Mammon," *Elizabethan Poetry* (London, 1960), where the parallels are numerous and clear and the relation suggested is not that of figura. My statements do not quarrel with the idea that Guyon "is imitating both Hercules and Christ." The relation of imitatio Christi, not that of "a Christ-figure," is the reason why we require no recherché theories to account for the next scene, where Guyon needs and receives the grace which all followers of the tempted and victorious Christ are promised—"And angels came and ministered unto him" as readers recall, and expect (Mark 1).

extend through their history the significance of his fiction; the golden apples evoke all those sad stretches of human history when men's concupiscence, for power of all kinds, had brought all the great typical "ensamples of mind intemperate" to their various eternities of frustrated desire. He uses what he calls the "present fate" of these long-dead persons to tell the powerful who have *not* yet left their mortal state for that other, "how to use their present state"; this is evidence that he wishes us to read allegorically of the relation between a virtue Temperance and what can happen to a soul, and not merely morally of a character Guyon and his confrontation of covetous desires.

In the Acrasia canto we are most helped by whatever we know of something common enough to Elizabethans—Circe as an image of man's betrayal of his spiritual allegiances to the intemperance of his other natural desires; our familiarity with this conventional Christianization,[14] enables us to catch the many insistences in canto xii that widen the image of yielding to "Voluptas." The basic meaning of man's loss of his humanity has such fundamental implications that no reader can quite miss the allegorical purport of a fatal seduction, breaking man's tie of fidelity. "Fidelity to a divine allegiance" is the continuation fitting both Spenser and *Comus*, for as the image widens from moral to allegorical, it shows its Christian heritage.

It is well to repeat periodically that we do not seek to define allegory as if it were some changeless essence, and then in turn use the definition to admit or shut out poems from the category. We seek something quite limited and historical—what was involved in reading allegorically to certain writers at a given time, and for reasons we can trace. My first conviction, that certain definitions and distinctions were inherited mediaeval distinctions passed down to sixteenth-century writers and readers, arose from reading a late mediaeval book systematically, and consciously handling and exemplifying these matters. Christine de Pisan wrote her *Épitre d'Othéa* at the end of the fourteenth century;

[14] This inherited Christianization of temperance comes out with special clarity in *Comus*, late and by a learned and conscious artist; much was pointed out by Bush in 1932 (*Mythology and the Renaissance Tradition*), but the essential Circe article is Merritt Hughes's in *JHI* for 1943, and we may save ourselves the numerous citations here since they are clustered and the problem discussed in R. Tuve, *Images and Themes in 5 Poems by Milton* (Cambridge, 1957), pp. 130ff.

she was an esteemed author, and her books, including this one, were accessible in more than one form and in more than one language. The *Othéa* is invaluable for our questions, because the author tells us outright how she expects to be read.

Christine tells one hundred stories, or rather versifies what she calls one hundred "Textes," and they may be mere story-moments or even personages, pagan gods, or dicta from ancient times; all are classical in provenance. She then appends a prose "Glose," and thereafter a short prose discussion she entitles "Allegorie." We read the hundred, each first as a history or straightforward statement (i.e. "in the letter") and up through the Elizabethan period this may embrace such figurative senses as the parabolic meaning, say, of the sower. And then if we read each of the hundred in the two prose interpretations, which are two ways of reading the significance of the letter, we have at any rate one invincible authority providing what our book is trying to find: what distinguished allegory from other ways of reading, to mediaeval and Renaissance readers. Christine satisfies the requirement of being famous and accessible enough for later writers in the mode to have been nourished on understandings she represents. And when one such writer exemplifies definitions before our eyes, in examples whose very phrasing we can check, we know we are reading as someone in truth did read, not as we conjecture "the mediaeval mind" must have. It is very rare to find documentation so precise on a matter of literary interpretation.

We will exemplify from a few of Christine's hundred merely to secure and confirm working definitions; her book as a whole suggests ideas about the imposition of Christian allegory upon classical materials which can wait for another chapter (Four). The *Othéa* has the additional merit of usually being illustrated, so we can observe what conditions permitted or assured the appearance of "allegory" (by Christine's own definition) or of moral meaning in the pictorial presentations of her hundred stories. Some of the manuscripts which illustrate all the hundred are thought to have been done under her surveillance, another lucky circumstance; the tradition in illuminations is interestingly constant, but of the early editions, Wyer's partial English translation does not follow early designs, and the Pigouchet cuts are not detailed.

FIGURE 9

Figure 9 shows an image we should unhesitatingly interpret
narratively; Perseus on Pegasus rescues Andromeda from the Sea
Monster. For the interest of an iconographical tradition preserved
through vicissitudes, I include the parallel pictures from St.
John's Coll.Camb.MS.208 in English (Fig. 10) and the French
MS.Laud misc.570 (Fig. 11) as well as Harl.4431. Christine's
Texte (No. 5) tells the aspirant to knighthood to emulate him
in this chivalrous behavior. In the Glose, we "make a figure of

FIGURE 10   FIGURE 11

it according to the manner *of poets*"—and we should notice that both this reading and the third are figurative. Like Perseus, every "bon chevalier" is to rescue those in peril, flying upon his steed of Good Renown; he must win his chivalric good name, then use its strength to succor the distressed.[15] This is a good moral allegory. But Christine proceeds to what she herself entitles Allegorie: Andromeda is his soul which he will deliver from the enemy of hell by conquering sin (in himself, of course, so that this Andromeda, like the other "maiden," may return to her parents). The Pegasus which carries "lesp*er*it chevalereux" is a Good Name since he desires to please God, for he must have no hint of vainglory, and his good angel who carries him through dangers here will make good report of him when his guerdon, like Lycidas', is finally to be enjoyed amid the singing companies of Paradise. Perseus is to be "read" first as bon chevalier, but secondly as bon esprit, that within the human creature which can help it to attain deliverance of its immortal soul.

We may turn to Narcissus, who so traditionally exemplifies Pride that we certainly know we are embarking on a series of the seven deadly sins (Fables 16-22). The moralized figurative reading in the Glose sees in the fountain where Narcissus looked at himself and was drowned, that overweening of himself which blinds him and makes his knightly good deeds of no account; we are instructed on Pride. But the Allegorie quotes from Origen a reminder of man's creatureliness, the absurdity of pride in one who has his being in so frail and corrupt a vessel. Then *Job* is quoted on the ignominious destruction that is the destiny of a soul of such quality—one possessing this quintessential Pride which sees no irony in the arrogance of mere creaturely earth and ashes.

---

[15] Pegasus as fame and good repute is discussed at pp. 189f. of M. M. Lascelles' "The Rider on the Winged Horse," which examines many other points, such as the connection with poets and with Bellerophon, and in much more important literary texts (see *Elizabethean and Jacobean Studies presented to F. P. Wilson*, Oxford, 1959, 173-198). Christine's source is the *Ovide moralisé*; our concerns here, definition and the setting of problems, discourage the complication brought in by source treatment, but citations to Campbell and other investigators appear in ch. 4 below. My descriptions and quotations are from the MSS., for there is no edition of the French text (one of Scrope's translation is promised by Curt Bühler), but Gordon's edition cited below n. 18 or the Roxburghe Club edition of Scrope's translation (ed. Warner, 1904) can be consulted.

FIGURE 12

Ceres is pictured as a goddess sowing in a plowed field, a goddess of grains (or, rationalized, une dame who taught men to plow before seeding). To be a liberal giver who gives with "abandon" is to have the "condition" of Ceres, says the moral Glose; but when we read the Allegorie in Ceres, we see in her the action of the blessed Son of God, chief exemplar of giving with abandon to men of his high good things. The good knight reads chivalric largesse in Ceres; the good spirit believes in, loves and imitates the condition of Ceres read as figure for the agape of Christ and its fructifying influence. Ceres does not "equal Christ." Her condition is agape, and He is that in its essence. When properly read, allegory does not need to turn some personage into Christ or into God the Father. We merely pause to notice that the relation is not quite that of a type either, and in a later chapter of this book we will observe that the distinction is kept, though it is a nice one. Figure 12 shows Ceres' action; the illustrator has not rationalized away her divine nature or there would be no cloud.[16] Rationalizations (like Ceres

[16] As is said in the verbal descriptions accompanying pictures in several manuscripts described in the article (Part II) cited in n. 9.

as teacher of plowing), which are traces of late classical forms of rationalizing divinities through "allegory," are frequent in Christine's Gloses. Though both the moral and the allegorical figurative meaning can persist despite the rationalizing, it does more damage to the classical figure than is done by the translation into Christian-deity terms, much as these might be thought of as a forcing of the meaning. The divinity lies in the loving abandon of the gift; belief in this as the very nature of God is strictly intended here, for Ceres is the second of a series of figures in whom we "read" the Twelve Articles of the Apostles' Creed, and the second is "And in Jesus Christ our Lord. . . ."

In Fable 54 we are shown a figure of Jason, who by Medea's help won the Golden Fleece, but ungratefully and disloyally (the same thing) deserted her. It is Jason's lack of fidelity, of troth owed to her who saved him from the death others met, which puts him outside the pale of chivalry, a warning to the bon chevalier. "Ingrate," "disloyal," "unnatural," are the key words of the figure, and we are not surprised when the Allegorie tells us to read in Jason what the bon esprit must hold to as its first allegiance: it must not forget Who made it. St. Bernard is quoted on the dry wind that shrinks up grace and mercy in a spirit that is ingrate. This is the prime arrogance in a soul, and untroth is regularly a first branch of Pride, as we should remember when we read Una (and Sansfoy).

Two general observations can be made, even with so few illustrations from Christine's hundred.[17] The simplest one touches the design of her book, commonly denigrated as haphazard and eccentric. Her general scheme is to take up classical stories in which we "read" the virtues, thereafter the seven sins, thereafter the Twelve Articles of the Creed, thereafter the Ten Commandments, thereafter a series of virtues and vices (Fables 45ff.). This has been noticed,[18] but nothing has ever been made of the fact

[17] Christine's deliberate action of directing us toward multiple readings of classical story finds an interesting analogue in Enrique de Villena's *Los doze trabajos de Hércules*, ed. M. Morreale (Madrid, 1958), facs. edition of 1499 edition, Madrid, ca. 1879, extant in numerous fifteenth-century manuscripts and editions of 1483, 1499, 1502?. But its divisions into *Historia nuda, Declaración, Verdad, Aplicación*, do not offer us so comprehensive a view of the ways of interpreting classical figure as we find in Christine's less pretentious piece. See below ch. 4, nn. 38ff.

[18] By James Gordon in his very useful edition and discussion (unfortunately

that this structural design relates Christine's book to one of the commonest kinds of earlier mediaeval works—to those "Summa's" which were a major source of doctrine on the virtues, their contents being enjoined in concilia as a minimum of knowledge for the faithful, from the thirteenth century onward. This undiscussed fact has many implications. When for other reasons I very shortly take up the most popular of all exemplars of that common group, the *Somme le roi* (in its English form), we shall notice one of these important resulting similarities: an emphasis upon the "two chivalries," a natural part of a virtues-treatise and a pervasive figure in other forms of mediaeval literature also. It encouraged an understanding of the human situation and of human nature that made a place for the theologian's allegory, reading *spiritualiter*, in secular literature. In Christine we find the idea of double chivalry giving a kind of rhetorical currency to figures which are just classical images read *mystice*. Among lesser implications, we remark that the formlessness of mere casual didacticism is removed from Christine's list of demerits. One trait surely enjoyed by her audience is the originality of this use of classical materials to shape a scheme so thoroughly familiar in the handbooks, for it surprises, provokes new realizations of the meaning of old doctrines and mnemonically is quite amusingly efficacious.

The second general observation is important because it points to a broad distinction we find silently upheld in other literary works, one that is helpful in determining how allegory as used in literature of the time was usually read. One of our toughest problems is whether allegory strictly so-called, a mode of reading useful for centuries to theologians and suitable primarily for scriptural interpretation, could be drawn over into secular literature, and if it could be, whether or not it was. If it was not, and the modern flurry of interest in such matters has merely produced readings that were no part of the pleasure taken in allegory in its heyday and not intended by authors, it would be salutary to discover this.

When we read all one hundred of the *Othéa*'s sections as innocently as possible, we find that whereas the first reading, in the

---

out of print) of *The Epistle of Othéa to Hector* in the translation in MS.Harl. 838 (Philadelphia, 1942). But I wait with fuller bibliography until ch. 4 below.

Glose, has to do with building a character (preparing the Good Knight to enter the moral tournament of life), the simultaneous additional second reading, the *Allegorie*, does not use literature or vicarious experience for that purpose—though advice on the good life is often near at hand as a by-product. The Good Spirit (bon esp*e*rit chevalereux, "soul" often in MS. Harl. 838) reads in figures the reminder of its true condition as a creature, sometimes seeing its need of rescue, often seeing in the figures a repetition of the news of its way of deliverance or some definition of the nature of this deliverance. The author herself is these two readers. Hence the peculiar usefulness and authority of the *Othéa*, since we are almost ubiquitously in the perilous situation of conjecturing how writers expected to be read, from evidence that is largely implicit.

It may not be practicable to keep Christine's terminology and distinguish allegoria as she does; although I try to maintain roughly such a distinction in this book, mediaeval books do not so limit the word itself. However, many do characteristically so frame their allegorical images, which are thus distinguishable from moralizations, and whose function is to discuss the ultimate destiny of man as bon esprit. Some figures are clearly more amenable to the second reading than others; Christine sometimes flounders as she seeks to supplant a reading concerned with moral conflict and substitute the Good Spirit's fulfillment of some other concern inseparable from being human. Some classical figures resist the natural Christian twist—that human beings not only have moral responsibilities but belong to that Kind which is not debarred from regaining the lost resemblance to the divinity which created them, or belong to a Kind beloved and sought and espoused and owing fidelity to, a loving Creator. This is the aspect which was bound to enter Christian images of Temperance (governing the famous ones created by Spenser and Milton), since these ineluctably choose to speak of the *end* of temperate behavior. Indeed, it is merely one appearance of the universal stress on wonder and gratitude as the proper "temperate" response of a rightly reasonable man toward the book of the universe, emphases so familiar up through the arguments of Bacon's *Advancement* and Milton's *Paradise Lost*, and destined to become so ill-understood soon thereafter. Earlier acceptance of these commonplaces is often phrased in ways that show us that they greatly strengthened habits of "reading" the creatures in the universe allegorically, confirming us in right belief. They emphasized the notion, such as we see in Christine (and I think in Spenser), that the virtuous disposition of the soul is its adornment and beautiful raiment, not only its hard-won guerdon after conflict.

The *Dialogues of creatures*, in a preface, and citing Isidore, states thus this operation of figures which rather than instructing man morally, reveals meanings to him as spirit. Though outwardly the creatures do not "playnly show" their "inwarde meanyinge," yet these are shadowed in them, in order that "by the same path that man erryd from God, he may . . . retourned to him agayne, for as man was "pluckyd by his inordinate love of the creature/ from the greate love of his lorde & maker, so, by inspectyon of the great beawte of creaturys, he owith to be refourmed and to gyve lawde & worshippe to the incomparable Creator." Also quoted is Augustine's great sentence on how all things He made "crye to me, and sece not, that I owe to love the, my lord god and maker above all othir thinge."

Christine has a "Prologue a Allegorie" between her first Glose and Allegorie. What draws us "a ramener a allegorie le propos de nostre matiere" is "l'edificacion de l'ame." Because all things are created by the sapience and power of God, "raissonablement doivent toutes choses tendre *a fin de lui*." Because nostre esperit is God's image in us, and most noble (after the angels), it is meet (*convenable*) that it be *adorned* with virtues, "parquoy il puisse estre convoye a la fin pourquoy il est fait." She contrasts the droite chevalerie of the struggle here on earth with "l'ennemy d'enfer" with the parfaitte chevalerie whose heroes are "couronnez en glorie"; this speaking of lesperit chevalereux is "fait a la louenge de dieu principalement."

This decking of the soul for its heavenly destiny, this seeing the virtuous action of the bon esprit as a fitting form of louenge de dieu, produces (as we saw briefly) images quite distinct from those urging or portraying moral improvement—however much the decking improves us. The Gloses fasten their attention upon the latter, but the Allegories of Perseus, of Ceres, Narcissus, Jason, had a different end in view, though the same virtuous course was commended. The Caxton translation of the *Somme le roi*—or any form of that popular treatise—[19]makes with great naturalness a similar distinction between man as a moral creature and man as a spiritual creature. Treating of the virtue Prowesse, rooted in us by the Fourth Gift of the Holy Spirit, Fortitudo, Frère Lorens says, "More ferthere coude not the philosophres the vertue of prowesse leden" than simply to "destroie and overcome vices and wikkednesses and to wynne vertues." But "oure gret philosophre Ihesu Crist" and His disciples "gon moche forthere"; for He said "Who-so endureth in-to the ende, he schal *be saved*," and His disciples seek to be righteous and true *to Christ*. That is, they give their lives "for hym that gaf his lif and his deth for me," a virtuousness we may desire here but never attain, for though the motive for virtuous action is a gratitude which simply makes men try to imitate His acts of love, we shall not match them here, nor "paie it pleynliche," the debt we owe. This is why the Fourth Beatitude, in parallel with the Fourth Gift, speaks of a hunger and thirst after righteousness which "goes further than" what ethics commends, the struggle for attainable moral virtues. We have moved from questions of ethics to questions of fealty. Again, in elucidating the beginning of the Pater Noster, the words "Our *Father*" involve a "travaile to be like hym"—to be "large and curteis, swete and deboner" as He is, *so that thou go nougt out of thi kynde*" (pp. 169, 99).

It is not by fortuitous chance that we here meet independently the same turn to the orthodox Christian tenet as we heard in the fable of the fish Regina. Virtues as qualities natural to a child of God, beautiful in a spouse of Christ, expected of the chevalier Jesus Christ, are an inevitable result of this conception of man's nature and metaphysical position. For such a notion of his nature and "end"—a familiar doctrine, but one accommodated in dozens of phrases and in many books to mediaeval chivalric ideals and society—the imagery is likeliest to be that of a Quest, of knightly devoir, of Pilgrimage (seeking the final home of the spirit, born of heavenly lineage). The image of the two chivalries, briefly seen

---

[19] One can quote from Caxton (1486), or Frère Lorens' French text widespread in manuscript and print, or from the only convenient modern printing of an English version in *EETS*, vol. 217, as I have ordinarily done, with references in text to pages; in sections which appear in all, differences are minimal. All these points of bibliography are handled more responsibly in ch. 2, on the virtues literature. I do not take up Christine's sources, even in ch. 4, but for example, the Prologue mentioned is paralleled in the *Livre de Sagesse*.

in Christine and more movingly seen in romance materials which we reserve for a later chapter, is based on this understanding of man's moral and spiritual nature and is a common carrier of the distinction. And Christine's "Prologue a Allegorie" showed how clear and easy to her were such relations between man's raison d'être and this figure of allegory—to us a most curious observation. As we have seen, figures of speech that deal with man respectively as moral and as spiritual formally obey the difference in purport. I think we are justified in interpreting these conceptions as ordinary popular understandings of the learned differentiations we know well. Touching figurative writing, the resultant difference is that between moral instruction and exhortation through tropological writing and allegory more strictly so-called.

The Pater Noster quotation from the translated *Somme le roi* was actually part of an image of the higher chivalry. "Gretter nobleie may non be than to be so gret an emperoures sone as God is"; the imitation (of God) to which we set ourselves is admittedly impossible, and yet we say *Our Father* just as "whan a newe knygt goth to a bataile or to the turnement, men bidden hym thenke whos sone he is."

Although the imagery of the Knight battling for virtue, and the distinguishable imagery of God's Knight imitating a divine original, is structurally fundamental in all the portions of this easily accessible book which were most naturally attractive to later writers (as we shall see in Chapter Two), it is made especially clear in a treatment of another ancient commonplace, the Three Goods. These receive countless statements from the time of Augustine and Ambrose onward, but here they are denominated: small or temporal (ephemeral, of Fortune); the middle or mean goods, of Nature, or acquired by study; and great or "true." *Verray* Lordship, Freedom and Nobility are described, and when we read what constitutes verrey nobleie or true gentillesse, it is proper that we think of Dante, of the "Franklin's Tale," of the *Roman de la rose*, for these enormously popular didactic manuals, like the *Somme*, were important channels by which patristic and scholastic doctrine or classification flowed into vernacular writing. We are not surprised to hear that verrey nobility comes of "a gentel herte," that there is no gentle heart "but it love God," no nobility therefore but to "serve" Him and no "vilenye but the contrarie ther-of."

The basis for this is always the same:

Non is rigt gentel and noble of gentrie *of body*. [For as far as the body goes] we ben alle of o modre, that is of erthe. . . . [There is not] *rigt gentel ne free but our rigt fadre*, that is the kyng of heuene, that . . . maade the soule to his owne ymage and to his owne liknesse. . . .

[And because like an earthly father he rejoices to have sons like him] . . . he sente vs . . . Ih*e*su Crist, for to brynge vs the verrey saumple bi whiche we mowe schappe us to his ymage and to his fairenesse [like those that already dwell in the high city of heaven].

This quest of "the holy men of this world" for "the verrey nobleie that a man bigynneth heere bi grace and vertue" is "fulfilled in ioie," in eternity. But "than hath he the ymage and the liknesse of God, as [much as] a man may have in erthe" when "ther is no thing bitwene God and hym but o wille."

And this is the grettest nobleye and the grettest gentrie that any man or womman may come to . . . (pp. 85-87).

Such, then, is the quest of the chevalerie celestienne. It does not at all preclude, in Christine, in the prose *Lancelot* and in the *Queste del saint Graal*, in moralized fables and books inculcating the virtues, an attention to the Good Knight's earthly combats with vices. But I think it may be apparent that the large literature of virtues battling with vices, which we are accustomed to think of solely as a great tableau of the psychomachia we call the moral struggle, had running through it another kind of image as well—the spirit's quest for a lost but native noblesse, regainable ultimately but not here, a noblesse which every soul had as belonging to the "kin" of the sons of God.

The result of this double attention is especially interesting in Christine because her book also belongs, by direct intention, to a kind—the "regiment of princes"—which had a great Renaissance flowering and development. What Christine wrote was a double courtesy-book. She asks us to read each figure as assisting the Knight, who is a person fighting evil on earth and in his own mind, and as assisting the Pilgrim-Knight who is a journeying soul, the chevalier Jesus Christ. One notes that the difference is not between this-worldly and otherworldly; both kinds of courtesy are double-worldly. Both knight-readers read figuratively, for the distinction is neither between literal and figurative, nor between didactic and non-didactic.

Even the Gloses are not mere example; they go beyond "be not like *him*" to universalize faulty or admirable human behavior and thus take in even our own forms of it, though experienced through very different particulars. As with any Spenserian exemplum—Fradubio or Sir Terwin—Christine's personages, being moralized, operate as metaphors to generalize upon experience. Writing as did Spenser, to "fashion a gentleman or noble person in vertuous and gentle discipline," she clearly has in mind a particular social group; these are courtiers who must wage the moral battles described, under conditions localized in the France of 1400. But by the usual action of moral allegory (which is simply a strengthened form of the action of any metaphor), we cannot avoid applying her Gloses or moral readings to all men, who all emulate Perseus, turn from Narcissus' self-love, meet Orgoglio or Mammon or Despair.

The second way of reading the same Textes, "allegorie" in her terminology, while not more universal than this extension of moral meaning, is more profound. It concerns the reasons why the psychomachia is entered upon. The actor is not only a Knight, an Everyman who fights for Christian ethics, but a "spirit," that within any man which is in quest of his ultimate or his timeless destiny. This is why the second reading is—to use one of the oldest words for distinguishing it—spiritual; for moral readings are equally concerned with what are now called spiritual values, editors and commentators to the contrary. I do not think the distinction when it operated in secular literature is quite the same as the familiar distinction between tropological or moral, and allegorical, in interpretation of Scripture; but it does seem to be a more loosely understood or relaxed variant of that distinction.

We are of course entirely familiar with this habit of distinguishing between figures according to their sphere of action, in Scriptural interpretation. Most students of late years, resembling in this no doubt most mediaeval students, have found the famous distich the neatest and most memorable way of reminding themselves of the main difference in few words: "Littera gesta docet, quid credas allegoria,/ Moralis quid agas, quo tendas anagogia."[20]

---

[20] The distich was popularized by appearing in Nich. de Lyra, but they are twelfth-century phrases, already used in the *Catholicon*, and evidently orig-

It would be false to think that mediaeval readers always agreed on where the line could be drawn between these two functions we are emphasizing, for they could not always separate quid credas and quid agas.[21] It can be grievously and harmfully oversimplified, as can (and sometimes is) the whole method of reading in the four senses. This was not evolved, or thought of, as a way of reading secular pieces, at least with any rigor or consistency; and when this method is so used in the centuries of its popularity, it is applied with delicacy and restraint, suggestively and not tightly. It seems to me we should try to match this restraint, going only as far as earlier writers give us warrant. The restraint is peculiarly necessary in dealing with the basic conception underlying allegory's power to teach us true belief. This is the relation, caught in the word "type," between history itself (actual persons, events) and revealed truth, so that the actual people and events pre-figure or shadow what later comes to pass, and thereby fulfill the figures. For this is a firmly religious conception, requiring a characteristically Christian conception of God's relation to history, and is tied closely to a necessary other concept, the Old

---

inating with Augustine of Dacia; see the careful and well-documented "Introduction" to H. de Lubac's *Exégèse médiévale: Les quatre sens de l'Écriture* for the history of this ubiquitously quoted tag (2 parts; Paris, 1959-64). There has been an extreme growth in the very last few years in the materials available for accurate study of religious allegory; I cite but this here, for its completeness and its inclusion of the Latin so that we may assess points of view, and because its recentness insures citation of others. I might add the English translation of J. Daniélou's *The Bible and the Liturgy* (Notre Dame, Ind., 1956), and studies cited therein (cf. also his *Sacramentum Futuri*, Paris, 1950; or V. C. Spicq's *Esquisse d'une histoire de l'exégèse latine au moyen âge* (Paris, 1944), introductions to the pertinent texts in the *Sources chrétiennes*, ed. H. de Lubac, and J. Daniélou). Given this plenty, and because the figures we study show the influence of general understandings not theological information, I do not discuss subtler aspects or religious materials, but count upon readers' study of these.

[21] It would seem to me not only unnecessary but harmful in our context to attempt to accommodate the differences concerning four, or three, or more, senses, with English terms, or to fence off the three other senses from the allegory. Influence was too unselfconscious and too loose for this. An anagogical sense sometimes looks confusingly like what I keep the word "allegorical" for; though we admit overlapping in all categories, religious writings, which alone allow truly anagogical imagery, would show its difference ("religious" passages like the image of Lycidas in heaven with the saints, are as close as secular works come).

and the New Law. The present ease with which the relation of type is claimed argues a verbal rather than profound understanding. Nevertheless, it seems to me that these long centuries of practice—very common practice—and acceptance of Christian allegorical interpretation left a mark on the ordinary understanding of allegory. The more so because careful theory, New Testament sanction and doctrinally necessary safeguards kept the religious definitions of allegory incredibly pure, moving and deep (considering that we deal with the wide breadth of Christendom and at least twelve loquacious mediaeval centuries).

We should not lose sight of the fact that certain commonplaces of Christian doctrine have much to do with the current overeasy detection of types (usually of Christ) in some secular writings, often Shakespeare's or Spenser's. It is a doctrinal commonplace to think of the faithful Christian who tries to "imitate" Christ as attempting an image of Christ, as restoring through grace the relation to God which man held before the Fall—when he was truly and recognizably "in His image." Typology is not needed to understand the most important way in which Red Crosse "becomes" or "takes on" Christ; the Pauline terms describe what is supposed to happen constantly in the life of any Christian, and it is a misuse of a word needed for its own meaning to find types in all these. Types properly precede the figure that fulfills them, Moses before Christ. Only a divine Author can so write history that the types foreshadow the revelation of pure truth in another historical occurrence, and the serious use of this figurative relation requires a religious conception of man's reason for being.

As a natural and living figure it could not outlast, in the secular literatures of the Western countries, the unselfconscious acceptance of such basic ideas as universally valid and relevant. If Spenser had not been so much influenced by mediaeval ideals and materials, he might be outside the circle of influence as well, but he seems to me to come just within the time when the long tradition of exegesis and of reading spiritualiter could still impel a secular but Christian author to write images with a truly "allegorical" impulse. The relaxation of definition, which is bound to accompany the secularized use of a figure with such *ends* as this one, makes possible a much more general or large gesture toward the doctrine which we are to realize and believe instead of the exact doctrinal teaching familiar in Biblical allegory. In fact, the chief contribution of its theological background may be not its didactic force (which it shares with many types of figures) but the unrelaxed insistence on the importance of the literal sense.[22] This is absolutely constant during its mediaeval history, and it is easy to see why. If the history itself is not true, the "quid credas" of the figure is nonsense. Herein lies the main difference between it and the grammarian's allegory, the allegory of late classical tradition, which did not undergo this long Christian development. These allegories are frequently content to substitute the allegorical for the literal meaning, having no truth of Old Testament history to preserve, and no such understanding of the relation of revelation (the New Law) to history.

When we learn "beliefs" from non-religious pieces, our lowered demands—almost shrunk to a notion that the image should speak to us insofar as we are souls, or of our eternal not temporal health—admit of application to classical or worldly materials and purposes not ecclesiological or strictly dogmatic. Many among Spenser's figures which truly operate to make us see "what we are to believe" and are strictly allegorical by virtue of this function, yet invite a reading couched more in Platonic than in Christian terms. But the reason for the increased depth, power and permanent interest (the "importance") of the figures are much the same in either case. Usually the well-known commonplaces of both bodies of thought are all that is called upon, and Spenser is not the first poet who has been more Christian by being more Platonic. There is yet a seriousness about the philosophical and metaphysical purport of the images in the *Faerie*

---

[22] It seems wise to take every pertinent opportunity of reiterating this fact, for whether in ignorance or in wilful disregard of the care taken by mediaeval theory and instruction on this point, even mediaevalists can be heard to characterize a "typical mediaeval allegory" by its *substitution* of allegorical for literal senses, its disregard of historical, literal, or fictional reasonableness, or its schematized and devitalized paralleling of abstraction with concretion. There is no protection against an unwillingness to separate unimaginative, or decadent, or careless allegorical writers from good ones, especially if we will not consider what men advised or intended to do, but only what they do for us. There was the usual number of run-of-the-mill pedestrian writers making use of popular modes, then as now. A chapter (vii) citing texts is in de Lubac ("Importance de la lettre," part 1, 2), but treatments of single writers and their texts can be more specifically informative (e.g. Hugo of St. Victor, III, ch. iv). See also "La nouveauté chrétienne" in part 1, 2, ch. viii.

Queene which is somehow causally different from the many idealized disquisitions which commend the same virtues or vilify the same vices.

Here lies the power of the change which comes over the *Faerie Queene*, which I should also call a double courtesy-book, when we allow its major fictions and figures to speak with such a double voice. Spenser's design, whereby knights should show forth virtues in their very shape (or look for them), was uniquely suited to the figure of allegory strictly defined, for such "ideas" of the virtues can be seen pure only in deity, but are shadowed in all types and images of deity. The relation to Book I is so evident that I need not take space to particularize it; Red Crosse clearly figures forth both kinds of noblesse—in Christine's terms he is both bon chevalier and bon esprit. The imagery of the House of Holiness, the vision of the Heavenly Jerusalem, the rescue of Una-Andromeda-Regina-Eurydice or whomever you choose, the marriage made in heaven—all this shows both the use of the great expected ancient images and the ambiguity of the chevalier Jesus Christ who takes on a divine (redemptive) office without ceasing to be a human character. But Book I, with its religious direction, its sources in Revelation and in morality plays, its presentation of the basic theme of allegory (salvation through holiness), may be felt to be so special a case that it lies outside discussion.

Guyon and Britomart, too, are images of a quest more than of a conflictus, and their books show not only the confined method of a Guillaume de Lorris staging inner experiences in new and piquant terms—though of course Spenser does this too, and frequently, and well. They show equally well the difficult and dangerous method of a Jean de Meun, a kind of weaving dance-like movement, a dialectic in which no figure is Auctor but in which all the possible positions are shown to us on the great questions of: What is man's nature? Can such a thing as bon amour exist? What are Temperance, and Reason, and Fidelity, and Love? Spenser stresses more often the crying Renaissance problem, What is responsible Power? But even Book V, the one most evidently concerned with the moral discipline of the bon chevalier and good ruler, shows as well, or shows primarily, man's quest for a divine condition—the union of Justice with Love. All the characters, hero and all, constantly only approximate it. They learn what these are and look on them to admire and follow after them.

That Britomart comes closest to approximating this condition is part of a long differentiation of Love from very many things that look like it. In Book V a chief differentiation is self-will, in the relation of love to desire; it is Britomart's own first error, and Radegund's final one. But Britomart's long discipline, her manifest excesses and mistakes, and the kinds of loving acts she nevertheless consistently lays aside in order to perform her own purposes and desires—all point to an allegorical meaning in Britomart's attempt to understand the nature of Love and to pursue it. In Book III of the *Faerie Queene* we are not, nor is Britomart, learning the sex role, to use the modern psychologist's phrase. Neither are we set to re-define this role by translating it into idealistic terms or to re-shape the relation to Artegall by pouring it into Platonic or Christian molds. We are asked to watch Britomart at tasks which turn her away from finding Artegall as her raison d'être, though the place of passionate love between the sexes, in relation to all kinds of love that can be thought of, is always a theme kept before us. Whatever notion Spenser had when he began what has turned out to be the complex of Books III and IV, it is clear that before long he is examining the Idea of Love with the complications which had been brought into it by Christian thought; it is hard to retain the complexities in the one worn English word, but we catch sight of philia and agape as well as eros, or caritas when amor seems to have inextricably entwined it with concupiscentia. It seems to me a most happy part of Spenser's design that Britomart's pursuit of Artegall is interrupted and her union with that Just Knight deferred; he makes good use of these conditions, though I would be surprised if he did not come upon them rather by default, a universal artistic experience.

Allegorically, a Knight of Love is quite properly (and quite traditionally) a Knight who learns chastity, learns the nature of fidelity.[23] Britomart does not cease to be the faithful human

---

[23] Virginity as one of the forms of fidelity, "the sage and serious *doctrine* of Virginity," has its place, though this would not be as eminent as in Milton's *Comus* where the Lady's part was written for the young girl Alice Egerton; far less had to be conveyed by the allegory and its figures, and the nature of Temperance is the focus, only one of the elements to be known about the nature

lover in quest of a particular person—maintaining the literal sense is understood as an element in the figure of allegory—but the fidelity she comes to understand is not simply keeping-to-one-human-attachment; and the misdefinitions of love she meets with go much deeper than the infidelities of lust, to show the root of these infidelities and of others in the antithesis of love—self-worship.

All Spenserian figures of this size and importance are both moral and allegorical in a stricter sense; this is absolutely usual, for of course Scriptural figures were not written to be "tropology" or "allegory," and for centuries, untold numbers of them were read as both. Mammon's cave is most surely a moral allegory showing the evils of concupiscentia (in its most embracing sense, as well as covetousness in a narrower sense). But both the imagery of the canto and the extraordinary freedom and grace of the following vision of Guyon's angelic protector prove us right in our feeling that we have been in hell, where there was nothing *but* concupiscentia, and have seen the Beast himself, who thinks he is a god. It is better not to dilute these poetic experiences to moral allegory only—fictions which convince us we should fight greed or strive for chaste love in marriage; they portray men faced with the death of the soul or learning what its freedom depends upon.

The notion of a double chivalry of course developed quite independently of these two functions of figurative language. It is interesting that Christine should see and use the parallel between two sets of ideas whose relation lies in a common understanding of human ends. The hierarchy of man's allegiances, his two knighthoods, is paralleled in a literary theory which differentiates figures according to whether they are addressed to one sphere of man's

---

of Love. But no one learns so much as Britomart, and in the end it turns out to be what allegorical doctrine thinks of as saving knowledge. If Britomart were chiefly faithful just to *Artegall*, she would have acted very differently in the actions of the two books; and she *learns* how to deliver him. Of the many explanations of one of her great lessons, the delivery of Amoret, none is perfectly satisfying and perhaps none is utterly without contribution to our understanding (except those which see lustful flaws in Amoret to be cured); see most recently T. P. Roche's *The Kindly Flame, A Study of the Third and Fourth Books of Spenser's Faerie Queene* (Princeton, 1964), for a felicitious explanation and also for a very clear exposition of allegorical reading as this century could still understand it.

spiritual life or another. The two chivalries naturally gained currency in mediaeval writings which wished to show the more than moral nature of man's pursuit of virtue. It is proper to leave until the next chapter (on the virtues and vices) the further demonstration of uses of the double knighthood in connection with specific virtues—especially with the conception of Magnificence as the highest virtue of the Christian Knight, and the one possessed in perfection only by Christ himself. However, although we also give the whole matter of romances a chapter (Five), I would not defer so long the point that in the most powerful of all allegorized romances, the *Queste del saint Graal*, the strictly allegorical reading which is to be given to all important images is attached to a deliberate and declared presentation of the two chivalries.

The *Queste*, which was incorporated into the so-called Vulgate Cycle of the Arthurian romances between the prose *Lancelot* and the *Mort Artu*, is the most open treatment, and one of the most poetic and original treatments, of a fundamental motif in mediaeval writing—the tension between the earthly chivalry and heavenly chivalry. It creates a new Grail knight, Galahad, and it tells the story of his successful achievement of the queste del graal, here a fully Christianized symbol but not therefore fixedly equated with an historical chalice; it tells of Lancelot's moving, often piteous, failure and of Gawain's utter incomprehension, and Bohort's and Perceval's different kind of success. Neither Christine nor Spenser finds it necessary, as does the *Queste* author, to see the soul's quest as the sum of the human adventure. But quite aside from any subscription to this idea, or to the *Queste*'s narrow definition of chaste fidelity in the soul, the long advance through the very many symbolical episodes, which culminates in the final allegories of the marvelous Ship of Solomon and the Grail liturgy in the castle, is better preparation than any theoretical treatment of the nature of allegory for anticipating and understanding those larger metaphysical significances which we cannot persuade ourselves are absent from Spenser's large culminating allegorical images.

I am thinking less of the great mystical scenes of the *Queste* than of the constant double texture and the resulting complexity and variety of human character portrayal—and thence the poignancy with which we realize (always through figurative presentation) what it is to attempt the second kind of noblesse Caxton spoke about. As we take our way through the scores of tiny incidents, they cease to seem like fantastically curious marvels and become, under a surface as puzzling and dark as that of our real lives, a clear record of the meaning of men's half-understood choices. There are the small choices made on grounds of human bravado or self-assurance: Meliant decides to take the left-hand path he is warned against, thus testing his new knightly valor (alas, says the hermit, the warning spoke of the celestial chivalry, and you acted by the code of the chivalry of the world); Hector rides his horse up to all gates, as Knights do, and sees nothing to remark, notes no lack of the humility which marks out the chevalier Jesus Christ. There are the choices made on inadequate grounds which are obscurely blameworthy, or, the choices that are not reasoned but follow upon some commendable habit in the will and affections. We see the first sort in Lancelot as he helps the black knights that seem to need it most. He does by second nature what accords well enough with the codes of earthly chivalry, but is fatally inattentive to what the battle is about. The second sort can be seen in Perceval naïvely acting rightly—half by habit, half by chance, but protected time and again by the innocent and all but thoughtless way he looks to Heaven in his puzzles or his perils. There are the more complicated dilemmas, like Bohort's anguished hesitation, or there are the characters unaware of the presence of a choice, as with Gawain's courteous blind ironic answers to those who if heeded might reveal to him the secret that makes his journey meaningless.

The usefulness of irony is apparent in figures like these large fictional images where the persons are unaware or only half-aware, or at least less aware than are we, of the significance of what happens to them. Irony is native to the figure, and where significances are so quickly grasped that the mind moves with real freedom (as here), this must have been an important part of the pleasure taken by mediaeval audiences in such works. The same reserve and understatement which makes irony successful is responsible for the fact that the worst illegality in allegorical reading is to re-tell the images as I have just done, making the significances apparent. The hermits of the tale confine their explanations to those who have just lived through the experiences. For we have again in the *Queste* the unimpugnable evidence of readers *within* the work. We soon become accustomed to take the pleasure mediaeval listeners must have taken both in confirming our understandings by the hermits' interpretations of events, and in observing nuances we had neglected. We even learn readily to detect the fake hermits who rise up to apply conventional symbolic mis-explanations and lead knights astray. The allegorical critic we know so well, who announces "represents Evil!" as soon as he sees black objects, would quickly lose his way.

The *Queste* shows with what power the idea of a double chivalry could be used in a great literary work (a description we should never think of using for Christine's piece). But because it is so extreme and so consistent an example of reading a fiction allegorically, it amounts to a kind of discipline in the sort of double comprehension which this kind of figurative writing demands—and which some Elizabethans demanded, some of the time. The Lancelot of the *Queste* is a great psychological creation. That is by no means all. For as we take our way without hurry through all the things that happen to him, taught to see allegorically the double meaning of all that he does and all that the others do and say, we begin to read (as though under the flowing water of events) a great design, not of the drama-in-men's-minds but of the meaning of men's lives, lying there to be read under a transparent veil.

As we see slowly in many happenings what it means that Galahad is an image of Christ, that is, as we slowly take in the allegory (for allegories cannot be arrived at by the short cut of equations), we also see that the way to understand Red Crosse as a Redeemer is similar—though Galahad and Red Crosse are not the same image and do not mean the same thing. All the symbolical dictionaries we could consult will not convey the mode of action of such figures, which takes place phrase by small phrase within a work—but comparably acting figures do illuminate each other.

The double action, and hence the double reading, which I have suggested as typical of figures that can be both moralized and allegorized, was not, of course, spoken of under such carefully distinguished terms, though Christine was useful because she did so distinguish them. But even in the high mediaeval period, when such reading was common, the word "allegory" can refer to either; the *Ovide moralisé* is a prime example of what we must expect, being a tissue of the kind of interpretations Christine (and I following her) called not morals but allegories. I have wished to distinguish between two things, not two terms, and do not recommend trying to maintain Christine's terminology; it is too late. But it is not too late to keep the two kinds of figure roughly separate, since we have indisputable evidence that this was done, and done in secular literary works, much later than we would have expected. These understandings, which were to hand in popular and accessible forms for sixteenth-century men to take in and follow, will deliver such writers as Spenser from the slicing machine which reading on different "levels" has turned into of late. It will sometimes at least restore the depth of a reading that does not reduce human life to a psychomachia, spiritual life to morals and images to axes and hammers.

CHAPTER TWO

Allegory of Vices and Virtues

EDMUND SPENSER is not the inventor of the idea that Magnificence is the virtue which "is the perfection of all the rest," or even of the idea that it "conteineth in it them all." It was somewhat rash of him to ascribe this to "Aristotle and the rest," for Aristotle scarcely makes this claim, though indeed it is literally true of a good number of "the rest." When, in the Letter to Ralegh, Spenser gave this as the reason why "in the person of Prince Arthur I sette forth magnificence in particular," he probably meant his words very precisely, that this virtue is the one by which we designate all the other virtues if perfected, if brought to their completion—virtues in their absolute or perfect state. For that is what is said by the most interesting of "the rest" who after Aristotle write so copiously of the virtues.

We may look first at a firm, clear statement of this conception of Magnificence. I choose a manual or handbook sort of text, for they are long lived, and quote from Caxton's English translation of the famous French *Somme le roi*, reprinted later by Wynkyn de Worde and Pynson. Though the text is familiar in many forms, I use books available to sixteenth-century men, as the French text would also have been. I could as well quote from a fourteenth-century translation now more easily accessible to us, for differences are unimportant.[1] "The vi degree of prowesse is

---

[1] Caxton's "Ryal book," STC 21429, *ca.* 1486, was reproduced by Wynkyn de Worde in 1507. As men who rescued and passed on a large bulk of mediaeval romances and semi-didactic works, extending the fame for example of Malory, Chaucer, Gower and Lydgate, these printers received some of the kind of veneration felt for Camden by students of England's antiquities; and Drayton's use of de Worde in Ecl. 4 of *Shepherd's Garland* almost to typify "Romants" and mediaeval literature, in a lament for old things, is a case in point. For readers of the 1560's or 1580's it is always important to note a Caxton connection even if other editions were available, and the point will often come up throughout this book. Information on the French author and text of the *Somme* (dated 1279) will be given later; the most accessible version for us is the translation printed in *EETS*, vol. 217 by W. N. Francis (*The Book of Vices and Virtues*, with informative introduction); when later this is used for convenience of readers interested in context, differences from texts accessible to the men of the sixteenth century have always been scrutinized. Here the passages are Caxton, ch. cxxiv (sigs. N8v-Ov); *EETS*, vd. 217, p. 168.

magnyfycence. this vertu expresseth & declareth also the phylosophre sayeng Magnyfycence is an hye werke and happy achyevyng. Our Lord Jhesu Cryst the soverayn phylosophre *calleth this vertu perseveraunce* by whyche the good knyght of God endureth the evulles *unto the ende in that hye waye of perfectyon* whyche he hath emprysed. Of thys vertu sayth saynt poule that al the vertues renne/ but this vertu wynneth the swerde Alle they fyght but this hath the vyctorye & the crowne. Alle werken. But thys vertu of perseveraunce bereth awaye the rewarde and the meryte. For oure lord Jhesu Cryste sayth. who that shal persevere unto the ende he shal be saved & none other." The context of this understanding of Magnificentia, including the reasons for the pervasive chivalric imagery, and the total organization of the book are the most interesting and influential matters to consider, but we must approach them piecemeal.

Meanwhile, it is to be noticed that although the outright identification of Magnificence by name with the unnamed New Testament virtue, which alone deserves the incorruptible crown of 1 Cor. 9, is not to my knowledge a commonplace in text upon text, the Christianization of Magnificence and its pre-eminence is so. A Spenserian with an eye upon Prince Arthur's Magnificence in the *Faerie Queene*, perfecting all virtues through grace, is much more comfortable in the neighborhood of such definitions and conceptions than in trying to contrive a close relation with texts such as we are used to in the *Ethics* and *Rhetoric*: "Magnificence . . . a virtue concerned with wealth" extends only to those actions "that involve expenditure"; "For, as the name itself suggests, it is a fitting expenditure involving largeness of scale" (*Ethics*. iv.2). "The magnificent man . . . like an artist . . . can spend large sums tastefully. . . . Magnificence is an attribute of expenditures of the kind which we call honourable, e.g. those connected with the gods . . . and proper objects of public-spirited ambition, as when people think they ought to equip a chorus or a trireme . . . in a brilliant way." "The magnificent man spends not on himself but on public objects . . . will also furnish his house suitably to his wealth . . . what is most magnificent absolutely is great expenditure on a great object . . ." (iv.2). "With regard to money there are also other dispositions—a mean, magnificence (for the magnificent man differs from the liberal man; the former deals with large sums . . .), an excess, tastelessness and vulgarity and a deficiency, niggardliness . . ." (ii.7). "Magnificence is a virtue productive of greatness in matters involving the spending of money," its opposite "meanness" (*Rhet*.i.9). These were well-known passages long before the 1580's.

Frère Lorens in his *Somme le roi* has occasion to treat of Magnificence because from Cicero onward it had been a famous "part" of Fortitude, and one which was never omitted, whatever the other variations, throughout several centuries of well-known treatments by almost every important Christian thinker. One did not ignore the united authority of Cicero and Macrobius. To Cicero, Magnificentia is the first part of Fortitude; the others are Fidentia, Patientia and Perseverantia.[2] It has already lost the emphases which have made the purely Aristotelian Magnificence so troublesome a virtue for the Christian Arthur to "sette forth" in a poem like the *Faerie Queene*, which though inconceivable as belonging to any era except the magnificent Renaissance, is yet profoundly imbued with a distrust of the pretensions of vainglory, famous form of Pride, the vice of Book I. Cicero defines Fortitude, that double virtue "by which one [1] undertakes dangerous tasks and [2] endures hardships," and Magnificence under it as "the contemplation and execution of great and sublime projects with a certain grandeur and magnificence of imagination."[3] Influential as Cicero was, Macrobius was yet more so, and partly for the interesting reason that he leaves his subdivisions undefined, so that they were all the more open to the idealization and Christianization fully apparent in those who followed and used him.

Macrobius' brief and memorable treatment of the cardinal virtues occurs in that piece of his which most became common property in all succeeding centuries: the *In somnium Scipionis*, i.8. It is referred to ("Macrob.liber 1") by one successor after another, and even when it is not, we yet see its marks, for every-

---

[2] I must ask the reader's indulgence touching one barbarism repeatedly found in this chapter and elsewhere: the use, without italics, of any or several languages for names and subdivisions of virtues and vices. Translation is very hazardous and obscures alignments; redactions being cited can be wordlessly made clear in multiple citations, and the like.

[3] This is the Loeb Classics editor's translation of "Magnificentia est rerum magnarum et excelsarum cum animi ampla quadam et splendida propositione cogitatio atque administratio." The wordings are to re-echo through all following centuries, though not unaffected by other influences. Copied out as commonplaces, they do not always argue direct contact with Cicero's text.

one passes on its statement that Fortitude is manifested in Magnanimitas, Fiducia, Securitas, Magnificentia, Constantia, Tolerantia, Firmitas. Frère Lorens in his *Somme* has done what great
numbers of learned theologians, encyclopedists before and after
Vincent, devisers of iconographical programs and vernacular
popularizers, have done; for what we meet is a combination of
the two great early authorities, in his six "degrees": Magnanimity,
Affiaunce, Surete, Patience, Constaunce, Magnificence.

Macrobius' series is the staple of Lorens' list, but his selection
was probably not original with him, though he must have known
both authors. The use of Cicero's Patientia, omitting Macrobius'
Tolerantia, had become customary in the series of treatises that
cluster around 1150—at least three of them, very popular, by
known authors, were translated later, used in the arts, and are
extant in numerous manuscripts. And in any case, this famous
name of a virtue, with its scriptural uses and eminence as Christ's
special form of Fortitude, ousted other names for the aspect of
Fortitude we call sufferance, in lists of the cardinal virtues and
their parts; it also became prominent in another famous series of
quite other virtues, wherein Patience became the most frequently
appearing opposer of Ira, especially in art. As we have seen
from the quoted English passage, Lorens had a conception of
Magnificence as Christian Perseverance, perfecting the virtue by
carrying it through to the end, which took care of the remaining
subdivisions, Cicero's Perseverantia and Macrobius' Firmitas.

No one, Latin or vernacular, writes a discourse on virtues
that ignores these two founts of wisdom; but in all probability,
Lorens did not deliberately set himself to sort out and pair their
essential divisions, but merely decided that a sensible choice had
been made—exactly the six he has, and so named—by the author
of an exceedingly long-lived treatise, the *Moralium dogma philosophorum*. That author was pretty certainly Guillaume de
Conches, who wrote shortly before 1150; but the *Moralium*
was constantly re-copied, translated into French and Italian and
German, quoted by fourteenth-century and fifteenth-century
writers both learned and popular—and for that matter, accessible
to sixteenth-century men in at least five editions.[4] For though

---

[4] The survival of this extremely popular piece in some ninety manuscripts,
the early editions, the translations, the forty-odd manuscripts of the French
version (thirteenth to fifteenth century), and so on, are discussed in John

Guillaume de Conches, or John of Wales, or even Alain de Lille, and Frère Lorens may sound like recherché sources for conceptions held by men writing on the virtues in the sixteenth-century, two points must be kept in mind: that learning or indeed any serious study was still fed from sources of this kind, rejuvenated by the late Renaissance editions which old libraries and especially collegiate libraries can show us were bought and used; and secondly, that vernacular versions and popularized uses had steadily channeled memorable parts of learned traditions into the stream of accepted common knowledge, with arts other than verbal acting as a special factor in such conservation.[5]

Though as yet I have had occasion to specify but two among the incredibly numerous mediaeval treatments of virtues—Lorens' and the *Moralium dogma philosophorum*—an important general observation might well be kept in mind from the outset. If a Renaissance writer treats the virtues or uses them to frame a literary piece, if he is learned and not only pious, our first thought has been that we will find his ideas in Aristotle. No first step could be more sensible, given the undoubted pre-eminence of the *Nicomachaean Ethics* to men of the Renaissance, and the step is usually assisted, as it is in Spenser's case, by the author's declaration of his dependence. It behooves us not to forget that Aristotle, and only Aristotle, is actually named by that poet, though he himself declares he found that Aristotle was supported by others. But there was not merely one vital and revered classical tradition by which Greek and Roman conceptions and learning about the virtues were carried to men of later societies. There were certainly at least four great streams to which men gave conscious attention. The other renowned name and our natural second thought, Seneca, directs us to the sources of a large bulk of the general moral advice rife in Renaissance writings on the

---

Holmberg's edition (Uppsala, 1929). It can be read in *P.Lat.*171 also, and an informative article on it by Delhaye appears in *Recherches de théologie ancien et medieval*, vol. 16 (1949), 227-58.

[5] These general statements are better documented in Tuve, "Some Notes on the Virtues and Vices," *JWCI*, vols. 26, 27 (1963, 1964). The last claim is exemplified in two cases of the influence upon the graphic arts of the *Moralium dogma philosophorum*, one impeccably supported by inscriptions in the illumination, the other a more conjectural connection with the famous "Good Government" fresco in Siena.

subject, though not to the source of their systematizations and schemas. In fact, "Seneca on the virtues" refers to a specific text so familiar to mediaeval students that he has assumed something of the same natural first place for those who investigate earlier times, as has Aristotle with his *Ethics* for the Renaissance. Any mediaeval four-virtues treatise is first suspected of being some form of the *Formula honestae vitae* ascribed to Seneca but written in the mid-sixth century by Martin of Braga (M. Dumiensis); we shall meet it again.

In both Middle Ages and Renaissance we must add to these two favorites, and usual hunting-grounds for sources of ideas and conventions, a Ciceronian tradition and a Macrobian tradition which were lively and extremely influential. Both were peculiarly important for the classification and definition of the virtues, that is, the great ancient series of the cardinal four—discussed with specificity, "divided," differentiated and characterized, envisaged.

Both authors were thoroughly acclimatized and integrated into Christian thought through a long development. Their pervasive influence wound down like a growing vine to influence the ways in which the other two "classical" authors were understood. Like some other authors in spheres distinct from the tradition of virtues, their "mediaevalization" made them all the more good classics—attractive, intelligible and comfortable to the many Renaissance writers who were not in revolt against all mediaeval thought. This greater acceptance and tolerance of mediaeval ideas is always a difference to consider between England and (e.g.) Italy. A framework, a terminology and definitions are always long-lived for mnemonic reasons; but also their influence on held conceptions, though subtler, is often as important as that of consciously imitated propositions.

The Ciceronian treatment which was so steadily recalled was not the longer and less schematic one in the *De officiis* but the brief summary in the *De inventione* (ii.53-4). What the *De officiis* has to say about the cardinal virtues was widely used, of course, in both Middle Ages and Renaissance (and also I here speak of only a minute area of that book's total influence). The *Moralium dogma philosophorum*, which we have had occasion to notice was based upon it, interweaves vast numbers of quotations from it with other classical passages, in verse and prose.

But the rapid presentation of each virtue with its "parts" in the *De inventione* was a locus classicus; what they cite as "rhet.1.li.ii" provided names and definitions which do not cease to echo through mediaeval treatises. Meanwhile, the Macrobian framework seems to have been universally used; classifications which order the analyses in treatment after treatment are controlled by the brief set of lists in *Somnium Scipionis* 1.8.

The importance of these named subdivisions to later conceptions of what the four virtues are and include becomes apparent even in a cursory study of treatises—which we choose for such adventitious reasons as that they remained accessible, or were popular in the vernacular, or were used in the arts. To Prudence, says Macrobius, belong Ratio, Intellectus, Circumspectio, Providentia, Docilitas, Cautio. And later treatises line up behind him like those who walk a trial (as was the case with the seven virtues we looked at under Fortitude), very often preserving even Macrobius' order as subsource copied from subsource. One of the most famous manuscripts in the history of the iconography of the virtues is a Rouen copy (Bibl.munic.MS.927) of Aristotle's *Ethics* in Oresme's glossed translation. It has been thought heretofore to be the earliest occurrence of the "new iconography of the virtues" whose development in the post-middle and late fifteenth century was outlined with some distaste by Emile Mâle. It is scarcely a demonstration of Aristotelian influence that at Book II the *seven* virtues stand in a row, strangely accoutred after the fashion of "the new iconography," in this manuscript which we can now date *ca.* 1454. Less puzzling but yet more revealing is the illustration to Aristotle's Book VI, on the intellectual virtues. We find there a large representation of Prudentia (see Fig. 13), with four damsels with scrolls who "belong to Prudence." But they are the un-Aristotelian figures—Circonspectio, Providencia, Cautio and Docilitas—and on their philacteries (and on Prudentia's) are verbatim definitions in Latin from that same *Moralium dogma philosophorum* of the earlier twelfth century.[6] One reason (besides my desire not to mention too many

---

[6] These inscriptions are given in the article referred to above in n. 5, with further data on this manuscript's history and date, on reproductions of it, and of the pictorial tradition in other *Ethiques* manuscripts. Guillaume's dates are 1080-*ca.*1154, but manuscript copies and translations spread over the later centuries; there is not a tradition of illuminations for his piece.

FIGURE 13*

texts) why we have already encountered it twice as a borrowing place, for a thirteenth-century Dominican and a fifteenth-century artist, is that it set an early pattern for definitions of Macrobius' undefined subdivisions. And here is the early pattern "lighting up" the meanings of Aristotle, in one of the most sumptuous of fifteenth-century manuscripts.

A slightly different popular pattern was dispersed through a treatise bearing a name more famous in literature—Alain de Lille (*ca.* 1160). His framework, divisions and inclusions are yet more firmly Macrobian, for he generally omits none and keeps even the order of names; but he depended for definitions on still another much-copied treatise, the *Ysagoge in theologiam*, through which ideas of the virtues prevalent in the Abelardian school were widely disseminated.[7] This particular tractate of Alain's, which

* Please see the List of Illustrations and Sources following the text.

[7] The swiftest way to refer to these treatises, their alignments and their modern editors (whom I shall not always give unless I quote) is to cite the series of volumes by Dom O. Lottin, *Psychologie et morale aux* XIIe *et* XVIIIe *siècles*,

was spread, like all these materials, through being taught (preserved abridgments proving to be student's notes), did not get into print; yet as late as the turn into the fifteenth century, an author who was no stranger to Renaissance readers, Christine de Pisan, saw fit to translate it into French. Described as "les diffinicions des .iiii.vertus cardinales et de leurs parties selon loppinion des hommes ecclesiastiques," it appears attached to her *Livre de prudence*. This place for the tractate (in two of the best and earliest manuscripts)[8] is important to our concerns as well, for the *Livre* is her version of the Braga-"Seneca" text.

The texts I shall be able to refer to are a mere fraction chosen for exemplification.[9] Thus, when Macrobius says that Temperance has in her train Modestia, Verecundia, Abstinentia, Castitas, Honestas, Moderatio, Parcitas, Sobrietas, Pudicitia, we are to think not of one author's isolated statement on the nature of that virtue, but of a well-established group of Temperance's manifestations that had become fixed by centuries of repetition. For these duly reappear in the *Ysagoge*, the *Moralium dogma philosophorum*, in Alanus, and of course in Christine, and in a string of

6 vols. (Paris, 1942-60), especially III, parts 1 and 2, and VI. Important problems not relevant here dictate his organization, which is not author by author, and I therefore do not attempt full references to his recurrent data. Lottin is also the most recent editor of Alanus' *De virtutibus et de vitiis et de donis Sp.Sancti*—in vol. VI, but previously edited in *Medieval Studies*, vol. 12 (1950). It is truncated both in the abridgments and in Christine's translation (which of course may be someone else's, appropriated by her); these are described in the article referred to in n. 5 above.

[8] It is described, with manuscript references, in Part 1 of the article cited in n. 5; there is no tradition of pictured virtues for the Latin or vernacular versions of "Seneca," and none in the ornate early Christine manuscripts, though another French version is curiously linked to "the new iconography."

[9] Small study of the authors and texts referred to in Lottin's volumes (cited in n. 7 above) will show how many and yet more famous writers could be made use of here. I am choosing texts made iconographically prominent or interestingly popularized in vernaculars, and make no mention of Albertus Magnus, Guillaume d'Auxerre, Jean de la Rochelle, Simon Hinton, Guillaume d'Auvergne, Chancellor Philip, Ambrose, Bonaventura, Thomas, and many others, all of them variously related to the two traditions.

Once recognized, it is curious in how many connections known series pop up, often making some problems nonexistent. For example, the subspecies of virtues are fundamentally those of the two traditions studied here; on page 22 of an article on "The Passage on Sins in the *Decir a las siete virtudes*" (D. C. Clarke, *SP*, vol. 59 [1962], 18-30), some questions touched do not arise.

others—including a group as yet unmentioned who took Cicero's lists as the base of organization but dutifully added Macrobius'. Moreover, Alanus, like some before him and many after, could not forebear to add Cicero's first part, Continentia, as one of the accompaniments which "follow" Temperance. Though Cicero's second, Clementia, is largely confined to his imitators, his third and last, Modestia, is also in Macrobius, so that once more we have a merging of the two.

Also we simply circumvent, in most of the treatments conventional for centuries, that quarrel so space taking in Spenserian criticism—whether Temperance *or* Continence is some character's virtue, and which of them is, which not, designated as "A Virtue." Long, long before Spenser's time, in materials remaining current, Continence had been accepted as one of the forms of Temperance, and pseudo-Seneca (Martin of Braga) could simply use her name to designate that virtue, as he refers to Fortitude the second cardinal virtue as Magnanimity, first Macrobian facet. It is best, unless an author himself comments on newly aroused doubts, not to attribute too sharp a sense of responsibility for differentiations and characterizations which the centuries had not kept alive; and particularly it is not safe to grasp at distinctions we can turn up in Aristotle or others to explain puzzles in Spenser's allegory. Three names it would surely be ill-advised to dare excise from Spenser's claimed body of authorities, "Aristotle and *the rest*": Cicero, Macrobius and "Seneca."

With Justice, matters are yet more complicated, for it is the most interesting virtue, the one most related to metaphysics and the definitions of Deity, most caught up in doubles entendres during centuries (including the sixteenth) when every Western man was conscious of the Vulgate uses translated iustitia: righteousness. It is the virtue which most violently resists the attempt to denominate virtues classical or Christian. The amalgamation under this head took place early. Cicero's parts were Religio, Pietas, Gratia, Vindicatio, Observantia, Veritas; his names are retained and their purport is Christianized. Macrobius began with Innocentia, Amicitia, Concordia, then inserted Cicero's historically very important two—Pietas and Religio—and finished with Affectus and Humanitas (all of them, as usual, undefined). Even writers who are faithfully Macrobian insert some of the Ciceronian names, as does Alanus, who apparently started an important modification—the introduction of the three theological virtues, Faith, Hope and Charity, as under or manifesting Religio.

The *Moralium dogma philosophorum*, before embarking on subdivisions, used the *De officiis* to outline a basic division between Severitas and Liberalitas. This did not cease to have reverberations; it became useful when, after the full text of Aristotle's *Ethics* became known (roughly during the time Albertus Magnus was writing), writers wished to introduce ideas of Distributive and Commutative Justice and yet not lose the inclusion of penal justice which both mediaeval and Renaissance treatments find reasonable. These famous two terms, however, usually indicate true influence of the *Ethics* itself, which increases not only with St. Thomas but at the time of Oresme's fourteenth-century translations of Aristotle. Meanwhile, the idea of Liberalitas, even Largitas as in Abelardian materials, takes a completely accepted place among notions of how justice is manifested; terminology varies early, as we see from Macrobius' last two names. Lottin notes the importance of Peter Lombard's adoption of one of Augustine's defining statements, that Justice lies "in subveniendo miseris." For thus Misericordia became not occasionally but commonly and properly one of the faces of Justice.[10] This traditional alignment makes a Mercilla canto in a Book of Justice read rather differently than it would if we assumed that men had no habit other than our own opposition of the just and the merciful, much as the earlier-mentioned inclusion of Caritas induces some new thoughts about Britomart's quest.[11]

These divisions and refinements did not remain locked up in the Latin treatises but, in the train of that "dividing" into aspects which became completely habitual, both the names and the ideas

[10] Lottin's chapter on Justice in vol. III of the series cited in n. 7 above is helpful not only for information but to save the citations from treatises that would engulf our purposes here. His discussion of Aquinas comes at pp. 323ff., and for interesting remarks on the effect of Peter Lombard's espousal of Augustine's dictum, see p. 286; the quotation in my text is from *De trin.*14.9 as given in *P.Lat.*42:1046.

[11] I do not argue that the earlier periods did not often make our habitual oppositions; these are the times which developed and made wide literary use of such allegories as that of the Four Daughters of God, with its debate for and against man's salvation, between Mercy and Peace his champions and Justice and Truth his accusers. But a many-faceted Justice was a commonplace, not an idiosyncrasy, before Artegall's story was imagined as a way to show it forth.

were passed on and became rhetorically useful, mnemonically fixed, almost schoolboy's property because of the lucky combination of authority behind them. Religio and Pietas never lost ground; and as a result of the basic definition of Justice as giving "ius suum" to all, an interesting arrangement became current in which Religio shows as the Justice of giving God his due, Pietas giving due to parents and nourishers, Amicitia—to equals, Innocentia—to subordinates, Concordia—to our fellow citizens, Misericordia—to those in need, and Reverentia or Veneratio or other names for proper recognition of elevation—to superiors. If we found such alignments only in a Guillaume d'Auxerre we might dismiss the notion of their influence, but they are loud and clear in a much-copied book like the *Moralium dogma philosophorum*, re-appear independently stated with variations (as in Alanus), are handed on to influence graphic portrayals of Justice and to give Concordia and Discordia special relevance when the vice opposed to the virtue forms the way to define it. If Amicitia is surprising to us, certain other usual inclusions are superficially more so: Alanus' Humilitas, the Obedientia which we must justly offer where it is due, the Devotio which St. Thomas conceives of as justly God's—so that Religio is a subdivision of this moral virtue not of a theological one. "Sanctitas," too, finds a place to which we are quite unaccustomed. The context formed by such inclusions (and it was Cicero's Religio that furthered them) is a context in which Holiness could not seem the kind of eruption, among virtues where it does not belong that it seems to modern readers of the *Faerie Queene*. The obvious connection of all these "just" virtues with the infused theological virtue of Faith is not loosely but nicely understood.

We are not making any attempt so foolhardy as to outline the development of the idea of Justice in the centuries which preceded sixteenth-century allegories of her. It is our presuppositions and unexamined associations, not our sophisticated definitions, which would profit by some of the earlier flexibility—our opposition of Justice and Love, our sense of a courtroom virtue, the law's creature, which "sees Justice done," by ensuring fair play with cool objectivity. With each virtue of the four, we experience this same re-settling of assumed boundaries. It is obvious to a reader who works back from the popular treatments and artistic or vernacular appearances to what they adapted or translated, that the sixteenth-century web of lore about virtues is truly formed from uncut threads, and that certain unusual slants of thought remained to help us explain later anomalies, modes of organization, or things seen by us as peculiarities or even flaws (like Spenser's odd list of virtues, or the pre-eminence of Arthur's own).

Niceties of distinction will be blurred, of course, as centuries advance. Yet, figurative expression of ideas is remarkable for conserving nuances, and both the graphic arts and the large controlling images of poems perform this task easily. For example, in Lorenzetti's famous fresco in the Palazzo Pubblico in Siena, the appearance of the three theological virtues in an order above the cardinal-virtues-and-Concordia, that are grouped around the "Common Good" or Good Commune, conveys the difference between infused virtues and those natural acquired virtues which they partially cause; and "under" Securitas the landscape of that commune shows life and death with safety, "under" Timor it is shown in peril (see n. 20). In general, we may well beware of assuming that these copied and re-copied lists indicate a rote-memory mechanization or a jejune conception of the nature of the virtues. The problems which the theological discussions argue, with tickle points of niceness, are those which are still the difficult ones in later treatments. Which virtues are natural? How and how far are they acquired? Which come by gift? Which are the private ones and which public? Which overlap? Which have priority to others? What are the relations between them? For the recognition of Justice as especially cardinal, the hinge of the others, is as common as the observation that St. Bernard rightly called Prudence the auriga or charioteer. Or, though the *Moralium dogma philosophorum* rightly denominated Prudence the "Lantern" who goes "before" the others, still Temperance or "Evenhede" must be said to be the one necessary before any of them *are* virtues ("Seneca"-Martin of Braga shows this; the *Somme le roi* discusses it under the virtue opposed to Wrath, Equité, the virtue with the plumb-line, measuring all—which we must admit into our too-legalized Equité, when Artegall must learn it from Britomart).

Another much-argued question, quite rightly, was the propriety of the word "parts" (it was Cicero's) for the subdivisions we have been noting. Macrobius avoids the word, presumably from a deliberate wish not to imply that the cardinal virtues are wholes made up of the constituent elements he lists. His implication is that these elements, which follow from, or come of, or show, or declare, the great quiddity he is dividing, are aspects or faces in which the virtue is made manifest. At any rate, this is the understanding maintained with a curious clarity even in popular treatments using Macrobius. This is a typical mediaeval way to view such a matter, and it is figuratively fertile. It makes allegory a natural mode in which to portray the visible action of such universals, which were difficult to grasp and hold in a definition. The degrees or steps that we quoted from the *Somme le roi*'s treatment of Fortitude are not at all a favorite locution or image; the divisions within virtues make no hierarchy (though some sets of virtues are so seen). Some form of the figures in "born of" or "in attendance upon" is most usual; the subdivisions are living evidences which display the quality of, or make apparently operative in human affairs, the abstractions whose nature is thus exposited. Some uses of Cicero's wordings persist, but the unease shown in the discussions and the prevalence of other locutions warn us that a more subtle idea of the relationship was common. Therefore, there is no fuss made about the overlapping of aspects or manifestations; no one boggles at how a child overlaps its parent, or how two adumbrations of the nature of a thing are too similar to separate neatly. Thus, what we might have thought to be old classical bottles safely held a remarkable amount of new Christian wine.

Important for iconography was the fact that while Cicero's nomenclature and definitions were frequently kept, the understanding of the listed abstractions was related to a perfect and divine virtue in ways Cicero could never have meant. The offspring, or attendants, or embodiments of the virtues are frequently personified and portrayed. The effect of a shift from parts to manifestations upon the verbal portrayal of a virtue is a strictly comparable effect. It betrays itself in that stage of composition which these epochs called invention. We shall notice this later in the *Faerie Queene*, where this habitual view (quite truly a view and nothing propositional) much affected the structures of the Books.

Dependence most upon Cicero or most upon Macrobius varies, and one doubts that either stress is more humanistic than the other. A thoroughly mediaeval writer, John of Wales of the late thirteenth century, organizes his *Breviloquium de virtutibus* primarily according to Cicero's divisions and illustrates each with many exempla from classical history; yet he adds, and usually treats, Macrobius' named aspects. Very popular in manuscript form, and spread abroad in printing up into the 1500's, this little treatise was put into Italian four times and into French at least twice in the early and mid-1400's.[12] The circumstances of the French translations re-emphasize an attachment clearly intended by the author and consistently important to the study of virtues—the connection with advice-to-princes literature. In illuminated manuscripts the adaptations of John, somewhat by chance, were more frequently attached to "the new iconography of the virtues" than to other texts. An abridgment in French of the *Breviloquium* was tucked into a vast historical compilation by Jean Mansel in the 1450's or '60's, the *Fleur des histoires*, which was designed to teach men in power, through history; certain illustrated manuscripts picture the virtues in the new way. An independent abridgment of John's treatise appears in a manuscript (of good lineage and authentic connections) of Christine de Pisan's compilation of advice, the *Othéa*; this manuscript of these two pieces offers us the first clear example of "the new iconography," dated 1450—and illustrating, oddly enough, Christine's(?) abridged translation of John on the cardinal virtues (see Figs. 14, 15, 16 of Prudence, Fortitude and Temperance in Bodl. MS. Laud misc.570). I think the twice-seen connection with John's treatise fortuitous,[13] except that the factor of vernacular popularization for a rich spon-

[12] A. G. Little mentions manuscripts surviving to the number of 150 to 200, 12 editions by 1520—but these figures do not separate the *Breviloquium*; however, more than 40 manuscripts of this are listed in M. W. Bloomfield's "Preliminary List of Incipits of Latin Works on the Virtues and Vices" in *Traditio*, vol. 11 (1955), No. 821, and it is even now easy to find it in print. John was in Oxford *ca.* 1259-62, went to Paris *ca.* 1270; see A. G. Little, *Studies in English Franciscan History* (1917), ch. 5; we now have the valuable addition of W. A. Pantin, "John of Wales and Medieval Humanism" in *Mediaeval Studies Presented to Aubrey Gwynn* (Dublin, 1961), pp. 297-319, and B. Smalley, *English Friars and Antiquity* (Oxford, 1960), pp. 51-55.

[13] The identification of the Mansel and "Laud" texts as translated adaptations of John's *Breviloquium* is shown in the author's article cited in n. 5 above, where their contents are described, and the genesis of the iconography is much more carefully treated, with data on the manuscript exemplars which show it.

FIGURE 14

FIGURE 15

FIGURE 16

sor (hence sumptuous illustration) came into conjunction with
the really operative point—organization around the parts or accompaniments of the virtues, which induced the curious attempt
to show their nature in attributes and pictured offices. As I have
intimated, Spenser's series of appearances of a virtue first in one
manifestation, then in another, has precise connections with this
development.

The other text which we find illustrated by this elaborate and
fussily allegorical iconography shows an equal divorce between
text and pictures—for as in the case of both abridgments of
John, no words of the text could evoke the strange habiliments
and symbolic objects which surround the virtues. In this instance
the unsuitable sets of pictures are to be found in a manuscript of
the French translation of Martin of Braga's *Formula vitae
honestae*, more often entitled *De quatuor virtutibus*. The translation was made for the Duke of Berry (as was the manuscript
of which Laud misc.570 is a copy) by Jehan de Courtecuisse, in
1403; but the manuscripts are late, and there is nothing to tell
us whether an early exemplar was being imitated by the illumi-

nator of B.N.MS.fr.9186, whose bizarre set of cardinal virtues is reproduced in Fig. 17, their late date of *ca*. 1470 casting suspicion on the verses of "explanation."[14]

There is even less reason for attaching such an iconographical program to this treatise, for the "Senecan" tradition does not enter upon the division into ancillary virtues or facets which might conceivably, in some lost work, have provoked the illustration of these usually personified aspects through symbolic objects—for example, Prudence's sieve for the Circumspectio which Prudence is, though she has other natures and offices; Fortitude's tower for her appearance as impregnable Constancy, and her press for that aspect in which she is Patientia; Temperance's clock for Moderatio. But Martin did not organize his treatise as all our others have. The glosses, Latin and vernacular, have not been studied, for Jehan de Courtecuisse's version has found no editor, and Christine's in the *Livre de prudence* has not appeared, and although when read in manuscript these seem to reveal no secrets, we cannot accurately gauge the full importance of the "Senecan" tradition of the virtues. But it was an enormously popular small tract in manuscript form and in print, and there can literally be no doubt whatever that Renaissance authors interested in the virtues knew what it said about Prudence, Magnanimity, Continence and Justice. Chiefly it gave generalized moral advice about the usual four, two designated by their derived names, springing from important facets. This tradition, already known to be pseudo-Senecan in some mediaeval manuscripts well before Erasmus entered the fray, was a schoolbook for Rabelais and was quoted by Dante and Chaucer; yet it is (I consider) the least interesting and least fundamentally important of them all, for sixteenth-century writers. The text makes estimable and wise observations, and we listen with interest as our forebears did; there the interest for literature seems to stop—though it takes some temerity to state that a work of which there were 635 known manuscripts is

---

[14] The replica of *ca*. 1475 in MS.Chantilly 491 is evidently copied; for references to reproductions, support of dates, and other Courtecuisse Manuscripts, see the citation in n. 13 above. The verses accompanying each virtue are printed by E. Mâle in *L'art réligious de la fin du moyen âge* (5th ed.; Paris, 1949), pp. 313-17. I do not think them explanations of the origin of the pictures, but inventions after-the-fact.

FIGURE 17

unimportant.[15] It did not exhibit that strange marriage of classical and Christian presuppositions which is the secret of so many fertile figures.

We see, then, that a man of the 1580's, or earlier, or later, who wished to make the virtues an important vehicle of his thought would find it unnatural to avoid certain inherited bodies of material and traditions for treating them. These obviously still lively traditions were classical in their inception (or thought to be) but were changed and vivified and made all the more congenial by developments during Christian times, which were no longer separable from the resulting amalgamations. This account has been extremely restrained in pressing the accessibility and long life of the traditions described. What we know about education at the time, what we can still see in the arts, influences we detect in popular manuals or in the very color left upon the language (once we are alert to these classifications and definitions) combine to prove that classical lore about the four cardinal virtues was manifold. Moreover, these treatments and listings were not rivals; from the beginning they illuminated and corroborated each other. This could not have been true if men had kept to the Ciceronian rigor of four wholes divided into their constituent parts. Modern discussions could well re-introduce some of the flexibility, variety and richness of definition that accompanied these examinations of a many-faceted abstraction under headings which indicated the multifarious forms of behavior whence it could be abstracted.

Similarly, there is not a shred of antipathy sensed or shown between classical virtues and some Christian set that ought to be substituted for them. There exist two peculiarly Christian sets. The integration is effortless. It operates equally well in the classifications and basic definitions of treatments taking up some exclusively Christian problem as in the more patent classical dependence of a John of Wales with his hosts of exempla, or of a

---

[15] The modern editor is Claude Barlow, *Martini Episc. Bracarensis Opera Omnia* (1950), though it may be read in very many places, incl. *P.Lat.*72:21. Anything which ran to over two hundred manuscripts and forty printings before 1500, with comparable figures after, has escaped obscurity. I have denied place in this book to any materials whose accessibility was conjecturable. The long life of traditions described sometimes has to be confirmed through references given; when editors show popularity by lists of manuscripts, early printings, and translations, I have not thought it necessary to reproduce proofs of so indubitable a vitality.

Moralium dogma philosophorum with its dozens of quotations from the ancients.

It has been quite proper that scholarship on Spenser has attacked the question of the relations of the *Faerie Queene* to the *Nicomachaean Ethics* first and foremost, and with extreme care for detail. The poet's own statement directs us to this. We need not have stopped there. Moreover, touching what "Aristotle" thought and meant, the uncontaminated, warranted-truly-Greek Aristotle that a modern student tries to isolate and read was neither a possibility nor a desirable possibility to Spenser. To be sure, scholars have been aware of the difference made by mediaeval and Renaissance commentaries on Aristotle's own text, but again we stopped too soon. For the other "classics" helped Spenser to what he thought Aristotle indeed meant—by a term like Magnificentia for instance, or Temperance and Continence compared, or the relation of iustitia to righteousness; and we may be sure he thought the later writers useful both for understanding Aristotle and understanding virtue. Much as we would seek for help in good modern editors, later classical expositions, books studying "classical conceptions of the virtues," so Spenser was certainly unlikely to engage in a vast work based on ideas so fundamental as the virtues without regarding the living traditions which explained what the ancients thought these were. All such sources were still being studied and conveniently to hand for all educated men, together with the books which students normally used to explicate them. We too, like Spenser in the Letter to Ralegh, would refer to the master himself as the spring of our ideas, think we had grasped them "as Aristotle hath devised," and feel no need to recite the interpretative helps we had in understanding what Aristotle devised; similarly, Spenser must have felt no need to refer to a Castiglione or all the Stoics when he tells us what Virgil and Homer devised—though we now think he rather tells us what these later men read into those poets.

Spenser's easy reference to "Aristotle and the rest" shows how unselfconscious his attitude was. Were we primarily and seriously interested, as he was, in what the virtues are, rather than in Aristotle's ideas of the virtues, Cicero's ideas of the virtues, Aquinas' ideas of the virtues, we would find these attitudes more natural ourselves. He is not an intellectual historian but a poet thinking; it makes us erratic guides to his thought if we care less

about the exact quality of his ideas than about their pure line of
descent. This was scarcely a preoccupation of the time. Spenser
wanted to know what Justice and Temperance are, and he surely
took assistance wherever he found it. The places to look were
no secret to any educated man. The *Faerie Queene* is of all
things not naïve; it is an eclectic Renaissance literary-work-not-
treatise, by a sophisticated author, classically oriented and university trained. A single and exclusive view is not proper to a
subject with such a history as the virtues have had, nor to such
an author. I do not believe the Renaissance student was over-
careful about where knowledge from one source of ideas on the
virtues stopped off and another source took on, especially touching
semantic problems. After these centuries of discussions (often
several per decade, as time went on, and printing revived many),
of treatises, artistic uses, subliterature, school-definitions and
scholarly ones, popularizations, handbooks, it is quite impossible
to envisage a Cambridge M.A. making single-minded forays into
his Aristotle to draw forth his list of twelve, then depending for
his conception of each upon further explorations into that great
book.

But we do not find wasted the enormous amounts of work done
on the relations of Aristotle to the *Faerie Queene* and have no
substitute source to propose and no candidate for Aristotle's
place.[16] Looking at the widened field will not present us with

16 The *Variorum Spenser* appendices, commentary and bibliographies offer
sufficient documentation of the studies done on this ancient problem, ever since
Jusserand, de Moss and Padelford (all cited in *Variorum Spenser*, ii, App.)
wrote the treatments whence so much other work and so many corrections and
debates have arisen. The work which would seem closest to the emphases being
made here, V. Hulbert's, we have known in the restricted form of the one
published article on Temperance (in *SP*, vol. 28 [1931], 184-210. Influences
upon our study having been thus confined, I did not try to find out what the
unpublished dissertation would have made available to us—but never has—about
mediaeval treatments). But in the cited article, substitution of "sources," denial
of Aristotle's influence, etc. are the issues in view, rather than my quite different
understanding of the influence of intervening centuries. As in Dr. Hulbert's
roster of mediaeval names, so in Jones' work on mediaeval Aristotelian commentaries, or some of M. B. McNamee's factual data in *Honor and the Epic
Hero* (New York, 1960), facts are put forward which I, too, use. But in general, writers on the subject seem taken up with what seems to me impossible:
putting a finger exactly on the origin of Spenser's conceptions of the virtues, from
their names (despite the problems of language) down to the smallest detail of

feuding philosophies, hard choices to be made between irreconcilable alternatives; not rivalry but accommodation is usual. When such long-shared, easy and commonly known inheritances are being drawn on, in the suggestive, imprecise way proper to poets and objectionable to philosophers but much more so to historians of philosophy, competition and delimitation are very little to the fore; we in turn wish not to introduce them, but speak out instead only against the impossibility of confining a man of the 1580's, interested in defining virtues through his poem's action, to one text and one set of understandings. The reprehensible corollary of this—and it has happened so incredibly frequently that we propose it as the next-to-last infirmity of noble minds—is that we attempt to force his poem, willy-nilly, to mean whatever that text does.

Against this background of constant new weaving of strands never quite certainly assignable, we may look again at the popular work whence I first quoted the developed idea of Magnificence. It can show as something of a test case, for I doubt if Spenser thought his portrayal of Arthur's Magnificence engrafted new and great improvements onto Aristotle's earlier Greek conception. Rather he probably saw it as evading the pagan narrowness which greatness had to those who had not our chance to view perfect Magnificence unveiled, as carrying on a good beginning to a natural end, and getting at the kind of lavish spiritual generosity Aristotle would have meant if he could have seen plain this virtue's relations to grace now apparently revealed. Frère Lorens' *Somme le roi* typifies the largest single category of mediaeval works through which conceptions of what was included in the subject "the virtues" and the demands they made in terms of human action, filtered down to the completely unlearned, lodging definitions and lists and images in people's minds—part of the common intellectual apparatus like multiplication tables or phrases of etiquette.

---

his views. E. Sirluck's "*FQ* ii and the *Nicomachean Ethics*," *MP*, vol. 49 (1951-52), 73-100, should be mentioned because it summarizes usefully and detects untenable and forced points in the many previous studies which it conveniently cites. My remarks are written against the background of all the previous work done on this relationship, re-studied, and many of my points will seem adventitious or oddly chosen unless the questions raised by that work are in the minds of readers.

The *Somme le roi* was scarcely originated for the unlearned, since the Dominican confessor of the King of France compiled it in 1279 for Philip III, "le hardi." It filled an acute need of those particular decades. After the order requiring annual confession in 1215, there came the important orders of the thirteenth century, touching the obligation of parish priests to instruct their people—four times yearly, in certain specified elements of the faith. In England the several directives are represented by the famous Constitutions of 1281, often associated with the name of John Peckham, the then Archbishop of Canterbury. These manuals, containing such materials as expositions of the Creed, the Ten Commandments, the Pater Noster, treatment of the seven sins, seven virtues principales, seven works of mercy, seven sacraments, were so useful that we find a whole array of such works. Some of the first were for priests, while later books were used by laymen as confession manuals.[17] Their basic organization was dictated either by the list of essentials to be taught, or by the materials chosen as the basis for one's repentant meditations. One reason for the *Somme le roi*'s extremely wide dispersal and centuries of vitality is indicated by these historical facts, but another reason lies in its lively imagery and its combination of Christian symbolism with one large image, that of the Christian Knight. This depended on a regnant conception of man's service to God as a higher chivalry, serving as vassal of Christ the most "debonair" of all lords and the one most free of Largesse; terrestrial chivalry in its most ideal form is but a faulty reflection of this primary allegiance. A handsome and long-preserved iconographical scheme, developed very early, played some part also in the wider dispersal of this particular text, among the several of its kind.

A main reason why we must attend to this text and its kind,

---

[17] Various treatments help us to pursue details on this historical matter, and on this large branch of mediaeval literature whose effects on English literature we not only see in Chaucer and Gower but well into the sixteenth century. Studies are cited and texts described in H. G. Pfander, "Some Medieval Manuals of Religious Instruction in England," *JEGP*, vol. 35 (1936), 243-58; D. W. Robertson, Jr., "The *Manuel des Pechés* and an English Episcopal Decree," *MLN*, vol. 60 (1945), 439-47; relevant sections in M. W. Bloomfield, *The Seven Deadly Sins* (Michigan State College, 1952), may be found through his index. The bibliography in the last-named is exceptionally valuable for tracing information on vices-and-virtues treatises.

when our concern is to scrutinize what Elizabethans knew about
the virtues, is that they give us a different seven. The odds are
heavy that if an Elizabethan were asked to name the virtues, he
would get as far as his memory served on this set, not those "four
cardinals" and "three theologicals" we think of as so conventional.
Nashe used them; Lodge used them; did Spenser? There are
several things we must know about this mediaeval book before
we understand this difference, for it lies in nothing so simple as
a different idea of what conduct would be virtuous. The *Somme
le roi* is a compilation making use of other treatises besides that
half of the book which Frère Lorens is thought to have written
himself. The last section of the six, the one most certainly Lorens'
own, is by far the longest and most attractive; the usual com-
posite is: Ten Commandments; Creed; seven sins; an "Art of
dying and living," with a "garden of the virtues"; Pater Noster;
Seven Gifts of the Holy Ghost, with the virtues they nourish.
This kind of book drew upon, but is very different from, the kind
of virtues-literature we considered earlier in the chapter. Instead
of the roster of philosophers and theologians demanding mention
there, the great name as far as Latin sources go is that of
Peraldus (Guillaume Peyraut), whose *Summa de vitiis* (1230's)
et de virtutibus (*ca.* 1249) has come down to us in so many
manuscripts and editions that its great circulation is undoubted.
Peraldus' thorough use of both Ciceronian and Macrobian materials helped to ensure their later mediaeval vitality; nevertheless,
both his works and Raymund de Pennaforte's *Summa* a decade
earlier, the *Somme le roi*'s other source, are landmarks in the literature of penitentials.[18]

The tradition in virtues-literature typified by this category of
important books is no less interesting and powerful than the
other traditions, indeed not separable from them, but it contributed emphases and imagery and "postures of the mind" that
are subtly different and had different sixteenth-century results.

[18] Dates from Bloomfield, *op.cit.*, p. 124. A. Dondaine's list of manuscripts,
incomplete, occupies four and a half pages of close print, and he notices fourteen
incunabula and twenty-one editions in the sixteenth and seventeenth centuries
(see "Guillaume Peyraut: vie et oeuvres," *Archivum fratrum praedicatorum*,
vol. 18, 1948, 162-236). Students of English literature have long known both
Latin authors superficially as sources of Chaucer's *Parson's Tale* (references in
Bryan and Dempster, *Sources and Analogues*) and of Gower (see R. E. Fowler,
Une source française des poèmes de Gower, Mâçon, 1905).

I would like to watch this happen by looking at our first example, the Magnificentia inherited by the *Somme le roi* ultimately from Ciceronian and Macrobian discussions, compared with the same mediaeval virtue from the same sources when not set in the frame which the *sommes des vices et virtus* treatises provide. We shall not only watch how a classical virtue is inescapably Christianized by Christians long before Spenser got Holiness out of Aristotle, but we may watch it in the case of the perennial stumbling block of Spenserian criticism—classical Magnificentia with its hint of plain Pride, tied up with Christian grace. To many, this is only understandable if we take the desperate way out of supposing Spenser to have shut eyes and ears as in Blindman's Buff and fancied he was leading out her well-known companion Magnanimitas.[19] This was quite simply impossible at his date. But like other virtues, this one grew with slow naturalness, not seeming to alter.

We paused upon and partially described the popular *Moralium dogma philosophorum* (n. 4 above) because it was probably the immediate source of the order and inclusions in Lorens' list of the aspects of Fortitude. Its author, Guillaume de Conches, like so many writers (Alanus, John of Wales), treats both the Macrobian Magnanimitas and the originally Ciceronian Magnificentia (found in both). (I do not attempt to go into likenesses to Aristotle, of obvious interest to later writers.) Electing the Macrobian order, Guillaume writes first some three pages "De magnanimitate," and after short definitions of Fiducia and Securitas—the latter startlingly enlivened by the famous dialogue excerpted from Seneca's (?) *De remediis* and given here to Securitas and Timor[20]—he arrives at "De magnificentia." The

---

[19] The problem has bedeviled Spenserians for decades, and what Spenser could possibly have thought Aristotle meant by his virtue of Magnificence has been discussed in every treatment of their relation, with varying amounts of candor and accuracy in allowing Arthur's portrayal to elucidate that question. M. Y. Hughes confronts the difficulty most openly and helpfully in "The Arthurs of the *Faerie Queene*," *Études anglaises*, vol. 6 (1953), 193-213; I cite here none of the many other witnesses to the difficulty of the problem, because I remark later upon the illegality of our evasions of it, when possible explanations have become more apparent.

[20] See the close of Part I.A. of the article referred to in n. 5 above for conjectures connecting this with Ambrogio Lorenzetti's frescoes in Siena, depicting landscapes reigned over by Securitas and Timor. These were not the usual inter-

author is true to his Ciceronian model, the *De officiis*, and the discussion of Magnanimity (though she is a Macrobian contribution to the facets of Fortitude) is made up of sentences from that treatise of Cicero's interspersed with other classical quotations. They are chosen from about ten pages of Cicero's discussion of Fortitude, generally mentioning magnitudo animi, viros magnanimos, etc.,[21] and they extol a highly moral disregard of reward, and avoidance of cunning or of avaricious or craven or foolhardy behavior.

What does this twelfth-century Chartres master do when he arrives at Magnificentia? He discourses on its Officia in peace and war, and again his mainstay is the *De officiis*. But the process of his dependence is interestingly different. He seeks out in one of its more general sections a Platonic declaration that the good of the people comes first; he then goes far back to the treatment of Justice for the remark that the only excuse for going to war is that we may live in peace, then finds warnings concerning care in preparation, and the dangers of ambition. Guillaume selects a distant declaration that death is better than turpitude, returns to the much earlier discussion of Justice to emphasize sparing those we conquer and keeping promises even to enemies. He then extracts Cicero's defense of the achievements of peace as more important than those of war, and ends with the statement that the goodness we seek "ex animo magnifico" is secured by fortitude not of body but of mind or spirit, "animi . . . non corporis viribus."

Nothing here is Guillaume's own. But one finds very striking the way the author of the *Moralium dogma philosophorum* has opened the nut of an earlier man's observations and contrived that it should contain understandings of Magnificence which firmly emphasize the usual meanings of Christian charity as the Powerful are advised to practice it in their use of their Force—great things always and only for others' benefit, mildness and a forgiving temper, absence of vindictiveness toward enemies, absence of self-aggrandizement or other ambitious motives, power only defensible as the agent of Concord.

---

locutors, but the piece is extant in extremely numerous forms. Timor is an anomalously introduced opposite to the Macrobian Securitas, appearing in her proper place.

[21] They range from §xix to §xxiv; the references supplied by Holmberg in his edition (Uppsala, 1929) make a check of their derivation simple.

The pure process of selection has provided a good Christian princely virtue of Magnificentia for the twelfth-century church-man, entirely from classical sources. All this cannot but commend itself to those who for many years have tried to avoid the embarrassments of the Greco-Italian Magnificent Man as an explanation or libretto for Arthur. With each succeeding century this particular treatise became more popular, and was entirely accessible; but in this part it is especially striking for its ordinariness. With Cicero and Macrobius to lean upon, plus, in centuries like the twelfth, a list of theological definers which swells from tens into twenties and longer, and in later centuries their descendants and popularizers, we have had five or six centuries of a classical virtue of Magnificence that could fit the kind of Fortitude suitable to Arthur—the modest and chivalrous mediaeval hero—before Spenser ever chose to couple the two. It will make the age and ordinariness of the Spenserian Magnificence apparent if we at this point compare with this Chartrian Ciceronian's description that discussion which we half-quoted from the *Somme le roi*—no more Christian, no more mediaeval, but set in a different frame of reference.

Magnificence does not enter the *Somme le roi* as part of the treatment of the cardinal virtue of Fortitude at all. From the common treatments (like that of the immediate source) came the notion of such a facet or form of Strength or Prowess, and its elevated character, but we here meet Force in so different a setting that it may not be she despite her familiar parts. It is a symptom of the difference that opposed to her there stands not Cowardice but Accidia. The Fourth Gift of the Holy Ghost was Fortitudo, and the virtue it nourished was called by that name or translations such as I use; prouesse is the natural choice of the *Somme le roi*, with its pervasive and typical knightly language and imagery, and relation both to idealization of chivalry and to mediaeval ideas of the hero is obvious. It is natural and usual for the division into Ciceronian-Macrobian parts or manifestations to be taken over from the cardinal-virtues treatises and attached to the Fortitudo of the quite differently conceived series of gift-virtues, at this one crossing-point, a mere chance of terminology. But it gave Magnificentia a perfectly astonishing new milieu. For one thing, the direct relation between Magnificence and Grace, when it is a form of the Holy Spirit's Gift, is immediately obvious, in all this *summa* literature and its innumerable popular descendants.

None of the sevens, except possibly the seven corporal works of mercy (which Spenser works into I.x.), came more popularly into the graphic arts than the seven gift-virtues. None received more frequent mention, none crept more pertinaciously into ordinary devotions and ideas on the virtuous life, for reasons that will soon appear, leaving the cardinals-set in a more academic position. The Gifts of course find their origin in the verse of Isaiah (11.2) which is the continuation of almost the best-beloved of all Christmas prophecies—"And there shall come forth a rod out of the stem of Jesse": "And the Spirit of the Lord shall rest upon him, the spirit of wisdom and understanding, the spirit of counsel and might, the spirit of knowledge and of the fear of the Lord." By developments far too complicated to rehearse here, the seven (for Pietas is not omitted in the Vulgate)[22] became very early not only a fixed series, which may be read in either direction, but progressive or hierarchical, a scala of the good life. This is felt even in Augustine or Ambrose, and it is attached—again as early as Augustine—to two other sevens: the petitions of the Pater Noster and the Beatitudes. The word "attached" is both careless and unsuitable; the ideas behind both connections were powerful and of permanent importance. Though much about the Gifts has never been declared dogma, there is practically no fluctuation in the list of spiritus descending upon Christ and upon man: Timor Domini, Pietas, Scientia, Fortitudo, Consilium, Intellectus, Sapientia.

Two famous sections of the *Glossa ordinaria* fixed the Gifts as those for which we pray in the seven petitions of the Pater Noster: in "Hallowed be Thy Name" for God to strengthen in us the Gift of Timor Domini (drede, peur), in "Thy kingdom come" for Pietas (pitee, pitié), in "Thy will be done" for Scientia (cunning, science), and so onward. The alternative version of relations begins rather with Sapientia; thus petition two, "Thy kingdom come," asks that the spirit of Intellectus (understondyng, intelligence) may shine like the sun in our hearts (the *Somme le roi* says that the good heart seeing its darkness, takes

[22] Vulgate, Isaiah 11.2-3: ". . . spiritus sapientiae, et intellectus, spiritus consilii, et fortitudinis, spiritus scientiae, et pietatis; Et replebit eum spiritus timoris Domini."

"pick-ax and shovel" and mines away sin, to make itself a fit kingdom. "Thy will be done" asks that the Gift of Consilium confirm us in this difficult identity of wills, and so onward. This possibility of reading the parallels in either direction depends on a fairly typical mediaeval notion of what a relationship can consist of; enforced by the prior decision to find sets of relations between series not initially related at all, the relations are un-covered, with some belief in the marvelous correspondences that are part of the very structure of truth. Though sixteenth-century men are not given to these sets, except in sermons and for witty effect, there is something of this belief, in a principle of analogy, under Spenser's presentation of allegory (quite vanished by Bunyan's time). Both readings of the Pater Noster are intelligible, profitable and unforced, and I do not here dissever the Anselmian and near-Anselmian origins of the two, but only note that both are common from the time of Anselm of Laon.[23] The English transla-tion of the *Somme le roi* most convenient for moderns to read, like the Migne edition of the *Glossa ordinaria*, has the Sapientia-to-Timor order in its Pater Noster tract.[24]

In common listings, the order beginning with Timor Domini is frequent, partly because of the verse "Initium sapientiae, timor Domini" (Eccles. 19.18), and partly because a ladder had been common since Augustine, with Sapientia at the top of hierarchically arranged Gifts and virtues. The supreme Gift is to contemplatives, and Sapientia tastes or savours God's own nature. The idea of Timor Domini as the basic Gift, and the first one, is so extremely common that we realize a conventional image is to be recognized with pleasure when the "usher" Peur turns up in Christine de Pisan's *Othéa* (it is a common image), or when the janitor-porter,

---

[23] See the Appendix to vol. VI, 444-77, in Lottin's series (*op.cit.* in n. 7 above), largely from a reprint from *Recherches de théologie ancienne et mediévale*, vol. 24 (1957), 267-95.

[24] In *EETS*, vol. 217 (see n. 1 above); see pp. 104ff. Pater Noster tractates were naturally numerous, and manuscript materials of the *somme des vices et vertus* type introduce one to complicated variants as yet unordered (at least in the vernaculars). The fact that Lorens' final (Gifts) treatise uses the opposite order (Timor Domini to Sapientia) would not to my mind be an argument against his authorship of the Pater Noster tract (see *EETS*, vol. 217, p. xxvi n.). The places to look in glossed Bibles are *sub* Matt. 5.3 (Beat.), 6.9-13 (PN), 12.45 (spiritus vs. sins). The *Glossa ordinaria* is found in *P.Lat.*113-114, because of the mistaken ascription to Walafrid Strabo.

who is the first to converse with Guillaume de Deguileville on the strange Ship (of religion), is Fear-of-the-Lord. Indeed, this scala leading ultimately to a more-than-human perfection indicates one of those unobtrusive presuppositions which give our thinking its shape; Red Crosse, too, has his ascent crowned by Sapientia. Discipline in virtue commonly takes the form of a gradual education with steps of growing difficulty, while the cardinal virtues largely escape this kind of ordering.

From Augustine onward, it was commonplace to connect the Pater Noster with the seven gifts, a connection firmly engraved in men's minds by its appearance several times in Bonaventura, in the *Glossa ordinaria*, in the *summae* or tractates of writers in all schools (Simon Hinton, Hugh of St. Victor, Alanus, St. Thomas).[25] It is very common in the vernacular devotional or moral handbooks. This is no doubt partly because it was a mnemonic help, and things that became rote-memory habits, whether for purposes of prayer, confession or written definitions and schemas, could not disappear the moment a Protestant sovereign mounted the throne; this is plain from the conventional sets in Spenser's House of Holiness, or from any Elizabethan's treatment of the seven sins, Nashe's or Lodge's or Dekker's or Spenser's.

But the linking with the Lord's Prayer has nothing like the importance of another Augustinian connection: the great fundamental spring of spiritual instruction about the Gifts is their con-

[25] Although ascriptions which I make, like these, depend always on verified actual passages, such documentation in a chapter like this would quite obscure our further purpose, of observing the post-mediaeval transmission of such traditional conceptions. I must therefore ask that those interested in a closer re-tracing of my steps should consult the well-indexed volumes of Lottin cited in n. 7, and especially the long section on the *dons* in III, part 1, pp. 329ff. Three secondary sources which I use but seldom cite in detail should be added: Gardeil's article s.v. *dons* in *Dictionnaire de théologie catholique*; J. de Blic, "Pour l'histoire des dons avant S. Thomas," *Revue d'ascétique et de mystique*, vol. 22 (1946), 117-79; J.-Fr. Bonnefoy, *Le Saint Esprit et ses dons selon S. Bonaventure* (Paris, 1929) (Études de philosophie mediévale x). This general note is of most importance in connection with the most basic point immediately following—the connection with the Beatitudes. I may include now the citation of Augustine's sermon, in *P.Lat.*34:1229, 1234. A few later works were so important in setting conventions for art, general knowledge and literature that I shall refer to them directly; notably Hugh of St. Victor on the five sevens (*P.Lat.*175:405-414) John of Salisbury on the seven sevens (*P.Lat.*199:945-964), Bonaventura's *Breviloquium* (in v of the Quarrachi edition).

nection with the Beatitudes of the Sermon on the Mount. Augustine's great sermon on that was a head-fountain, but there is an important reason why the connection, universal in all later centuries, was inevitable, and allegorically fruitful. Christ provided in the Beatitudes the New Law, that is, the New Dispensation, which stood opposed to the hopelessly unfulfillable Old Law— that contrast which is the most powerful and inclusive of all mediaeval Christian symbolic images, perhaps is fundamental to all of them. The Gifts dispose us to, and bring to their possible earthly height, those seven blessed conditions or divine strengths or virtues of which the Seven Beatitudes speak. Augustine established these as seven, by amalgamation and interpretation; we move from the Timor or Humilitas of "Blessed are the poor in heart" on up to the highest gift, Sapientia, knowing God through the beatific union of the highest mystical state, a Pax ("Beati pacifici . . .") not long maintainable by frail earthly man, though Wisdom nourishes the virtue Sobrietas which leads temperate man to desire only that perfect concord.

The whole complex of thought provided a set of seven virtues —totally different in aspect from the set we know best, and more important than them not only for the arts but for theology. It is clear from my statement of the seventh virtue that the delimitations and alignments of the cardinal four cut across these others confusingly. The confusion is welcomed, for there is not the slightest hint of rivalry between two sets, or need for substitution; and the integration, through the use of both sets for definition, defies later separation.

These other seven virtues, called "the spiritual virtues," or given other epithets like "evangelical," are those which Christ by His nature had in perfection, and which were bequeathed in "the new testament." The Virgin Mary (and the Church) possessed them—pre-eminently endowed as both Christ and His mother were with the seven gifts that nourish or induce or water the virtues from the well of grace. We are now ready to understand more completely Fig. 7, where we saw the petitions (as seven maidens) water the virtues that were made to burgeon by the Gifts. But our interest there was in the nature of truly allegorical pictorial language.[26] "Cest li iardins des vertuz. Li vii.

[26] Cf. Fig. 6, from MS.Bodl. 283 of the *Miroir* version of the *Somme*, with Fig. 4 in *The Parisian Miniaturist, Honoré* by Sir Eric Millar, who owns that

arbre senefient les .vii. vertuz dont cist livres parle. Li arbre du melieu senefie ihesu crist souz qui croissent les vertuz. Les .vii. fontaines de cest iardin sont les vii. dons du saint esperit qui arousent le iardin. Les .vii. puceles qui puisent en ces .vii. fontaines sont les .vii. peticions de la paternostre qui empetirent les .vii. dons du saint esperit." This series affected all treatments of virtues so persistently that it must be considered by anyone who wishes to understand such discussions, literary or theological, at least as late as the sixteenth and seventeenth centuries, and by anyone who wishes to recognize the significances in graphic portrayals through some five centuries at least.

One thing which made this series so broadly important is that these, and not the "three theologicals" and the "four cardinals" of our own commonest knowledge, are the virtues which are set over against the seven vices. Because they are the roots nourished in the heart by the Seven Gifts or spiritus we pray for in the seven petitions, they displace the evil roots which are the seven capital sins, the vices. They truly oppose these, as the ordinary (to us) seven do not except by awkward forcing; and they oppose also in that they are utterly contrary as conditions, rather than in that they promote the image of a fight (though that imagery is used). The imagery of plants, trees, the semina of Hugh of St. Victor's enormously popularized treatment of the Five Sevens, is very usual, very potent for art as our example shows, and appears again in the later Gifts treatise of the *Somme* (I have taken this illustration and quotation from the fifth treatise, anonymous, and supposed earlier). The imagery of the vices as poisons for which the seven gift-virtues are remedia or antidotes is also completely commonplace. We have only to think of Spenser's various books of the *Faerie Queene* to realize how different a treatment of virtues will become if it encloses this idea—not fundamental to classical treatments—of an evil condition, a vice of Pride, or Avarice, or Luxury, which is ousted by a blessed condition, not necessarily fought and conquered by it, but rooted out, substituted-for, displaced, by it.

---

incomparable work, Honoré's *Somme le roi*. The manuscript is more carefully described, and others reproduced in part for comparison, in the same author's Roxburghe Club publication in 1953, *An Illuminated Manuscript of La Somme le Roy*. Millar's Fig. 4 is the usual garden picture, Delisle's picture #5 (see n. 5 above).

A yet more fundamental conception, far less naturally linked to the seven which are the "three-plus-four," is that of the imitation of Christ as the mode of developing these virtues, or as the definition of the attempted virtuous condition. This results in a different imagery—pilgrimage, quest, copy, shadow, slowly constructed temple. Spenser's basic image in the whole *Faerie Queene* —the knight-errant in quest of virtues—is of this sort, with its greater emphasis on end and allegiance than on attributes and process; it is an inherited image, for his vast attempt is one in a long series, not to be isolated from its many predecessors (however they may differ, as they assuredly do).

That earlier virtue-quests often come closer to the great Pilgrimage-of-Life theme than Spenser's (except in Book I)[27] is only one of the results of another fact we must equally never lose sight of: his eclectic amalgamation of classical sources, to which he was equally sympathetic. Though he is full of Aristotle, yet the great Aristotelian principle of a mean as defining and constituting virtue will not fit the basic structure of his book or its parts; Spenser uses it, but it has not shaped his poem. He uses (even subverts) "Plato" to his purposes, just as he also uses fragments of most of the variant mediaeval images that had developed— the psychologized mansion or house (of Pride, of Alma), the garden, man as a castle, the actual vice-virtue combats, the otherworld journey, the enfances motif.[28] His several quests are

[27] I have deliberately abstained from reading the posthumously printed work of my friend and old teacher, S. C. Chew, *The Pilgrimage of Life* (New Haven, 1962), since it was too late for my own studies to be helped by his work, and I believe our concerns and approaches are very different, and the temptation to cross reference our probably vastly numerous relations would have overloaded this different work. That difficulty is apparent from the richly loaded article in *Studies in Art and Literature for Belle da Costa Greene*, ed. D. Miner (Princeton, 1954), pp. 37-54, on a subject which could not be more relevant, as this chapter begins now to show: "Spenser's Pageant of the Seven Deadly Sins." We had used some of the same late mediaeval books for our different purposes (for Dr. Chew's inquiry into just why the sins *appear* as they do is one I have not attempted), but I resist cross referencing, since there is not the slightest pretence to completeness or coverage in this study. His article is tied at scores of points to this chapter's materials and is an invaluable addition.

[28] Historically speaking, I am convinced that his major image, which acts as a structural principle, of knight-errants who seek, learn the nature of, fail to encompass, meet opposites of, finally achieve or do the work of, some virtue, came to him through his saturation in the romances, directly; yet those themselves

those of a Christian knight who seeks perfections he will never entirely possess here, because they are knowable only in a divine Exemplar; this sense is conveyed (e.g. in Books IV, V, VI) despite the fact that Spenser is more thoroughly impregnated than most with classical learning and ideas on the virtues. Not only do the choices of virtues to seek differ, but the end of doing so and the intervening revealing experiences are different. If Spenser's heroes accomplish labors of Hercules, they do so as the mythographers' transformed Hercules did—their deeds achieved by personages who shadow and present some essential of divinity or universal embodied in a deity, not the simple heroic accomplishments of a superlatively heroic protagonist. This makes the allegory of presented Virtues differ from Stoic or late classical allegory. Pre-Christian ways of allegorizing ancient story can equate personages with some virtue. But when we so equate Spenser's characters with the Justice, or Holiness, or Chastity, or Temperance, of their quests, instead of seeing the virtues as shadows of unseizable essences which the characters incompletely attain, the proof that we are misreading lies in all the leftover poem we cannot squeeze into our wrong pattern. This can be said of Red Crosse, of course, but also of Artegall (who is not Justice but her faulty knight), of Guyon, Britomart, Calidore.

A large reason for this difference is the inescapably post-Christian understanding (in the *Faerie Queene*, for example) of the relation of man to the ground of virtue, and this different aspect of the last point is another fundamental distinction which sets off the acquisition of the four cardinal virtues from the unending seeking of the seven spiritual virtues. Spenser does not need to mention God, even as Jove, or even by talking about the divinity of the virtue of Justice, for us to realize that his conception of these sought virtues in their perfection is supernatural. That they exist as the Ideas exist does very well, though his Platonism is more Christian than Greek; but at any rate, the mode of existence of Natura, or Concord, or true as against false Love, the Garden of Adonis—his greatest images—requires postulating another dimension of reality from that of the phenomenal actual

developed an allegorical dimension only late (except for the superb early *Queste*)—whereas Spenser *chose* this unallegorized image for its allegorical power. But these are convictions which must be supported in a later chapter.

world, and to him this world exists with its virtues, not only in his questers' imaginations or in his own. Perhaps it is not necessary to stress here that this basis for allegory is inescapably Christian (despite its relation to myth, it is not the same). Again, this grasp of the nature and crucial reality of the quest is inherited along with the spiritual virtues and with human beings who owe and give allegiance—God's Knights—not simply battle areas for conflicting ideas of behavior, or human types of this or that moral trait. This is less a point about sources than about the complications we must expect because virtues had had several centuries of history, under more than one religion.

I wish to name and list the seven virtues drawn from the Beatitudes, those against the vices, by using the *Somme le roi* phrasings, which show the linkages. The mediaeval wordings should not deceive us as to the absolute commonness of the series, as ordinary in devotional books and moral treatises as it is in iconography. We find this set in Chaucer's *Parson's Tale*, in Gower's two works which use the virtues structurally; it is the set which remedially opposes the vices in Lodge's *Wit's Miserie*, and the set of seven good spirits which opposes the seven devils named by Nashe in *Pierce Penilesse* (another common named seven). It is the set usual in the popular diagrammatic wheels or trees, in manuals that give the branches of virtue and vice, almanacs like the shepherds' calendars, in numbers of treatments where the vices, rather than the virtues, are the principle of organization, like many notable now only for their pictures.[29]

Because this set of virtues is conceptually tightly attached to two great motifs—the Gifts and the seven sins—it follows these two motifs into iconographical schemes where they are important. We therefore meet the series on fonts (as at Southrop); by name or personified where the descent of the seven spiritus (or the Doves) is figured; opposing the vices in illuminations (those accompanying the Penitential Psalms, as in the Bedford missal, Add. 18850); in late City of God manuscripts like the famous B.N. fr. 18-19; in illustrated devotional handbooks like the fifteenth-century *Examen de conscience*, or Legrand's *Livre de bonnes moeurs*, in tapestries, in sculptured reliefs (on the twelfth-century capitals of Clermont, or on the north porch of Laon— often, as here, with inscriptions to make the identity of the set

---

[29] Like several in S. C. Chew's article (*op.cit.* in n. 27 above) *passim* and n. 5 and the tapestries of n. 6.

quite questionless). The assumption that the virtues always included the cardinal four has produced mistaken identifications,
and forgetting this set in favor of the "three-plus-four" more
familiar to us has made unnecessary puzzles in well-known
series like those of Paris and Chartres (complicated there by the
appearance also of "parts" of the classical four).

We become accustomed to their turning up in any sort of text,
so that we are not surprised when Gringore's *Chasteau de Labour*
and Barclay's translation show them both pictorially and verbally,
and when in Chapter Five of *Le Petit Jean de Saintre* "My Lady"
discourses on them as opposed to the vices she considers. Unlike
the Gifts which have the inflexible nomenclature of a verse of
Scripture, these virtues have variants of terminology and order.
This flexibility is what covers up the fact that Spenser had read
some such orderly traditional scheme; otherwise his Red Crosse
would not learn Holiness (the function of this scala of penitence
and repair), in the House of that name, from seven helpers who
gradually oust the wicked conditions and substitute blessed ones.
They properly start with the porter Humiltà, include the franklin
Zele, the leech Patience, make much of Misericordia with her
usually included seven works, and culminate in Contemplation;
to him usually belong the last two Gifts, and as we expect, the
seventh (Sapientia) is not to be finally possessed until Red
Crosse shall return to the Heavenly Jerusalem.

Frère Lorens says in the *Somme le roi*—it is an absolute commonplace of doctrine—that the Holy Spirit "by the seven gifts"
"doth away and destroieth the seven deadly sins" in the heart
of a man. The Gift of Drede (Timor Domini) is first in this
sixth and chief and most beautifully illustrated tractate,[30] and it
destroys the root of pride, and sets in his stead the virtue of
Humbleness; this is the virtue Christ spoke of when he said,

---

[30] See n. 24 above on the other order in the fifth tract (on Pater Noster) and
on text used. Using a translation is unhappy, but the French is in manuscript,
and amplifications or contexts make accessibility worthwhile, for they are vivid,
interesting, or useful for noticing conventionally attached motifs—many not
lost on Spenser: the five senses as defended gates of the body's castle, the degrees
of Humility, the seven battles under Fortitudo, of which Patience is one form
under whom we meet the common trio Repentance-Penance-Amendment (see
Faerie Queene, Bk. I.x.23-7), the seven works of misericorde, the seven-headed
Beast, etc. The rubrics or prefatory summaries declare the paralleled Gift, virtue,
vice, and (toward the end of each section) Beatitude. The seven main passages
are at pp. 126, 143, 148, 161, 188, 222, 272, in *EETS*, vol. 217.

"Blessed are the poor in spirit," "that is the gostiliche pore" (spiritualiter). The Second Gift "maketh the herte swete and debonere & pitous," being that of Pietas, Pite, which casts out the root of Envy, by the virtue "good *love*" (Amitié) or mansuetude or benignity; this virtue, loving one's neighbor as oneself, Christ taught in saying "Blessed be the deboner, for thei schulle be in possession of the earth" ("Beati mites. . ."). The Third Gift (Scientia) is "science, that is cunnynge," making a man measurable in all things, and it casts out Wrath (Felonie); the virtue planted in its place, since it puts Reason and Will in perfect accord, is Equité, evennesse, temperance—whether we think of guarding the five gates of the soul's castle, or of maintaining "discretion" and measure in all respects.

It is characteristic that this third virtue (Equité) is not only accommodated in the discussion to Temperance—as is also the seventh virtue, Sobrietas—but because of its radical connection with "resoun" and its Gift, Prudence with its old Ciceronian parts comes in for description. Authors commonly do not try to force the other division on this later one by limiting and truncating descriptions, and thus willingly cross lines. Under this Equité we have the almost unmanageable inconsistency of a division into seven branches, based evidently on the idea that virtues lose "the name of vertue and bicomen vices" without reasonable measure and claiming as branches or parts of Evenhede "the sevene principal vertues that answeren to the sevene vices": "meknesse agens pride, love agens envye, debonnerte agens felonye," Prowess against Sloth, Largesse against Covetise, Chastity against Lechery, Soberness against Gluttony (p. 159). One notices that some sleight of hand was necessary when under his 3 Lorens arrived at our third. Meanwhile, the discussion of this Evenhede-Temperance-Patience-against-Ira has an expected description of harmony in the soul—perhaps one reason for "Peace" in the iconography—but also includes Bernard's commonplace that it is Prudentia who is auriga ("maister cartere"), for Temperance is pre-eminent in a different way. A perfect use of Equité's line or plummet is not possible to us (this line of the masterbuilder brings in a variant citation for the Gifts—Zach. 2, on the stone with seven eyes and the plummet-line). Our inability to achieve the virtue is met by Christ's "wel curteis" rule: Blessed are they that weep, for knowing their defaults, they shall be comforted.

FIGURE 18

This Third Gift is more variously treated than most. Gregory's opposing of it (Scientia) to the evils of Ignorantia, and Hugh of St. Victor's abstraction of the virtue of Compunction from that Third Beatitude, are not the most popular variant interpretations, though the latter is often found in diagrams because of the popularity of Hugh's *De quinque septenis*. Such chart-like aids to memory were certainly known to sixteenth-century men.[31] The most familiar virtue answering to Wrath is Patience, and it is the plant set by this Third Gift in John of Salisbury's *De septem septenis*; that is scarcely the explanation of why it is so common in the arts and in popular manuals, but the accompanying *Somme le roi* picture of Abel's death reminds us that he was the type of the most important of all patientia under suffering, and the ark "which signifies Peace" (the church born of that Passion)

[31] Gregory, *Moralia* 2.44 (*P.Lat.*75:592), *Glossa ordinaria*, sub Job 1.19; followed by Hugh of St. Cher, Chancellor Philip, Simon Hinton and some others. The influence of this very early scheme (of course Gregory and Hugh were printed) sometimes shows in the opposition of Stultitia's temptations to Sapientia as remedy, of Praecipitatio to Consilium. Hugh of St. Victor's text is in *P.Lat.*175:405-414 (a useful partial translation by J. Wach in "Hugh of St. Victor on Virtues and Vices," *Anglican Theological Review*, vol. 31 [1949], 25-33); illustrated schemes using it turn up unattributed here and there in manuscripts (one such in Bodl. MS.lat.th.c.2[R]). John of Salisbury, next following, is in *P.Lat.*199:945-964.

FIGURE 19

confirms the suggestion (see Fig. 18). Basic similarities underlying these variations are quite obvious, and of course Spenser was
not the first to connect the leach Patience with Compunction.

The Fourth Gift is the most stable of all—Fortitudo—and
with this sole doublet, present in both traditions, we encounter a
true mingling, with both Fortitudes somewhat changed in their
natures as a result. Most important for later vernacular literature
was the pronounced stress on suffering-of-tribulations as Fortitudo.
Even Cicero mentions both active strength and passive endurance,

but when Fortitude the acquired virtue mingled with Fortitude
the Holy Spirit's Gift, supremely shown in Christ's passion, we
may anticipate a chivalric virtue in God's knights wherein suffering evils is the truest mode of courageous fight against evils.
When we have met this emphasis under Fortitude some dozen
times, such definitions of heroism (e.g. in *Paradise Regained*)
cease to seem like Miltonic forms of seventeenth-century inward-
ness opposable to Renaissance active fights for glorious great
intents.

The Gift Fortitudo (Strengthe, Force) sets in the place of the
vice Sloth (accidia, paresse) the virtue Prowess (see Fig. 19).
Authors see that this virtue, too, has claims to pre-eminence
(semantic this time); "for vertue and prowesse is al on."
"Prowesse in knyghthode is cleped doughtynesse," and a very
great deal is made in this section of chivalric relationships, language and ideals. Although the special Gifts and virtues of the
contemplative life are the last two (Intellectus, Sapientia), a
hierarchical distinction is sometimes made, and is here, for at the
Fourth Gift we take leave of those in the lowest of the Three
States, those whom Lorens compares to "the burgeis" who chaffers
and thinks of gain, and who does indeed manage to save his
soul. From now on we speak of those Job meant when he said
that the life of man or woman "fareth as knyghthod"—those
who despise the world, undertake the way of perfectness, try to
fulfill supererogatory commands, and in general go "al a-nother
weye" from the burgeis. For these, like "the newe knyght," aim
rather "to be curteis and geve largeliche and lerne knyghthode
and pursue the armes and suffre moche woo to schewen doughtynesse."

Each of these phrases is to be understood of the chevalerie
celestienne. Yet I am not sure that Lorens speaks of men of
religion only in the many passages about the master of our field
(Jesus Christ) that assayeth his new knights, or the described
obstacles and the Holy Ghost arming his knight "in his vertue"
as he did first on Pentecost—and what He provides him with
turns out to be the Macrobian-Ciceronian facets of Fortitude, the
cardinal virtue. They are ascribed to "the philosophres"; first,
He gives him a noble heart, to despise the world as a mere
nothing and undertake truly great things, like the hard way to

God's hill, then good hope (fiaunce) from his burning desire to follow God, then "sikernesse" like the lion's, not fearing peril and pain but desiring it, just as a new knight does a tournament, welcoming even torment (the martyr's desire). This last shows what was quite honestly seen in Macrobius' Securitas, while the first, which was the interpretation ready for the ancient Magnanimitas, reminds us that "greatness of spirit" changed its look too; and if Spenser had indeed chosen to write about that in Arthur, it would not by the 1500's have looked quite like Aristotle's Magnanimity.[32] The sixth of this series is the transformed Magnificentia, identified with Christ's perfecting pursuance of virtues to the end, which we strive to follow, though unable to do so (unless we embody the attempt, like Arthur); the fourth and fifth are regular, Suffraunce and Constaunce.

But there is the important addition of a seventh, that our Master Jesus Christ, who "made the philosophres and philosophie," himself "put ther-to, for to that the philosophres myght not atayne"; He added as part of Fortitude the hunger and thirst after righteousness of the Fourth Beatitude. The description of how "the maister of oure feld," knowing our power insufficient, makes our Strength "to wexe" when need be (that we shall have in the end the crown that comes with perfected virtue) confirms and particularizes this whole Gift's relation to grace. The relation is clearest in Magnificence which is the perfecting of the rest, the persevering to completion. It is equally important to notice that other mentioned aspect of the virtues' gradual Christianization, brought in here by the use of the Beatitude (as happens in other cases) and important to the conception of virtues in the *Faerie Queene*—in fact, otherwise Spenser would have needed no Arthur.

The virtues are not fully attainable; their ground is Deity. Christ did not say, blessed are those "that don" righteousness, but, "more curteisliche," those that hunger and thirst thus to do;

---

[32] I quote in these paragraphs on Fortitude largely from pp. 164-66, 161, 163, 170, 187, if it is desired to notice in context this superlatively interesting discussion, humorous, vivid, modest and delicate. The eloquent discourse on the world's and man's littleness is not a foretaste of the supposed distress after Copernicus removed from us the comfort of geocentricity. These typical mediaeval reflections, with their quotation of Austin, Isaiah, Seneca and Solomon, fitly introduce the common image of the littleness of the world seen from outer space, "in bigness as a star . . ."; all that surprises us is the use in defining Magnanimitas.

for our radical pouerte is such that we can never pay what we owe in this world. I am to "geve my lif" to Him who gave His life for us is what all the virtues ultimately boil down to. As a description of the process of achieving a virtue and the end of a quest for one, this adds a dimension not in any classical conception of the striving or the attainment. Here is the reason why "more ferthere could not the philosophres the vertue of prowesse leden"—but the disciples of Christ "gon moche ferthere." For the *end* of Fortitude, the end of righteousness "which is iustice" (Iustitia), is that man by saving his soul comes to participate in that condition of divinity (the perfected virtues), is one with it, receives the crown, and is victorious in the seventh and last battle against the devil himself. It is *this* battle of which it was said, "To hym that venquiseth I wole geve hym to ete of the tree of life . . . that is Ihesu Crist,"—made one with God, the end of the quest for a virtue.

Of course, Red Crosse fights this battle in terms like these, and could not have won without the repeated additions to his strength through "vertue itself" stooping to him—when Arthur by grace adds on to the waning fortitude he had, and when that rejuvenated strength twice needs added vigor on the plain where he fights the Fiend. But grace that makes strength sufficient is channeled through Arthur in other Books, too (though Spenser did not grasp how intelligibly he could use him until Book I), and a virtue in its essence—not Christ, of whom that would be an imperfect definition—comes to some human being for the instant of power that is all that is possible to him. Only in allegory could Arthur be both the person Arthur (which he certainly is) and the perfected universal, wherever those quiddities that we write about and strive for have their being. The experience is common enough, and most of us have glimpsed that Christ-like Perseverance which endures to the end, called by Lorens Magnificentia, if that was the whole nature of its being. This final definition of what kind of strength is "great" is not unrelated to the fact that several important writers, notably John of Salisbury, give the name Perseverantia to the virtue nourished by this Fourth Gift. It appears quite commonly. The Perseverance who was Cicero's fourth part of the virtue Fortitudo quite early became this Christian kind of Strength, magnificent and great for the special Christian reasons. It takes an Arthur to pass on this Christ-like power, sufficient to a crisis, for much the same reason

FIGURE 20

that the human heroes never become the virtues, but only locate
them; their quests end in knowledge, not possession, though
these unearthly perfections lodge in them as tenants, showing us
their nature.

The Fifth Gift, Counsel (consilium), especially enables men
to follow the chief counsel of the New Law: Misericorde
(largesse, mercy), dislodging Avarice (covetise), imitating God's
own liberality to us, and of course, related immediately to
"Blessed are the merciful." It is inevitable that the seven works
of mercy should be introduced and that iconographical counters

like Dives and Lazarus should be persistent. Sometimes the virtue herself is portrayed as giving a cloak to a naked man, and sometimes all the works are pictured. The sermon cliché from Matt. 25 of Christ's identification (at the Last Judgment) of Himself with the recipients is to be expected, as is a discourse on alms, a frequent attachment to the virtue of Mercy, as here in the *Somme le roi* (see Fig. 20).

The Sixth Gift is Intellectus (understanding, intelligence), and there is some fluctuation in these materials generally, in attaching to six or alternatively to seven the last two pairs of vices and virtues. The *Somme le roi* introduces here the virtue Chastity and its displaced precursor Luxury, but some later popular books show Sobriété replacing Gluttony here, and Chastity-Luxury under the next Gift, Sapientia—as we find them in various authorities as important as Bonaventura's *Breviloquium*.[33] We are surprised less by the fluctuation than by the fact that the two greatest Gifts, endowments primarily of contemplatives, and attached to the mystical states illumination and perfection, should nourish these seemingly simplest virtues, that they should "be against" these two plain fleshly vices. But all the terms are extended and read figuratively, and the connections are with the "pure in heart" (having true Castitas) of the Sixth Beatitude, for they shall see God, by the light of Intellectus; in the seventh set with the "Blessed . . . sons of God" whose love and knowledge of Him, per gustum sapientiae, is mystically a union.

The Seventh Gift, Sapientia, opposes in the *Somme le roi* and elsewhere a gula which desires to taste not God's nature but only the things of the world and the flesh; Sapientia supplants this by nourishing a Sobrietas which is the complete harmony, the ineffable Pax, of unity. The "Beati pacifici . . ." verse is quoted, and much is made of the "*saverous* knowynge," of the inebriety of love and union, the last step on Jacob's ladder of "perfectness" (p. 273). There is widespread use of Pax as the seventh virtuous condition (cf. the Third Gift; and not *this* Pax is a virtue but

---

[33] *Breviloquium*, Part V, ch. v, and Simon Hinton's *Summa*. Alleg. New Testament, ascribed to Hugh, has concupiscentia carnis as the opponent of the Sixth Gift (*P.Lat.*174-176). Whatever changes, the sins do not, but are "interpreted"— a point which had its effects on later writers. Since Bonaventura at least, the relation to mystical states has been common, and Purification carries at least through four, Perfection is confined to the seventh and supreme Gift of Sapientia.

only the Concordia-Temperance-Sobriety sort); and this only emphasizes the fact that these seven virtues are not so rigid and schematized as the "three-plus-four." But the broader and more beautifully articulated scheme of which they are a part offers no true inconsistencies, and conceptually is clear, tough and resilient to allow of theological elaborations, without important modifications over many centuries. Literally numberless authors and artists treated the Gifts.

Two great ancient images, structurally important in the *Somme le roi,* deserve mention now that the context will make their importance clear without much quoting. One of these, the Garden of Virtues in the heart, is a figure only readable or intelligible allegorically (understood *spiritualiter*); as we saw in Chapter One and in this chapter when we met it and its illustration in the Pater Noster tract. We shall presently briefly recall it, though it did not survive whole except in devotional books and in the tree-image with branches, in so many vices-and-virtues lists; it had one important Spenserian use in Book I. The other, which I describe first because it has never been lost, is the Beast of the Apocalypse, seven-headed, interpreted as Satan with his seven sins or vices or heads.

For once, "identification" is the proper term, for the Beast as Satan, and thus quintessential evil, is understood as John's literal meaning. This identification, and the *figure* of the heads symbolizing the sins, had been utter commonplaces since Gregory, in Richard and Hugh of St. Victor, in Honorius of Autun, in Albertus Magnus and Bonaventura, and in Biblical glosses and vernacular treatments. As we saw in Chapter One, the simplest exemplum of the Regina-fish and the hydra was interpreted in the Moral on the assumption that readers would immediately recognize who was trying to seduce the well-ruled soul; pictures make his "many heads" seven. The small third tract in the *Somme le roi* on the seven sins naturally begins with a description of John's "beast that arose out of the sea," the one force that has power to fight with the hallowed ones and overcome them, and continues as did many a parallel Latin treatment with a description of how the seven heads are the "sevene chef synnes, bi whiche the devel draweth to hym welny al this world." This is the signal for an illustration in practically all redactions, and the beautiful series of the late 1200's which established the

FIGURE 21

iconography with its persistent set of verbal descriptions gives us
a Beast whose identity is left in no doubt; some earliest exemplars
have a legend on this picture, "Ceste beste senefie le deable."
Our illustrations show it from a manuscript of just before 1300
(Fig. 21, B.M. Add. 28161) and a fifteenth-century English
translation of the *Miroir* form of the text (Fig. 22, Bodl. 283);[34]

[34] I cannot here go into these questions of redaction; it is pertinent to state
that I do not feel confident in erecting whole theories of filiation on "contamina-
tion" of the Beast image and the tree-and-boughs imagery, as does Tinbergen,
followed by the editor of *EETS*, vol. 217. It was already a most ancient commonplace that the Beast's picture was applicable, whether in the text or not, the

FIGURE 22

for good measure and the amusement of it, I give as Fig. 23 the latter's Gluttony boozing on his swine.

---

moment the sins were discussed. The heads portray them, as clearly as titles. The mentioned *Somme le roi* descriptions, discovered by Delisle, are given, and the iconography in all manuscripts studied, in Part II of the article mentioned in n. 5 above. The quotation on the sins is from *EETS*, vol. 217, p. 10. For the commonness of the Beast's-heads—seven-sins image see Bloomfield's *Seven Deadly Sins*, pp. 85, 89, and notes and index.

FIGURE 23

Figure 24, from the latter manuscript, is a just representation of the very Knights we meet in the *Faerie Queene*; it follows the description of Magnificence as the sixth part of Fortitude, and of that seventh part which Christ "the maister of the feld" gives to his knights (quoted above p. 99), and illustrates the seven battles which are as boughs on that tree of Fortitude, the first being the battle "the cristen man and womman" hath against deadly sin (this is pictured) and the last the one which wins for him a place forever in the garden where is the Tree of Life. It

FIGURE 24

is difficult to see why so many writers on Spenser should have
quarreled with the impeccable sense presented by the fiction in
Book I. vii, that the Knight of Holiness, like his predecessors
the "halewen" of saints (Rev. 13.7), dedicated to the pursuit of
the holy, should find his strength or fortitude insufficient when
here for the first time he encounters the apotheosis of evil for
which one of our names is Satan (the symbol names him again).
It is most proper in allegory that the Knight's actual opponent
in the field should be Orgoglio the giant, the very idea of the
diabolical sin, radical Pride, given a metaphorical body, and that
Orgoglio's creature is the Satan-Beast—once literally and *historialiter* incarnate in Lucifer whom Michael fought (Rev. 12.9),
living again on earth in another body that was an extant human
institution (so Spenser thought: the then corrupt Roman Church,
whom Falsehood-in-essence is given to have for her own).

As is usual, allegory does not equate a concretion with an abstraction, but shadows or mirrors essences. Quite properly, Orgoglio is not the Roman Church but a figure for the basic and
radical ur-sin of Pride, usurping Godhead, which has taken over
that once-luminous creation of God, a Church on earth—just as it
took over Lucifer the bright, and can take over any other creature,
Elizabeth or her England or the post-Reformation Church or
Red Crosse or any other knight of Christ. Similarly, Duessa is
not an image for the false church; rather that church (and Queen
Mary is another such) has become an image of her. She mirrors
falsity pure. We can see her nature as an image by watching
Malbecco turn into the sort of figure Duessa always is, when he
turns into Jealousy itself. From being a human so filled with
the humor of jealousy that he represents it, like the persons of
Every Man in His Humour, he becomes—as Spenser transcends
what is possible for novelists or dramatists who must keep their
characters particulars—the very quality itself in its universal
aspect. Jonson is not to be read allegorically, but these are different ways of avoiding the relationship of equation, which is not
figurative. This more correct reading of the figures is one answer
to problems some writers bring up of Spenser's "repetition,"
especially in Book I, where the number of times "pride" is met
has caused much grumbling. Furor, the very essence of Wrath,
is differently handled—as an image of Ira from the obsessed
victim of the same appetite, Pyrocles, though he also mirrors

that one aspect to which he is sheared down, as a particular. We can see this difference by asking ourselves what a tawny beard has to do with it. So every case of Red Crosse's despairing self-blame is not like the meeting with the naked quiddity itself in the Despair canto. We may not so reduce images to their same significance that we do not see what shape they came in.

The meeting with pure quiddities is different again from meeting the very source and fountainhead (perhaps only as men's modes of thought differ). The largest figures are the latter: Acrasia—Circe, Mammon. Orgoglio is both and it is too much for Red Crosse. In this sense, at least, Orgoglio is Spiritual Pride—he is Pride spiritualiter. When we leave the imaged duels, the psychological cases, the meetings with forms and aspects, and confront in its very shape, as a symbol, that which made Satan act satanically—then we must expect Red Crosse to succumb, and to be lost without Arthur's intervention; the "perfection" of Pride's opposite, Holiness, confronts the perfection of the vice. For such encounters Spenser generally uses public symbols which openly take us into the realm of the vast and crucial conflict between heaven's strength and hell's. Orgoglio has not this public character except as giants or Titans have always signified hybris, and his creature is the overt symbol thereof. If we are in doubt as to why he subdued Red Crosse when another form of him (in canto xi) will not conquer but be conquered, the *Somme le roi* explains it outright: "And therfore seynt Iohn seide that hit had power agens halewen, for ther nys non so holy man in erthe that may parfgtly kepe hym to forsake alle manere of synnes that cometh out of thes heved synnes, with-out a special ... grace of God." The special grace comes through Arthur, the Christianized Magnificentia which is Fortitudo to-the-very-end as Red Crosse hadn't it.

Of course, the great example of this extended significance is the dragon fight of canto xi: we consciously view the great duel taking place once again between life and death, Christ and Leviathan—seen in a copy (man as Christ's Knight fighting evil pure; Red Crosse as "Christ figure" is far in the future, after canto xiii). In the dragon fight the entirely public and unmistakable images of Eden and Serpent and heaven's rejoicing hosts make the huge image completely foolproof. It is inescapable that we read it allegorically. The moral reading and the extra historical reading (as it adumbrates events referable to Spenser's own time; the first historical reading is as-a-fiction) are held within the greater allegory, which presents them as it presents all other particular such struggles subsumed under it, today's or any century's. I think Spenser still had the sense a mediaeval allegory-reader had, that *these* actualities present the religious doctrine to those who could see. These readings are not parallel floors of a house as the levels image would have it, but shapes that the same great conflict takes, eternally the same yet never twice alike.[35]

Besides the Beast, the second great common image, the Garden of Virtues in the heart of man, is the climactic and beautiful image of the fourth tractate of the *Somme le roi*. From its first rubric it has received the modern titles of "on virtues" or "ars moriendi," but both of these really belong to quite other kinds of common mediaeval pieces. The treatise especially takes up the "three kinds of goods," and it defines true fairness, true strength, true lordship, true freedom, true noblesse or gentilesse. In the last it has not only been markedly influential upon authors we know better, but shows that the image of a double chivalry received vivid statement in a popular place.[36] It culminates in a figure of the good man or woman *as* a "fair garden ful of grene and of faire trees and of good fruyt," planted by the great gardener. The "graffes" in it are that second set of virtues which comes with the Holy Ghost's Gifts of grace; "Goddes sone, that is the

[35] The complaint about repetition is not infrequent, and a fairly recent example by an expert will suffice: V. K. Whitaker's censures in "The Theological Structure of *FQ*, 1," *ELH*, vol. 19 (1952), 151-64. But Lucifera is not a double of Orgoglio; she, like Archimago, figures a branch of one of the heads (Pride) of his creature the Beast (Archimago is, in our text, Hypocrisy the sixth sin, she is Vainglory [and Ambition for it]; these are utter commonplaces). Despair has no true doublet; Error is what her accoutrements, behavior and name declare. We keep meeting the Beast's shapes, but only in that sense of Leviathan himself. There is no repetition in Book 1 except as men eternally repeat the First sin, never recognizing it again when they see it—surely one of Spenser's points.

[36] The three goods, ultimately from Augustine, were well spread and much used; Lottin (*op.cit.*, III, part 1, 143ff.) gives some references to learned discussions whence spring the interesting popular commonplaces. On the garden-image see Fig. 6; also on noblesse and double chivalry see ch. 1, p. 39; it is based on the sevens we have looked at, and is so closely tied to the Gifts-treatise imagery and the Pater Noster tract that if it antedates Frère Lorens, we must think its imaginative imagery inspired his. The treatise is on pp. 68-97 in *EETS*, vol. 217; I quote from p. 93.

verrey sunne bi his vertue and brigtnesse," makes them grow;
this "paradis rigt delitable" in "the herte" is the image of the
other: ". . . rigt as God sett ertheli paradis ful of goode trees and
fruygt, and in the myddel sett the tree of lif . . . *Rigt so doth
gostly* to the herte the goode gardyner, that is God the fadre,
for he sett the tree of vertue and in the myddel the tree of lif,
that is Ihesu Crist, for he seith in the gospel, 'Who-so eteth my
flesch and drynketh my blod hath lif with-out ende.' " (Italics
mine.)

The roote of this tree is God's "outrageous charite," and by
virtue of the "gerde of the roote of Iesse" all the other trees in
the garden wax, blossom and bear fruit. The branches were His
own virtues, taught to disciples in the Beatitudes, and a good
heart sits in their shadow and beholds them with joy; moreover,
of His "grete curtesie" He taught the seven perfect petitions by
which the seven graffs in each man's garden receive the water of
grace, the only other necessity for their fruitful growth besides
the Sun's warmth of love—and we join the image of the well in
seven streams and the damsels, quoted earlier. This whole complex of theologically careful and acute understandings is taken
in through the symbolism, elaborating effortlessly from a few
simple images and doctrines known to every ordinary Christian.
Yet there are real reasons behind the long, learned tradition
which provided the image of germinating, watering, tree-with-
branches, displacing of a vicious plant by its opposite virtue;[37]
compare the process of acquisition of the cardinal virtues with
the kind of imagery that we have seen grown up around them.
We are so used to "A paradise within thee, happier far" as Miltonic, just as we think of the pun in "son-sun" as surely so *likely*

---

[37] It is very early, but a typical wording is that of Hugh of St. Victor speaking
of the "semina virtutum jactata super terram cordis nostri," the spiritual Seven,
the ones against the vices ("contra illa septem vitia sunt virtutes"), "quasi seges
quae ex ipsis consurgunt," the process of growth being initiated by the Gifts.
See *Summa sentent*.iii.17, *P.Lat*.176:114-15; John of Salisbury has virtually
the same phrasings (*P.Lat*.199:954). Bonaventura's popular tracts consistently
use this elaborated Biblical imagery, which has iconographically a great past and
greater future; the Tree-and-branches cliché in so many diagrams and manuals
pulled back in the paradise-garden source which was theologically so much more
interesting—reminders of strains some of which are relevant, and of their vast
dispersal, are in "The Child in the Tree" by E. Greenhill, *Traditio*, vol. 10
(1954), 323-71.

a Metaphysical invention, that we cut ourselves off from the imaginative springs of images. Imagery and common doctrine alike are peculiar to no branch of Christianity.

This common imagery is very much more illuminating and suitable as a way of reading the Well of Life in which Red Crosse bathed, and the Tree with its stream of balm (1.xi.29,48) than the forced and awkward equations with the two sacraments that were accepted by Protestants, baptism and communion—an interpretation surely partly motivated by an interest in proving Spenser to be Calvinistic in temper. Baptismal water is from this well, to be sure, and the imagery is in a sense sacramental, but the "baptized *hands*" and their "secret vertue" (force and size), the strength that had hardened even the brandished steel blade when it fell therein (stanza 36), are details which fit no scene at a font, but do read lucidly of added fortitude received through grace in extremity. We harm the poem's action when we introduce notions of the new Christian's first renunciation of the devil (he has fought him already for one whole anguished day), first entrance into the body of the faithful (making nonsense of the far other stages of canto x), of infancy, of the birth of the church (also in each heart), of a sacrament wherein we die to be reborn (the death of stanza 30 is not the one shared with Christ). Every familiar emphasis of the traditional image we have been pursuing is in Spenser's well of life—its ancient paradisiacal place "before that cursed Dragon got That happie land" of Eden (or the human heart, *gostly*) whose King and Queen Red Crosse now rescues, its medicinal strength (remedium is the common metaphor of the treatises), its power to wash away guilt and restore life to those who have met the adversary and failed, the new access of strength with which to resume the fight.

Even more precise is the suitability and exact theological purport of the anointing and the dew in stanza 48. The balm flowed from "that first tree," the tree of life planted in the first garden, "loaden with fruit" said to have powers over all, for eating it bestowed everlasting life (and Spenser does not evade the ambiguity of saying this tree was charged with the reproach of causing the fall)—this is most certainly the tree of which we have just read in the virtues-literature, who *gostly*, is Christ in the heart and so operates. As in the *Somme le roi* passage, this bath of saving balm decorously presents the conception of

the Christian healed and revivified and given sufficient final
strength through access to more than human strength poured out
for him, whereas the attempt to force this into a solely eucharistic
image merely confounds and embarrasses us. Of course, Holy
Communion is a means of grace, and Red Crosse doubtless "fed"
on the fruit, but not in stanza 48, where it is pernicious to import
troubles about "he fell," bathing not drinking, balm and anointing; these intrude into the most unchangeable image in Christianity (the elements of bread and wine).[38] Spenser has rather
used, with simplicity but plenty, imagery completely usual and
universally meaningful to all Christians—we have been studying
the imagery of grace, and there is no great marvel in Spenser's
using it too when that is his subject. The imagery in stanza 48
of dew, balm, rain, curing, bringing to life the "corse appointed
for the grave," saving Red Crosse from that same death when
he fell into the stream which had overflowed the whole plain,
suits as it should Christ the Tree of Life and the operation of
grace; moreover, great tact is shown regarding the choice of concretions possible to his "literal" fiction and yet weighted with
all the old habitual meanings.

Our trouble has been the same old bête noire of imposing
equations, quite properly maligned as a cheap game of one-to-one

---

[38] The eighteenth-century critics were more careful, but the nineteenth- and
twentieth-century readiness to equate these incidents with the two sacraments
may be followed in the *Variorum Spenser* notes and appendices, from Keightly
and Dodge on to the unquestioning assumptions in later studies, in Padelford's
"Spiritual Allegory of the *Faerie Queene*," *JEGP*, vol. 22 (1923), p. 17, or
even seen in Whitaker, *Religious Basis of Spenser's Thought* (Stanford, 1950),
p. 52. Padelford's readings of both historical and ecclesiastical allegory are
especially obscured by this persistent reading of allegorical imagery "in reverse."
I have tried to substitute truly traditional ways of allowing this figure to operate.
The same habit of seizing on equatable—or even just associatable—concretions,
is responsible for misreadings (I think) in A. C. Hamilton, *Structure of Allegory
in the Faerie Queene* (Oxford, 1961). Compare, e.g. the interpretation of the
passages discussed above as a Harrowing-of-Hell—the *meanings* of the Harrowing of Hell are here impertinent and useless, and all the Three-Days references
one can count will not get in the patriarchs, the "death," the adversary's nether
kingdom, in a story where they have no propriety. Yet he is more careful than
most on the relation of allegory to Christ-figures, and perhaps clearer examples
of the modern form of forcing images to convey particular meanings are found
in A. D. S. Fowler's "Emblems of Temperance in *The Faerie Queene*, Book II,"
RES, vol. 11 (1960), 143-49; I find evidence for these meanings notably insufficient.

correspondences—under the mistaken assumption that this is what allegory does. If baptism and communion, during this fight, did not hamper the clear progress of meanings in this canto, as they painfully do, allegory at least would have put them *not* in the form of events that stand for them but in the form of further shadowings of the idea the story is conveying to us—assistance from heaven needed and given to the weakened struggling image-of-God-in-man (his "Knight") who has on his hands the fight only Christ has ever completely won. I would point to the evidence for conscious use of the figure allegory in the *Somme le roi*'s phrase, "rigt so doth gostly to the herte the goode gardyner," planting Christ in that garden, as detail for detail and insight for insight we "read" the one image so that everything in it means the second inner image as well. The first remains quite valid and firm and is not replaced. The author, of course, translates the *spiritualiter* or *mystice* of scriptural exegesis; we cannot possibly misunderstand how he thinks allegory works. It is impressive that all Spenser's readers do this transmuting, and universally stage the action of the *Faerie Queene* within the human heart; the battle perhaps is keeping the poem at least double (or triple) and not settling for a dwindled *gostly* half.

It is convenient, as we leave the garden-image based upon five well-known sevens, to mention the fact that mediaeval discussions had made several other groups of seven very usual as figures. A whole complex of ideas, often about the relation of virtues and grace, is intimated often when we least suspect it. The Gifts were regularly connected with the seven pillars of wisdom, and the seven horns and seven eyes of the Lamb who signified Christ in Rev. 5.6, or the seven eyes in the stone of Zech. 3.9; similarly the doves descending or those around Christ's head were seven (to be read as the Gifts in windows and illuminations, in Jesse-trees and the like, probably without exception). The seven lights of the candelabrum (Christ) in the temple were read allegorically very early, as in Bede; like some other figures, this found its way into the *Glossa ordinaria*. Connections with the seven days of creation—found often in writers both more known and less known than Bonaventura (the *Breviloquium*)—caught the interest of writers reprinted in the Renaissance (like St. Antoninus) or writing them (the Englishman Bonde's *Pilgrimage of Perfection*, 1526). Certain liturgical parallel sevens achieved more acceptance or less, though it would be hazardous to conclude too much from the extreme beauty of the iconography: parallels with the seven penitential psalms (illuminations relate the seven vices and the seven gift-virtues), with the seven o's of Advent, with the seven Matins divisions of the psalter, with the seven-times-said "Dominus vobiscum" of the Mass. Some Biblical connections I have met less frequently: the seven women of Isa. 4.1, though treated by Origen and in the *Glossa ordinaria*; the seven steps to the interior or vestibule in Ezek. 40, though in Gregory; and even Gregory's quite famous early tie, which never caught popular interest, with Job's three daughters (theological virtues) and seven sons (Gifts; *Moralia* 1.27).[39] I think we can rest assured that the sevens were brought so frequently to men's attention that they could not have become by the sixteenth century mere old mediaeval learned lore.

It may by now appear worthwhile also to remind ourselves of the very large output of books like the *Somme le roi*. I have mentioned the historical necessity for their composition. We have concentrated on Lorens' *Somme* because of its liveliness, vast popularity and accessibility in print, its beautiful iconographical tradition maintained for two centuries, and because all English students are subjected to its first translation in the *Ayenbite of Inwit* and can now repair this experience by reading another (of the eight attempts) in *EETS*, vol. 217, the nearest approach in several languages to a chance at acquaintance with the text. But if we are trying to gauge the enormous influence upon common readers of this body of materials and its conventions of imagery, we must not only recall the vast spread of Latin summae of vices and virtues like Peraldus' and Pennaforte's (which were the main sources plundered), but all kinds of variant compositions in the same category as the *Somme le roi*—William of Nassyng-

[39] As early as Cassiodorus, a series of ties is made between the Seven Gifts and the seven uses of "Vox domini" in Ps. 29 (Vulgate; Kg.J. 29). The many powers of the Lord's voice, "in virtute," "in magnificentia," "to break the cedars" (the proud), etc., are accommodated to the Gifts from Sapientia down to Timor. I could cite the particular theological writers and the passages referred to, but it seems preferable to recall the general discussions cited above in notes 7, 25 (especially those of Blic, Lottin and Bonnefoy), where references recur, though scattered. Certain suggestions, like the iconographical and liturgical examples, can be pursued in the article cited in n. 5 above. The *Glossa ordinaria* in *P.Lat.*113-114, since it ensured centuries of familiarity, I usually cite, by Biblical reference; the "candelabrum" passages are Num. 8.2, Exod. 25.37.

ton's *Speculum vitae*, the *Pore Caitif*, other specula (to stick to England) such as *Speculum Christiani*, St. Edmund Rich's *Merure de sainte eglise*, the common ones like the *Parson's Tale*, and Gower's *Miroir de l'omme* and *Confessio amantis* (both organized around the sins and their opposing virtues—*not* the cardinal and theological virtues). There was also the swarm of small popular devotional or moral works, sometimes with a manuscript history and sometimes not, sometimes iconographically interesting, which dot the printing lists of the 1500's and show this tradition expiring: Jacques Legrand's *Livre de bonnes moeurs* (a Caxton version; STC 15394); *Le Livre de saigesse* (these two books use the gift-virtues, not our ordinary set); Alexander Carpenter's *Destructorium viciorum* (studied by Owst, and not to be confused with the *Dialogues of creatures moralized*, using this title); Guy de Roye's *Doctrinal de sapience* (with Creed, Ten Commandments, Pater Noster, vice and gift-virtues, sacraments; a Caxton version, STC 21431); the *Ordinaire des crestiens* (Creed, Ten Commandments, vices and virtues, seven works of mercy, sacraments and other series; a Wynken de Worde version, 1506); the *Examen de conscience* (Creed, Ten Commandments, Pater Noster, vices and virtues, Beatitudes) a poor book by the time of a Paris, 1529, edition, though a vellum copy shows the "new iconography of the virtues" (fifteenth century); Bonde's *Pilgrimage of Perfection*, London, 1526.[40]

The attachment of named demons to the "seven other spirits more wicked than himself" of Matt. 12.45, plus the idea we have seen, that these vices must be routed by seven spiritual virtues ("virtutibus spiritualibus contraria . . . septem vitia") provides the kind of tie responsible for, say, Nashe's treatment in *Pierce Penilesse* of the seven vices under the heads of the seven devils with the appropriate virtues. The spiritual virtues were perhaps somewhat affected by the list of Fruits of the Spirit.[41] Attention

---

[40] I leave citations to the usual bibliographies, but all these pieces have been studied in order to build an accurate idea of the tradition. On Peraldus' enormous circulation see n. 18 above; on "Peckham's Constitutions" see n. 17 above.

[41] In conception and perhaps some names; the list is in Gal. 5.22-23: caritas, gaudium, pax, patientia, benignitas, bonitas, longanimitas, mansuetudo, fides, modestia, continentia, castitas. It is interesting proof of the continued strength of traditions discussed early in this chapter that the King James version has conflated the three last Macrobian facets of Temperance (modestia, continentia, castitas) into one fruit "temperance" (hence not twelve fruits but nine). After

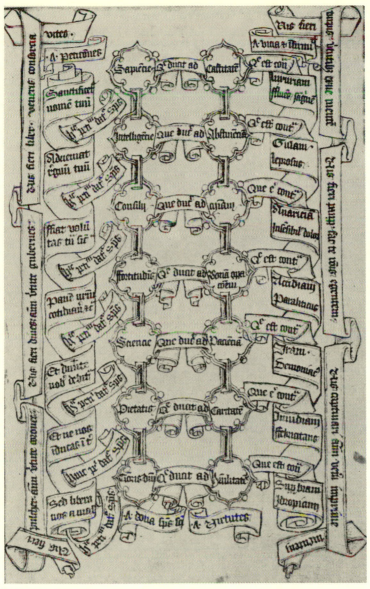

FIGURE 25

Bonaventura's famous *Arbor vitae* and some other diagrammatic reiterations, these images and relations became elementary commonplaces to literate Christians. For a typical scheme see Fig. 25 and citations in article referred to in n. 5 above. Fluctuations of terminology for virtues in Spenser perhaps reflect less his odd translations of Aristotle's Greek than this situation of the existence of several well-known series. On Fig. 26: no sixteenth-century Englishman, but some fifteenth-century men, had seen this magnificent book and its verbal "Exposition" of its symbolic pictures, for it was sent back to Jean Duke of Berry by King Henry after its owner Richard II's death, and is now B.N. lat.MS.10483, fol. 53r; but these trends are absent neither from English writing or arts (see both parts of the article referred to in n. 5 above).

to the commonness of all these series would have obviated
McKerrow's (and others') criticisms of these passages in *Pierce
Penilesse* and *Christ's Tears*. One parallel of considerable importance for the arts was that of the seven sacraments with these
other sevens. What St. Thomas propounded could not remain
obscure, though the same scheme occurs apparently earlier in
Simon Hinton. One superb pictured scheme in a manuscript of
great fame, the *Belleville Breviary*, deserves recall, and a reproduction (Fig. 26), for its own beauty. It also illustrates the last
parallel I mention, which remaining unfixed was the least useful—the attempt to attach the "three-plus-four" usual virtues.
Found in both authors just mentioned, attempted by many, and
include the writers of such subliterature as the ars moriendi books,
these burgeoning sevens for which we claim no great seventeenth-
century popularity were yet important, given their number, in
that they made virtues or vices into whole complexes of imagery
and conceptions. Use of one member pulled in much else, if not
the whole lot.

Unlike other sevens, an accepted and familiar order of parallelisms was never established for the "three-plus-four." They
are likeliest to be given a separate little treatment, as in the
Somme le roi. The first inescapably well-distributed listing was
perhaps Bonaventura's in his *Breviloquium*; he takes the four
cardinal virtues first, others reverse this. I do not pause to show
the differences in meaning which order (hence parallels) causes—
whether a connection transpires between Faith and Baptism, Charity (Pietas) and the Eucharist, or whether we begin "Temperance,
Justice" with those sacraments and Gifts. We note the naturalness
of introducing Fidelia, Speranza and Charissa in i.x of the *Faerie
Queene*; it is almost equally natural that Spenser left out the
four cardinal virtues in a context where the supernatural virtues
belong, as do the spiritual ones (his Humiltà and the rest). The
point should be made again here that accommodation rather than
rivalry or substitution was the accepted procedure; Holiness and
Friendship and Chastity are not out of place beside Justice and
Temperance. They had long been seen to overlap, to be identical
in some branch and have innumerable subterranean relations.

In sum, the important fact stands out: the virtues defined from
the Beatitudes and nourished by the Gifts were the ones that
were "against the seven vices," and most suitable for choice if

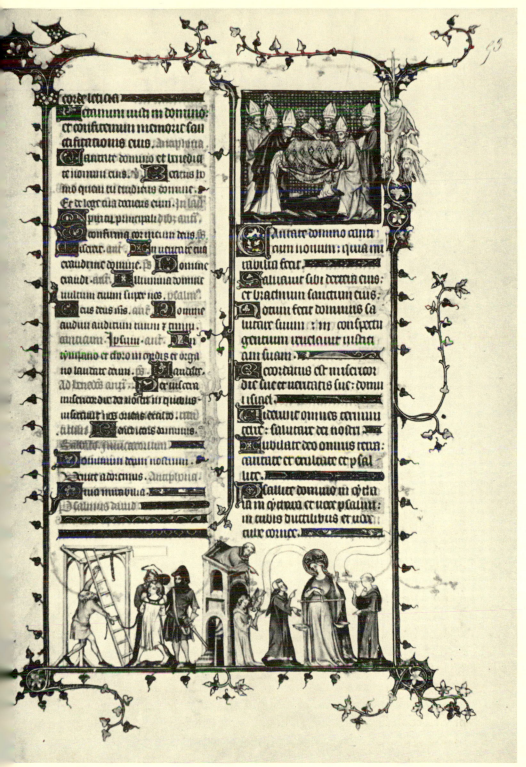

FIGURE 26

such situations were the subject. The more ordinary seven do not work out as opponents; as a set they have no place in a large complex of imagery carrying subtle and profound conceptions, and hence a less fertile endowment of associated relations. The now less known seven held the field absolutely firmly, as the virtues truly opposite to the seven famous modes of evil-doing, and this could be documented fully, from the time of Gregory on Ezekiel up through the centuries to the little books I named and the children's sing-song lists. It is typical that at the beginning of the gifts-virtues-vices treatise of the *Somme*, Frère Lorens tucks in the "three-plus-four" in four pages, saying, "But er we fall to speke of vertues that ben contrarious to the seuene dedli synnes, we wolen schortly speke of seuene othere vertues, wher-of the thre ben cleped diuine vertues, and the foure ben cleped cardinal vertues" (p. 121). Citations in other connections have shown how unchanging are the language and the conception —"against the vices," contraria, opposita, with innumerable instances of images of supplanting, remedying, leaving no room for, and far fewer of fighting.

It makes a great difference in a poetic treatment of a quest for a virtue if a presupposition exists that it has a famous proper opposite, and it made a great difference to Spenser—though he was not intending to present seven opposing actions against Christianity's seven modes of evil but twelve virtues from Aristotle. When he chose to use out of his varied heritage the errant and contending Knight and the quest-image with its implications, and partly impelled by this, chose also to set over against his figures their famous great opposites (thus further determining the nature of his virtues), and finally, chose the mode of figurative language that asks for allegorical reading, it meant that most of his structure of meanings and means of portrayal were lined out for him.

To be sure, no matter how firm his intention to delineate the Aristotelian virtues, a man of 1580 would find it all but unnatural to depict a quest of a virtue without depicting a conquest or escape from a particular opposing vice, without demonstrating the latter's nature and allowing that in part to define the virtue. This has affected Spenser's design markedly. It has often pressed his selection and his conception of his virtues over in the direction of the set that were truly against the vices. He handles all his inheritances with a proper freedom, and I am not in sympathy with attempts to find the total series of seven sins in the *Faerie Queene*.[42] Yet his Temperance has been pushed toward a virtue more resembling Sobriété with its connections with a rightly directed love despising the world's lures, by the stress put on Luxury and Avarice as chief embodiments of concupiscentia; it is the *intemperateness* of Acrasia that becomes apparent to Guyon; and psychomachias concerned with temptation to the sin of Lechery come elsewhere, just as in the *Somme le roi*, Lecherye riding on her goat occurs in a later section. The temptations of Red Crosse are to Pride, not Luxury. Book I is dominated by the idea of countering Pride; Discordia, every form of Ire, is more investigated in Book IV than the nature of Friendship; and there is a clear attempt to set Luxuria against Castitas in Books III and IV, mingled with the equally common emphasis, but peculiar to Christian tradition, on Chastity seen as related to Fidelity (the pure soul faithful in allegiance to God, to the good, to the right loves, to creatures loved through the creator), only very secondarily related to Virginity, and related to marriage only because of the concern to define love as it exists in a knight who always makes the choice that is not self-indulgent. These extended meanings of luxury, of avarice, of wrath, belong of course to Spenser's predecessors, and were perfectly habitual.

The way in which an opposed vice has affected the *definition* of a virtue being sought is very clear in Book I. The Book has always forced commentators into tight corners, not simply because a virtue of Holiness is out of line, but because Pride in its relation to self-reliance (and even to condescending benevolence) is not vicious to Aristotle and his like, and because the great deliverer Arthur has as his *virtue* that Magnificentia which in its Aristotelian

---

[42] Although it is true, as J. Holloway says, that the structure of Book II is affected by the use of sins to oppose virtues, too much forcing of the text is necessary to get Gluttony in (in the apples) and meanings are squeezed or inflated (to get Braggadochio from Vainglory to Envy). But this hunting down of possible carriers is more apparent in R. Fox's article, and the great structural principle which Spenser observes so carefully, of major highlighted images, and minor images and ideas, is obscured very damagingly. See "The 7 Deadly Sins in *FQ*, II," *RES*, vol. 3 (1952), 13-18, in which Holloway does indeed call attention to a relation too much forgotten, and *RES*, vol. 12 (1961), 1-6. When Miss Spens long ago took up these ideas, results were exhilarating to read, though somewhat highhanded in dealing with plain facts.

exposition is suspiciously akin to the very vice itself of Book I. This is aggravated by the fact that meanwhile, if we forsake an Aristotelian for a Christian frame of reference, its vice of Pride ought to be the special temptation of a Knight on a quest of Humilitas, rather than one especially in love with Truth.

The radical Christian definition of Pride, kept to the forefront (given the persistence all clichés have by the mediaeval virtues-and-vices literature), is strictly to the point here. Why is Red Crosse's first enemy *Error* not arrogance, his first conquered knight Sans*foy* not Sans-humblesse, and why is Truth, which is seemingly the *goal* of the intellectual virtues, here the special *guide* to Holiness, and that which Holiness' patron must espouse, while Duessa or *falsity* in one form after another is his constant temptation, rather than vainglory? We may profitably recall the exemplum chosen by the *Somme le roi* illuminators to set forth Pride typified: Ahaziah. Now Ahaziah or Occosias was not a vainglorious, proud tyrant; he was a king of Samaria who, having injured himself by falling through a lattice in his upper chamber, sent to Ekron's god Baal-zebub—instead of the prophet of the true God—to know whether he was destined to recover. That was the sin which caused Elijah to declare God's judgement, "Thou shalt not come down from the bed . . . but shalt surely die." He is always pictured coming down in no uncertain sense, but actually his miscreance was the "fall" of Pride, not the one from the lattice.[43]

For the same reason, the first branch of Pride is commonly untrewth—that is Spenser's Sansfoy, the Sarazin, Infidelity. For the same reason, Error with her filthy poison of false books and papers manifestly figures the first mistaken way in which those err and wander who worship falsely by believing in the wrong things. Hence Una says during that first fight (1.i.19), "Add *faith* unto your force" (Fortitudo). For the same reason, Hypocrisy, proud Lucifer's quality, plays so large a part, being again a

---

[43] "Ocozias" and numerous variant spellings label him with certainty; he is not unusual as Pride, but dates might show him dependent upon the early and popular iconographical program of the *Somme le roi*; he is not verbally in French *texts* I have seen, but it is unedited, with its 80-odd manuscripts. His story is told in 2 Kings 1 (Vulgate; 4 Kings). No doubt many saw in his pictured fall the same simpler significance we read in the falling horseman who often represents Superbia. Some characterizing phrases are taken from the *Somme le roi*'s separate seven sins treatise, pp. 12, 11. They are legion.

prominent branch of Pride in all the lists. Archimago the shape-shifter (evil is multiple) hates Una, who is single in her nature (Truth's nature) and in her devotion, because she is his exact opposite—one true to the Truth.

The meaning of the word "truth" which connects it with troth to an allegiance, and makes it include both veritas and fides, is a very important meaning in incident after incident of Book I. Both sides of Una's trueness are continually played upon. When Red Crosse in the second dream "suspects her *truth*" though as yet "no untruth he knew" (stanza 53), fidelity not rightness is being spoken of, yet it is "faire falshood," both as false religion and as duplicity, who steps into Truth's stead (prefatory verses). Fradubio, because he was in doubt which to think more beautiful, his frail but true faith or the meretriciously attractive, untrue mistress, saw his true love turn into a wooden, lifeless thing and met both deceptiveness and infidelity in the untrue love; Red Crosse learns nothing from seeing the exact parallel to his own situation because he has lost truth through failing to keep troth. The double emphasis on Truth and Faith is indigenous to all treatments which discuss the fundamental spring of the sin of Pride, which is not self-conceit or arrogance or vaingloriousness but the cause of those (all are branches)—an unwillingness to worship the true God, Lucifer's flaw. "This is the first synne that assaileth Goddes knyt," "the lioun that al swelweth and biteth," and it is perilous "for it blyndeth a man that he ne knoweth not hymself, ne seeth not hymself."

The blindness is certainly being used to define the nature of "sight." Pride's special blindness is to man's true nature and limits; as a creature he must first recognize the true God to whom he owes allegiance, and secondly, maintain this allegiance with no trace of rebellion (basic humilitas) because he sees God's nature rightly. This understanding of Pride's failure of sight accounts for the stress throughout on darkness: Night and her forces are arrayed against Red Crosse, "old *Aveugles* sonnes" are her nephews Sansfoy and Sansjoy, and the Lucifer-parallel of the rebellion against Jove is recalled; blind Ignaro has the keys to Orgoglio's castle; Corceca's blind heart cannot achieve the first recognition, while her favorite Kirkrapine robs the body of the faithful, replacing right allegiance with idolatrous whoredom. The three brothers can stand by one another loyally enough, but this is not an alleviating characteristic to give them human complexity. This kept faith to wrong instead of right underscores their blind faithlessness as miscreants, the opprobrious term cast at them when Sarazin is not preferred. Yet every sight image is not attached to this concept, and it is just as natural in allegory, which asks us to discriminate between the significant and the casual, that when Una is momentarily blind to the identity of Archimago, unable like Milton's Uriel to see through devilish Hypocrisy, we must refuse to read this as a confusing error made by Truth. Una, too, is a creature, and does not equal Truth but shadows Truth so far as may be; she is not God Himself come down from heaven, the only perfect Truth.[44]

The emphasis on clear sight of the true is accompanied by images showing rather firm faith to it. The "salvage nation" who can see enough of truth's beauty not to destroy her is neither an idealization nor a condemnation of man's nature, but demonstrates its insufficiency to Una's double discipline "of *faith* and *veritie*" (1.vi.31). Spenser plainly means to leave undenied the connections with lust and brutishness, even in Satyrane's heritage, and the latter's story shows us, without overnervous constant translation into ideas, the reasons why he alone could learn, and be "plaine, faithfull, true." Spenser keeps as close as ever in these sections to his theme of the virtue that is against Pride, but the kinds of pride he thinks it is against have helped to define it. It is cunning of him to introduce the humble who are without all trace of Humility by the radical definition of the Book, and dis-

[44] In part, this shows one of those tacit unmarked differences from late classical allegory (and also some mythographical descendants), resulting from the long Christian history of the figure. Sidney's description of the way particulars to see" and hence love, puts it in terms of poetic theory—allegory being the shadow universals, those forms which the poet can seem to let his reader "steal extreme of this metaphorical dimension. The same long history warned that the needs of the literal meaning must be respected. Spenser is busy portraying Una's love for Red Crosse, who, if he is dead, sees nothing left remarkable neath the visiting sun, and her lament decrying eyes and sun (1.vii.22-28) will be found to be so written; only by main force can we turn it into a temporary desertion to the forces of darkness, truth herself mistaken, and then vilifying the eye, symbol of man's sight of God. The image does not contain within it indicators to such meanings, and it is highly illegitimate in allegory to tie every story detail to the metaphor, and by reading details of a history *spiritualiter* make nonsense of its primary meaning. This problem is handled with more care in ch. 5 (and see ch. 4, n. 36).

tinguish among his miscreants. In apprehending such nuances, it is a disadvantage to see too morally; Book I is so often strictly allegorical, letting moral allegory take its chances.

Yet a hint of these conceptions, rather than an ironbound system of correspondences, is profitable. This comes out apropos of the Lion, whom we have had to take as only too many obfuscating equivalents. Lions "as Nature" would have astonished any Elizabethan; they are no more Nature than chickens or scholars to those who have not yet identified savage, uncivilized, irrational, ungoverned, with natural. Spenser also avoids the irrelevancies of that famous character, the Grateful Lion. To be sure, he is not ingrata, in the sense which made Ungratefulness one of the branches of Pride (a human sin, man's unkindly [unnatural] resentment at owing service to God, manifest truth; long after the Elizabethans, it was still a cliché that brute creation escaped this diabolical perversion). A reasonable link connects the many references to Christ as Leo, the strong sun in Leo, the Lion upon whom Wrath rides in Spenser as in so many places, Leo as Pride. Spenser's phrasings show that he thinks of how the "mightie proud" has once more yielded to the "humble weake" (iii.7), as in the innumerable allegorical pictures of virtues standing upon, exacting submission from, their opposites. The power of truth against princely puissance, its simplicity and divine grounding compelling proud submission, is felt throughout but elsewhere not so specifically depicted. It is the theme all over again, but the different ideas brought in prove how far from repetitious it is; the choice of concretions must be intelligently managed to secure this—though Leo is Pride, we may try to imagine Spenser using him as the devilish apotheosis of the vice pure that he can make of Orgoglio. But the nature of the vice is providing the differentia which define the virtue.

It is notable that we are not given a story of man's temptations to power. Red Crosse does not lapse into vainglorious tyranny; he lapses into trusting in his own powers to get on with his quest and know what mistresses to offer his help to. We do not see him captived by Lucifera, for he walks through her court as one who "Thought all their glorie vaine" and their Princess "too exceeding prowd"; we see him the spoil of Untruth and Untroth, far more basic causes of Pride; and it is therefore that he *takes his armor off*, "poured out in loosnesse on the grassy grownd" (vii.7).[45] That he was carelesse was his Pride. Spenser's inclusion of temptations not felt as such by his protagonist, as in the more famous example of Guyon, shows a poet interested less in dramatic struggle than in investigating through actions and images the nature and the definition of a virtue. (Of course, we could be simultaneously reading Spenser's thoughts on the present state of England, declared in the images.) I attribute the inclusiveness not to a moralist's effort to be tidily complete, but to a true pleasure in distinguishing varied motivations, effects, moral nuances, doctrinal profundities. Before Red Crosse's almost fatal captivity, there is no warning tale of a psychological temptation to Sloth, and battle against it lost; he fell victim to "foolish pride" and "weaknesse" (viii.1) and *their* nature, not his, is exposed to us.

The form taken by proud power is not pride-in-power but usurpation. This is not only stated of Lucifera (iv.12) but made clear before the statements by use of the common figure of Phoebus, a metaphor for presumptuous usurpation of divine prerogative. This theme is never dropped, for it is radical Pride which Spenser shows us. Of course, he shows it finally in the ancient images used for Satan the prime usurper. The greatest temptation scene in the Book, with Despair, is quite fitly that temptation to a misapprehension of the nature of God, denying His mercy, which veritas-fides must save him from. These qualities were exactly what Dr. Faustus did not have. That Una seizes the knife and pulls her knight back from danger with the words "thou . . . that *chosen* art" is the fundamental Christian answer to *man*, common to all Christian churches, who all conserved the Judaic faith in God's relation to a chosen—if a faithful—people. It is a pitiful diminution of this great scene to use it as proof of Spenser's Calvinism merely because we hear so loudly the echoes of a peculiar use of that universal word.

These later developments in the Book make it the more ap-

[45] When he drinks of the fountain, he is still the "guiltlesse" man Spenser understands but does not exonerate in vii.1, and he was not expected to know better than to drink those particular waters. Spenser commonly faces his knights, as in the romances, with tests not understandable, not moral in the usual sense, and the reasons for this subtlety in dealing with the human situation will be clearer later. Of course the graile is the wet gravel and pure and simple (see n. 44 above and Hamilton, p. 74; citation in n. 38); but the tissue of the half-canto is delicately symbolical, directing us not to wring the necks of the figures, when Red Crosse's tired desertion of his quest and his allegiance is so clear.

parent that what Red Crosse receives in the House of Holiness is knowledge of the virtue truly opposing the radical vice of Pride; he also receives that condition of the spirit which would lead him to strengths to piece out his own (as he shows in canto xi). The first of the Seven Gifts, we recall, was Timor Domini—the beginning of Wisdom to which it ultimately could lead, the Sapientia of the beatific vision. The virtue it nourishes is Humility. This radical virtue (for instance the prime virtue of Christ and of the Virgin Mary, and the root in many a diagram) is to be defined in its opposition to radical Pride and has very little to do with self-deprecation; it is what we watch slowly taking shape as we read Book I—a virtue built of clear-sighted realization of man's dependence on and grateful faith in his divine Lord.

I believe Spenser's dependences to have been usually very general ones, his inheritances to have been typically more uncircumscribed than precise, almost never schematic and often unrealized. He certainly realized this one, and chose to send his first Knight in quest of Holiness not Humility. It turns out to be a better name for the special humilitas he means. I am sure he thought to avoid some misunderstandings, wanted a chivalric virtue, and knew that the virtue of the First Beatitude, complete contrary to Pride, is the virtue Holiness begins with—recognition of the Truth of the Godhead and a perfect Troth kept in that owed allegiance. The treatises declare this to be the case, but indeed, the matching of names makes little difference. We see that the whole set of awkwardnesses disappears (e.g. Holiness is not a Christian virtue any more than a Greek one, neither it nor Truth is opposite to Pride), when we read the still-accepted double meaning of Truth-Troth, true contrary of fundamental radical Pride.

The demonstration of ways in which the use of an opposing vice has affected the portrayal of a virtue's nature has drawn us some distance from my related statement: that the design of the *Faerie Queene* has been affected by the existence of another famous set of virtues, best known as the contraries of the seven vices. A Spenserian must find some interest in a series of virtues that includes Amitié, Chasteté, Debonnerté and Largesse, when so much difficulty has been made about Friendship, Chastity and Courtesy as truly eminent Aristotelian virtues. The names, I think, had their influence, but the nature of what was signified by the names had much more—their relations, characters, wherein "virtues," and the like. This point may be conveniently woven in with another: the effect on the structure of treatments of virtues of an element in the Ciceronian and Macrobian traditions which was perhaps strengthened by men's natural desire to find places in each tradition for the other. From the beginning, the character of these two traditions had something to do with the universal mediaeval habit of dividing virtues, and later vices, into aspects and branches, though many typically mediaeval reasons kept the habit lively (mnemonic convenience in confession, and in debate, for example).

One large imprecise related point stands out, for causes of such results are bound to be multiple. Spenser in the *Faerie Queene*, insofar as it is a work examining virtues, wrote something comparable to many lesser preceding pieces: a work that exposes the nature of these great abstractions which interested him. He exposes them by opening to us through fictional adventures or great speaking pictures facet after facet, manifestation after manifestation. This is a key to his design—an unclassical structure and one very unlike epic. There are other reasons for his choice, but it suited phenomenally well the presentation of virtues as they were customarily presented.

He does not undertake a vast psychomachia, nor a series of smaller ones, though one result of the definition via opposites is that multitudes of minor incidents each have the motive if not the form of a Prudentian psychomachia. Sometimes these great posed oppositions occupy his climactic places—about the middle, and toward the end, of each Book; sometimes they are undynamic images of great antithetical principles, for the hero is not always the principle in action but a learner who thus comprehends what it is. The Mammon and Acrasia and Mutability and dragon cantos present such oppositions; but the Garden of Adonis rather reveals like a vision, while the House of Busyrane and Masque of Cupid lay out false love in all its operations and adjuncts ("displayd"), and Venus Temple sets before us all Venus had come to mean, as if resolving the ambiguities were part of our responsibility. The history is in abeyance, the characters all but stand by and wait, poised precariously on some narrative link that is tenuous but important, while we learn what we need in order to understand the story. The existence of a great contrary vice is often the immediate cause of such great imaged expositions, but what gets exposed is the complicated multiform nature of the virtue involved. No mode has ever existed, perhaps, which could match the power of allegory to accomplish such tasks. The intervening parts of Books, so famously episodic in structure, are taken up with interlaced presentations of each of the many faces the virtue and the vice can wear. This, too, is a natural operation of the figure of allegory, but also, since the time of Cicero, it had been the way to go about understanding a cardinal virtue—with no notion at all at first of allegorizing the manifested shapes.

We end by seeing into the general, the principle, the quiddity "in its universall consideration" as Sidney phrased it, and feel that we see it in essence, whole. But we do not see a whole with all its parts; we see chosen, salient, often deceptive or just recognizable forms in which something can appear—universals in their this-world shape, i.e. bodied in particulars, countless, deceptive, needing translation, but real, and being virtues, grounded even in *ultimate* reality. For here, in the mode of existence that virtues were assumed to have, the pressure of the set which were Christ's own attributes is felt in the treatment of all of them; all Spenser's knights are in quest of fundamentally divine attributes (in their perfection), and all are what Yeats called "making their souls." This would not have happened if there had not been a set of spiritual virtues which needed gifts of grace, just as Spenser's great oppositions would not characterize so many treatments had we heard only about Prudence, Temperance, Fortitude, Justice and their parts. They are not definable by the nature of their contraries, indeed have none, though they have dissimilars.

It was important that Macrobius departed from Cicero's name of "parts" for all the divisions he gives us for each cardinal virtue. Spenser opens out the virtues in just this way, showing rather than naming the manifestations, but it is very lucky that he and others did not think they were analyzing into parts, or sterility and rigidity would soon have killed the virtues for literature. Overlapping, misapprehension, "knowing" virtues, are problems with much the same meaning as they have when applied to experience. Red Crosse learns to comprehend Fidelity and Truth by experiencing the nature and import of falsity as men do in life, time and again a similar idea in different guises. We see Justice in very many shapes, opposed to an In-Justice which is partially defined by iustitia as "righteousness"; they are not parts at all, but forms that the long years of dividing and defining have made familiar to men as shapes of Justice: Artegall's misjudged *liberalitas* being his un-*just* character, yielding to Radegund; Equity seen as the quality of being "mesurable" which provided her with her plummet and line (v.iii.36;i.7); distributive justice, justice as *vindicatio*, penal justice, cases involving unusual refinements on *ius suum* (Braggadochio's undeserved honours, unjust *vereratio*); the commonplace about Munera's deflection of Justice, that face of Justice which is Misericordia; unjust characters who lack *veritas*, lack *humanitas*; or the unexpected importance of Envy and Detraction as the unjust obstacles to *concordia*, which is public *iustitia*, as *amicitia* and *pietas* are private justice (*ius suum* seen and granted, that which is due to friends, kin, human fellows). These are not examples but appearances; Justice is "in" them all, and she is what we see.

Envy as the named foe in Book V. xii.31 does not forbid the idea, which has much to be said for it, that the opening out of the nature of Friendship in Book IV deliberately uses the traditional great opposite of Amitié—Invidia. The conception would enlarge the virtue, for Amitié is the form of Love which is the special *remedium* for Invidia—one of the forms of Envy. The theme of concord and discord culminates in the great set-piece on "*Concord* . . . in common reed," the great figure in Love's temple; it is set forth in one revelation after another of the faking, or the destruction, or the contrary, of the virtue, seen in those who are entirely possessed by hatred of others' good, *detractio*, *susurratio*, venomous words, treason to companions, obduracy—all famous forms of Envy, as *discordia* usually is. All are set in opposition to the absence of self-regard which is the root of the true friends' behavior. Agape is mother of this *philia* in the three brothers who give their lives each to the others; this is a most unusual detail, certainly showing deliberate and purposeful originality,[46] and her special kind of love is given

---

[46] This and related points have just been handled with more care in T. P. Roche, *The Kindly Flame, A Study of the Third and Fourth Books of Spenser's Faerie Queene* (Princeton, 1964), who gratifyingly avoids those ways of misreading allegory which have most dogged us since the unsympathetic nineteenth century—impatient with mediaeval developments in religious allegory and given to the Coleridgean definitions got from German thought.

the heavenly birth it always has by the hint hidden in her being a fay. This love is very much the kind nourished by the Gift Pietas, variously named caritas, amitié, pitié, love, pite, benignity. The good characters, full of pitié, all save each other: Britomart saves Amoret; Amoret comforts Aemylia; Marinell is transformed by ruth; Cymodoce gives up her hard-fought battle, out of pitying love when she sees her son's suffering; the bad characters all devour and exploit and defile. The story's persons are set on to vicious acts by the fully abstract creatures, like Ate, who is Envy's branch, Discord in essence. Corflambo, with his basilisk eye that kills all it looks on (a familiar image for Envy), burns with rancour, his heart consumed by self-indulgent lust. The frequent use of poison-mouth imagery, the description of Sclaunder (she is the most famous of Envy's daughters), the persistent flashing of light upon envious motivations and behavior in these swarms of Amity's enemies, help to make it plausible that Spenser had in his mind the ancient contrariety of Envy to Amitié or Douceur or Love, the virtue nourished by the Gift Pietas, and the second of the other seven.

To be sure, he treats in Book IV one of Aristotle's supposed twelve. Yet, except for the need to fit his Book to Aristotle's ideas upon Friendship, no one would think of looking, as critics feel called upon to do, to see if the love is between equals or unequals (in Britomart or Amoret), or of looking for ideas on the merit of persons—these are not problems. Though Blandamour and Paridell are no doubt accidental friends and therefore impermanent ones, no one would independently find this to be the stress in their story of comical shifts of allegiance (iv.i.2) based on self-concern, despite, hatred of the good of others (stanza 39); these are opposed to generous loyalty and love displayed in the following friendships. True, Amyas and Placidas, twins, can show us the value of likeness between friends. Yet who, reading without trying to think of Aristotle on this matter, would miss the portrayal of loving-another-*as-thyself* and the burden of Placidas' voluntary incurring of danger, "greater love hath no man than this, that a man lay down his life for his friends"? Many students admit without comment that Spenser departs markedly from Aristotle's text; this is striking in that he introduces so much material delineating Friendship's contrary, equally so in his neglect of most of the philosopher's puzzles and problems—the dangers of dissimilarity, breaks in friendships, affection for those benefitted, relations to happiness, friendship wrecked by using friends, the famous three kinds of friends.

It does a good deal for the much-criticized structure of Book IV to see these connections (one does not know how planned) with materials in which Friendship is not a state to be analyzed but a true virtue to be sought; this Spenser makes it too. It could be no surprise to anyone who knew the old frame of reference for this virtue that the climax shows Concordia, Harmonia, in the porch of Love's temple.

Similarly, we come closer to Spenser's understanding of a virtue if we do not force upon him the structure of the Aristotelian mean with excess and defect. This is not the design of any Book, though Book II has large portions where the idea is Spenser's theme. Even there, Medina is not better than Elissa because she is less of what Elissa is, or has "more of Perissa"; all the tempering in the world will not make them virtues. Spenser's vices are vicious, not overdone. His thought is inescapably colored by the Christian pre-eminence of caritas, and as Bacon said, it admits no excess but only error. Nothing but forcing the comparison with Aristotle could have made anyone think of a Holiness that would be just enough, but not too much, or of Chastity as a mean between license and celibacy, or Holiness as a mean between Infidelity and blind Superstition. Celibacy is not love in the defective extreme; infidelity and superstition are considered intrinsic evils, related to faith as contraries not as extremes. How otherwise than by trying to make the *Faerie Queene* "fit" could it occur to a reader to see in Red Crosse one who avoided Pride by precisely hitting a just estimate of his own worth? Pride in moderation is recommended by no one. Red Crosse learns to be humble; he does not learn to be proud for the right reasons, for there are none such.

These ideas that would not arise from the text itself have all been seriously put forward as Spenser's intended points. The example advanced with most confidence, of extremes portrayed to commend the mean in the moderate high-minded man, is the incident of Braggadochio in Book II (Padelford thinks Spenser developed the character with an open copy of the *Ethics* before him). But there is no foolhardiness portrayed, no one adumbrates Courage, the cowardice shown by the characters is incident to

their being Bad Courtiers, a half-dozen of whose other characteristics appear, irrelevant to the supposed pattern. Braggadochio
is vainglorious, an unrelated excess, and the subject is not Fortitude anyway. The subject is Temperance, and instead of being
shown excesses and defects which help to define a virtue between
them, we are told about this idea but advised to govern our
passions (the virtue is closer to Sobrietas). Then, as we hear more
of Reason governing Will, the discussion becomes overtly one
of faculties which keep order, and the mean becomes one more
virtue, as it had in the *Somme le roi*—Evenhede—and we can set
out on a quest for it.[47]

When, upon that quest, we meet Maleger, we have not met
an insufficiency but a vice, though here, if anywhere, the pattern
should show clearly. But Maleger is a propensity in the mind, and
Woodhouse's brilliant connection of him with original sin fits
what we have to fight as sons of earth—Im-patiens, and Im-
potens, our inability to suffer or to do, right. Like all Christian
thought, Spenser's faces such an impasse with grace; the ill must
be transcended, not simply re-measured. Time and again when
Spenser seems to speak to us of excesses, we find he is talking
about a wrong allegiance. When Temperance, too, is handled
with these suggestions, we realize that vast influence of Augustine's
discussions of temperance as rightly directed love. Guyon does
not have to learn how to have just enough love of the world, a
reasonable amount of lust. He is to love good *instead*. And we
assent without overmuch shock to a presentation which, like the
Somme le roi (and innumerable such bodies of material), in
treating "Of temperance," first mentions the law of mesure and

---

[47] Instead of referring separately to these infelicities, each of which has been
definitely advanced, one may cite the *Variorum Spenser* wherein all appear at
length: in Book I, see App. I, esp. 327ff., and in Book II, esp. App. IV, the
virtue of Temperance. Examples and phrasings are from Padelford, de Moss,
Jones (in that order). The prior paragraph citing Spenser's presumed interest
in accidental friends, unequal friends, excessive friends, likeness in friends, uses
discussions by Jones, de Moss, Davis, which are sufficiently to hand in *Variorum
Spenser*, IV, App. I. These named authors are the merest few out of a long suc-
cession. The remedy for overemphasis on the *Ethics* has often proved to be the
same as the ill-substituted influences; one quotes Calvin enunciating common
doctrine in entirely general terms (Padelford), another produces Melanchthon
as a key and turns the poem into a "will" morality (Jones), another adduces
all the mediaeval writers but mines them for "source" points so as to argue
thence Spenser's ignorance of Aristotle (Hulbert).

reason, but concludes that this virtue keeps a man from being broken and defouled in these three things—"synne of flesche, pride of herte, covetise."

Though it may seem repetitive and inartistic, compared with the tightness of a mean-and-extremes design, certain advantages accrue from the habit of dividing to define, for all its pedestrian results in the branched trees and lists and abstract descriptions of Renaissance and mediaeval vices-and-virtues literature. It lends itself to the making of distinctions—the kind to be made between Red Crosse's fights for "glorious great intent" or virtuous thought and Sansjoy's fight for blood and vengeance, or between this zeal in Red Crosse, a corruptible thing as it proves, and Arthur's true Fortitude at its height in Magnificentia. It allows for the necessary interrelations between subvirtues without repetition. It allows the minor aspects to be presented as the psychological incidents enacted on the stage of a man's mind, while the great images may yet keep the huge scope and timelessness we sense in cantos like the dragon fight or the Garden of Adonis. No other design could allow with so little awkward confusion for a Red Crosse who remains a struggling everyman (in whom virtues are good qualities and vices are bad ones) and for the poet who can present through him the very duel between Christ and Satan in that Christ-in-man fights Evil. The valuable thing about the variety of figures which is born of this habit of coming at the nature of a thing by observing facets of it, is that each exhibits some form of the relation of particular to universal. We have seen Spenser use personified qualities, men who shadow an idea, characters whose traits make them representatives, principles embodied in living acting abstractions—each "is" in some way the universal it shadows. The clusters of personified aspects interact in the story or the complex of ideas. It is usually as a habit of thought that this influenced poets. But, for example, in the case of Magnificence, the very name and character of this special and superlative aspect of Fortitude apparently touched more than one imagination; its Greek and Roman and mediaeval and Christian history is visible from its users, and surely attractive to Spenser. I have quoted above a few striking uses, but the role of this virtue and its exponent is so basic in the *Faerie Queene*, and the image and conception so unusually dependent on its history, that I think the naturalness of Spenser's choice should be made apparent by a little fuller treatment of this particular division.

There was a long tradition of a Christian Magnificence, uninterrupted by silences, and it was kept accessible. Since it was Cicero's first part of Fortitude and Macrobius' fourth, all the theologians I have had occasion to cite—and a crowd I have not—had it: the Abelardian *Ysagoge* had it, Guillaume d'Auxerre had it, Alanus and his abbreviators had it, the *Moralium dogma philosophorum* had it as did its translators; so had John of Wales and the versions of him, the *Fleur des histoires*, the Laud misc. 570 treatise, Christine de Pisan and the branched trees of a score of manuals and diagrams, and the whole *Somme le roi* corpus of widely dispersed and long-lasting books. We have looked at such texts always for other reasons, but whenever we looked, there was Magnificence. It would be hard to overemphasize the fact that it found a place in *both* sevens, because when Fortitude occurred also as the Fourth Gift, men thought it wise and valuable to cite its time-honored forms. Thus it had vastly increased currency, and there was a Magnificence which was a spiritual virtue, and it displaced Accidia and Sloth, but most of all, it became a grace-implanted virtue. We had certainly not thought to see Magnificentia growing in that garden we have described, where Christ in the center and the dew of grace made the trees grow, nor see it be an aspect of the kind of Strength asked for in its own parallel Lord's Prayer petition ("give us this day. . ."). For that is the Strength or Force to "do grete thinges for the love of God," and it puts a different complexion on definitions like "joyous clearness of courage administering things laudable . . . high or great." And just what did men think of as essential to the Magnificence they encountered under Force in all the run-of-the-mill lists, say of a *Kalendrier des bergers*?[48]

We realize that the often-met virtue of the common lists is by this time the transformed conception of Magnificentia. This is suggested in the definitions of more respectable works; no longer

---

[48] The 1493 Marchant *Compost et Kalendrier*, facsim. ed. (P. Champion: Paris, sg. g7, h), has Force divided into Magnificence, Confidence, Tollerance, Reppos, Stabilité, Perseverance, Raison—a very Macrobian list; an accompanying chart of the *tour de sapience* (familiar diagrammatically) emphasizes yet more the Gift-virtues and the Christian sevens. See the Sommer edition, pp. 98, 94 and the article referred to in n. 5 above, which will explain any citations that may be puzzling.

does the least stain of vainglory or pride or condescension or calculation of reward cross the face of a thoroughly Christianized Magnificence. A primarily Ciceronian treatise, entirely secular, like John of Wales' *Breviloquium*, says (in the French of the abridgment in MS.Laud misc. 570): "Magnificence est administracion de haultes et grans choses avecques magnitude ou grandeur de courage/ ou autrement magnificence est consum*m*acion et perfection de nobles choses et de grans fais" (f. 22r)—Spenser's perfected in, the *perfection* of; obviously the idea we have seen elsewhere of "carried to the finish," "persevered in to the end." An elaborating sentence will do very well even for an Arthur: "Et de ce est denom*m*ez homme et dit magnifique pource quil est noble & glorieux en gra*n*s fais." This consummation or perfecting is emphasized in the influential places; the *Moralium dogma philosophorum* (again meticulously "classical") has "Magnificentia est difficilium et praeclarorum consummatio," a wording similar to that in the *Ysagoge*, or in Alanus' treatise; "*maine affin* grandes et hautes emprises," says Christine's translation of Alanus. And so in many—Peraldus and the hosts he influenced; and the procession of schoolmen "on the virtues" (either set); but I keep to names already familiar to us to avoid new citations. We remember that Macrobius does not define his listed aspects. Echoes of Cicero sometimes bring in other imagery: "Magnificence est quand ladministration des gra*n*s choses & excellentes aussi ample & reluisant propos de couraige . . ." (the *Fleur des histoires* version of John of Wales; B.N. MS. fr. 54, f. 396v).

Or, for a reputable English author we are sure Spenser knew, Chaucer's Parson, in the fully developed context of gift-virtues versus sins, defines under the Fourth Gift, Fortitudo or Strength, "magnificence, that is to seyn, whan a man dooth and perfourneth grete werkes of goodnesse; and that is the ende why that men sholde do goode werkes, for in the acomplissynge of grete goode werkes lith the grete gerdoun"—that is, the Pauline crown rewarding the perfecting of Fortitude in "perseverance" to the end.

The transformation of this virtue, like others, was not a matter of changes in qualities thought admirable or in kinds of ideals; as was suggested earlier, the Christianization was rather a matter of a few basic assumptions. A redefinition of greatness accompanied them, affecting notions of what is strong, in several facets. Though Seneca or the "philosophres hethen" are the ones quoted in support of it, Magnanimity as the virtue which "maketh to despise the world" is high-mindedness with a difference. Constancy is imaged as a tower (our dead metaphor "tower of strength" preserves the cliché *turris fortitudinis*); no wind or fortune can shake it—but that is because the constancy is divinely founded ("steadfast and *tristy to* God"). Magnificence is greatest of all "highness" because God's knights persevere in the quest "right to the ende"—therefore a quest unfinished here; the victory over death is pointed at.

The basis for these differences is no simple "ascetic Christianity" or supposed Christian or Calvinistic idea of human depravity, or mediaeval unawareness of the self and the world—but a view of the end and ground of virtues as divine with virtues "followed" or sought or imitated (mirrored) by men, rather than defined, located, then pursued and acquired. Similar assumptions can be present without talking about "God" at all, indeed could be put into Platonic terms, especially those of Renaissance Platonism, which had half-Christianized the incapacity of man to see and seize Ideas pure. Changes which had come upon the old classical abstractions were old long before Spenser used them, but it is differences of this imprecise order— like making loyalty to good as important as analyzing the nature of good, or conceiving of it as man's destiny to be restored to immediate relation to the divine, or virtues practiced for love of their maker more than to turn oneself into a virtuous person— which make Arthur's Magnificence no longer the classical virtue. Equally, they give Guyon's refusals of Mammon and overthrow of Acrasia a significance uncaptured by the phrase "temperate behavior," and make Love in Books III and IV a form of something which can be named Chastity, and preserve to Justice its "righteousness" while it is perforce a divine virtue, *encompassing* Mercy in action (this Mercilla could not do, but only wept). The Christian aspects of the *Faerie Queene* need not be sought in "symbolical" three-day fights, chalices, fruits, bits of re-lived *vita Christi*, knights turning into the Redeemer in person.

Arthur is not such a divine form of a virtue, not a Christ, "substituted for the Saviour" in Book I. He is just what Spenser says he is, "the image of a brave knight," who shadows Christ's fortitude because he shows what it is to become perfected in a virtue. What he has is not The Perfect Virtue; it is that special form of "Strength" which constantly strives to bring "all the rest" to their perfection, an impossible task without grace which operates to piece out men's inadequate powers. And this is why Spenser says with great exactness: "therefore in the whole course I mention the deedes of Arthure *applyable to that vertue, which I write of in that booke.*"

This is strictly true of the role of Arthur, "setting forth" Magnificence.[49] As usual, it is clearest in Book I. Of course, when Red Crosse forgets his quest, forgets man's raison d'être (to relate himself again to the divine—to be Holy), that absence of the fear-of-God *constitutes* meeting radical Pride, Lucifer's sin, the utter absence of humilitas, the basic humilitas. Arthur can rescue him not because he is a divine Redeemer shedding grace (no one in an allegorical poem *is* the Holy Ghost, or Christ), but because he is the image of God's own "form" of Fortitude, a Gift of grace with a virtue born of it. The notations that certify Spenser's relating of Arthur to grace have been so often mentioned I do not repeat them; they seem like little footnotes to the tradition we have been examining, when it is fresh in our minds (the diamond box with drops of "healing" grace, the remedium-image for the action of the Gift-implanted virtues, against sins; the symbolic relation to humility of the diamond of Arthur's shield, deliberately described with echoes of the "glistering" rays which "exceeding shone" in presumption its opposite). By the time of canto xi, Red Crosse has learned himself to eke out his

---

[49] I do not mean to imply that the role of Arthur was planned with the deliberation and clarity pretended by the Letter, or controvert later evidence presented by Mrs. J. W. Bennett, and W. J. B. Owen, for the non-seriatim composition of the *Faerie Queene*; it seems proven that not Book I but Book III contains the first stratum and that Arthur's significance has not yet been thought out, save that his devotion to "the Faerie Queene" makes him the *unresting* servant of unprotected beauty wherever met (III.iv.43-4). Even if we notice changes resulting from a poet's developing themes, Book III studies the nature of a kind of Love men do not perfect without gifts of grace; but Arthur is not pre-eminent in this until the continuation in Book IV. I wish to avoid a flaw, characteristic of recent study, that starts from imagery and works into total interpretations, a peculiar readiness to ignore our bank of factual studies, so that fanciful genealogies of ideas often tacitly depend for instance on the old assumption that Book I was written first, II next, etc. I do not, however, see Arthur's role as puzzlingly minor (nor as "the Saviour" as in Bennett, *The Evolution of "The Faerie Queene"* [Chicago, 1942], p. 59), nor the Letter to Ralegh as unsuited to the poem we have. Some other reasons are given in ch. 5.

human strength with God's own Fortitude; of course, Arthur's absence does not mean he is without that grace. That Arthur is off seeking Gloriana the Faery Queen ("glory in my generall intention" but "our soveraine the Queene" in "my particular intention") does not at all contradict his character as an image through which we see the form of God's grace. If Arthur, seeking the glory he saw in his vision, were to find Elizabeth in that "faery" England which is Spenser's vision of things hoped for, he would meet not glory perfected, but again an image of it. She shadows it, as Spenser says, with "rare *perfection* in mortalitie," mirroring divine virtue which alone is perfected always and to the end, and therein she is "th'Idole" or idolum "of her makers great *magnificence*" (II.ii.41).

Again in Book II, Arthur's deeds are mentioned, as Spenser says when the perfecting or perseverance in a virtue is beyond the questing hero; and Arthur must present the power of grace to graft heavenly strength onto that which the hero had shown, as this is "applyable to that vertue" treated in this Book. The keynote of the action in Mammon's canto is not conflict but revelation; when a human creature has seen the very root and ground of all concupiscentia, he finds it unbearable—only Dante has reported it, and he also found it thus. Throughout the Book, as Woodhouse says, classical imagery is preferred, to set before us the nature of a famous classical virtue. But instead of canto vii acting as a kind of watershed between a classical and a Christian struggle for temperance (as Berger thinks), the expectations and attitudes and inadequacies seem remarkably alike in both great scenes (cantos vii, xii); and the assumptions about what virtue is and how it is attained are alike and are those of Book I.[50] The

---

[50] Berger's thesis is expounded in Parts I, II of *The Allegorical Temper* (New Haven, 1957). See the article of permanent importance in the interpretation of Books I and II esp., by A. S. P. Woodhouse, "Nature and Grace in the *Faerie Queene*," *ELH*, vol. 16 (1949), 194-228. The interpretation of Maleger is of an unequaled brilliance, and the suggestions concerning Mutability not much behind it. That we read the allegory basically similarly seems true to me (and I hope to him, but if not I will correct my reading); but I do not think Arthur to be Aristotle's Magnanimity, and Woodhouse would probably not accept my more pervasive role in the *Faerie Queene* for Arthur-connected-with-grace. I find myself not always able to make out from Spenser his distinction between meanings i and ii (in n. 24), many of the latter seeming to intend reference to the Gifts of grace, and it may be that figuring forth "the power

nature of *In*-Temperance is two sins, Avarice and Luxury, not too much or little of some virtue. Both are defined with a maximum of extended significance, but the secret unfolded to Guyon during this display of Intemperance's nature is not that he should seek a mean but that he should not love the wrong things (not measure in one's covetise or one's response to a Circe, but no Mammon, no Acrasia, are recommended). When his strength is at its lowest, then Magnificence—which by grace can persevere yet further, however much has already been endured—takes over the unremitting battle; for Guyon, with just enough strength to "see" and realize the significance of the thing itself, seen plain, is left at the mercy of a flank attack by persons who embody forms of it.

Magnificentia always comes in when the hero is "used up"; although what he possesses of the virtue being treated has done great things, without Magnificentia, the final straw or a final enormous log would be too much for the hero. Spenser uses great skill in portraying a variety of situations as the moment of this need. In Book V, as in Book I, the hero cannot come up to the fight with the very root and principle of the virtue's evil opposite; Gerioneo is In-Iusticia in essence, but even if the topical meanings did not hint this to us, the portrayal of the intolerable Beast which Arthur must fight (in v. xi.), rising from under the idol which has a place upon the altar, has the character of Spenser's (and other poets') attempt to show Evil pure. I suppose the closest we can come is to say that he meets the very fiend. In Book IV, on the other hand, the multiplying, spawning brood of forms taken by the opposite of Amity has just reached a level beyond the good characters' power to cope with it, and Arthur, with a rain of good deeds which rescues one after another victim

---

and providence of God in the natural order" is accurate for some Books. I would be satisfied to claim that Arthur continues to be Magnificence, and rest upon its transformed meaning. Guyon does not represent the Christian version of temperance, but he learns about it. Agreement with Woodhouse's later animadversions concerning distinctions to be maintained (see *RES*, vols. 5 and 6, 1954-55) prompts the reminder that the point here is not sixteenth-century confusion of Christian and classical conceptions, but a distinguishable addition through some centuries of Christian development. That the decades when Spenser wrote preferred classical conceptions so enhanced, is a comfort when results are not logically tidy. The safeguard seems to lie in the fact that we find evidence in the poem that the Christian extensions were added; scores that developed were not used by him (see n. 38 above).

at his last breath in some situation where he is blocked and impotent, saves Amoret and Aemylia menaced by lust, evades Sclaunder's harms which next enviously threaten those gentle natures, kills Corflambo, that antithesis of the book's virtue who has one form of it in his power, quenches the many-headed strifes between a whole flock of knights who hold at bay the exponents of loving-kindness to others, Britomart and Scudamour, when "him selfe he to their aide addrest."

In Book VI we may not think the action serious enough to hold up, if we continue to read Arthur's Magnificence with these important implications; it might seem a very precious sort of world in which God's grace has to come in to deal with that swarthy stalwart Disdain whom we meet brandishing his hackneyed old club around the garden of the Rose. But this is too quick and superficial a judgment. The author wishes to keep within the conventions of courtiership, including its century-old images for the self-centered pride being castigated, but the seriousness with which Courtesy was taken as a virtue is not at all confined to romances nor to books on "the gentleman" and heirs of Castiglione. The "Debonnairete" called blessed in the Second Beatitude, ascribed to Christ as coming of the Third Gift, is a very fair representative of this Courtesy, whose opposite is seen by some theologians in the duritia which must be dislodged by the douceur or mansuetude which is born of the Second Gift, Pietas, by others in the discord which must be replaced by the harmony and patient peacefulness born of the Third Gift (see above pp. 94ff.). Sometimes indeed Debonnairete *is* the virtue born of the Third Gift; and in any case, the temper of books like the *Somme le roi* and Spenser's which stay within a chivalric frame is one in which the ungenerous cold self-conceit of Disdain is readily seen as antithetical to virtue. Turpine, the other object of Arthur's action in Book VI, is an embodied antithesis of the Book's virtue, as Disdain and scorn are important facets or principles of it; and when we see him go from bad to worse, from cowardice to falsity to treachery, he seems to sum up Dis-courtesy as a serious vice in that radical or essential form that characterizes Arthur's opponents. In all their varied forms in the different Books, these are always *that which* must be got up by the roots and cast out, before the virtue of the given Book can hope for firm and permanent rule. It is this getting at the very root of the weed which is the persevering to the end that gives Magnificence its special character. The extent to which the transformed form of Fortitude is intertwined with the conception of virtues that are *against the vices* is obvious.

There could be no better instance of this than calling upon Arthur to fight Maleger in Book II. The propensity to sin, the inherent twist in the branch, the taste for the apple—it is only natural that grace must help against such an enemy. The concern of the whole Book with disharmony has already emphasized the Christianized theme of passions usurping the government of reason through an infected will (discord in Atin and the variants of Ira; descriptions of the inharmonious perturbed mind; Medina's household with its lopsided characters, who do not present excess and defect since the whole quartet portrays qualities bad in any degree; the false "peace" urged by Phaedria; deceptive harmonies from start to finish in the Bower of Bliss). Arthur's first undertaking for Guyon had been the kind of fight the heroes can generally manage very well without perseverantia, the encounter with representatives of the virtue's opposite. Pyrocles and Cymochles are almost "humours," and we do not forget Guyon's earlier encounters with them both, in Malory's best style of conversational chivalric insult. They are not only moral enemies; they are "miscreants." The state of depletion we see comes not from flaw or conflict or failure but from shock at the magnitude of the enemies who threaten man's "temperance" for that includes not just measure but rejection of "the world" and re-direction of man's nature and desires. After Arthur has taken them on, and after Guyon has seen the "goodly frame of Temperance" (xii.1) as clearly as he was shown the nature of Intemperance, he like other heroes becomes equal to supreme demands made upon him in the area of the virtue concerned. They all learn how to exercise their special virtue carried to the degree of "Magnificence."

The harmony in the mind which is emphasized both positively and through the opposite of discordance and disproportion was, of course, part of Temperance long before Christians re-defined the Pax of desiring God and His will instead of the world, flesh and devil which the infected will pursues. I cannot emphasize too strongly the fact that I do not seek to "substitute Christian sources" for classical ones, particularly Aristotle. I do not recommend that we should forget Aristotle's own singling out of magnanimity as the master virtue which makes all the others better, or that Spenser studied "the Philosopher" with zeal and tried to understand his virtues and portray them. If a Christian view illuminated and bettered Aristotle's conception of a virtue, it is wise to remember that Spenser or any other sixteenth-century Englishman might quite well have believed the Holy Ghost responsible. They added the illumination. The kind of historical conscience which would remain "Aristotelian" at the cost of omitting Christian understandings of the operation of virtues, felt to be true, was absent. And very often the exact definition of being "Aristotelian" was not sure.

But Spenser did know Magnanimity from Magnificence. So did anyone. Our chief outright illegality, in the general attempt to get rid of differences somehow, has been the sleight of hand practiced by critics in substituting Aristotle's Magnanimity or high-mindedness for Spenser's Magnificence. Early writers were most highhanded, Winstanley and de Moss, or Padelford jumping the gap with a phrase like, Arthur, the Magnificence or rather the high-mindedness of Aristotle; later writers show a mild uneasiness but cannot resist using the Magnanimous Man to explicate the term Magnificence.[51] It is folly to suppose that two aspects of Fortitude which every tuppenny-halfpenny popularizer can list and distinguish—after some centuries of separate definitions, appearing not only in the slightly more academic set but in both sets of seven virtues which were commonplaces to the illiterate—would be confused by Spenser, and a major point of his allegorical treatment hung upon the confusion. A poet with the subject of virtues on his hands could have found treatments

[51] See notes 16 and 19 above, which cite work on the general relation to his sources, and Hughes' more forthright admission of the problem. But (to my knowledge) only Mrs. Bennett (p. 59), and Moloney, "St. Thomas and Spenser's Virtue of Magnificence," *JEGP*, vol. 52 (1953), 58-62, challenge with some strictness our juggling in respect of Magnanimity-Magnificence; the latter has some other relevance to matters occupying this chapter, and I would cite again McNamee's recent book (n. 16). Though H. S. V. Jones openly offered a solution to the problem, by proposing to investigate mediaeval commentaries, we soon edge over imperceptibly toward ideas that belong to Magnanimity. The often-suggested Italian humanist treatises on these subjects do not offer fruitful explanations of Spenserian puzzles; the more accurately classical they are, the farther from the *Faerie Queene* in feeling and usually in point.

as thick as blackberries on the same to set him right. The study of
fifty years in this special area, so necessary otherwise, so zealous,
has presented a somewhat sorry spectacle in respect of a willingness to read a poet as saying anything that would preserve the
source relationship. We are preserving something else by the
same means now, no doubt; and one hopes there is safety in principles as easy to apply as taking a poet's word as what he meant.

One point about these earlier materials needs only mention,
perhaps as a point of conscience, for it is hard to judge whether
Spenser would regard it. I have spoken as if listing and defining
were the major concern and contribution of the innumerable
earlier, mediaeval and Renaissance examinations of virtues. This
is far from the truth. A great many questions occur and recur,
in heated discussions. One which may make a difference, at a
point which Spenser isolates to give importance to, is the relation
of virtues to Gifts, that is, to grace. An influential conception was
popularized by Bonaventura, though earlier proposed, that the
Gifts are a habitus of the mind which "expedites" virtues.[52] This
is roughly Spenser's presentation of the relation he professes to
show between natural and supernatural strengths in the various
forms of virtue,[53] a common understanding and that, for example,
of Sidney or Tasso. That Arthur's role is to expedite the virtues is
an interesting concept; at any rate, it is sure that a long history
lay behind the poet's compelling interest in showing us the *exact*

[52] For example, Lottin's discussion of Albertus Magnus on this point is of
assistance, oddly enough, to the reader of Spenser (*op.cit.*, above n. 7; see III,
Part I, 398ff.). It may make considerable difference in both writing and reading images of Spenser's sort if it is stressed (as Alanus did) that virtues are inseparable *effects* of Gifts of grace, that such Gifts *are* virtues (as by Peter Lombard; an important decision, this would almost negate a secular work like the
Faerie Queene), and various other positions. The importance of the point lies
in its relation to allegorical reading; Bonaventura's expediting (which does not
claim originating virtues, nor identity) assists images in that extension of significance in which they discuss metaphysics, without turning all poetry into
theology.

[53] Many arguments asserted that what the Gifts of grace do is to super-
naturalize the virtues, and this has in a sense happened between Aristotle and
the sixteenth century, if not quite in the sense it was argued. But the *Faerie
Queene* does not seem to present virtues operating "according to a supernatural
order"; there is some tendency recently to overread Spenser's Christianizing of
virtues in somewhat this fashion, but the portrayals of the quests do not seem
to me to uphold such an extension.

nature and operations of certain abstract quiddities like the virtues and grace—the subject is more typically his interest than the drama of mental conflict. He uses the latter as a means to open his subject, to reveal, to engage us poignantly so that we join the inquiry.

When Spenser spoke of Aristotle and the rest, one doubts that he had in mind the long procession of theologians; I should be surprised if he did not remind himself of Cicero and Macrobius, and of those common Christian writers who simply seemed to pass on their learning, and add such further virtues and vices as would not have been visible to worthies who knew nothing about "grace." It would be equally surprising if he thought of those additions and Christian conceptions—say of Fortitude and Magnificence—as controverting Aristotle. We similarly learn what is most necessary if we too are willing to widen and make more inclusive the sources and kinds of Spenser's knowledge of the virtues. It can be called a certainty that his own eye rested on none of the illustrations for this chapter. He would have understood them, and when we have, it is my belief that we know better what he thought he was learning from Aristotle and the rest.

CHAPTER III

Guillaume's Pilgrimage

IT MAY seem ill judged structurally, after our preceding
chapter wherein scores of works were seen to present a ubiquitous tradition, to devote a chapter to a single work of one man:
the *Pélerinage de la vie humaine* of Guillaume de Deguileville.
It is in fact one of three parts of a trilogy; two succeeding *Péler-
inages*—*de l'âme*, and *de Jésus Christ*—will be but scantly mentioned. There are several reasons for giving Guillaume's famous
first work so eminent a place.

First, his book has as subject the basic allegorical theme, of
which most others are variants or parts: the pilgrimage man takes
through life to death and redemption (this last is, of course, the
ceaseless burden of scriptural allegories). It is perhaps the most
striking and well shaped of mediaeval treatments of the plain
total subject. That English literature includes a Bunyan has resulted in a close association between this theme and "allegory"
to English-speaking people, but the association is intrinsic, not
an accident of literary history. Familiarity with Guillaume during
the nineteenth century largely followed upon discussions of his
work as a possible source of Bunyan's; I believe the reader will
presently see this as unlikely, for the allegory in Guillaume must
be rather differently read. It is more truly figurative, more subtle
and closer to ancient ways of pursuing enigmatic truths, however
much it may lack Bunyan's moving simplicity.

A second reason for giving the *Pélerinage* a position in the foreground is its merit as a book. Here a great number of distinctions
must be made touching the changing literary qualities of its many
appearances, in new redactions, different languages, new media.
One such distinction lies in the fact that Lydgate's wordy translation has constituted "Guillaume" for most English readers,
and moreover he chose to re-clothe not Guillaume's 1331 redaction, but that of 1355, itself verbose and plagued with the faults
allegorical writing can develop, especially in long-pondered re-
vision. But the growth of modern interest in symbolical presentation of ideas and doctrines, both in literature and the graphic
arts, has put us in a position to take much pleasure in various
attractive forms of the *Pélerinage*. This renewed sympathy is

the major condition for another of the reasons why it is emphasized in this book: it shows better than most pieces, to the
sympathetic eye at least, certain natural operations of the figure
of allegory—imaginative or surprising ways it can work, an
unobtrusive conveying of conceptual subtleties, a network of
ancient symbolisms pleasurable to recognize and durable enough
to uphold the weight of doctrine taught. The whole fiction has
to be read allegorically; it does not use such figures on occasion
like Chrétien, nor ask intermittent but discontinuous such reading, like practically all symbolical narratives (especially the few
in romance), but comprises one great complex of imagery. It
has much to teach us about such reading.

We are at least the fifth century of readers to be so taught; and
in this count I omit not only the first century which neglected
him, the eighteenth, but also the nineteenth which reprinted but
denigrated him. The book was amazingly popular and long lived.
The evidence for this lies first in the number of manuscripts—
of the author's own two verse redactions and of the fifteenth-century prose versions; secondly, in the translations made (English
verse and prose, German verse and prose, Dutch and Spanish);
thirdly, in the number, the spread and the care taken with early
printings, of the verse and of the prose. Another kind of evidence
that the book was well known—allusions—may be exemplified by
the fact that an early fifteenth-century Book of Hours (now
Fitzwilliam MS. 62) could count upon the recognition of a series
of incidents in the *Pélerinage*, pictured in marginal illuminations,
without rubrics and of course without textual identification or
relevance (see below n. 26; the Apocalypse is usually the only
text so used on this assumption, to my remembrance). This reminds us of another reason for the long life of Guillaume's book:
a firm iconographical tradition had developed in the early manuscripts and was passed on to the woodcut designers of several
countries, as will appear. It also received the compliment of translation into later artistic styles, the subjects and "moments" chosen
for illustration (and usually basic designs) remaining practically
constant.

When Stürzinger edited the first French redaction of 1331,[1]

---

[1] For the Roxburghe Club in 1893; he similarly edited the *Pélerinage de
l'âme* in 1895, the *Pélerinage de Jesu Christ* in 1897. Pollard edited the French
prose version, mistakenly ascribed to Jean Gallopes, in 1912 (also for the Rox-

he enumerated some sixty-two manuscripts then known to him of the *Pélerinage de la vie*; only nine of them are of the 1355 redaction.[2] There are some thirty in the *Bibliothèque nationale* alone. The spread into other countries did not wait for printing, as is shown by the ownership and the decoration of some manuscripts and by the dates of foreign prose renderings; in the fifteenth century.[3] French printers of the verse chose to present

---

burghe Club), reproducing the miniatures put into a vellum copy of a Paris (Vérard) edition, which use the manuscript tradition but manifestly depend upon the woodcuts of the prior Lyons prose edition. In 1869, W. A. Wright had edited the English fifteenth-century prose version, most interesting to us, and fully discussed later. Twenty-two manuscripts out of all Stürzinger's list of seventy-two contain all three pilgrimages (like him, I indicate their inclusion when relevant by their initials, V, A, J).

[2] A more recent list appears in the study of John Rylands Library, MS.fr.2 (Lord Crawford's in Stürzinger's list) by M. Lofthouse; it largely depends on Stürzinger's, but she gives some of the prose manuscripts, and some Oxford manuscripts of the *Vie* (both are ignored by Stürzinger). I add Bodl. Add.C.29:V[2] incomplete at beginning, AJ; and British Museum MS.Add.38120 (once the Huth Manuscript). Since French prose manuscripts of the *Vie* get only chance listings, I add here Arsénal 2319, B.N. fr.12461, to Miss Lofthouse's fr.1137, fr.1646, Ste.Gen. 294. See below *passim* for manuscripts of English prose versions. Like Douce 305, fr.602 is the prose *Âme* not *Vie*, and Arsénal 507 is another manuscript of the Latin translation of *Âme*, mentioned below. This study appears in *John Rylands Library Bulletin*, vol. 19 (1935), 170-215; the author is unsympathetic to the allegory, reading it like unfigured narrative, but the Rylands Manuscript is unusual in text, though regular (and full) as to illustration, and her comparisons of the two author's-redactions are of use. Comparison of these has now been most completely done—showing clearly the greater excellence of *Vie*[1]—in Faral's treatment in *Hist. litt. de la France*, vol. 39 (1952), 1-132, dealing with the author and all his works. It contains more biographical information, topical allusions in the poems, and a completer analysis of the text, than any other treatment. But little is done with the English versions.

[3] German versions are fifteenth century; see A. Meijboom (ed.), *Die Pilgerfahrt des träumenden Mönchs* (Bonn, 1926), a Cologne manuscript in verse, and A. Bömer's edition, with same title of another verse version, 1915. The prose manuscript in Hamburg is unedited, but the pictorial tradition follows the French. The Dutch prose may be fifteenth century (Meijboom, p. 4*); there are printings in 1486, 1498, (?) 1516. Of these, I have studied the full and detailed series of cuts in 1498 (copy in Bodley); they are inventive in detail but still, for choices and often for general design, dependent on the early miniature tradition. Notices of a Spanish printed translation seem to stem often from a manuscript note of Douce's in his copy of Vérard's 1511 edition; but see *Hist. litt. de la France*, vol. 24, p. 542 (tr. Mazuello, Toulouse, 1480 or 1490).

Guillaume's own later verse redaction (hereafter Vie^2) which of course incorporates the livelier narrative of 1331 (Vie^1), but has numerous purely doctrinal insertions which almost destroy the fully allegorical and pleasurable constant double texture of the first version. It is marked proof of a continuously interested audience, however, that Vérard in 1511 chose to print Vie^2 in a handsome volume, for which he had made a new series of cuts and procured very full Latin marginalia (most often scriptural). There had already been a fat little edition (Paris, *ca.* 1510) of all three verse *Pilgrimages.* A 4,500-verse slice from a section where dialogue is lively (between Nature, Grace, Aristotle and Sapience) had been turned into a morality play, and as Cohen thinks, really performed.[4]

The French prose version was based on the original Vie^1, and done late; in addition to several manuscripts, it was successful enough in the Lyons (Nourry) edition of 1485 to be reproduced in 1486, 1499 (Lyons), to reappear in 1504 (Lyons, Nourry) and to be printed by Vérard in Paris in 1499 (?), accompanied by a prose *Pélerinage de l'âme.* The redactor of this *de l'âme* we do know and can date: Jean Gallopes, called "le Galois," who did his prose *de l'âme* at the request of John Duke of Bedford, while Regent (1422-31). Because Gallopes' prose *de l'âme* was well known, the prose *Vie* was ascribed to him also, and still sometimes is, despite the fact that we now know it to have been begun as late as 1464/65, in Angers, at the request of Jeanne de Laval, the wife of René d'Anjou (always an interesting connection for an allegorical book). This error was not disentangled until 1946, by Faral,[5] and we must therefore ascribe to "Anon. of Angers" (about whom I shall have more to say) this obviously popular prose rendering which, with its woodcuts, still traditional as to choice and design, made the *Pélerinage de la vie* an accessible book to sixteenth-century men. The warning may be interpolated

---

[4] See G. Cohen, *Mystères et moralités du MS.617 de Chantilly* (Paris, 1920), morality No. 5, *ca.* last decades of 1400's (by dating of the copyist). The section used begins about ln. 1,471 in Stürzinger and there are few omissions.

[5] See Edmond Faral, "Guillaume de Digulleville, Jean Gallopes et Pierre Virgin," *Études romanes dediés à M. Roques* (Paris, 1946), pp. 89-102. Several hoary errors are corrected, and specific data support one's conviction that much care was often taken by Renaissance editors when presenting materials of mediaeval provenance to ordinary readers. We have perhaps opened a little too wide the bins for the categories "chapbook," "slum-area" and "decayed-gentry."

here that we are too ready to think of mediaeval writings as recherché territory, solely for students to map and explore, and thus feel obligated to prove men antiquaries before we assume such acquaintance. Many were so. But it is from us that the 1490's are so distant.

That Lydgate translated Guillaume's *Vie*[2] of course made for its fame in England. Although it was not printed, it was well enough known. Stowe owned a manuscript and completed copying it (some 7,500 lines of it, in B.M. MS.Stowe 952); William Browne's signature is on it. Cotton owned two; Speght listed it as Lydgate's in his 1598 Chaucer. Yet this translation is not, and I think happily, the channel through which Guillaume's *Pilgrimage of the Life of Man* became familiar to those who did not read French easily (no vast number, certainly, of sixteenth-century literate men). There was also an independent English rendition into prose, done from the first verse *Vie*, and this is extant in several manuscripts, though unprinted until 1869.[6] Shirley took the trouble to copy it and his manuscript is now in Sion College. This fifteenth-century English prose version will be used for illustrating the points of the present chapter, since we have Wright's modern reprint and it represents the best-distributed redaction (*Vie*[1]). But the existence of these two English translations should not distract us from recalling the marked accessibility of French texts, especially in the several printed forms mentioned, when we pose to ourselves the question of whether later Englishmen learned something about reading allegory from reading the famous one by the reputable Guillaume.

Of course their predecessors did; everyone knows that Chaucer translated Guillaume's ABC, a prayer to the Virgin occurring in the *Vie*, and there is warrant for believing that there were more (or other and differently illustrated) French manuscripts

[6] See n. 1 above. Then, and frequently later, it was assumed to have been done from the mentioned French prose *Vie* wrongly called Gallopes', but the now-known late date precludes this, since some English prose manuscripts date from earlier in the fifteenth century. Some manuscripts of the English Prose *Vie*, of which only Laud 740 has pictures, are: Bodl. Laud misc.740, St. John's College, Cambridge 189, University library Ff.5.30 (Wright's text), Glasgow Hunterian 239, Sion College (old mark A15). But as with all problems touching the prose versions, much is undone, and other copies probably lurk under the often-met tag "Romance of the monk"; author and provenance are generally unhinted, although Shirley knew them.

in England than there now are. One large point should not be forgotten in estimating Guillaume's popularity in England: the interest taken in his second Pilgrimage—*de l'âme*. This work was bound to be spread about, with its use of so many favored motifs—the argument of the Four Daughters of God over man's salvation, the soul-weighing so popular iconographically, the Worm of Conscience, the Green and Dry Tree. I do not trace its several forms, but manuscripts were numerous. Gallopes' French prose must have been brought into England by the Duke of Bedford to whom it is dedicated (see, e.g. MS.Douce 305), for we know a Latin translation was copied for him in 1427 under the eye of Gallopes who also did the translation (the very manuscript he paid for is at Lambeth; another at Lincoln, both unillustrated); both the French prose and an English prose version were well distributed;[7] Caxton printed what he called a 1413 prose translation in 1483.

It is a matter for some chagrin that there has arisen no modern editor for a work so influential and so revelatory of fourteenth- and fifteenth-century ideas both in text and pictures, and of interest to both literary and art students of symbolic imagery in narrative. For the prose presentations, which were the book to

---

[7] It is interesting that two Oxford manuscripts of the English prose "Sowle" should belong to college collections (University 181, Corpus Christi 237); one must add Bodl. 770, and there are two in B.M.—Add.34193 and Eg.615—and one in Cambridge, University library Kk.1.7. All are illustrated except the Corpus manuscript (blank squares in University 181); so also is the Vérard French prose print of 1499, and no doubt they all depend upon the illustrations in the very numerous manuscripts of the original verse *Âme*. These relations should be studied, especially since these books were used for borrowing iconographical motifs; as a somewhat doubtful example, a Bellini in the Uffizi is explained with their help, by G. Ludwig in *Jrbh.d.Kgl.Preuss.Kunstsamml.*, vol. 22 (1902), 163-86; and see E. Harris, "Mary in the Burning Bush," *JWCI*, vol. 1 (1937-38), 285; her case is strengthened by the fact that it is this Jeanne de Laval, René's queen, who had Guillaume's *Vie* put into prose, some dozen years before Froment's triptych was influenced by the already prosified *Âme*. Another reason, which also concerns the *Vie*, is that some manuscripts of Guillaume are very famous in art annals—like Brussels B.roy. 10176-78, on which see references cited below, n. 24; or on Fitzwilliam 62 see n. 26. Caxton's "Sowle" and the manuscripts are uncompared; I have not seen his marks in any of them. A curious series of errors from Warton onward, including Lydgate as author of this prose, may be oddly connected with the faulty copy (a signature interpolated) described as owned by Wm. Robinson in 1931 (see W. L. Hare in *Apollo*, 1931).

perhaps a majority of later men, we are confined to the biased se-
lections and discussion of Miss Cust in 1859 (her presentation of
the *Vie* is equally slanted). But we have not space and time here
for the allegory of Guillaume's "Pylgremage of the sowle." Relations between the texts as well as within it bristle with problems,
if writers of theses could be persuaded to attack them. Who was
the audience in 1427 for a Latin *Âme?* What *kind* of changes
did the Anonymous Monk of Cluny make in preparing the *ca.*
1510 edition and why? Whence came the "St. Lawrence night"
beginning in the English prose? Questions touching the choices
made on aesthetic grounds are numerous, and not all are concerned with the illustration or the development of prose style,
or with dialogue, realism, psychological subtlety and the like. All
this is equally true of the various unexamined forms of the *Vie.*

There is one more very compelling reason why Guillaume's
Pilgrimage of Life should have attention in a chapter that seeks
to know how Renaissance Englishmen read allegory, and whether
they retained mediaeval habits concerning such enjoyments, and
how these were conserved. This book happens to provide one of
the most notable cases of the transmission of mediaeval literary
materials, for literary reasons and incontrovertibly supported by
documents, down into the middle of the seventeenth century. The
transmission includes iconographical imitation. It is not often that
we know with such precision what the seventeenth century made
of the fifteenth (already refurbished from the fourteenth), or
have data to judge securely what the later men felt to be enjoyable and of value.

FIGURE 27*

FIGURE 28

Figures 27 through 34 show four pairs of pictures. To anyone who knows the usual illuminations or woodcuts in Guillaume's *Vie*, they are immediately recognizable as four of the story-moments universally given illustration. Figures 27, 29, 31, 32 look thoroughly suspicious; they are from a mid-seventeenth-century manuscript in the Pepys Library in Magdalene College, Cambridge, No. 2258. Figures 28, 30, 32, 34 are from a fifteenth-century manuscript of the English fifteenth-century prose version of Guillaume's *Life of Man* (taken from *Vie*[1]). Three pairs of the four are clearly (or rather perhaps, obscurely) allegorical, and one indubitable point is that the seventeenth-century redactor, though he abridged markedly, showed no tendency to omit or tone down the allegorical fantasies of the original; he exhibits none of the nineteenth-century impatience with their credibility and obviously comprehends without difficulty this method of

* Please see the List of Illustrations and Sources following the text.

FIGURE 29

FIGURE 30

conveying conceptual niceties. But the most trustworthy way of claiming a clear understanding of fifteenth-century allegorical writing by these seventeenth-century men will be to thread our way through the story, and allow such points to appear where they can be exemplified. This is the more defensible since even Wright's edition of this English text is hard to secure and read at leisure; the seventeenth-century version has never been printed.

One fact about the seventeenth-century version should be stated before we look at the narrative, since it makes considerable difference whether we think of details as interesting to one lone copyist or to a group of readers. It was copied not once but at least four times, three of these dated between 1645–55. There remains one other seventeenth-century copy (Cambridge University MS.Ff.6.30, and its colophon gives important informa-

FIGURE 31

FIGURE 32

FIGURE 33

FIGURE 34

tion about the provenance of the earlier source and dates subsequent copies. What we make of this information may wait, but the colophon should be reproduced:

> Written according to the first copy. The originall being in St. Johns Coll. in Oxford, & thither given by Will. Laud, Archbp. of Canterbury: Who had it of Will. Baspoole who before he gave to the ArchBp. the originall, did copy it out. By which it was verbatim written by Walter Parker. 1645. & from thence transcribed by G.G.1649. And from thence by W.A.1655.

> Desiderantur Emblemata
> ad finum cujus capitis.

> in Originali apposita

We may obviously assume a fair number of readers, and we must ask ourselves as we proceed through the narrative why this many seventeenth-century men went to the labor of securing copies (the Cambridge Library copy runs to 242 pages of 33 lines each); we ask also what pleasures they took in the thoroughly allegorical presentation of very mediaeval attitudes and ideas in Guillaume's literary work. I address myself deliberately throughout to the latter question.

The person who commands a seated and standing audience from his Gothic "chaire" (Figs. 27 and 28) is the teller; he is ostensibly Guillaume de Deguileville of the Cistercian house of Chaalis near Senlis in 1331, but is really a naïve narrative persona in the best modern tradition of deliberately distorted point of view. The Protestant modernizer of the 1600's omits a section responsible for some of the most engaging details, and pictures, of the French books: a vision of the New Jerusalem, seen "in a mirror" as he slept; it is guarded all but savagely by a personage unceremoniously spoken of as Cherubin, whose flaming sword, with the aid of Peter and his keys, keeps back many of the little naked souls seeking entrance. But over the walls peep St. Austin, St. Benet and St. Francis, with ladders or with loans of feathery wings helping their followers in by special ways. Figure 35, the Lyons 1504 woodcut, shows what conventions can serve to portray graphically a dreamer having a vision (the city is sometimes mirrored upside down); Fig. 36 from a Dutch edition shows a convention nearer to that familiar in the *Roman de la rose* portrayals

FIGURE 35   FIGURE 36

FIGURE 37

of a quester seeing himself on his journey. Figure 37 from a
fifteenth-century French manuscript (B.M. Add.22937) can
add a second footnote to Milton's anger that those who "Dying
put on the weeds of Dominic" could be thought to have special
ways into heaven.[8] Actually, Guillaume's allegories rarely signify
anything so simple; he thinks of the true "ladders" and "wings"
of practiced humility or consecrated lives.

The dreamer is fired with a wish to seek this place, and we are
straightway set down in the situation of the Pilgrim—man just
born into his earthly life, entirely naïve, unfurnished with scrip
or route or staff. But he is sought out by an unnamed beautiful
woman who promises him all these helps; she requires him first
to go through the water to the "House" she shows him (in Figs.

[8] It is conventional in these manuscripts to picture a bright scarlet "cherubin," and since we know that Chaucer knew the text well and took his *ABC* from
it, the startling eminence of the bright-colored character (visible at left in Fig.
37 as shading) should be mentioned as an addendum to the note by H. Morris.

29 and 30, in the Pepys and Laud manuscripts). When he demurs, but is told that he must be cleansed of his nine-month sojourn in impurity, and that more children than men brave these waters, and that a great king assured the passage by fording it himself, we begin to realize that it is the "House" of God, to be entered through the mystical death of baptism, which was being pointed out by the unearthly helper we now identify; she is Grace Dieu.[9]

[9] We now observe that the object in the left top corner of the Pepys picture of the House of God (Fig. 29) is the font to which the Laud Manuscript gives a separate Baptism picture, Fig. 38. The Baptism pictures may be *less* properly allegorical (like this one) or more; if the former, they feel constrained to show the Pilgrim as an infant at the font. Allegorically, he is always (whatever his age) "The Pilgrim," and should appear so—as he does in Fig. 39 from the fifteenth-century French manuscript B.M. Add.22937, or in the Lyons 1504 woodcut, Fig. 40. These have no views to pass on about adult baptism, but properly illustrate "The Pilgrim's" entrance into the church when he was an infant.

FIGURE 38   FIGURE 39

FIGURE 40

It is one of the felicities of allegory that it can preserve without comment quite fine distinctions, here doctrinal ones, and the role of Grace Dieu is very different from that of Reason; particularly clearly conveyed are her sudden quiet appearances to give aid at the barest request and her loving openness to all seekers, comically misunderstood and resented by the novice Pilgrim.

The Lady Reason enters to give explanations and counsel, heard with profit by the Pilgrim but addressed to the interesting character who is consistently called Moses but is pictured either with the horns which traditionally identify that personage, or as a mitred Bishop (Figs. 41, from the early fifteenth-century MS.Douce 300, and 42, from Laud 740). It is typical of allegory in the stricter sense, grounded as it was in a typological relationship between the Old and the New Law, that we should be expected to read this character constantly as double, unobtrusively but insistently reminded that he is a "vicaire of Moses or Aaron," and that the cornua of the mitre were foreshadowed in the older lawgiver's horns.[10] Meanwhile, in the text and independently of the iconography, the Confirmation of the Pilgrim is reserved to Moses (episcopus), and he tonsures the servants who come for Ordination, though another "sergens Dieu" can perform a Marriage which fills out the set of sacraments, or the Baptism.

One form or another of such double reading characterizes the narrative method of the whole piece and gives it sometimes depth,

[10] See s.v. *mitre* in Cabrol and Leclerq, *Dict. d'arch. chr.*, and in the *Catholic Encyclopaedia*. The gradual development of this connection was accomplished well before Guillaume's time. A variant explanation of *les ii. cornes* may be read in the description of the symbolic accoutrements of Josephe, "novel evesque" paralleled with "mes sergans moises," in *L'Estoire del S.Graal*, ed. Sommer, in *Vulgate Version*, I, 35, 39. The explanation of "Pontifex" (see s.v. *evèque*) is another example of this habit—constant in Guillaume, and native to allegory—of the discovery or uncovering of symbolism in appurtenances, garments, and ritual actions. It is not mediaeval fancifulness, or triviality, but often results in our startled grasp of some nice or illuminating relation. An example is Reason's explanation, to the Lord's newly shorn sheep (the tonsured ones) of the Sword whose use is henceforth delegated to them. It is the sword we saw wielded by Cherubin (the Angel with Death in his hand, at the gate of the New Eden, where martyrdom transforms the sad promise of the Fall, "death," into a victorious entrance into life). But the new servants who are receiving it can also wield its cutting edge to bring death to the rebellious (excommunication); even then, however, it must always flame, and love is its flame.

FIGURE 41

sometimes comedy, sometimes acuteness. In this portion, the contrast between the rigors of the ancient Law and the love of the New Dispensation, never stated, is conveyed by the dialogue in which Moses maintains that he must have been given his horns to butt the sheep into line, while Reason dilates on the loving-kindness that must accompany all a bishop's acts of discipline; her speeches convey without sentimentality and with experienced good sense an ideal of Christian tenderness based on humility, in terms that keep the pastoral metaphor, and the colloquialism usual in the numerous dramatic encounters.

When we read the allegories of later men, not only this inculcated habit of pleasure in a constant double reading (unexplained and unglossed) is to be remembered, but another point easily made here. The sacraments I have mentioned are not all narrative parts of the Pilgrim's life story; he does not marry, and he is not here ordained. It is an error to bend and cripple an allegorical fiction into the shape that would be taken by a psychological biography, whether of Everyman or another. This is true even of a pilgrimage allegory, because it includes what the protagonist learns as well as what happens; it has many eddies and pools of this kind, where what we think of as the action stands still while something is examined, clarified, elucidated. We are often closer to *The Prelude* than to the morality play. The loosest sort of tie—the Pilgrim simply sees what goes on in God's House that he has come to through his baptism—is quite sufficient, and defensible; the unity is not that of a biography or of a particular personality's slow organic growth. For Spenser's *Faerie Queene* as for Jean de Meun's part of the *Roman de la rose*, it happens to be important that we should not insistently drive the poems, or portions of them, toward a kind of unity which demands biographical coherence and relevance of the incidents. Allegory is supremely fitted to examine closely the nature of great abstractions as they touch men's lives, and this generalized quasi-philosophical interest is asked of readers, while the method remains, in great writers, stubbornly literary. The story is truly primary; it is often a very large story. For the real theme of Guillaume's book, that he should understand the place of the sacraments in the life of the church, is not in the least digressive. Yet the numerous doubts and arguments posed are not the experiences of the Pilgrim, and this is not a narrative flaw. He watches, listens and learns; he is the quester. (A sentence which fits Guyon.)

In this portion, for instance, a little eddy or backwater in the action allows for a long duel between Grace Dieu and offended Nature, who cannot brook the notion of transubstantiation in the Eucharist, or of bread and wine that do not remain outright bread and wine. Reason, too, is put to a stop and cannot answer the Pilgrim's questions; angry Nature calls in her clerk Aristotle. His colloquy with his ancient friend, Sapientia, quite aside from reasons that must have given piquancy in the year 1331 to the dignified discomfiture of Aristotle, is an example early in the book of another marked pleasure in allegorical reading: the neatness of arguments that seem merely dramatically appropriate, and turn out upon reflection to be able to carry the weight of some doctrinally important point. Sapientia is the seventh and ultimate Gift of the Holy Ghost. Her spirited ways of suggesting how "all" can be in any merest part of the host, or of how men's small hard hearts can long for and even possess the infinite, are read with interest not because of the Pilgrim, but because they

FIGURE 42

suggest the problems posed by the natural reason and do not pretend to settle them. We never lose sight of the dramatic encounter; yet, is not the reason why we continue reading, conversations which go on roughly thus: You have seen the size and quantity of a man's heart? He has. How large, to your thinking? Serteyn, quod he, a kite, reasonably hungry, would scarcely be satisfied therewith. Yet the same heart, in the living man, contained ambitions insatiable. How shall we measure by nature's rules of quantity and space what can "be in the heart"? There is much lively repartee and skilful parrying, but we are kept in the area where suggestion merely starts a mind toward "proof."[11]

Two figures had come in while the Pilgrim is trying to comprehend what the food is which Moses delegates his shepherds to dispense, and which presently he too will be granted to keep in his scrip against his hungry journey. One woman is very strange, one very beautiful (Fig. 43, in Pepys, cf. Fig. 42). It is

[11] Furnivall twice objects with some contempt to things like Grace Dieu's telling the Pilgrim he must put his ears in place of his eyes if he would believe the miraculous; "De Guileville's main object was to expound and enforce Romanist doctrine by any arguments, however absurd, as when the Pilgrim has to get his eyes taken out . . ." and accept transubstantiation (see the *EETS* edition of Lydgate's translation, vol. 77, p. vi). Two nineteenth- and twentieth-century misconceptions of allegory show here: that keeping to a story means telling a realistically credible tale, and that the allegory of it is translated philosophy, logical discourse or argument simply set down in a picture-language. Granted, this section is infelicitously enlarged in *Vie*[2], but it amounts to a gloss on the *Adoro te*, St. Thomas's superlatively familiar Eucharistic hymn; Guillaume like other allegorists is not proving anything but vivifying (by re-literalizing an old metaphor) the common point about defects of the senses, and faith based on hearing the Word. He is also playing on "the Eye of the Understanding"—sometimes blind.

FIGURE 43

characteristic that the odd appearance of the first is remarked upon, by herself and by the Pilgrim, who is simply puzzled by the fact that she is not repellent—any woman with a broom held in her teeth ought to seem so. We do not know her identity until we begin to have shrewd guesses as we hear what she does; with her mallet she softens petrified hearts, beats on them as children make hard apples juicy, with her besom she sweeps out impurities—she is Penance. But the name is only the beginning of our understanding of what she means; indeed, this is perhaps to be evoked largely from our own experiences of contrition, for Guillaume is counting somewhat on the pleasure felt in recognition of identity, but more on the pleasure we take in recognizing the truth of something experience confirms.

This is a pleasure native to allegorical reading. So basic is it that those who find little enjoyment in deliberate reflection upon the meanings of almost *any* type of experience, had best avoid the form. It asks of us a most catholic interest in every sort of moral experience. It characteristically does not stop with apprehending the quality of experience, though this great literary aim is often superbly fulfilled. Many qualities of allegorical writings (some criticized as figurative excesses) depend from this expectation that readers enjoy recognizing and realizing what they have long known; it is to be distinguished from taking in information or receiving instruction, overstressed as aims of literary allegory, though present. It is true that if one finds Guillaume's problems immediate, one finds him more pleasurable; he addresses readers to whom the exact nature of Caritas is of immediate concern. Therefore they take more pleasure in recognizing the woman of great beauty who shows a scroll to Moses, she who never had any man in despite, great or small, who takes no vengeance, shoves not nor smites and sets her heart to forebear all creatures. And when recognition of Charity is confirmed by her announcement, the author anticipates that this honest concern with the questions will augment pleasure in the just delicacy of many details: that she is almoner of the heavenly bread, so that all come to it "through" her, the Pilgrim's amazement at the transformations she works in men—he looks at his fellow pilgrims, and "never saw anything so fair," she makes the ills of others all hers, it was she who caused Christ to spread his arms wide upon a cross. To those contemporaries in whose daily lives the numerous theological and moral problems occupied an eminent place, his book must have given more absorbing pleasure; nevertheless, any reader is better qualified by a natural bent toward examining the puzzles of human life than by a natural fondness for pious solutions of them.

The scroll that Caritas shows to the Moses-bishop character is the Testament of Christ, who in his death has bequeathed to men the jewel he brought from Paradise—Pax. Of course this comes from "My peace I give unto you," but Guillaume has introduced the reconciliation between man and God,[12] symbolized in the Eucharist, in the context of a famous mediaeval image, Christ's Charter or Testament, signed with his blood—a promise that is a warning to all mere human executors set in authority. Soon after, another famous and powerful image helps Caritas explain how the "bread of heaven" was made the spiritual food of earthly men; the image is the mill of the Crucifixion—almost as well

[12] The seventeenth-century abridgment omits the figure and picture of a carpenter's square formed by the letters P A X (reading left to right, and up to X at top)—one cannot tell whether because the initials do not fit in English or through Protestant feeling (other inclusions support rather the attitude we call a historical sense, toward mediaeval Catholicism). I think the reasons not aesthetic, though this "Jewel of Peace" is exactly the kind of figure stigmatized as showing mediaeval preoccupation with fanciful pseudo-relations—yet Guillaume contrives to suggest through it a number of the distinctions and insights which have made recent books on agape, eros, and philia by Nygren and d'Arcy of interest to a wide public. English must forego illustrating how le Prochain is loved as on one level with ourselves, how Anima is the little "anglet" wherein Charity can lodge herself, Christ crucified (X) must be "set on high." We may recall from ch. 2 the connection between the Ecclesia-ark "que signifie pais" and the virtue Equity with her builder's rule; this comes with the Third Gift, and supplants Wrath with harmonious Peace; see Fig. 18.

known as the wine-press image. Charity brought the grain from heaven, but in the "straunge berne" (Christ) where she put it, it was found, thrashed, fanned, beaten and buffeted, so tossed and so fanned that from the straw it was dissevered; naked to the mill he was borne and there he was ground, broken, and bruised. The kinds of differences between versions can be exemplified by the loss of the beautiful rhythm of the early prose: "Thilke mille was maad to the wynd, and with the wynd of envye grounde."[13]

We have met another characteristic expectation facing the reader of allegory: that he will recognize with interest and pleasure large ancient image-complexes, surprising him in new contexts and opening the view upon conceptions and subtleties which they were accustomed to shadow forth. This kind of recognition (and there are many such invoked conventions or suggested familiar series in Guillaume as in the *Faerie Queene* or any good allegory) is especially important, for thus the whole purport of a particularized fictional situation may suddenly be deepened; the extension may be metaphysical or may make relations that increase the emotional intensity. This typical literary method may be very unobtrusive, consisting of a single quick reference or well-known detail.

The Pilgrim now knows what food will keep life in him on his journey, but he has no scrip to put it in, and no staff to lean upon when he is faint. Grace Dieu finds these for him; as we have been learning, he is to carry Ralegh's "scrip of joy, immortal diet," and the immemorial tie between joy and faith is signalized

---

[13] From the edition by W. A. Wright, *Pilgrimage of the Lyf of the Manhode*, Roxburghe Club, 1869, p. 43 (hereafter Wright); this is flattened in the Pepys Manuscript to "This Myll was made by the wynde of Envy, and naughtiness." The mill-stones are the expected facets of Envy in the sins treatises. The fifteenth-century Laud Manuscript has a short list of translated archaisms (f. 1v) in the same seventeenth-century hand which has provided many marginalia, and the Middle English obviously gave some trouble; this mill-image includes one of the misunderstandings of Middle English which only enforce the absolutely certain dependence of Pepys *et al.* upon the fifteenth-century prose. Charity brought "the greyn" from heaven to earth and sowed it; in Pepys she "brought it green." For the "straunge" barn for Christ, that the Pepys Manuscript has "Strong Barne" may be added evidence that he used Laud 740, which reads "stronge." We must note that the seventeenth-century modernizer did find this image clear and worth keeping.

in the scarf it hangs by (Faith's set in opposition to Sans*joy*, only unusual in name). For the scarf is hung with twelve bells; the apostles put them there, though once no codified creeds were needed by the faithful; and it is green and lovely with a "verdure et vigeur" whose beauty the Pilgrim must cherish. He objects to the staff because it has no iron tip to fight off wolves, but when he learns it is to lean upon not to fight with, he learns something about the proper and improper uses of Hope.[14]

We will not linger over the details of the staff—its pommels, for example, one of which is mirror-like and reflects Christ, *or* the New Jerusalem—and it quite truly does not matter which, allegorically speaking. It is something of a strain to the modern visual imagination to introduce this flexibility, and it must not mean that we, or authors, become careless about the object-world, but only that we care simultaneously for significances. Given the information that the other pommel "is" the Virgin, and that whoever grafted it onto the staff "was not of this lond," but took this step when men seemed unable to hold firmly onto the staff, we are to think how justly this is said of the Incarnation; but the Pilgrim is all the while leaning heavily in his rough climbs upon his quite tangible staff, and in this form it enters into much subsequent action.

But the story advances rapidly to a long fitting-out of the Pil-

---

[14] It is more interesting that Ralegh uses exactly the kind of imagery native to mediaeval devotional treatises, in his "Give me my scallop-shell of quiet . . . ," than that his staff happens not to be hope but "my staff of *faith* to walk upon." Rigid equivalences do not characterize mediaeval allegorical practice, to anything like the degree we are familiar with in modern criticism of that practice. Guillaume was not interested in what staves "equal" (we soon hit a staff of Obstinacy), but in sending forth his Pilgrim with the aid of Hope-in-its-true-nature, hence the figure. The difference in *interest* is often at the bottom of modern misreading; it is significant that nineteenth-century critics' castigation of "mere allegory" usually touches *ideas* they thought were outmoded trumpery. Now that symbolical interpretation is so often a game, we are in worse case. Ralegh is surprisingly given to this kind of imagery and learned much of it from the Psalter. The similitude may be solely in functioning, the logical base less likely seen in a property than in some intellectually apprehended point (scallop-shell: requies, with which cup he dips up the living water; "my food shall be of care and sorrow made"—only ironically nourishment). Hence the characteristic pungency of such imagery, full of "points"—a characteristic shared with much metaphysical imagery, similarly formed, and for the narrowness of its logical base, sometimes styled "radical" imagery.

grim with suitable armor. With the example of Eph. 6 behind it, this is less covert allegorically than much of the book; it is filled with the kinds of small enjoyments I have spoken of. Sometimes we know why a helmeted pilgrim would be a temperate one, or why wearing the haubergeon would be like wearing Christian Fortitude, though we are struck by the novel detail (for an old idea; this is the Fourth Gift) that it was forged by "the smith of the hye cuntre that forgede the light and the sunne with oute tonges and with oute hamer" while the smith's son's blood tempered the iron. And sometimes we are surprised, as when the doublet which clothes one with Patience has an anvil set in the back; this in 1331 interests anyone who has tried to account for the anvil on Fortitude's head in the "new iconography of the virtues" of the mid-fifteenth century (see Fig. 15). Small additions change the seemingly purely moral meanings; when Grace Dieu says that this doublet was fitted to Christ and "on him was forged thi ransoum," we are not only quickly awakened to the real identity of the poor Pilgrim's great Enemy to come, but to the truly allegorical base of all these multifarious images, for each of his small victories figures the vast one—Christ's "Strength" in men, crushing blow by blow the serpent's head under His heel. Patientia, so often aligned with the sole ultimately triumphant virtue, Perseverance, was Christ's especial form or manifestation of the Gift, and the virtue, Fortitudo (Wright, pp. 61 ff.).

But the chief new attraction of this armor section is comedy. The Pilgrim is woeful from the start concerning what he is asked to wear, but when he is finally armed and cannot endure any piece of it for a moment's time, the comedy is deliberately broad. None of it fits him. When he says so, Grace Dieu says, "Serteyn . . . it were shape for thee ariht if thow were ariht shape." He is fat, has too much grease under the wing; she adjusts what pinches. He shoves his head into the helmet, and obediently clamps on the gorget; but the one makes him "astoned and blynd and def" ("I see no thing that liketh me ne hear no thing that I wolde"), and the other only torments him with the feeling of strangulation that sudden Sobrietas does induce. Meanwhile, the tough hard gauntlets cannot be pulled off quickly enough: "Youre gloves ben not for hem that han tendre handes and tendre I have hem." In these stiff articles he had "put on" the third facet (as Guil-

FIGURE 44

FIGURE 45

laume knows and says) of Temperance–Continence; we generally catch sight of these identifications just in time to be amused, or find them out after the action has made them guessable. The pictures share in this comic effect, and when, after feverish effort, the ludicrous small figure emerges from his embarrassing moral protections and stands in his shirt, confronting all his coming battles, the illustrators simply obey the tone conveyed by the text. The woodcuts only partly catch the ruefulness laughable in many manuscripts; see Figs. 44, 45 and 46.

FIGURE 46

We have not left the moral level for a cheerful interim of en-livened story; the comedy is an inherent part of this typical human behavior in these familiar circumstances. The Pilgrim's naïveté is depicted with relish in almost all the encounters which follow, but it is only the naïveté of one who has everything to learn, the universal human situation; he is more comic when he frequently settles for the comfort of a convenient rationalization. One difference from many uses of the method of a naïve narra-tive persona lies in the fact that if we do not time and again recog-nize, in him, ourselves as the comic figure, it is not the fault of Guillaume's sober ironic silences. When the Pilgrim rests back upon the thought that other respectable fighters have declined ar-mor, and fastens upon David the popular iconographical counter for Fortitude, Guillaume need not say anything overtly about the logic of human self-defenses. The armor, carried by the wench Memory, does accompany the hero. Since her eyes are naturally in the back of her head (portrayed thus, with desperate results), she shows how fitting a squire has been chosen to forewarn the warrior of coming dangers.

The incident in which the Pilgrim meets his first real obstacle is a good example of skill in prose conversation before Malory and also of one of allegory's natural advantages—the amusement and point of reading every speech and character trait "double," where it fits. This must not be forced upon all parts of allegorical fictions, especially in scenes where developing emotional power would be disintegrated and overintellectualized by such reading (as often in Spenser); but here where it suits situation and purpose it is highly entertaining. He catches sight of a rough churl, with "grete browes and frounced that bar a staf of crabbe tree" (deliberately apple); this evil-shapen thug is mumbling impreca-tions against pilgrims: "What is this quod he. Whider goth this pilgrim. Lord whider goth he? He weeneth he be now ful wel arayed. . . ." The Pilgrim wishes wildly for an "advocat; . . . gret neede I hadde of oon if I hadde wist where to have pur-chased him." For his first meek words are dashed down his throat as the churl accuses him of illegal carrying of scrip and "burdoun"; the King's orders were that no one was to provide scrip or staff for the journey. We know the scriptural injunction that is being taken so literally, but not yet the identity of the policeman. When the confiscation is interrupted by the arrival of a lady, who quietly requests his name and credentials, he is ruder still; "the cherl lened him on his staf and seyde hire What is this Art thou meyresse? or a neewe enquerouresse" and asks for her writ. When the Inquisitress produces one, it turns out that he cannot read; he takes refuge in bravado, and must listen while the more clerkly Pilgrim reads out the writ signed by Grace Dieu "in our year 1331" (dating the poem), providing for the arrest of a churl, Rude Entendement, who is a spier of ways and a stopper of pilgrims for he "wole bineme hem her burdouns and vnscrippe hem of here scrippes" (Wright, pp. 77-79).

There is a great deal of brash exchange, as that tough customer, the unskilled natural reason, puts forth his usual brand of undigested scriptural adjurations and weak logic, as close to actual vulgar speech as one of Ben Jonson's or Nashe's satirized Puritans. But he is discomfited by reason, though she cannot get his crab-tree staff away from him, for it is pride's own standby ("obstinacion," we learn). It is a perennial grief to Grace Dieu—but for it heretics would not hold out, the Jews would come to her of themselves, Pharaohs would not lean upon it and purchase their deaths.

This is a novel appearance of the apple. There is no mistaking the pleasure taken by the author in the combined task of telling a story and allowing a great number of witty simultaneous significances to nick the reader's understanding just as they move out of his sight. Neither aim hampers the other. Contrary to common apology, this co-operation is frequent in good allegory. It is not labored—if double meanings seem so, they are probably not there; rather, some broad simple analogy, merely lodged in the mind, makes a reader "see double," without effort. Some of the comedy in the boorishness of Rude Entendement evidently seemed a little indecorous to the late Renaissance; as does the Pepys Manuscript abridgment, Vérard's 1511 edition flattens it (but I have not compared manuscripts of *Vie*[2], where Guillaume himself flattened many things).

In a following incident there appears clearly a quite different pleasure, yet more indigenous to allegory, and very typical of its great masters like Spenser and Dante. Some turn of a situation or some question posed may pierce through the fiction with such arresting immediacy that we forget what century we are in, and our identity with the quester becomes complete and anxious;

we read as an allegory was meant to be read, conscious of a need to know what he is learning. An unusual response now, it was certainly once extremely common. The Pilgrim is puzzled that he cannot carry his armor, yet sees it borne easily by the wench Memory—not a riddle we feel any great concern about. But Reason rounds upon him with a question we do not answer easily either: "Wost thou quod she who thou art? Whether thou be aloone or double thou be?" He is too innocent still even to recognize the Pauline dilemma of not being all "oon"; he slowly realizes he does not know, and must find out, who he is. He hears with alarm of an enemy he lodges within, clothes handsomely and coddles; it is deliberately obscure and remains so to the Pilgrim, even after Reason uses the word "body," for he is untried man with all values and impulses yet to sort out. She breaks off again; were he in a delightful place, "good mete, softe bed, white clothes, ioye reste and grete disport," would he stay? "Serteyn," says the Pilgrim. "Aha, and leve thi pilgrimage?" *That* he would not, "for albitymes *afterward*" he would go. Reason plays on this "betimes" in a series of echoing ironies. "Allas, lady quod I, allas." The Pilgrim must assent to the radical doubleness of his will; he seems alive and touching because the basically metaphorical nature of allegory erases the distinction between him and us: "Ladi quod I, I pray you that ye sey me *who am I*" (Wright, p. 87).

Her answer only allegory could manage in a narrative. She helps him undo the "contract" between all these conflicting "I's" —and, with his body left behind, he seems to float upward light as air. Guillaume again is not afraid of comedy in his serious passages; men can not be "done out of their shap" easily, though "she drawh and I shof." Then what seems to him his real self looks at his "shap." There it lay, and neither heard nor saw; "I wente and cam al aboute him," tested his pulse (Fig. 47). This thing "was nouht, I seigh it wel," yet this is who keeps him from bearing his armor and flatters and commands him; in he must again. "Body" is not merely the gross temptations of the flesh. But Guillaume's conception of the human personality is not ours; the object here, however, is not to show him as profitable to read because he has our ideas, but rather to look at the interesting ways he found to shadow forth his own. There is a striking use of the

FIGURE 47

image Chapman makes so moving in *Bussy d'Ambois*, "Our bodies are but thick clouds to our souls" (III.i.78);[15] and Guillaume speaks like a Sidney of the enticing beauty of the soul's "goodness" if it could shine through to be seen fully.

Reason's chief answer to the Pilgrim's dismay is one we have already met in the *Somme le roi*: "Thow art of god the portreyture and the ymage and the figure. Of nouht he made thee and foormede thee to his liknesse. A more noble facioun mihte he not yive thee. He made thee fair and cleer seeinge, lightere than brid fleeing, immortal withoute euere deyinge. . . . God is thi fader and thou his sone. Weene not that thou be sone of Thomas. . . ." And here I would ask the reader to remember a crucial passage for later points. This passage reads in the original, "Ne cuides pas que soies fil a Thomas de Deguileville" (5,964), and in Wright's Cambridge Library manuscript, "sone of Thomas of Guilevile" (p. 90). In Laud misc.740, f. 56 this has been corrupted to "sone of Thomas & William . . . ," an obvious scribe's correction for the strange surname. Some variants will presently

---

[15] Chapman's imagery has been influenced by materials like those examined here in ch. 2; cf. the passages on Envy "feeding upon outcast entrails" in the *Bussy d'Ambois*, II.i.4-23, or "Sin is a coward, Madam . . ." or the plummet image (III.i.20ff., 70); Flattery, and Truth, and Bussy as hawk, or the set-piece characterizations, in III.ii. The other Elizabethan dramatist most visibly influenced by images with these qualities is Webster, and we note that the extreme concreteness combined with narrow or odd "radical" bases, noticed in both, is native to the sort of images Guillaume's methods produce.

help us to interesting conclusions about the French prose redactor "Anonymous of Angers" and the mid-seventeenth-century English manuscripts. But the major interest of the passage is its presentation of the same ideas about man, basic to the mode of allegory, which we encountered in Christine and in the vices-and-virtues literature: man's quest for a lost noblesse inherited from a heavenly Father, his singular relation to the divine, which gives to the merely moral allegories that extension of meaning which relates them to allegory strictly defined. The psychomachia shadows forth a larger struggle between all good and all evil; mankind's ultimate raison d'être is in question; heavenly powers enter the action both within him and on his side, and the stars in their courses fight against Sisera (Wright, p. 90).

This profundity and double-worldly (different from cosmic) importance of man as actor is felt persistently in Spenser's greater images. Even in those where the stage is apparently a character's mind, we are teased by significances which carry the action away from today's psychological conflict into the realm of the everlasting Platonic ideas, or of eternal verities grounded in a Christian God above all nature and informing it (including man the actor) with meaning. I do not think a sixteenth-century writer would have learned to do this from classical forebears, uncommented and unChristianized, nor from the methods *and aims* of late classical allegorizing. I would advance again the hypothesis that it is the trace left by centuries of familiarity with religious allegory strictly so-called—mainly typological, Scripture read mystice, history seen as God's dimly apprehended revelation of "truth." And I would suggest that secular allegory, during a brief efflorescence when it could still count upon being read with these unstated assumptions about man's value and his history's meaning, got thence its metaphysical seriousness and the symbolic force of its constituent imagery. It is a foregone conclusion that it should decline when full secularization removes man's ultimate destiny from its ancient place as the most interesting thing about him; we still have moral allegory, but the figure no longer operates symbolically if man's life does not symbolically speak also of an order of reality not seen. We have also, and it is part of the decline, the overt religious allegory of a Bunyan in which concepts and propositions about a higher order of reality get names from the real things we sense. A Spenser does not do this, though the two authors may look alike. The rule which will demonstrate and maintain the difference is that in the stricter and truer allegories like Spenser's we must not equate his *visibilia* with their counterparts, but allow them to retain their symbolical operation and revelatory power—attempts by an author to present the whole *significance* of that which we lamely and imperfectly *name*: Ignorance, for example, or Despair or Mammon or Acrasia or Venus. The name cannot display it in its being as it works, and the fullest conceptual statement leaves out not only what we call realizing a meaning, but something of its quiddity.[16]

It is notable that in the lively but after all fairly superficial work of a Guillaume (no genius) this larger purport of the moral allegories which follow should be clearly established first—by this vivid and even gay demonstration that the Pilgrim is a spirit, and his pilgrimage the return to his heavenly inheritance and parent. These are precisely Christine's assumptions; he is Christine's and Frère Lorens' chevalier Jesus-Christ. It is a taxing role.

We go on immediately to the most engaging and artful part of the book, the part whose illustrations (following the text with a closeness utterly heedless of credibility) were popular for over a full century in manuscript, and then for a century more in the woodcuts they influenced. With, or rather as, the Pilgrim we meet the Seven Sins. We meet them to learn their natures, perhaps a meeting truer to life than the more usual claim to have met and conquered them. We learn surrounded by minor amusements, for this is the most colloquially vivacious section; recognition of old friends is also at its most frequent, for the remedies (the gift-virtues), the daughters of this vice and that, even the Gifts themselves, steal upon us from unexpected corners.

The Pilgrim must choose his road; there are two paths, separated by a thorny hedge, which go in the right direction. One is

---

[16] The same reservation holds throughout this book, that no definition of what allegory "is" will take care of all the things it has been, and none is meant to. I have tried to pluck from among the valid understandings those pretty certain to be habitual among literary men, made so through accessible and valued earlier literature. The Renaissance writer was the more hospitable to large general conceptions such as those phrased above because they merged with ideas from different sources—e.g. the ideas so familiar from Sidney of the function of poets, their revelation of the bright beauty of "the forme" of things which doth "possesse the sight of the soule"; their creation of a golden world wherein accident did not becloud essence.

graced by a damsel twirling a glove, one by an individual who keeps ripping up a net to weave it over again. The give and take of conversation is too swift to retell, but the chief comic device is the double-talk that the Pilgrim as "I" has with "my body," who persuades him that he can go through the hedge to the laborious road any time he chooses, and he should therefore start off by the charming damsel's pathway. Body is this Phaedria's protégé; it is she who keeps the calluses off his hands, and takes him to the woods to pick violets. We have already recognized Paresse and Labor (seen so many times repeated in the *Somme le roi* illustration of Fortitude; see Fig. 19); not so the Pilgrim, who elects to leave the Labor or Diligence, which is the virtue nourished by the Fourth Gift; we foresee which deadly sin will be his first downfall. Meanwhile, the Pilgrim, sorry for old Body, looks for an easy spot to pass through the hedge if he should need to; too late, for he is caught in a coil of rope. There looms up one of the series of unnamed vile hags by whom the Pilgrim will now be assaulted, and he makes his usual bold complaint against her behavior, rope, person and anonymity. "Thou old stinking," quod he; well-bred people cough at least before intruding. What follows is the pattern in all these encounters.

There is a long speech by the unidentified old hag: "Olde stinkinge thou hast cleped me. Old I am. But miscleped me thou hast of that stinkinge thou hast seid me . . . In many a fair place haue I be both in winter and in somer. Leyn in chambres of emproures of kynges and oothere grete lordes. Leyn in corteynes of bishopes of abbotes of prelates and of preestes, that neuere was cleped stinkkinge . . . How durst thou speke thus? . . . I shal wel venge me . . ." (Wright, p. 107). When he insists on a name, he is given instead a long rhetorical portrait limning out the hag's exact character through plentiful concrete detail, and we slowly recognize who she is, not the Lechery we expected from the coil of rope and the bed-curtains. Nothing is missing, from the tangle of rope which is also that with which desperation hangs himself (Judas' rope) to the decoy-part played by innocent-looking Idleness, her daughter the glove-girl. We have seen her pictured, in similar designs two centuries apart (Figs. 33 and 34); the Pilgrim was prey to all manner of opposites to Fortitudo, once he declined trying to grow the virtuous root Diligence which it plants in a heart.

After she finally reveals her name, the tone shifts to that of gloating self-revelation, thick with specific particulars of her surreptitious work, from the children who turn over for more sleep after they are called, to those who fore-do themselves because Tristesse—for this is she—has taken away all savor of life. All that she sees is nought; "so go I grinding my self." This is not presented as temptation, and it seems to me we overwork the idea of a temptation in allegorical reading; we are being shown a general in its essence. But without quoting whole pages, it is impossible to reproduce the spate of colloquial specificity by means of which the abstraction shines through as a living form. This is one of Sidney's speaking pictures, and the method is that which some centuries of rhetoric had called "lighting up," "illustra-tion." It is not exemplification, though many instances are given.

The pattern is repeated with variations. The Pilgrim is assaulted by another unrecognized evil hag; one worse than herself rides in upon her. He is getting too much of Amazons; "Olde here, and olde there, I wot nevere whether I be in Femynye." This one only boasts of her age: "ther is noon so olde as am I," bred in the nest of heaven before the world was made—so that we conjecture whom we deal with, for she shoved her father out of that nest, falling with him, and then down in the new-made world used her powers upon "a werk there which was maad to clymbe an hy to the nest from which I was fallen" (the same stress on man's true kindred and home). But the guessed identity does not take away the slow excitement we experience in these sections where we meet intangible realities like this Pride, undisguised; it is pleasurable, with only one condition, that we honestly care to discover through the scores of pictorial details and suggested incidents the multiple nature of an abstraction hidden under a name.

It is more customary to enjoy aptness in the detail, and mediaeval naturalism. The old monster has a horn she gets men to blow—the one Braggadocchio blew with such absurd effect, the facet distinguished as vaunting:

"And thanne whan I heere swiche . . . avauntinge blastes myn herte hoppeth for ioye and lepeth and trippeth. Swollen and wombed thanne I bicome as thou seest and of gret beringe thei maken me place more than I hadde. Large chayer large benche sitte allone as princesse go bifore as duchesse be with folk envirowned a ferre with oute beeinge empressed. For anoon I shulde breste if I were any thing empressed. Feers I am thanne as Leopard and thwart I have my lookinge. A squynt I biholde the folk. And for feerstee I strecche my nekke and heve up the browen and the chin makinge the countenaunce of the lyoun. I go with my . . . nekke coleyinge. With alle myne ioyntes stiryinge and with all my sinewes I make it queynte. . . .

"I hatte orgoill the queynte . . ." (Wright, p. 115).

The colloquial liveliness which is entirely typical of Guillaume's style persevered into the translations: "I blowe also whan I haue take a pray. . . . As an henne that hath leyd kakeleth anoon so to eche wiht I telle it anoon Tprw tprw I sey tprw tprw have ye herd have ye seyn how I haue seyd What sey ye thereof Is it wel I-doo? thinketh yow I have properliche ydoon it, and sub-tilliche? trowe ye that thilke or thilke hadde doon it thus? . . ." (Wright, p. 118).

Her outer person is evidence that anyone could interpret, and it is a proper understanding of the simple figurative relation shown by the sixteenth-century marginal note (in the Laud Manuscript), opposite such another loudly expatiating hag: "A true *discripcion* of an *envious man.*" But this is only the beginning when a personage is allegorically read, just as Spenser's Malbecco only begins as "a jealous man." To the three pages opening out the traits of Pride before she declares herself, there are added seven after that, powerful with that tone of exultant revelation which each ancient evil exhibits as soon as she has said her name. Envy tastes and savors the fear of others at her basilisk's eyes. Detraction, Envy's daughter, gloats and rejoices that she has a throat bloody as a wolf that has just strangled a sheep in the fold, "I am of the lynage of the raven that hath mad his nest in hell. I love to eat caraynes"—the more stinkinge the better, for rottenness is her life and her nurture (Wright, p. 129). Fre-quently the long recitals are packed with very precise things "I" (Ire, Gluttony, Lechery) do or have done. What is so charac-teristically allegorical about these figures is not the element of an abstraction personified,[17] doing actions, but the fact that the suffo-cating, piled-up concretions define and realize a universal that has a life and a nature of its own.

These unabashed self-revelations convey pure evil with a mounting intensity which is shocking, even terrifying if we feel self-convicted, an effect something like that of James's *Beast in the Jungle*. The methods are not as different as they seem, for the secret of this power—more overt in allegorical writing—is its accepted right to abstract and present the very thing-in-itself. This cannot be conveyed by selective quotation; the hag Envy and her terrible daughters, and Avarice, are particularly fearful. Could I present the latter, readers too might share my suspicion that there is a relation here with the self-revelations of Chaucer's Pardoner. The blatant and exultant tone which has always been an embarrassment in explanations that stress some psychological "situation-al" cause (like Kittredge's) is completely proper if we are viewing the very essence of Covetousness in a human form. He shares an unmistakable ecstatic timbre with all those charac-ters who "present" an evil in Guillaume and parts of the *Roman de la rose*. This is the only tale of Chaucer's that is truly hospitable to such interpretations (witness the Old Man), though in others there is a good deal of simpler moral "signification." More figurative meanings do not here militate against our appreciation of his creation of full, living, complicated human characters (a different thing but no more literary). Even in Guillaume's truly allegorical fiction the line between a proud man, an envious man, and Pride or Envy embodied, is easily crossed, as we have seen. As we watch, the Pardoner becomes the very thing; when Malbecco does this we are told more exactly what to see. The open exultation in evil, in which Milton like hundreds of others saw the satanic character par excellence, is related in seven-

---

[17] Modern descriptions of works often seem to proceed on the assumption that prosopopoeia is identical with allegoria. This is quite as uninformed when six-teenth-century men, better trained rhetorically, are sometimes caught thinking it. The popular tag "personification allegory," usually used pejoratively, is espe-cially useless to make the needed discriminations; the simple glove-girl Idleness is a personification as are Grace Dieu and Caritas, yet the first is an idle person doing idle things, the latter two convey various niceties of theological doctrine. As usual, *function*—how it operates in the fiction—truly defines the form of an image, and thence comes its classification.

sins schemes to the set of seven devils who were these sins; but Guillaume makes much of this in only one instance, the most usual one—Mammon, whom Avarice has made her god.[18] The gloating and self-indulgence in evil is marked in her speeches.

She wears Mammon on her head, her "mahoun" or "mawmet" (i.e. false deity). This somewhat odd iconographical language for declaring affiliation with something is also maintained in the head-attributes of late vices-and-virtues iconography with much loss of what one guesses to be its original logic (see Figs. 14, 15 and 16; descriptions in the mythographers are partly responsible, overloaded with attributes, on the head and under the foot). It will be recalled that in the *Somme le roi* iconography only Mammon, among these devil-exponents, appears physically, seated upon the miser's chest of coins. Perhaps the most familiar sixteenth-century use of the old series is in Lodge's *Wits miserie*. What these sins, the old Beast's seven heads, want of their victim, is allegiance—not merely the victory in some single case of a tempted human being, but the worship of a false deity and thence his eternal death. This is the demand Mammon makes of Guyon in Book II of the *Faerie Queene*. The attachment to right belief is of course the fundamental concern of allegory. That Britomart fights a god too we have slowly realized, and yet with awful surprise, we hear it confirmed in the magnificent climax of her speech, replete with other suggestions and ambiguities we take in simultaneously: "What monstrous enmity provoke we heare,/ Fool-hardy as th' Earthes children, the which made/ Battell against the Gods? so we a God inuade" (*FQ*, III.xi.22).

It is extremely important to stress Guillaume's habit, not con-

---

[18] Many parts of Avarice's pages of bitter and vaunting revelation of what she *is*, being Covetise incarnate, make comparison interesting. It is not impertinent to quote her description of what kinds of activities she fosters through her sixth hand, trickery: "An oother time taketh ymages in the cherches that ben olde and maketh hem holes in the hed. And for to make the preest winne she dooth oyle or water or wyne . . . in the hole that she hath maad to that ende that whan the licour descendeth doun it mowe be seid that it swet and that the olde ymage mowe be named to do miracles. . . . And in swich wise I make hem come bifore the ymage and crye Allas holi ymage hele me. After God in yow I have grettest feith. And thanne al hool I reise hem. . . . But wunder is it nouht, for harm hadden thei noon ne sykenesse. Al oonliche myn euel thei hadden. But the folk weenen it nouht thei aretten it to the ymage. And thus the preest winneth . . ." (Wright, p. 151).

fined to him, of presenting the abstractions incognito and allowing us to recognize what we are meeting, with a slow unease or with sudden drama. Since this is one of the ways in which allegorical fiction is most like life, it is a pity that it became obscured. In our own days of handbooks and annotated texts, of introductions that schematically pre-publish the "meanings" of pieces, there is almost no opportunity for that initial bewilderment, mounting suspicion or hope, and final realization of full import, which is so like the way we find out what things are in daily life, wrapped as they are in cocoons of particulars or of situations difficult to interpret. That Guillaume names Envy sooner or later, or Spenser names Furor or Despair, is not a great point; it is "knowing" them rather than naming them that gives us trouble. Withholding the name often does intensify this pleasure in allegorical reading, in which identities and realities sometime seem to dawn upon us like suns and then shine out.

Although our century is worst about paraphrasing the experience of reading into a schematic synopsis full of named abstractions, and then castigating authors for "sterile allegories," earlier centuries also hoarded these neat little packages of dried meanings. Later printed forms of Guillaume's piece, like Vérard's in 1511 or the French prose, are fitted out with named dramatis personae or full rubrics or chapter headings. The fifteenth-century English prose version is like many of the manuscripts in abstaining from this, and thus helping the author to keep his secrets until he tells them himself.[19] It seems true that Guillaume intended it thus, for we have several columns before Pride or Grace Dieu identify themselves, odd appearance and puzzling lines before we

[19] This point would be worth study, like many others touching aesthetic effect which depend on comparison of versions. I have not scrutinized the very numerous manuscripts in the Bibliothèque nationale with this in mind, but two manuscripts which seem like good early ones do not show this excessive rubrication: Douce 300 (early fifteenth) and B.M. Add.38120 (*ca.* 1400; the Huth Manuscript). The Pepys Manuscript avoids it, perhaps by accident of format; B.M. Add.25594 (though the fourteenth century) and Add.22937 (*ca.* 1450) on the other hand are overinformative. Harl.4399 has little else, though it has this, which would indicate artistic care; see Figs. 48 and 49, as I take the occasion to show a characteristic picture not in Laud 740, for comparison with Pepys 2258. One extenuating point: in the pathlessness of texts in manuscript, rubrics or "persons-speaking" were felt to be as useful to the fifteenth century as we find them.

FIGURE 48

FIGURE 49

begin to recognize Charity or Penance, slow dramatized discovery of the notion of Rude Entendement, and a gratifying reticence apropos all image-conventions or familiar series, like those of the sacraments or vices or opposed Gifts, Charity's mill or her charter and the crucifixion, or the age-old branches we recognize when they enter narratively. Guillaume's impatience sometimes spoils the effect, but usually he adjusts these matters to the Pilgrim's situation and powers, deliberately varying between allowing us the humor of superiority to his naïveté, or engaging us seriously enough to learn as he learns. This variation in degree of self-identification is artful and removes the super-solemnity some modern readers reserve for allegory. All these niceties are general points about the natural possibilities of works designed to be allegorically read, and they can usually be applied with more profit to greater authors than Guillaume. That meanings should be slowly uncovered with a mixture of surprise and recognition is an advantage exploited by all masters of this mode of figurative writing.[20] It is the excitement of metaphor writ large. Rhetoricians show that they know this in their discussions of the necessity of obscurity in allegory.

One adventitious point that no longer affected even the sixteenth century should be mentioned, as effects were evidently planned with it in mind. Guillaume's first poem has divisions marked by minstrel-like tags and was apparently meant to be heard. No doubt the conventions lasted longer than the practice, but even if nothing remained but old habits of mind and attention, we lose something by not imagining orally these speeches of unidentified grotesques. This one is an example; she rides in on Envy's back, refuses to reveal her name or ugly countenance but claims she was well trained for what she does by schooling from her father, who presented her with the knife and box of ointment she carries, and a false visage, then "out of the scoole he wente. . . . Maistresse I am as me thinketh of al that hath be tauht me. Wel I can sette my fauce visage . . . lawhe with the mouth and . . . bite with the tooth. . . . On that oon side frote and enoynte and on that oother side smite and stinge. I am the addere that holt him vnder the gras til sum wiht cometh that I sle when he is sett bi me on the gras. . . . Men knowen nouht wyne bi the hoopes ne folk bi the clothinge. Many a wilowh is ofte clothed with faire leues that is with inne al holowh and al ful of wormes. I am a wormy wilowh . . ." (Wright, pp. 127-28). This lively behavior is what lies behind the dead metaphor the-ugly-face-of-*Treason*, and though mediaeval listeners would have found a clue in the knowledge that she is one of Envy's daughters, executrix of her wishes, still the amusement of deciding which does best as a Wormy Willow, before she unmasks, is augmented if we are listeners not readers.

Oral transmission bears a relation to the greater stress (than in our own fiction or poetry) on pleasure taken in recognition of commonplaces. Yet when we happen to be very familiar with the mediaeval ones, we discover to our surprise that we too experience

---

[20] Hence the attention throughout this book to what can be learned about allegorical *reading*, not about allegory as a mode of writing. Both eras are early enough for writers to be uniformly serious about regarding as their true subject *what is shadowed* in the figure; they do not write with some experiment in method or their own sensibilities as *subject*. "The Poetic Process" is the subject of no great allegory.

this same simple pleasure. When one is reading along innocently about the Pilgrim's decision to enter an order—that is, about his sight of the great Ship (ecclesia, of course) and his resolve to board it—one reads with a conscious little spurt of pleasure in the added meaning a conversation the Pilgrim has as he steps aboard and sees a man with a mace: "Porter quod I let me go I wole entre in. . . . Frend quod he if I wiste that it plesede the kyng I wolde wel suffre thee entre in. . . . Is thanne the kyng ther inne? quod I. Ye, certeynliche quod he I were not heere elles; . . . Whan I holde me at the dore it is tokne that with inne is the kyng of Paradys. How art thou cleped? quod I. Paour de dieu quod he I hatte. And am the biginnynge of wisdam . . ." (Wright, p. 192). Timor Domini has been the doorkeeper or the usher with his mace in many a text, for he was the first of the Seven Gifts and the beginning of wisdom in Scripture, and even in this book since studying the Gifts in Chapter Two we have bumped into the character in Christine's *Othéa* and in the *Somme le roi*.

FIGURE 50

FIGURE 51

Guillaume is full of these unobtrusive tacit uses of conventional series or figures to secure deepening of the meanings without further words. The two spears from Envy's eyes are the ubiquitously mentioned two forms of her malice: resentment at others' joy, delight at their adversity. Saul's attempt to kill David is universally an example of her work; she was the dragon Pietas stood upon in the *Somme le roi* pictures, and here, her daughter Detraction is "of dragownes kynd." The incestuous birth of the Sins (Envy the daughter of Pride by her own father Satan) is ancient, as of course Milton knew. Symbolic animals as mounts show already the interchangeableness which troubles those who like allegory to keep to immovable significances for given objects;

Lechery explains (riding a swine, not a goat, as in Figs. 50 and 51) why her "wunderful hors"—her own will which loves filthy places—is figured by this other swinish creature.[21] The most ordinary figurative horse, him of Good Renown, appears once as the Pilgrim's mount, to his surprise and to ours, for we tend to forget that the story must be allowed the odd incoherence of dream. The staff Rude Entendement had carried turns out to be Pride's, and several notions circle around her remark that her father found it "in the wodes of egipte"—which is always saeculum; but that obstinacy is of a hard craggy wood, to hand here below to serve the devil's uses, is as neat taken of Pharaoh as taken universally. Dozens of small images have simultaneous fitness in the history or in the allegory; it produces a witty surface but it was also a demand made of good allegory from Augustine onward.

Detraction, most famous of Envy's daughters, roundly confirms the accusation that she is a thief, stealing a man's good name which is worth more than riches ("Serteyn! A proved theef!" she asserts with the usual glee). The timeworn series of branches of the sins are brought in in part, surely, to provoke the interest of those who were accustomed to organize self-examination before confession by telling them over, or were instructed to do so. But they are so thoroughly concrete that they do actually achieve the purpose of raveling out the very nature of Ire for example—

[21] One does not know whether this way of putting it means that the horse-and-charioteer image had not been quite forgotten. The Pilgrim's horse (see immediately below) sometimes appears in pictures (e.g. in Harl.4399, in Brussels B.roy.10176), but I have not seen him with the wings he should have, descended as he is from Pegasus—as Christine, or Harington, or Boccaccio, or Comes, or anyone knew. Who Pegasus was they did not know quite so well, though Pegasus as Good Renown is very much a commonplace (see Perseus in Othéa, Fig. 8). But the larger implications and related ideas unsuspected by Guillaume, who rode no horse from Parnassus and merely thinks of a cleric of honorable report as the rider, should be pursued in the article by M. Lascelles cited in Ch. One, n. 15. The horse connected with the heedless will reappears infrequently, but perhaps just frequently enough to support the suggestion of parody of the virtues in the very curious four which appear in Lorenzetti's Martyrdom of Franciscans. Certainly Temperance appears to flick the liquid from her cup with ribald intemperance, and since the four decorate the *domus* of the cruel representative of False Religion, possibly the gaily undominated horse indicates ironically, also, that the tyrant is under the sway not of virtues but their opposites. The other two "virtues" are also very obscure.

which can look very different as Chiding, or as Despite, or Impatience, or Hatred. We do encounter what Sidney describes, "vertues, vices, and passions so in their own naturall seates layd to the viewe, that wee seeme not to heare of them, but cleerely to see through them." So Avarice's many hands (Ravin, Usury, Simony and the rest) present us in sum with a complete picture more real than any one-handed creature. These parts were much appreciated by Laud 740's sixteenth- and seventeenth-century marginal annotators, who rubricate them with interest. But in such attempts to describe content I come uneasily close to permitting the book's scheme to falsify its effect and character; as these images function they are anything but sterile abstractions to a reader with any experience of men's motives in action.

Safer examples of the way non-literary doctrinal traditions reappear unselfconsciously in literary situations are the occasional silent appearances of the familiar gift-virtues which theologians for centuries had opposed to the seven sins. The "lemman" whom Avarice destroys with relish is Liberality (the usual Largesse or Misericordia); it is Caritas (Love, Pietas, Mansuetude) that Envy does despite to; the sworn enemies, nastily vilified, of the swine's rider are Chastity and Virginity, distinguished here as was common up through Spenser and Milton. The common use of Pharisee-and-Publican as exemplum both of Humility and under Pride's form of Hypocrisy, as in the *Somme le roi*, is repeated here. Especially striking in connection with the last-named text is the re-appearance in Guillaume of the unicorn as symbolizing Pride. That this Gregorian (and Old Testament) significance, later displaced by a chastity connection to which it is not unrelated, was still understood in the mid-fourteenth century, though that is late, is proven by Guillaume's Pride wearing a unicorn horn in her forehead, and describing its fierceness and chiseling cruelty with zest.

As in all good allegories, and Spenser's is no different, we are at moments quite conscious of many meanings, at other moments caught and carried forward by what we afterward think of as pure story. That we were quite right in so thinking should, happily, be accepted, or allegorical fictions could never advance without constant hobbling. The "every similitude hobbles" was a commonplace in logic, and the continued metaphor of allegory is not to be insistently forced as the story moves. When all these

FIGURE 52

FIGURE 53

FIGURE 54

hags help each other to corner and throttle the Pilgrim we simply follow the fight; Guillaume gives no indication that we are meant to reflect, "he has fallen into gluttonous behaviour," "he became a dissipated prodigal, vanquished by all seven sins." We met them and learned their nature and their strength, as the Pilgrim did. When they disappear without remark, this means only that their relevance is concluded for the time, and our interest becomes the ordinary narrative-interest in the protagonist's trouble, lament and rescue. The writing slides effortlessly back into the sort that has more-than-narrative significances to convey. Grace Dieu comes at a mere thought stirring the mind's surface; he would pray if he could, she immediately throws to him a "scripture" that teaches him a prayer—it is the one we know as "Chaucer's ABC." His burdoun no longer resists his grasp; he bathes in a well that was the Magdalene's, for it is made of the tears of a penitent.

In other words, we read double that which demands such reading. The process is not constant. It is not coincident with images— like the present one of the human eye in the hard rock weeping—

which remind us of what is later to be spoken of as the baroque imagination. Though there surely was such a thing, the strangeness and emphasized physicality of this particular image were put there by the man who wrote the text in the 1330's. The seventeenth-century Pepys Manuscript artist has no more of the baroque quality we are conscious of than those who translated the image in an early manuscript (Fig. 52; cf. Fig. 54) or in the Dutch woodcuts (Fig. 53), though the styles of these illustrators certainly do not usually ask for that adjective. Other images where significancy is at a premium (as in some of the sin-portraits) elicit these same qualities of imagination no matter what the century. There are ties between religious allegory in its stricter definition and baroque qualities in graphic arts, theoretical reasons for the chronological anomalies, which have been too little examined.

Much of the closing portion of the story is to be given the usual kind of allegorical reading, being a combination of external and psychological biography couched in terms of a physical journey. The most fancifully figured part of the work has figures simplest in their nature; it is obvious that once the Pilgrim has become a religious, it pleased both the monk-author and the audience to trace out and half-guess at the many characters describing figuratively the cloistered life with its daily regime and habits, its values and bits of moral wisdom, ending with the trials of age and the infirmary where Death comes to the teller. Their aptness pleases; but a more interesting effect conveyed by all these joyful and kindly creatures who personify the aspects of conventual life, with their singing of ditties and playing of organs and their orderly goodness, is that release from tension, cruelty and ugliness which we feel here much as when we advance from Inferno to Purgatorio to Paradiso. Despite his ineptitudes, even this allegorical writer conveys something of the beauty of adornment with virtue, and certainly much of the plain ugliness of vice.

Certain functions already noted continue to be served by images carrying the narrative of these later more ordinary pages. Distinctions are still cunningly made in a concrete detail instead of in conceptual form. An individual who beats unmercifully on the anvil of the Pilgrim's doublet is both friend and enemy, she both forges Christian Patience and is yet a spiritual danger; she is Tribulation, and has not one commission to afflict him, but two—from the just King of heaven and from Satan, admiral of the sea. Colloquialism, and names withheld or hinted, keep the interest lively; Heresy has the loquacious passion usual in all her descendants who fish so eagerly for pilgrims to "unscrippe hem of here scrippes I hate scrippe over alle thing."[22] The connection, so persistent that it shows even in Milton's "Nativity Hymn," between Christ's Misericordia and the rainbow is based not on some situation likeness but on a real allegorical figure of Christ *as* the-mercy-of-God residing in that Judge who will be the only one ever to combine perfectly justice with mercy, losing no drop of either.[23] The fondness of the author for word-plays could have been frequently remarked upon. One disservice we have done him by re-telling is that another of allegory's native powers could not show in our short quotations—the way sharp points of wit prick through passages that are emotionally moving, the effect being not deflation but enhancement. All figures that keep a secret ("enigma" being the strongest) show this, but allegory especially strongly because the intellectual logical base often contrasts with deeply felt import.

Such a book as we see this is, if illustrated, must necessarily have pictures that give pleasure on grounds not primarily visual. The illustrators accepted with alacrity this somewhat reprehensible restriction and chose for portrayal the very subjects which depend most on the literary text, so that a series of irritating visual puzzles would unroll before the eye of one not interested

[22] We too feel the interest (here courted) of noting the aptness, accuracy or exactitude of detail; it *is* what the "scrip" signifies that rouses Heresy to such ire; she sits helping the devil at his fishing. Youth has winged feet but drops the Pilgrim incontinently into the dangerous sea. Tribulation confesses that she can end either well or ill because "I work after that I find in the hearts of men." There is nothing made of these tiny little true touches; they are slipped into the images as if they had no reason for being there except characterization, and they are present in scores, extremely simple aesthetically but in the mass, effective for realism.

[23] The Misericordia of the first historical rainbow prefigures Mercy which will "come after all judgements"; God's Mercy speaks, who made Him "sette a bowe withoute corde in the hevene for cause of accord. With the corde which the bowe was corded and I have uncorded, I drawe and bringe out the wrecches of [from] miserie whan I fynde hem ther inne . . . I hatte Misericorde that is to seyne corde of wrecches for to drawe hem oute of foul wrecchednesse. My moder Charitee was cordere and thredere of this corde . . ." (Wright, p. 204). I am not familiar elsewhere with this play on *corde*-heart-heartstrings; usually more is made of the *dew*-of-Thy-mercy, God's Misericordia since as the Fifth Gift it falleth from heaven, "as the gentle *dew*," immemorially, in prayer and liturgy. That is what Portia had.

in reading the book. The story cannot possibly be followed with any finenesse through the pictures, and the allegorical significances are too precise, numerous and specialized to be elucidated from mere common knowledge (of sirens, or seven-headed beasts, or virtue-attributes, or other public symbols). Since, in several cases, later artists of notable talent chose to illustrate the book without departing from the established choices by so much as one added pictorial experiment (so far as I have found), it is apparent that pleasure was long-lived in this close interdependence between verbal and graphic painting. The details that the hack illustrator desperately crams into his figure of Pride or Envy or Penance are all there in better work, wildly at odds with credibility as they may be.

The constancy of iconographical traditions is always astonishing, and nowhere more so than in this book where dozens of lively passages offered chances for the realism of genre-pictures or the stylistic changes and taste changes which accompany passing years. The talent for brutal and grotesque realism shown by the Artois artist of Brussels Manuscript (B.roy. 10176-8) is expended upon the countenances of the same familiar figures we have seen in virtually all the manuscripts, in pictures illustrating the same chosen story-moments, with personages similar in disposition, number, even stance.[24] Envy's eye-spears and her daughter Detraction, with the spear strung with the row of doughnut-like ears,

[24] In *Early Netherlandish Painting* (Cambridge, Mass., 1953, esp. p. 108, but see index), Panofsky discusses this Brussels manuscript, B.roy.10176-8, using M. Lyna's phrase "le réalisme pré-Eyckien" and his alignment of it with contemporary work from Bruges, esp. with B.roy.11041 of the *Somme le roi* (Envy from the former, and the Equity-Ire set from the latter, are reproduced). A possible departure from the antecedent tradition, especially in spirit, seems to me very much more accurately claimed in the case of the *Somme le roi* (even though the famous Instructions are followed, for the usual quadripartite pictures; for a more detailed examination of this iconography than was possible in Ch. Two above, see the article cited in Ch. 2, n. 5). The manuscript of Guillaume was produced *ca.* 1390 in the Artois. Lyna's interesting treatments of the several related series of works are found in Gaspar and Lyna, *Principaux MSS. à peinture de la Bibl.roy. de Belg. Soc. fr. de réprod. des MSS. à p.* (1937, 1945, esp. #159), and "Le réalisme pre-Eyckien," *Scriptorium*, vol. 1 (1946-47), pp. 106ff. Points here would only be repeated by more prints, or we would add the melee from B.N. MS.fr.823, the Pride from fr.376, the Gluttony from fr.828; all emphasize the attempt to paint the vices as grotesquely ugly. That is the single objective of the text's author.

FIGURE 55

FIGURE 56

FIGURE 57

have become very familiar to us; Figs. 55 and 56 are merely two from rather early manuscripts (*ca.* 1400), but we would know them in any crowd of monsters, having seen them in book after book. Here they are again, in the Brussels Manuscript; and if the three proponents of Envy by the Artois master have faces grotesquely distorted by a "brutally overstated" ugliness, this seems to fit well the intention of each artist who has drawn them. It seems less a difference or innovation in spirit than a more skillful portrayal of the superlative ugliness these hags are customarily given. One may look at Figs. 60, 61 and 62.

In Guillaume it is necessary to take into account the fact that the allegorical elements enter the imagery in the form farthest removed from ordinary realism and closest to "realized idea"— pure Envy, pure evils, are presented. Panofsky's admirably descriptive phrases, "physiological overstatements—crass by a very excess of veracity" suit also Guillaume's verbal portraits, and suit pictures attempted earlier by far lesser craftsmen—for the excellent reason that essential evil is the subject. Envy has this wildly unnatural and overstated ugliness in common with the other embodiments of evil because they were firmly believed to *be* so. Few artists can manage incredible ugliness with the genius shown by the Artois master, but in Fig. 57 from an early fifteenth-

FIGURE 58

FIGURE 59

century manuscript the melee of vices who have the Pilgrim
down is not far behind the monstrous inhumanity of the Envy
and Gluttony figures. The parallel picture (Fig. 56) in the Huth
manuscript (*ca.* 1400) had very ugly customers; the concentrated
malice of other figures is as bad as the characteristically monstrous
features of Gluttony, who can often be known by his unbelievable
nose (it is shown in Figs. 50 and 51; I do not reproduce a worse
one which is in B.N. MS.fr.828). But Tristesse (Accidia, Sloth) is
no less unnaturally deformed in countenance, in Fig. 58 (again
ca. 1400), and noses are a favored feature to show deformity, in
Sloth with her axe (Fig. 59) as well as in the disgusting, vomiting Gluttony.

The churl Rude Entendement is another character who traditionally was monstrously ugly; this is completely regular. But

he has not the direct demon connection which is responsible for the monstrosity of the illustrated sins. He does often look a monster, but has the wild hair, insolence and bestial features of the low boor; he is not a universal in person. (See Fig. 60 for the facial overstatement we have been noticing.) If there were a dawning readiness to accept the lowly, ugly and grotesque "as part of God's creation" (see Panofsky, *Studies in Iconology*, p. 106), the test would come, in these books, in pictures portraying the good or innocent thus, or at least the merely ignorant and rude. Both the mediaeval works discussed in the note and in the present book do declare, quite overtly, the beauty of the lowly and even the seeming ridiculous; but as far as I have seen, verbal and pictorial ugliness is reserved for the morally ugly. The total text would need scrutiny, and the scattered manuscripts are not in the great libraries. This notion is supported, however, by such earlier evidence as the deliberate similar effort at outrageous ugliness in portraying such named evils-in-their-essence in an entirely separate text—the *Roman de la rose*. Time and again, the portrayals of evils kept outside the Garden show this attempt;

FIGURE 60

see Figs. 61 and 62 for examples from MSS. Douce 332, Douce 371 (both fifteenth century but not late, and good manuscripts). Haine, Vilenie, Envie, familiar members of the usual sin-series, when seen in their essence have the same distorted, even deformed, unnatural ugliness which later marks certain Guillaume illustrations. This is not, I think, to be interpreted naturalistically or as a by-product of developing acceptance of all God's works.

Constancy in subjects is not unusual, but conformity in detail is more marked than some traditional series show. The rock-and-eye-and-tub picture varies little, or the sea of this world with floating or sinking pilgrims; there is a standard first picture of the narrator at his reading-desk before his auditory, and we can expect Penance with her broom or Pride with her horn riding on Flattery with the mirror, to show us where we are in an unfamiliar manuscript. Even the old-fashioned rectangular frame remained usual, so that the seventeenth-century illustrator of the Pepys Manuscript perhaps used it because he had seen nothing else, though my plates show it was not ubiquitous. Those who avoid it are not linked together, by date or style (e.g. Douce 300, Add.25594 and a Hamburg German version).[25]

It is natural that the accepted choices of moments to be illustrated fall into certain well-remembered series, after the universal first few—the New Jerusalem pictures, the set of sacraments, the fitting-out with armor, the sins, the ship, followed by the set showing the Pilgrim's monastic life and his death. Possibly the way this book's illustrations fell into large memorable groupings is responsible for such facts as their use as a decorative series in MS.Fitzwilliam 62, to be "read" with understanding and pleasure though separated from text or rubric. This set also in-

[25] Large numbers of fifteenth-century manuscripts have this old format, while the two without it listed in the text happen to be from the early fifteenth and fourteenth centuries. Again in the Hamburg Stadtsbibl. Manuscript (reproductions may be seen at the Warburg Institute) a translation still follows traditional choices and usually composition. I have seen only one picture from the Geneva copy, with Envy, her daughters and the string of pierced ears as expected, though set in a most unexpected detailed landscape. Brussels B.roy.10197-8 is dated 1375-80 by Gaspar and Lyna (#164; see n. 24 above) but has very few pictures. This is unusual, though one distinguishes one group with maximum illustration; it is as though one could order the minimum set (as in Laud misc. 740) or the very-full set (Douce 300).

FIGURE 61

FIGURE 62

cludes the famous series from the second Pilgrimage (*de l'âme*);
the set from the *Vie*, which the artist must have imitated from
some manuscript of *Vie²*, is fairly inclusive, though he is aiming
for the evidently familiar arming-series and sins. He may have
been influenced by the currently emphasized habit of introducing
vices-and-virtues series into liturgical books in similar contexts
(his series accompany the seven penitential psalms, Hours of the
Cross and the Holy Spirit). The pictures would not have been
very enjoyable if not understood. This manuscript of the early
1400's offers a striking proof of the currency of Guillaume's
literary work and the pleasure taken still in highly allegorical

representations;[26] also it gives us information on the kind of artist and patron who favored both.

The manuscripts we have been using in the double task of presenting Guillaume's work and considering its English fortunes, do not move in this high company at all, as has been obvious from the plates. The illustrator of the Pepys exemplar of the seventeenth-century abridgment, like his fellows W.A. and G.G. and Walter Parker, certainly never saw anything so splendid. But this illustrator did see and copy fifteenth-century manuscripts, and he saw more than one. Despite the constancy I emphasize, it is remarkable that within the small range of variation the differences or similarities can stand out with such eminence; this will appear when later we make a few more comparisons of the seventeenth-century pictures with their fifteenth-century predecessors. When we look at the text itself, the word order of the later abridgment, the archaisms and consistent verbal agreement, show the source to have been indisputably the fifteenth-century English prose version we possess.[27] We shall notice cases in which

---

[26] On the date and provenance of MS.Fitzwilliam 62 see J. Porcher, *The Rohan Book of Hours* (London, 1958), pp. 11-12. The author allocates this work done in the atelier of the Rohan Master to his years in the service of the house of Anjou, a book done for the younger Yolande. We cannot but remember that it was René d'Anjou's wife Jeanne many years later (1464-65) who commissioned "Anonymous of Angers" to transform the *Vie* into French prose, but any search for a connection would be too tangential to this book's interests. If the beautiful decoration of Fitzwilliam 62 later awakened anyone's interest in a text it used, it must have awakened that of Isabel Stuart—owner of the book and daughter of James I of Scotland—who married in 1445 the duke of Brittany. This provenance clouded ideas of the date of the manuscript's decoration until it was pushed backward by Fry in *Burl. Mag.*, vol. 7 (1905) and in the most detailed discussion, that by A. Heimann on "Der Meister der 'Grandes Heures de Rohan' u.seine Werkstatt," *Städel-Jahrbuch*, vols. 7-8 (1932), pp. 1-61. On sins-and-virtues in liturgical books see ch. 2 and for reproductions, n. 5.

[27] Relations between manuscripts of it (see n. 6 above) are unstudied. But Laud misc. 740 and Wright's edition of Cambridge Ff.5.30 agree, with minor scribal differences, in all the many passages I have compared. Cursory examination of Shirley's Sion College copy indicates no different version, though much added rubrication. I do not understand Wright's remark (p. xi) that St. John's Cambridge 189 is a translation "clearly distinct from" that he prints, as variants in his notes seem explicable from the former's dialectal provenance and some slight elaboration. In Hunterian 239, also Northern, we again miss the word-for-word correspondence we find in Laud and Wright, but I doubt if fuller

the late Middle English puzzled the later writer, so that he made some mistaken substitution of what he guessed to be the probable meaning. There is no ground for supposing an already shortened early form of which all manuscripts are lost, "Will. Baspoole's" book. In any case, we can prove that the writer of Pepys 2258 handled one illustrated fifteenth-century manuscript of the fifteenth-century prose text, which we too possess and study.

It is naturally of the greatest interest to students of literature and figurative language to notice the number and the kinds of changes felt necessary by the seventeenth-century redactor. He adds extremely little in the way of explanation, and what he keeps in is far more surprising than what he takes out. We may state rapidly first the important fact that though he is strenuously trying to cut down a very long text (Wright prints to 207 pages), he has room in his 58 folios for verbatim reproduction of all the liveliest conversations, and for uncut presentation of the concrete particulars and the gloating self-revelations of characters. To exemplify from the mere few we were able to quote: Sloth the old stinking one, Pride's speeches, the Wormy Willow, the faked miracles, the porter Timor Domini, all appear, weakened only by the less piquant seventeenth-century rhythms, not by dilution. He is even careful to preserve telling phrases—minor occasional ones like "hard bed hard life and hard passage," when he is shortening most desperately in the House of Religion (Pepys, 157, Wright, p. 199). He does not cut or water-down allegory, and tempers no winds of outrageous imagery to seventeenth-century lambs. I think his motives for inclusion and omission were literary.

The necessity of abridging explains by far the greater number of changes. Other deliberate omissions can be rather quickly pointed out. The ABC prayer to the Virgin of course disappears; it was as little suited to the new literary tastes as to the new doctrines. The figurative elaboration of the triangular PAX is one of the few images which vanish, plus the lengthy description of monks and friars getting into the New Jerusalem. But we may not overstress the Protestantizing, for we still meet Pontifex as a needed bridge-builder, the tonsure symbolically connected with a hedged enclosure and a victory over the world's enticements,

---

examination would prove it a distinct version. Its late marginalia could be studied, though owners' initials are unfamiliar.

the two pommels (Blessed Virgin Mary and Christ) on the staff of hope, and the circumstantial description of the House of Religion which the Pilgrim entered for safer achievement of his journey's end. It is patently entrance into a religious order in the late version too. Although this is the part most nearly a paraphrase because the abridgment is severe, the characters, still praiseworthy, are all left in—Obedience and Discipline and Wilful Poverty and Study, a Dame Blaunche the washmaid who does up the "dortour" (she is Chastity), a "pittancer" and "freytoureere" (Abstinence). The dead who feed the living (through endowments) in a re-literalized image which would surely qualify as baroque if the desire to surprise were as trustworthy a criterion as critics make it, is in the abridgment but not illustrated, as it often is in manuscripts with bizarre results. Benefactors are even thanked by a Lady Orison who makes return by feeding the dead—though references to shortening their time in purgatory are missing, as are names of Cluny and Cîteaux when the Pilgrim chooses which "castle" on the Ship of Religion he will try to enter.

One can observe only few and minor deliberate revisions on possibly doctrinal counts. There is no attempt to diminish the number of sacraments, but Penance may have been acceptable as "Penitence" and the redactor may not have caught the reference to Extreme Unction in the talk of several ointments that help the Christian. Where Christ's will is read bequeathing his jewel Pax, we hear only that "Conscience is the true informer" as to whether we do or do not have Christ's Peace (are of the elect); added is a rather striking series of those who haven't it. Where Penitence talks of confession (the besom in her mouth sweeps all clean), the Pepys Manuscript reads that she casts out all "by the whole Christe without fraud or exception," but we observe that what stuck in the throat was only Middle English and handwriting, when we see in Laud 740 "by hale schryft *wit*howte frawde and *wit*howte excepcion."[28] This is misreading, not Puritanism.

---

[28] Laud 740, f. 22; Wright, p. 34 reads "outtakinge," cf. P. ch. 8. The Pax-image is in ch. 9; cf. Wright, pp. 37-39. The song next mentioned is not recognizable as verse in Wright, pp. 194-95, the rhymes being lost in translation. I observed no evidence that the seventeenth-century redactor consulted the French text when in doubt (at 12,719). But though the Laud Manuscript is also cramped here, it repeats "I wyll syng, I wyll syng," f. 121, to make a

Where a song sung by happy Wilful Poverty is amusingly re-versified the original point is kept, that she is safe because being naked she can get in through the wicket to Paradise, but an ad-dition emphasizes that the Redeemer's blood is free and opens the wicket to all. Added phrases in the ditty in the Laud Manu-script are imitated. Altogether, it seems to me, we must concede that the later refurbisher took that attitude toward the forms and ideas of an earlier English church which we think of as re-sulting from an historical sense, though that is usually denied to the period concerned. Connections with Laud's circle would be insufficient to explain the inclusions, and the piece is not recusant.

This point touches nearly the difficult matter of how a majority of men in the late Renaissance and the seventeenth century read mediaeval literary pieces. Even more interesting evidence upon that matter is seen in the fact that there is no deletion of the peculiarly radical images which were famous mediaeval Catholic devotional figures. Such a one is the image of Christ's breasts, milk and wounds (Wright, p. 205), and we have noted the Testament of Christ and the mill of the Crucifixion, while the whole long treatment of the heavenly bread has much of this character. That these were fully comprehended is one observation to be made, and that they were deemed worthy of keeping and transmitting is another. It argues a need for some readjustment of our categories when the *conventions*, and not the oddities, of an earlier time show so often the methods and qualities of what we think of and term the baroque imagination. They are not identical, but the likenesses cover the very traits used for defini-tion. It may be that we should recognize certain reasonable af-finities responsible for the likenesses, drop our preoccupation with chronology and the baroque tensions, and observe how the methods and the subjects of religious allegory—and the traces left by exegetical theory pushing figures beyond didacticism to mys-tical truth—produce *at any time* imagery with the qualities we had thought were those of the seventeenth century. The phenom-enon may be literary instead of psychological.

Only very occasionally does the late Protestant redactor miss some nicety of doctrine that recommended an image to earlier Catholics. For example, when the first Gift, Timor Domini as

---

singable ditty, and the later reviser writes "I will sing, I will sing, I dare wel venter" to get a rhyme for "enter."

porter, converses with the Pilgrim, the conversation shows that
the later author did not catch the double reading in "*if* I, timor
Dei, am here, that *shows that the King is in residence*" (possesses
the ecclesia of the heart, by a gift of grace). He did not seize
the typological point hidden in the uncording of the bow set in
heaven after the Deluge, when the just man of one dispensation
is succeeded by the loving spirit of the other. But usually the
modernizer not only comprehends the relevance of the concretions
within the "fanciful" and audacious mediaeval images, but so
consistently retains these, despite severe cuts for brevity, that we
must conclude that the taste of a later day found them palatable
and interesting.

This is related to a special characteristic of much allegorical
figurative writing, usually scorned. Panofsky's phrase "the literal
pictorialization of verbal imagery"[29] well describes a habit or
technique that produced many of those audacities of allegorical
imagery which most quickly became unpalatable (though of
course allegory by no means always uses this literal pictorialization). Literary results of this process especially lend themselves
to contemptuous remarks about "fantastic" flights; but mediaeval literature has so often been read with an inner contempt
for the *subject* being treated that we have discriminated but poorly
between our own misreading thus caused, and examples of bad
writers who commit crimes against any era's taste. Guillaume
has had his share of such disdain, and it is true that he consistently
re-literalizes metaphors, small and large, pursuing within his

---

[29] *Op.cit.* in n. 24 above; see p. 357, where he speaks of "such truly
Boschian phantasmagorias as a big rock shedding tears from an enormous eye
into a bucket, or severed ears transfixed by a barbed skewer." Both of these were
among the universally included choices for illustration, varying least in com-
ponent elements and disposition; see Figs. 52-54, 55 and 56. Some artists had
the Boschian powers possessed by the Artois master being discussed, some had
not, but all were following exact directions. We never learn anything by merely
pushing back the tastes and tendencies of, say, a Bosch onto earlier men, yet *ca.*
1390 (the date of MS. B.roy.10176) did not mark the invention of these
pictorial images, and it would be odd to think they expressed the spirit of later
men but not of their inventor. The problem is complicated by our not knowing
how much of this peculiar type of imagination we should assign to the man
who did, in the unsuitable year 1331, "imagine" them, in verbal forms all but
pictured; we cannot know how Guillaume would have wished his manuscript
illustrated. I think no guess has been hazarded as to any manuscript done under
the author's eye.

verbal text a method which illustrators sometimes apply as they make verbal images graphic. He pictorializes the old horns of pride and darts of envy, mirrors of flattery and tears of sinners; his motive is surely to realize and re-vivify dead language, making his larger image, the personified abstraction, more acutely comprehended, since the conceptual discriminations which produced the original metaphors are thus reinstated. This ought to be distinguished from a mere playful translation of named elements into visual terms.

The relation does not always appear successfully, but this technique in images is related to the basic functioning of allegory as a mode that could make notions and ideas interact narratively by imaging them in their symbolical forms. We destroy this functioning if we do not follow story and symbols simultaneously, if we sacrifice the sense of something happening, for instance, to the moral meaning. The pleasure of a double apprehending of two kinds of real meaning is felt in images or pictures which do not tell proper stories, but there too the apprehension of tangible world-of-sense objects and of symbols of ideas must be simultaneous and unremitting. Otherwise we lose what produced such art—the suggesting of a world of (true) spiritual significances adumbrated by the (real) phenomenal world. The small electric shock of recognizing this is persistently repeated in imagery using the method discussed, whether visual or verbal. The continued metaphors which make up allegory keep being enacted. I will exemplify from a curiously interesting missal, Douce 313, because the complications of fictional allegory are not present, and because I have never seen any non-fictional manuscript which so consistently pictorializes verbal images. Here, these are the liturgical propers for the days, and the sense of two worlds of meaning gradually becomes very concentrated. The mysterious power of language to convey this is extremely impressive. After Freud and after Joyce, we can perhaps expect greater hospitality to such explorations of meaning in language than used to be the case.

If the Introit is "Rorate coeli . . . aperiatur terra, et germinet Salvatorem," then from the Deity horizontal above, the dew is seen descending upon three objects emerging from the fertilized earth—two trees and a being with cruciform halo. If it is "Introduxit vos Dominus in terram fluentem lac et mel," a field with two beehives and cattle shows Christ shepherding a flock of human creatures; if it includes "et de petra melle saturavit eos," the beehive with its flying bees is in a niche of a mountain. When the blessing of the water on Holy Saturday includes ". . . et sitienti populo de petra produxit . . . ," Christ's torso appears on a rock, and from an opening four people drink, plunging their drinking-vessels into the living waters which were his blood.[30] It is difficult to draw a line between illustrating a story and this translating of words, but the experience itself is different enough, for wherever Old Testament imagery conveys Christian story or doctrine, that typological meaning in the original image is thus suggested; wherever words symbolize something beyond the object they name, that is conveyed by handling the language on this double plane. Whatever the origins and other manifestations of this habit of literalizing figures of speech into terms so graphic that illustrations need only record them, it was certainly Guillaume's habit. The special point of stressing it here is that we have some right to be surprised that his seventeenth-century readers enjoyed it. It is equally surprising that a seventeenth-century illustrator copied it. It demands a firm disregard of any barriers between naturalistic and symbolical presentation of details.

Another general question is raised by the fortunes of this text. Despite certain great manuscript collections like Arundel's and Dee's and Parker's (to name three with different motives behind them), and despite occasional facts we know, like Lodge's use of manuscript materials, we normally assume that when printing had become established men ceased to use manuscripts seriously or take pleasure in their contents or decoration. Possibly it is time to question this assumption. Our own cleavage between mediaeval

[30] Liturgical places are: fourth Sunday in Advent, Easter Monday, Whitmonday, Holy Saturday; cf. many other examples. If a lectio is "Popule gentium . . . ," the people sitting in darkness, do sit there, veiled; some look up to the rays of the "great light" that shines out above. The famous image of the Holy Ghost entering through the Virgin's ear may exemplify this same process; though of course it is found in the great hymns *Alma mater redemptoris* and *Ave maris stella*, it appears here with "Missus est angelus . . . ," fourth week of Advent; God visibly blows forth his *spiritus*, down which descending lines a dove comes to Mary's ear. Oddly enough, this very same Bodleian manuscript, long neglected, and textually of course unrelated, has recently received attention for quite other reasons than mine (see M. Meiss in *Gazette des Beaux Arts*, July 1961).

and Renaissance studies has made it seem natural to us—a very strange piece of nature—that we can often find out all the extant manuscripts and relations between them, of a mediaeval work being edited, but know nothing of its fifteenth- and sixteenth-century appearances and what form of the work they represent. Though the Renaissance man thought himself very definitely not mediaeval—which was quite correct—this may only have made him less self-conscious about books in manuscript form. A more just idea of the relations between these two periods waits upon sounder information regarding the accessibility of early works and facts which enable us to judge whether large numbers of sixteenth-century men regarded manuscripts as books—as we do not—and read them.

We hold one provable set of such facts in our hands touching the text handled in this chapter. The man who did the Pepys Manuscript of Guillaume—whom I shall hereafter call P.—had read and used MS.Laud misc. 740 (which I hereafter call L.). This can be amply proven textually. We do not know what else P. used—he did know other manuscripts of Guillaume in some form—but at least he read L. with some care, and he may even have corrected it to match some of his misreadings.

Someone has tampered with a passage in L. (f.49r) on how kings govern by the grace of God, erasing and then in a fake Gothic hand substituting a reading more complimentary to kings. P. follows the tinkered form (ch. 13). L. makes an error not in the French text or Wright's manuscript (p. 198): one of the personified monastic virtues is called in a marginal note "Lady Latrina," and the text reads "In latyn latrina sche is called" (f.123r). The Pepys copyist (ch. 26) similarly and comically enough does not know she is Latria. Laud 740 and Wright's manuscript are close, but in certain differences P. reads like L.: for example, the Pilgrim's last evil "Vieillece la [re]doutee" is mistranslated "Viletee the dotede" (Wright, p. 202), but L.'s correct *Eld* is found in P. Or a misspelling in L. will explain an error in P.—the former's *stephys* (f.5v) provides P. with *stepps* instead of *steples* (Wright, p. 7) for the house Ecclesia, though it hung in the air surrounded by waters. More strikingly, in L., Grace Dieu "lough abaysched a yerde that she helde" (she low abased it; *lowe* in Wright), an ambiguous spelling which certainly helped P. to the unintelligent "And then Grace Dieu *laughed* when she beheld my fear, and a rod . . ." (L., f.108; Wright, p. 172; P., f.133r). The writer of P. uses the marginalia that dot the pages of the Laud Manuscript. The porter's statement that had he no mace "little would folk sett by me" comes from a marginal comment in the "pseudo-Gothic hand" (f.120r), not from the text; and so with other short phrases.[31]

More astonishing—for MS.Laud misc.740 has been in the care of Bodley's Keeper of Manuscripts since 1635—are instances in which the fifteenth-century manuscript has been corrected so that it has misreadings to suit changes made by the Pepys text. Where the commandments are osiers that hold the Ship of Religion together, a phrase (f.118v) that read like the Wright Manuscript (p. 191), "slakkyd for defaute of ourseeres" (default of "oseres") has been corrected in a later ink and hand so that it suits P's "the neglect of the *over*seers," quite a different point (L. had surely meant "oosers," using that form on f.119r,v). In passages on this folio a misspelled or altered *byng* for *bynd* used with *bounden*, hence clearly meant) is twice corrected to *bryng*, P's reading.

Finally, the same hand has written the same marginal comment in both Pepys 2258 and Laud misc. 740. We are warned against "Idelness stepdame to uertu. Barnard" in Fig. 63 from L., f.65r, and in Fig. 64 from P., p. 78. I do not reproduce what is surely the same hand on the Laud MS.76v adding marginally, "Flattery. prydes Supporter," and on the Pepys Manuscript (ch. 17), "Flattery, the supporter of pride." If not the same hands, these are attempted imitations, which would make the same point. Moreover, in the body of the Pepys text there appears in the Italian hand which writes frequent marginalia in MS. Laud 740, the long rubric to ch. 25 (see Figs. 88ff.).

These late marginalia in the Laud Manuscript have their own

---

[31] Also from seventeenth-century marginalia, not text, come short additions not in other texts: "the devil . . . fishing in troubled waters," L. f. 109v.P. ch. 23, not in Wright, p. 177; the "kings of the earth," changing the sense on L. f. 87r and P. 111, cf. Wright, p. 139. The first tinkered passage mentioned, where a derogatory phrase about kings ruling by grace is removed, is rather interesting. We find "Grace dieu by whom governen hem, as thei seyn, the kynges, and regnen" (L. f. 49r) transformed into "by wham is governid all waye, bothe Kynges & Regions," obvious adlibbing to fit the phrases to the handwriting. P. follows this presumably unique alteration, "Grace Dieu by whome alwaye is governed both Kings and Regions."

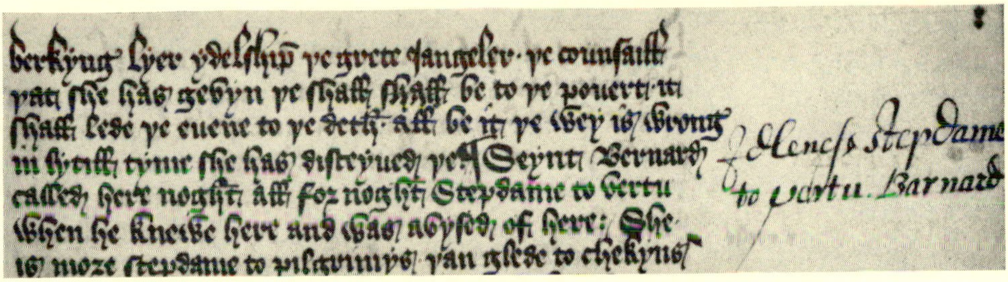
berkyng lyer ydelship ye grete Jangeler · ye counsaill
yat she has gevyn ye shall shall be to ye pouert · it
shall lede ye euene to ye deth · all be it ye wey is wrong
in synfull tyme she has distryued yes Seynt Bernard
calles here noght all for noght Stepdame to vertu
When he knewe here and was aduysed of here: She
is more stepdame to pilgrimys yan glede to chekyns

Idlenes stepdame to vertu. Barnard

FIGURE 63

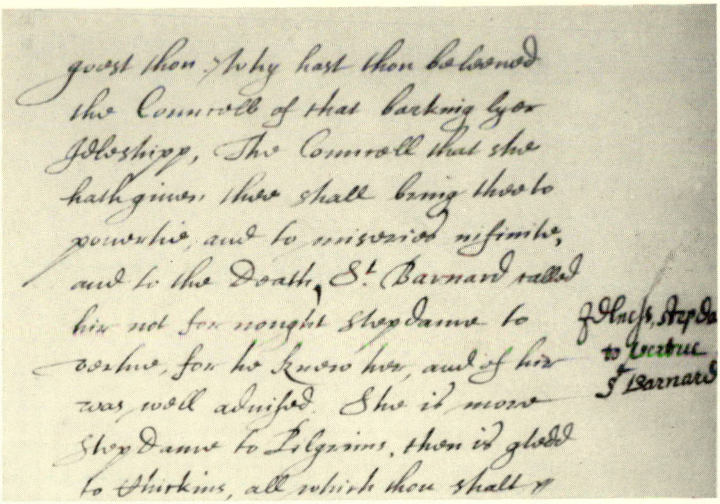
goest thou. Why hast thou beleeved
the Counsell of that barking lyer
Idleshipp, The Counsell that shee
hath given thee shall bring thee to
povertie, and to miseries infinite,
and to the Death, St. Barnard called
her not for nought Stepdame to
vertue, for he knew her, and of her
was well advised. Shee is more
Stepdame to Pilgrims, then is glede
to chickins, all which thou shall

Idlenes, Stepdame to vertue St Barnard

FIGURE 64

interest for our general question of how mediaeval works were read. Two, probably three, hands stand out, one which either imitates black-letter or is considerably earlier (called here for convenience the pseudo-Gothic hand), and probably two writing Italian script.[32] The first was that of a reader more alert to pejora-

[32] Not all the extremely numerous Italian-hand marginalia seem surely in the mentioned hand. Such scripts are famously hard to distinguish, and deliberate imitation complicates the matter. But cf. the almost identical "Religion" on Laud 740 f. 119v, Fig. 90. The marginalia I cite in this paragraph may be seen in the Laud MS. folios 93r, 94, 116v, 54r, 26v, 57v; the simile praised is an image for the soul, of a ship invisibly led by a governor within (Wright, p. 93).

If we could gather and organize the data on sixteenth- and seventeenth-century readers of mediaeval books which we have in the form of marginalia, known especially to editors, we could substitute a considerable body of fact touching attitudes and appreciation of early writing for the present guesses, based on a famous remark or two. A cooperative scheme would probably be necessary, but it would be an easier first step if editors always noted annotated manuscripts and always regarded early printings as part of the history of their mediaeval texts.

tive points about the mediaeval church, who is given to remarks like "note. ye abuse of tymes past" or "this monke was no frend to the Church of Rome." I believe he was post-Reformation, but he inveighs against "presuming" on faith without works and tells us to "Read with patience" the next seven leaves, "then judge" (the section on the body and soul separating). Since he comments "A Monkes opinion of ye Sacrament, 300 yeares since," and the piece is flatly dated 1331 by its author, he cannot be as early as he tries to look. He likes to add sententious morals, and to rubricate, organize, tell us to read twelve pages with care, or sum up with a heading; but he makes some literary commendations like "a good similly. reade."

The Italian-hand marginalia show more literary concern. Long passages, often descriptive, are bracketed, with the word "noat." This reader (or the two) rubricates persons or subjects, and inserts an occasional distich or proverb; the hand which recurs in Pepys 2258 is probably the one responsible for a little glossary of archaisms on f.iv in L. He was late enough to mention that the thorn (he says *y*) is to be read *th*.[33]

We may assert then that MS.Laud misc. 740 was read with much care, and as if it were simply an enjoyable and profitable book that happened to be handwritten after the invention of printing, and after the revolutionary changes in religion, taste, institutions and the arts which have always been thought to constitute barriers seldom crossed by later men. Since it was a story that depended for its entire power, zest and point on being allegorically read, easily and without fanfare, this reliable evidence is of importance to those of us who would like to know whether such interest and comprehension lasted down into the period of Spenser; for by teaching men how to read, it also taught them to write. Another point is of less general import. Whoever illustrated Pepys 2258 had the pictures of Laud 740 in his hands.

Did he also imitate them? Not as an historian, archaizing his version to suit its original date; the drawings, just as examples of draftsmanship, try to follow conventions of their own later

---

[33] I give his list for students of language, since such odd scraps of evidence on semantic change so seldom see print, but do not copy his equivalents unless they involve ambiguity or offer surprise: y, sweven, syne, hyrne (corner), saule (saulee: delight), algatiz, gab, yerdis, mowe, leve, recch, hate (call), sygh (sawe or see), hele (cover), araine, behight or hight.

FIGURE 65

day. He imitates the iconographical program of the piece, and with extreme care the allegorical significancy of the detail in single pictures. The Pepys illustrator did not simply imitate this and that picture; he copied a set, as any earlier manuscript decorator was accustomed to do, and we can draw up the traditional series of chosen moments to illustrate as well from his manuscript as from any other. He makes no new choices—except one, which will receive comment in its place. When eminent members of the series are missing in L., he gets them from elsewhere. His single pictures are always allegorically readable, and he has understood this aspect of his models before he imitated it. A seventeenth-century illustrator who copied manuscript illuminations instead of simply illustrating a story on his own would be interesting enough; that the pictures he copied had to be allegorically read to be worth imitating much increases the interest of the situation. We could not have better luck than to possess this unique body of evidence on how allegorical images were understood in three successive centuries after their composition.

Some outright comparisons should be given room. The reader may first look again at the pairs we can now localize in the story, Figs. 27 through 34. The elements in the Narrator picture are fairly standard, but other manuscripts (e.g. Fig. 65) show how P. with his Gothic chaire and benches supporting a few types of listeners does keep to the elements in the cruder Laud Manuscript picture (Fig. 28). The real differences came with architectural frames, new conceptions of situation and audience and speaker, not with P's mere addition of a few persons to the crowd.[34] When Grace Dieu points out God's House, the surpris-

[34] Or cf. Brussels B.roy.10197.

FIGURE 66

FIGURE 67

ing thing is how differently the simple elements can be combined in others than our two; Fig. 66 from Lyon 1504 shows how a different disposition of figures and elements makes a contrast with the firmly parallel Figs. 29 and 30. Figure 67 from a French manuscript of *ca.* 1450 reminds us how illustrators could, and did, unlike our two, change the quality by addition of detail.

The pairs of Pride and Sloth (Figs. 31-32 and 33-34) again show subjects one would think could differ but little from illustrator to illustrator, yet two or three random examples make clear that small differences in disposing the persons and in detail unfixed by the text do make appreciably different pictures. We take the opportunity to exemplify the format of Vérard's 1511 edition in Fig. 69; to these three (Figs. 68, 69 and 70) should be

De la Vieille sa porteresse
Aser la faisoit ou Vousoit
Et Vng mirouer sup tenoit
Afin que dedans regardast
Et que sa face elle p mitast

La tres plus Vieille et appellee
Auant que se monde fust fait
Et que se ciel fust tout parfait
Du nyd du ciel ie suz couuee
Hy suz conceue et engendree
Et Vng oysel quon appella
Jadis lucifer mp couua
Et iamais si male couuee
Daucun oysel ne fut couuee
Car si tost que esclose ie fu
Et que congneu et aperceu
Mon pere, si fort se soufflap
De ce soufflet que Vois que iap
Que du hault nyd ius trebuchier
Le fis et en enfer plungier
Blanc oysel par deuant estoit
Nobse gentil et plus suisoit
Que le soleil en plain midy
Di est de present si noircy
Tant sale deuenu et ort
Que plus est lait que nest la mort
Et te dy quant ie seuz ainsi
Mis et boute hors de son ny
Auecques sup trebuchap ius
Et ou ciel ne demourap plus
En terre Vins qui de nouuel
Estoit faicte dont pas moult bel
Ne me fut car Vng euure p Vp
Homme estoit fait pour hault ou ny
Monter dont trebusche iestoye

sunt species:
sclz interior t
intellectu l
affectu: et ex-
terior i multe

Jnitium iois
peccati est su-
perbia. Ecclr
siastes. ir. ca.

Michaes an-
geli eius pre-
liabant cum
diacone:7 d:a
co pugnabat
et anguli ei°:
et non value-
runt neq; loc°
inuetus est eo
ru amplius i
celo. Apoca-
plis.rii.ca.

Uidi de ore
diaconis 7 de
ore bestie.7c.
exire spus im-
mundos.7c.
Sunt eni spi-
ritus demo-
niorii. Apoca
lipsis.rvi.

Uant ces deup Vieilles ainsi Vy
quest ce dis ie/doulp dieu merci
En ce pays que Vieilles na
Vieille de ca Vieille de la
Ne scap se suis en femenye

FIGURE 69

added Sloth in Figs. 58 and 59; the similarity between L. and P. in the two pairs (Figs. 31-34) stands out against these differences. Yet all have in common the large list of "significant" detail from the text. We may add the pair formed by Figs. 42 and 43, of the pilgrim with Penance and Charity showing the charter to the Bishop. Again the allegorical elements are all "givens" from the text (though L. unaccountably omitted Penance's besom); two woodcuts (Figs. 71 and 72) demonstrate that, with all the likenesses, persons in a different order or altered attitudes make pictures that bring out the similarity in our pair. Two illustrations from separate manuscripts re-make the point (Figs. 73 and 74).

FIGURE 68

FIGURE 70

FIGURE 71

FIGURE 72

FIGURE 73

FIGURE 74

FIGURE 75

We may interrupt these more meticulous comparisons to state outright that the Pepys Manuscript illustrator did certainly see copies of Guillaume's *Vie* other than Laud misc. 740. These were French, unless we have lost some illustrated manuscripts of the English prose redaction that had a fuller series.[35] Notable among the other pictures P. adds, entirely conventional in the iconography but not present in L's series, are the ordination or tonsuring picture, the donation of scrip and staff taken from a chest, the armor hanging on a rod or in a wardrobe, the hedge with glove-girl and weaver, the assault of Death with his scythe. I reproduce P's tonsuring picture (Fig. 75), that someone may run into a good analogue, but do not give others, adding only that they are usually outside, have several onlookers and very visible shears. We have already seen that P., in illustrating how the Pilgrim received his staff (Figs. 48 and 49, in Harl.4399 and P.), keeps to the pictorial elements often used by others; another example of a conventional picture taken by P. from some manuscript other than Laud is shown in Figs. 76 and 77. The curtained

[35] I attempt no conjectures as to all he saw; we have observed how numerous (and attractive) were the forms in which the text was accessible, but I do not think comparative study was given to either text or pictures. French manuscripts *now* in England were rarely there so early; the tradition is clearest in the innumerable French manuscripts. Though French printed editions were available, I detect no influence of Vérard's cuts, and those I reproduce from 1504 and from the Dutch edition of 1498 show that extreme simplification would be needed to produce likeness. Nevertheless, P's added pictures (not in L.) are not invented but traditional. He doubtless trimmed the series to the number of chapters to which he abbreviated the text (I do not find his divisions paralleled; in rigidity they ape a printed book, though he had no printed English model—but we can see how MS. Laud misc. 740 could give him the idea of a picture per chapter).

FIGURE 76

FIGURE 77

recess with the armor is common; exemplified are B.M.Add.MS. 25594 (fourteenth century) and P. But Laud 740 does have the picture of Grace Dieu fastening the scrip on the pilgrim (Fig. 78), and it compares in composition and detail (tree, crown, stance) with P., ch. 11, Fig. 79.

A very few pictures from the series as imitated in P. are left unrepresented.[36] The set of sins primarily, but sometimes also Rude Entendement the churl, are as grotesquely ugly as the skill of their depicters could make them. But this is often far short of the demoniac and gleeful ugliness "painted" by Guillaume in his text. The various figures looked at, of Gluttony, Sloth, Envy, hags in a melee (Figs. 56ff. and 50-51), may be allowed to carry this point of early realism (cf. n. 24 above); I merely add the melee from L. and P. (Figs. 80 and 81) to bring out their similarity in composition, vertical accents, gestures, stance, masses, despite the enormous possibilities for variation, exempli-

[36] It will be remembered that one of the few incidents the Pepys Manuscript omits is that of the Pilgrim viewing his separated body. The hedge-pictures are customarily rather obscure and uninteresting, and the one from P. is not given, nor are the conventional illustrations of late experiences like infirmity, age and death.

FIGURE 78

FIGURE 79

FIGURE 80

The pilgrim heere surprised by wrath and by all the other things overthrowne complaineth

FIGURE 81

FIGURE 82

FIGURE 85

FIGURE 83

FIGURE 84

fied in some of our earlier examples. The Gluttony picture in P. is drawn by another hand, according to James's description; whatever the explanation for that, the misinterpreted and unclear representation of Gluttony's vomiting vessel and drinking cup (as in L., Fig. 83) surely has the look of a copied error. Lechery is on her swine (Fig. 82; see also Figs. 50 and 51), and the pictures of these two are telescoped, as is frequent. The 1504 woodcut, Fig. 84, will remind us of how these creatures more frequently look.

This redactor's strong stomach for strangely imagined allegorical images, shown in his well-of-tears picture, is that of the text's author and of his mediaeval predecessors (this picture is very constant; shown only are Figs. 52-54). One is added here from the 1504 edition to show another textual and therefore frequent element—the Pilgrim bathing in the tears (Fig. 85). Two angels with bright red wings not typical, floating in the world's sea where defeated pilgrims drown, outlined under water, are very striking and odd to one handling the Laud manuscript; they may have caught the eye also of the Pepys illustrator (cf. Figs. 86 and 87).

FIGURE 86

FIGURE 87

FIGURE 88

FIGURE 89

Both Ships of Religion are given (Figs. 88 and 89); banners, mast, "frets," and Pilgrim generally differ much more widely than these. But Fig. 89 is chiefly given to show the hand which has added the long chapter rubric, mentioned a few pages above in discussing the marginalia. Hence Fig. 90, in which the word "Religion" is almost identical, is added that similarities in the hand may be judged.

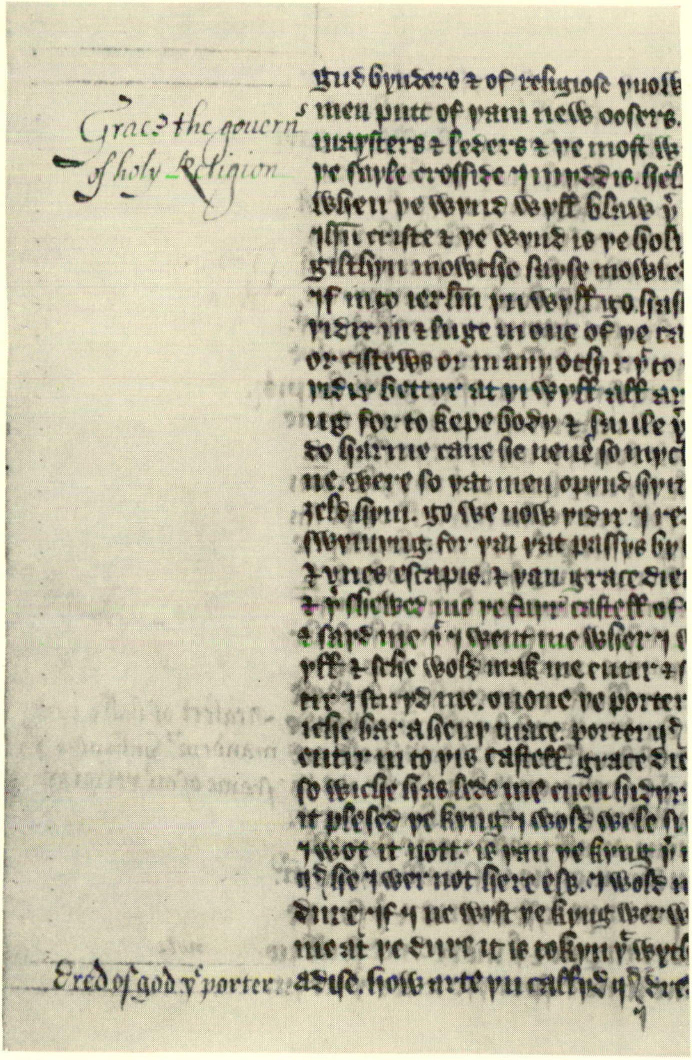

FIGURE 90

The reader may decide, if he can on these evidences, whether or not the seventeenth-century illustrator of the Pepys Manuscript was copying the fifteenth-century illuminations of this manuscript Laud had owned, elaborating its sketchinesses and improving upon its crass tastelessness, but producing pictures that in general say the same things. The point would have little artistic importance, since we deal with men of little talent, but it would tell much about something we must chiefly guess about: how the seventeenth century read and regarded writers of the fifteenth, who were modernizing some monk of the fourteenth.

I have been speaking in the last pages as if "P.," or those responsible for the writing and illustrating of Pepys 2258, represented the only interest in this early text, and this was not true. We recall that the colophon printed above (p. 155), from a different Cambridge manuscript of the same abridgment, named four seventeenth-century men who copied out the whole; and this shows at least a persevering interest, as anyone may test by trying it (the Pepys Manuscript runs to 62 pages). Pepys 2258 has not this colophon. Where is that first copy which Will. Baspoole made before he gave his old book to Archbishop Laud? And were the Emblemata at the end of each chapter those pictures we have been looking at in Laud 740, duly *apposita* in that position?[37]

To be sure, Laud misc.740 is not in St. John's College in Oxford, and was not there in the 1640's and '50's, but in the Bodleian. We know when it was given, for in the catalogue of Laud's donations on 22 May 1635 there appears under *Libri Anglicani*, no. 16: "Anonym: Pilgrimage of Man."[38] It may quite well have been in St. John's library first, between the time when Laud wrote his name and "1633" on the first page, and 1635. Laud's benefactions to St. John's are well enough known; during these same decades the magnificent second court was newly erected and the handsome library referred to as Laud's library was built. It does not seem fantastic against this background to

---

[37] For so they appear, preceding the indications of division in the text; actually the subjects belong to what follows. This is not common—but I have not made much attempt to discover what is regular as to this element of format. But I would add here, touching similarity of the pictures themselves, that after looking at the familiar and conventional series in several dozen manuscripts of varied date range (for the manuscripts preserved in France are vastly more numerous and have a far wider range of date), parallels between our two stand out much more convincingly.

[38] See Laud misc. 1705, f. 116. The title occurs only in a long marginal note at the commencement (in the "Gothic" hand). I think one has no right to be surprised that twenty years later a man who had never seen the original (the colophon writer) did not know it had left one library for another. Equally one has no right to cavil at his saying Baspoole "copied out" the original; surely we need not assume the existence of some other prose rendering to take care of the fact that the copies we have are abridgments and modernizations of the fifteenth-century text, not "copies." The abridger does copy when he can, and with extraordinary fidelity for one working after two centuries of language change.

FIGURE 91

suggest that if the person who made up the book form of Pepys 2258 wished to compliment Archbishop Laud, Fig. 91 with its teasing likeness to the second court of St. John's would be a neat way of doing so. Designed to represent the author's true haven and place of sanctity, his "monastery," it makes even now a pleasing quip between a group of St. John's men or men interested in St. John's library, if Will. Baspoole anticipated that his old book might end up in the library just then being assisted by the munificence of the man he hoped to please by giving him an old copy of the Pilgrimage.

By a most curious chance, we know one more fact about the man who worked over the Pepys Manuscript version. When Reason told the Pilgrim that he had a divine Father and only in the body was descended from "Thomas de guilleville" (many spelling variants), we noted that the Laud Manuscript copyist (f. 56r) corrupted this to "Wene noght that thou be sone of Thomas & William"—an easy error for someone faced with that improbable surname, but less easy to understand except as copied error when we find the doublet also in Pepys 2258 (but not in Wright's manuscript). Now, there is a German version of the *Vie*, which at this verse (5988) reads, to our astonishment, "En dencke neit dat du son sijs Peters van Meroede. . . ." The editor discovers that the "priester Petrus" who did this version was indeed not only God's son but the son of a "Peters van Meroede" of Köln.[39]

<hr>

[39] The editor, A. Meijboom, can thus date the version in 1444. See *Die Pilgerfahrt des träumenden Mönchs* (Bonn, 1926), esp. pp. 21*-26*.

He has cunningly indicated his identity, much as Guillaume had inserted verses that revealed his name; incidentally, this self-identification with a fictional character in an allegory shows how unselfconsciously the mode worked.

If we look at the French prose rendering no longer wrongly attributed to the earlier Jean Galoppes, but done in 1464-65 by "Anonymous of Angers," we find Guillaume's original changed to read: "Ne cuydes pas *que* tu soyes filz a thomas de guilleville ne a *pierre gautier*" (Lyons, Nourry, 1504, sg.h iv verso). It would seem safe to conclude that if sufficient search were made in the records of Angers, the clerk who put Guillaume's *Vie* into prose for Jeanne, the wife of King René, would not need to remain Anonymous of Angers. I suppose we might even now call him X Gautier.

One looks with some interest at the same passage in MS. Pepys 2258. Unlike the other extant seventeenth-century copy in Camb. Ff. 6.30, it reads: "Wene not thou art the sonne of Thomas, nor of Willia*m*, nor of *Richard*. . . ." The most in-curious reader would perhaps, at this juncture, find some interest in looking about for a Will. Baspoole son of a Richard.

Heraldry collections point to a Norfolk family, and the *Index of Wills . . . Proved in the Prerogative Court of Canterbury* provides: Baspoole, William, gent., Norwich, will proved *1658*. We recall the dates of copies—1645, '49, '55. In the *Visitations of Norfolk*, we find: Baspole, Richard, of Potter Higham; m. dau. of . . . Turner, of Hadley in Suffolk; sons Walter, Richard, Rafe *and William*. And Blomefield's *Norfolk*, describing the church at Potter Higham, copies from a gravestone in the chancel: Hic jacet . . . Richard Baspole, gent., June 19, 1613. This is a proper date for the death of a Richard the father of a Will. Baspoole who copied a manuscript between the early 1630's and 1645, and died in 1658.[40]

---

[40] One thinks he *may*, as the former owner, have used Laud 740 before or after it went to the Bodleian, but it is not necessary to suppose this. For the first citation, see *Index of Wills. . .*, vol. 8 (1657-60), Index Library, vol. 61, ed. T. M. Blagg (London, 1936); year 1658, f. 149. The *Visitations of Norfolk* are published in *Harleian Society*, vol. 32 for 1891; the ref. (pp. 19-20) is from MS.Harl.1552. That in Blomefield's *Norfolk* is at vol. 9 (London, 1808), 314. The lordship of Sutton was connected with this parish; on the last folio (129v) of Laud 740 we find "This is Ambrose Suttons booke."

FIGURE 92

One teasing clue we leave to be followed: there is an unidentified heraldic shield on the flyleaf of Pepys 2258, described in James's *Catalogue: "argent,* a cross fitchee *sable,* a chief indented *or* W W. Above the initials R.*P.*"—the last letter questioned. I reproduce this as Fig. 92. It seems unlikely that Will. Baspoole, son of God and of *R*ichard, presented this "copy" to his earthly father, if he had none after 1613; we know nothing of *R*afe or the second *R*ichard. But whether or not the other Baspoole's cared to read this final appearance of the romance written by the monk of Chaalis in 1331, three further copies testify that it lived and was appreciated until 1655.[41] It is odd to recall that *Paradise Lost* was then being written. It may remind us also that it is never safe to conclude, from a major work of a period, that a quite different past had become incomprehensible and antipathetic—or in this case that allegory had died and no one knew where it was buried.

[41] I have not investigated the identity of the other copiers. Some marginal hands in Laud 740 do not look like those of learned men. Miss Martin at the Bodleian tells me Laud had a chaplain G. G., Geo. Gibbs, but his "Dithyrambus" to Laud is penned elaborately in a presentation copy (see MS.Lat.misc. e. 102) and probably we dare not trust likeness seen to the Italian-hand marginalia. A "Geo. Goodman" wrote his name in MS.Add.34193 of Guillaume's *Pilgrimage of the Sowle.*

CHAPTER IV
Imposed Allegory

THE reason for reading any piece allegorically is to come at meanings which are truly in the work—but hidden therein; in our early periods, at least, the raison d'être of symbols is that they symbolize something, that they can carry from one mind to another significances, relations, insights, which are truly part of the subject and not arbitrarily and forcibly imposed upon it. But the words "truly in the work" refer us to a baffling critical difficulty. I ignore entirely the pseudo-problems raised by reading which regards symbols as a sort of quarry or game, to be pursued, shot down, bagged and brought in, inducing chiefly a feeling of achievement on the part of the hunter, who may care but little about the poetic subject presented and feels this no disadvantage. But the least responsible reader, if he is at all serious about the integrity of art, is under an absolute necessity to face the thorny problem of whether the allegorical meanings are "there." For a meaningless symbol is a contradiction in terms; if the meanings are not conveyed by the work itself as the author left it, the symbols are not "used in it as mere figures" or "used for their own sake" but quite simply not present. A few simple ones can creep in unconsciously, but none can be put in by us, and none was used just to have symbols.

Yet when it comes to allegory, it would be folly to claim that we can answer this question of whether a piece means X by endeavoring to see whether its author meant X. Even if we could find this out fully and for sure—which no intelligent critic to my knowledge claims to be able to do—we must realize that some of the greatest allegories in the world's literature were not the consciously intended meanings of the original writers. It is nonetheless the best habit to persevere in—our ordinary habit of looking at every suggestion which may reveal an author's own understanding of his matter, of studying the decorum of a piece to keep from perverting and abusing it, of seeing a work in the context of an historical moment in which it was born. We do not thus ensure a complete answer, but do prevent more than one bad answer; fashionable modern worries that one may thus substitute wilful notions of "the author's intention" or "the period's predilections" for the work itself are surely the product of over-attention to the naïvetés that come forth in classrooms. Still more infelicitous naïvetés and substitutions have resulted from the remedy applied—a general inattention to the evidence which could declare what an author may have meant. This and the consequent substitution of the critic's intention for the work itself, though a danger which no critic has ever entirely avoided, has been the special plague of recent critical interpretation of the *Faerie Queene* as well as of Shakespeare. An undisguised pleasure in symbol-hunting generally characterizes these re-makings of masterpieces, accompanied by much deceptive paraphrase. Nevertheless, we should declare at the outset that numerous symbolical readings of great pieces of literature, famous allegories we should only impoverish ourselves by renouncing, have been imposed upon works by later readers rather than deliberately written into them by their authors.

It is the thoroughgoing metaphorical nature of allegory which makes this possible. Like the neighboring trope of irony, metaphor implies what it can not overtly state without losing the formal character which defines it as a figure; both figures are, as it were, open at one end, allowing interpretations which can be supported by proper evidence but not proven. An extreme, perhaps a peculiar, complexity is given to the openness in the case of allegory by the fact that as we read the "letter" figuratively, meanings appear which we can arguably claim are and were always there, though we may know without doubt that the writer of "the letter" did not see them.

If we think of examples, this is immediately apparent as is the additional fact that we would be the losers if we relinquished such late-seen meanings on the ground that they were not intended. Who would forbid to Paul his allegory of Hagar, or Jerusalem "the mother of us all" in Gal. 4 because Genesis knew nothing of the second covenant? Who would give up the meanings of "Surely he hath borne our griefs, and carried our sorrows," "And with his stripes we are healed," as these verses from Isaiah 53 have been understood by generations of New Testament readers; who would subtract from the liturgy or even the sung text of Handel's *Messiah* those added poignancies which Isaiah could not have known since the events had not happened? History has made it an impossibility to millions of people to reduce the words "agnus dei" to what they meant to the writers of the verses that contain them. The arts, and literature especially, would be strangled by such a conception of meaning. However well we may know that Miss Weston's theory of the meaning of "The Waste Land" and various symbols connected with it is not supportable for the Middle Ages, Eliot's use of it has made some of those meanings inextricable. It would take a very complicated argument to convince one that the penitential psalms, the 22nd for example, ought to be pared down to what David had in mind when he wrote "All they that see me laugh me to scorn." The most problematical example of an imposed allegory, the Song of Solomon, offers a more complicated question, yet few persons would willingly delete from Western arts the written and painted and musical results of the transformation of that profanely intended love song into the great repository of texts adumbrating divine love for the spirit of man.

However much we may agree that it would be folly to cut ourselves off from our inheritance by a stubborn insistence that meanings later imposed by figurative reading are not "in" the works, there is a look of equal folly about the subjectivity of allowing every reader to claim that works of art mean whatever he sees in them. Examples would only show us every age pointing out the absurdity of what the last age made of great permanent works. Very occasionally, however, this condemnation would prove to be an error. Not only is it hard for a man to tell if he is an Origen rather than the exegete of a moment, but his contemporaries cannot tell either; the acceptability of readings always goes in waves—so that nothing is more open to faddism than symbolical interpretation. Meanwhile, the intelligence revolts from the idea that great writings have no life of their own but must eternally thus be killed and offered up as sacrifices to conceptions and values currently attractive, then with difficulty brought back to life, to be re-sacrificed to another reigning notion of the profound and the significant. Yet we recognize cases where we would not willingly return to the original meaning as the complete one even if we could. There is, then, a quite genuine problem, not to be solved by the simple exercise of good sense or by humility and austere conscience among critics.

In the largest category of examples wherein historically later events have filled ancient images with unanticipated allegorical meanings, the problem disappears. Where typology is in question, God Himself is conceived as the author of the relation between history's literally true events and the meanings they figure forth. That Melchisedec in giving Abraham the bread and wine prefigured the Last Supper and shadowed its eucharistic meanings, that Abel suffering death at his brother's hand and Isaac carrying the wood for his sacrifice prefigured Christ's passion, that the children of Israel delivered from "Egypt" by Moses is a figure of every deliverance of a soul from bondage by Christ—all these examples of the "letter" of history are conceived as embodying their meanings when they happened, even though those who enacted or recorded them could not read those meanings, which were yet to be revealed when later also-literal historical events drew the veil from truths always there but hidden. There is no question of a substitution of figurative for literal meaning; all doctrine touching allegory, varied and irreconcilably different in some other respects, is unanimous in claiming the validity of both the literal historical event and its allegorical significance.[1]

[1] This is especially well substantiated by patristic and scholastic quotation in H. de Lubac's recent volumes (though it has been tirelessly reiterated for years by critics whose knowledge of allegory is not confined to belles lettres); see citation above, ch. 1, n. 22. This heritage from religious allegory, the "importance-of-the-literal," descended into secular fictions (where historical truth is not claimed for any meaning) as emphasis upon the integrity or acceptance of the story as such. Most stories to be read allegorically are superlatively fantastic, but either very unselfconsciously so or presented with some care as to be credited (cf. *Gulliver's Travels* or the *Faerie Queene* or *Piers Plowman*). It seems to me to have been grasped early as a principle that narratives would necessarily be *intermittently* capable of allegorical reading. This is best exemplified in the romances (see ch. 5); current readers of allegory are often much more unwilling than earlier writers of it to allow some characters or some portions to serve simply and only the story-or-historical reading.

See n. 36 below for reference to the work of P. Alpers, soon to appear in book form—who almost alone, but with extreme tact in the reading of Spenser, treats this difficulty. I wish to disclaim once more, early in a chapter, the attempt to fasten *one* definition upon this word used over many centuries and for numerous needs. The notion of "one correct meaning" being of course untenable, a useful reminder of the differences between questions of *origin* and of sixteenth-century *meaning* (against the background of mediaeval developments kept familiar) is R. M. Grant's *The Letter and the Spirit* (New York, 1957), ch. v, especially the Greek exegetical terminology defined in App. II, terms which antedate mediaeval use but whose later influence was nevertheless shaped thereby. Differences in the later, influenced meaning become apparent especially in the

The profound and beautiful development of typological reading of the Old Testament, since it was well established by Paul
and common for seventeen centuries, could not but affect the
figure to which it gave its name of *allegoria*, when it appeared
in other than religious books, especially since this accepted reading of Scripture was not the target of Protestant complaints
against allegories (the narrowly fanciful and peculiarly ecclesiological readings were much denigrated). But it does not include
all the kinds of allegorical figures which are characterized by
symbolical interpretations not apparent to their first writers. The
largest other category is that of the allegorized classical figures,
both those from pagan myth and those from ancient story. It
seems to me unquestionable that the mode of thought in religious
allegory encouraged the appropriation and deepened the "true
meaning" in classical materials figuratively understood; still,
Hercules accomplishing the labors is not a type of the saving
Christ in the same way that Samson is, with the carried-off gates
of Gaza proclaiming, at the instant they yielded, the fall of Hell's
gates before the power of Hell's eternal harrower (historialiter
in A.D. 33, mystice or spiritualiter in any heart since). The shadow
of a later revealed truth is indeed most commonly and widely
argued to be truly present in imperfect pagan visions of it, and
this sense was far more important in the conservation of classical
story for us through the Christian Middle Ages than was any
cunning plot to hang onto the delightful lies by accommodating
them to reigning conceptions—a picture of the mediaeval mind
frequently offered to us. Nevertheless, this Greek and Roman
pantheon and history was not thought of as God's special manifestation and care as was His slow sure redemption of man as
recorded in His chosen people's history and Old Law and New.
A deity's authorship was not customarily seen in the late classical
and Stoic allegorizings of ancient myth; even when such readings
seem "true," we are conscious of the willed imposition of meaning.

Two or three large kinds of new meaning distinguish themselves, providing an unremarked classification of differing opera-

clear light of a book which seems to me to embody an almost perfect explanation
of allegorical reading at this date: T. P. Roche, *The Kindly Flame, A Study
of the Third and Fourth Books of Spenser's Faerie Queene* (Princeton, 1964)
(see its earlier chapters).

tions of allegory, in any handbook we pick up—Natalis Comes'
thoroughly popular *Mythologia*, or Sandys' late Ovid with its
capacious notes. Some ways of reading are barely classifiable
under a term "allegory" by any definition that has come down;
others offer a meaning for the figure "allegory" which is much
less profoundly figurative than that common in Christian materials; others show the influence of those materials. The same
unorganized bouquets of quite varied flowers greet us in the less
tidy texts of the many mediaeval progenitors, Fulgentius and the
several "Vatican mythographers" and the commonplaces of the
"Libellus."

Cosmological or natural-philosophy translations are favorites
that were given an extended life by Renaissance fondness for their
fantastic physics and their air of rational demythologizing. Circe
is sensual appetite in that she is born of heat and moisture, daughter of sun and ocean; Argus is taken for heaven with his eyes the
stars and his movements procuring earth's fertility; any sun-god
begets life in a passive and moist earth-goddess, and as vegetation-
god or initiator of a fertility-cycle, he can seem a scientific explanation of the conditions of life rather than an awesome
mystery or a childish fancy. Such "wisdom" was peculiarly that
of the clear-seeing "ancients" to a Bacon, and the dissemination
of it was so nearly universal in the West that such readings have
become second nature. Given a small capital of key notions which
are much repeated, children first encountering pagan mythological
imagery will readily make and accept these translations; ideas
of the origin of myth (to explain "Nature") promoted them.
Closely similar,[2] but more evidently euhemeristic, are the histor-

[2] Indeed, students may already have felt uneasy at the fact that distinctions
are more accurate and analyses more meticulous in the treatments which study
the history of these classical images, such as J. Seznec's *Survival of the Pagan
Gods* (New York, 1953, translated from the French edition, 1940), which
conveniently summarizes earlier work; or one of Panofsky's volumes late enough
to cite recent studies, like *Renaissance and Renascences in Western Art* (Uppsala,
1960), though less directly concerned than several others since his early *Studies
in Iconology* (New York, 1939). Work in this area includes, e.g. one after another
of the Warburg Studies, and much of Saxl's, Panofsky's, Liebeschütz's, Wind's and
others' work, but must be counted upon as familiar to the reader rather than
constantly interwoven, for we only raise here the points that can be related to
the small number of popular texts studied for their contribution to the sixteenth-
century man's experienced literary pleasure in allegorical reading. We deliberately

ical rationalizations that turn all gods or heroes into famous kings
who procured this or that benefit for the race of men—inventors
of tillage, discoverers of navigation. Similar, too, are the rationalizations which simply explain away myths by a step-mother's
resentment or a manorial lady's arbitrary sentence of punishment
or a cattle-owner's invention of a device to protect his huge
wealth. These attempts to return to "the letter" proved for later
literature the most sterile of all ways of reading intelligible sense
into alien symbolisms or mysteries, and often produce most
laborious awkwardnesses in the narrative. But we should not
forget that Christian writers learned this kind of reduction of
meaning from late classical men when we find ourselves annoyed
with the unconvincing Daphnes who by yielding "under a laurer"
made Apollo seize its leaves for a crown signifying triumph, or the
King-Phaetons who cannot control—not a sun-chariot—but the
fierce commons, or the Cadmuses who establish universities,
killing serpentine error beside a fountain.

When moral allegory is the nature of the figure combined with
this tendency to re-literalize and re-interpret, the better allegorists
made new and potent stories almost as profound in their way as
the ancient inexplicabilities, and extremely fertile. This is by
far the most usual form of the imposition of new meaning. A
case in point is the fruitful development of the figure of Circe,
from before Boethius onward, which made it finally amenable to
use in discussing with figurative indirection the whole complex

---

avoid that completeness which would support a description of the actual total
state of knowledge touching sixteenth-century reading of all classical figures,
verbal and seen.

The importance of several kinds of "reading," especially of a third sort
soon considered (astrological interpretation), has been more easily seen in the
history of art. But one needs only to consider the important relation to mythological imagery of an inheritance indicated by Saxl's *Catalogue of Astrological
and Mythological Illuminated Manuscripts*; of course, at our dates meticulous
knowledge and unshaken belief are less to be looked for than just the preservation
of serious meaningfulness in a dead religion's god and stories. One is increas-
ingly aware that the rise of the natural sciences and technology did more to
weaken classical figurative language than the change in religion. We have no
real use for, and hence no real interest in, the cosmological knowledge or
mysteries Spenser or Chapman or Drayton might clothe in such images; this
may be one reason why (unlike moral allegory) such imagery has not been re-
invigorated by the studies of it, but remained sterile or only historically interesting.

problem of sensuality versus temperance, of naturalism versus man's spiritual allegiances. Or, to seize a late example that shows an original mind in process of giving a moral re-reading to a figure, see Milton's Isis in *Areopagitica* and the scattered limbs of truth, with the opportunity it gave him to intimate certain sophisticated elements of doctrine. When later we become engrossed with examples in a context, it will be possible to see why imposed meanings of this kind enriched rather than impoverished what was inherited.

A great imaginative allegorist like Spenser will combine these various ways of trying to read truth in ancient images—seeming to evoke rather than impose, making full use of significances which had come to inhabit an image by virtue of its post-classical history of use. His primary method is to deepen meaning by reading moral images symbolically (not symbols in origin), so that they bring into play large conceptions of the moral order of the universe, and the actions debate or portray before us men's profound spiritual dilemmas. This is done with Acrasia, Mammon, Duessa, Cupid, Venus. He skimps or detours around all readings which stress euhemeristic or historical rationalization, and his cosmological readings are enlarged by neo-Platonic impositions of meaning (developments which are outside the limits of this book).

Other newly accruing or imposed meanings which preserved the importance of classical images, especially the pantheon of pagan gods, do not do so by moralizing them into forms which gave them universal applicability. The simplest way this was done was to use a plain event in the history of thought: the gods kept their empires as stars. Astrological reading of the power of the planet-gods is universally present in books of interpretation. What Jupiter or Saturn meant and could effect, being so understood—and nothing was commoner—may not look like an allegorical reading to us; but one form of exactly that operation of mind is involved, and belief in the stars' power over men's destinies gave complete meaningfulness and often a frightening truth to innumerable stories and conceptions of the power of pagan deities, which would otherwise have glanced off the shield of a different religious faith. Even a late author, partially satirizing and playing with the conceptions, like Chaucer, shows the translation of the images into thoroughly believable meanings. There is surely no question that Saturn or Venus or Mars were living and powerful realities to centuries of human minds; the pervading ordinary uses (in medicine, in what passes for psychology, and of less daily importance, in alchemical language) ensured complete comprehension and habitual use of this whole figurative translation of dead deities into actual powers.

Whether a writer disbelieves in judicial astrology or not, he will use the classical language with the figurative extension which men's thinking had imposed upon it and value the seriousness and the contemporaneous significancy thus possible to the figures. The last forty years of study, in the arts, have made it clear that we cannot safely ignore the vast "scientific" literature through which later men were made skillful in such "real meanings" of pagan images. We note that curiously little of Spenser's enrichment of classical figures is gained by using this extended dimension of their meaning, considering his early date and fondness for Chaucer. Perhaps I need not remark that all the ways of reading classical images so far mentioned were thought by the allegorists to be true meanings, that is, *in* the stories and not imposed by later men, though sometimes only truly understood by them because the ancients supposedly took in just "the letter" of their own myths and pantheons.

One final kind of important imposed meaning is the kind which this chapter will chiefly examine. It is blatantly an imposition.[3] It produced page upon page of bad allegory, and

[3] I am not attempting to enter silently and without names the current too-heated controversy over what is sometimes referred to as "patristic" interpretation of literary pieces (the collection of talks published as annotated essays, papers from the English Institute 1958-59, *Critical Approaches to Medieval Literature*, ed. Bethurum, can serve as a survey, though some major additions are later). The issues and the nature of evidence necessary seem to me often confusedly grasped, by entrants on both sides, the more so if kinds of figurative language must be distinguished, and the theory behind them. The overemphasis on moral point, which is often what opponents of D. W. Robertson *et al.* find untenable, is for example not the kind of "imposition" we here speak about at all. Conceptions of allegory's nature and functions are too narrowly dependent on few texts on one hand, but unhistorically and unsympathetically not even faced and studied on the other; tropology and typology are treated in one move by some, the praised habits of the century are assumed to be the literary credo of every author by others. I do not wish to argue the disagreements, which are temporary; but the sum of facts in the present book, helping us see what of "the tradition" was undeniably popularized and entered the vernacular, and claiming only what evidence overtly supports, should clarify the issues. The points made here about *principles* of "imposing" meanings often suit the

little that was good. I do not find it used by any great imaginative
writer, yet the impulse behind it is responsible for some of the
greatness in all the Christian, but secular, writers in the allegorical mode, and it was current, familiar, and enjoyed in some
famous books which refused to die when the mediaeval tastes
which produced them had met death in the forms we find most
ignominious: ridicule and silent neglect. This kind of reading is
the imposition upon classical figures and stories of Christian
doctrinal interpretations, the claim that the images "mean" dogmas or revealed truths—the Incarnation, the Passion, Christ's
loving pursuit of man's erring soul, the virgin birth.

Milton found it silly; he does make use very occasionally of a
kind of detritus which it left as the tide receded—there seems no
doubt that his giants and Titans are proud Lucifers, though
from ancient story; and his Ceres and Proserpina figure seems to
have its poignant stab of loving compassion from unmentioned
suggestions of the love of a truer redeeming Divinity that seeks
us through the world. But these are not the wrenching of classical
contents to Christian significances, but uses of inherited parallels
originally made on grounds of analogical relations between elements literally in both stories. Spenser to my mind avoids such
allegorizing, fastidiously. Pan may be Christ in an early pastoral
poem; but in the fictions of the *Faerie Queene*, the God of Love
with his arrows is not Jesus, the Tree of Life grows in a recognizable Biblical Eden, and we need not ready ourselves to meet
things like "for Socrates dying nobly in Athens, *read*, Christ
suffered in Jerusalem." Spenser uses Christian terms for Christian doctrine, but not necessarily "Christian terms for Christian
allegories." All Spenser's allegories are Christian, but not ecclesiological or doctrinal; and many are in classical terms.

Usually these classical terms and figures have been universalized by their truly always present, and unimposed, moral meaning. Pilate the proud unrighteous judge is in quite reasonably
similar company, suffering with proud Tantalus in a river in
Pluto's Hades—which is Hell because Pluto the ravisher lives

---

mediaeval situations currently discussed. The careful and learned ones among
the modern exponents (it has suffered much from faddist disciples) do not
desire to "impose" but to interpret, and quarrels with them belong to the
history of taste not of scholarship.

in a hell, with the victim he has raped and subjected, like the other similar Ravisher, with *his* subjects, and *his* loves. But in some larger images the classical terms or figures are understood "in their universal consideration," not on grounds of some moral element (like the hybris of Pilate's and Tantalus' blindness to the difference of deity from man), but because they have shed their local particularity and appear before us as essences, the very Ideas themselves. The very idea of Concordia, Venus as Beauty incarnate, Love in essence—or for that matter Intemperance itself or Falsity or Pride, appears indifferently in Circean classical guise or as the invented Duessa or in the satanic Beast of Revelation; the ideas are apprehended by the intellectus but require the body of a symbol if they are to be "presented" (symbols do not represent). I have argued that Spenserian images would not have had the metaphysical reach and the powerful extension of significance which they possess without a development in Christian thought and writing (which we met in Ch. One), even as late as Christine de Pisan. We saw in her the barefaced open translation of classical images—of a Ceres into a figure signifying Christ's love, an Andromeda who was the soul being delivered— in order that these might all bear allegorical meaning; and though Spenser and other poets of the English Renaissance use this bold method very little, the same impulse motivates their deepest symbolic images: i.e. to convey allegorical meanings, important and saving knowledge touching man's spiritual as well as moral life (to use the definition Christine and others preserve). But why did Spenser abstain from imposing precise doctrinal of Christological readings as what we may understand classical images to mean (Christine's phrase)? Because of historical fastidiousness? Or because he had a keener understanding of the nature of allegory as a figure and did not need these forced parallels?

Though English Renaissance writers do not show much hospitality to this form of allegory, they had good precedent for such writing. Moses, Orpheus, Hermes, Plato, were linked in the prisca theologia; the Orpheus figure had had its Christian significance since earliest centuries; Ronsard could write a long poem on *Hercule Chrestien*.[4] The habit of classical-Christian identifica-

---

[4] The point is somewhat confused by the relation these particular two bear to "types," as it is by the seriously understood prophetic element in the Messianic

tion was entrenched in pastoral (where it is powerfully used by both Spenser and Milton, perhaps because each desires to use the great timeless image of the shepherd which spans many cultures and transcends religious differences). Certainly there was common belief in the idea of a partial revelation of Christian truth to inspired pagans. The historical conscience which makes a modern student uneasy about attributing unborn meanings to earlier materials, was undeveloped. The handbooks include what must have been stereotyped examples of this kind of converted meaning in images. It is closer than other kinds of allegorical reading to the strict definition of allegory in Scriptural interpretation, for it makes figuratively apparent not moral injunctions but "matters of belief," fundamental doctrine, Christ's new "Law" seen shadowed but present in the older dispensation—veiled but reliably demonstrated by exegesis. Yet it was avoided by the great artists. It seems to me that their reasons were aesthetic.

There may be principles which govern the success of an imposition of meaning upon already extant images through allegorical reading, and the principles may be related to the nature and the powers of allegory as a figure. We may be able to see what these are by examining famous and popular books built upon the practice. They will not merit our attention for reasons of their literary excellence, but I propose to examine three such, entirely current in the early Renaissance, with the expectation that they will shed light upon our problem: that some deliberate later impositions of meanings seem fruitful, others (no more forced but somehow foolish) are a travesty; some extend the life of earlier products of men's imaginations by enabling them to refer to living questions with a vital contemporaneity, while others only kill the ancient life and anger us by strained and slavish misreading that deadens as well the new Christian meaning imposed on them.

Before we become engrossed in specific texts, I would add one more category of meanings imposed by allegorical reading in which recalcitrant materials were this time firmly and permanently

---

4th Eclogue, but many simpler examples could be substituted. D. P. Walker's "The *Prisca Theologia* in France," *JWCI*, vol. 17 (1954), 204-59 is indispensable for understanding the state of mind underlying these phenomena (as is F. Yates, *Giordano Bruno and the Hermetic Tradition*, 1964; and see her *French Academies of the 16th Century*, London, 1957).

converted to Christianity. It is a slender category, and indeed one great text will be (in Chapter Five) the only completely satisfactory example; yet the translation was so successful that "the Grail" has become a religious symbol familiar to any Western child. Despite the tangles in the question of origins, elements of Celtic mythology in the Grail legend and its symbolic objects and events are now seldom entirely denied. There are clear reasons why the imposed structure of Christian meaning had a fruitful effect, and why one of the fruits was a literary work of such beauty and originality (the Old French *Queste*) that even its unclear footprints in abridgments and in Malory's superb but incomplete retelling compel the unwilling to admiration. We shall find, I think, that a main characteristic of this converted symbol will help to explain the lack of success of other allegorically imposed meanings. It is a characteristic which is harder to illustrate from the examples that appear in the texts of this chapter. We may find that allegory can successfully and permanently impose a meaning too valuable to give up only upon an object which was already an important symbol in the original context, and when the general drift of symbolic meaning remains similar. The abundance of life, the spiritual nutriment and strength, the saving power—part of that which is symbolized by the Christianized Grail—were part of what it carried as a pagan symbol, however differently understood; and it may be that if this overlap or similarity in basic purport is important enough, *that* allows an old symbol to live a further life, as a carrier of those meanings as they are understood by the new religion or the new metaphysics. This basic similarity in what is symbolized, which of course eludes verbal formulation, will be seen to characterize other successful and lasting cases of attributed meaning.

It is interesting that neither the pious fervour of the allegorizers nor the avoidance of farfetched allegories seems to be a factor. No distance could be much more radically astonishing than that between pre-Christian magical tokens and the most sacred symbols of Christianity; but a closeness in significance made far more difference than an outward diversity. Greek thought, already a sibling, seems on the face of it so much more naturally relatable as to make the proselytizing of images also natural. It was popular for centuries, but it was artistically successful only when certain principles were not transgressed. When we note these, we may find that they almost solve the problem of when a new allegorical reading is valid and when invalid, and that they all involve the question of what meanings are truly present in the original image. It is a complication that these are not always identical with the meanings intended by first authors, but we shall find the safeguards against a chaotic subjectivity to be reasonable and capable of formulation.

The three texts are representative of clusters of habitually allegorized materials, but they are chosen because they were not only accessible but very famous. One wonders if perhaps two of them were more talked about than read, but at any rate, all were mediaeval in origin, all had the kind of later history which has determined inclusion of materials in this book: translation, modernization, re-publication in printed form, wide circulation, usually the development of an accompanying iconographical tradition—all the circumstances which made it feasible for them to influence the taste for allegory and the understanding of it in sixteenth-century England. The first is the *Roman de la rose*, doubly allegorical; the reasons why Molinet's moralized *Roman* was least current of the works handled, despite the large continued sale of the original allegory, may prove to be the reasons why we, too, find it chiefly a warning of how not to read. The second is Christine de Pisan's *Othéa*, valuable because images whose new imposed significances show insight and life are juxtaposed by others that are lifeless and seem arbitrary (all actually are arbitrary); we may detect some guiding principle from this work. She is also valuable to us, as she must have been to sixteenth-century readers, because she has not lost the distinction between moralizing and reading allegorically, which I have already borrowed from her. The third cluster we can refer to as the *Ovide moralisé*, though I do not mean by this the vast metrical text with that title, whose influence may have been negligible. But both examples and comment can be dovetailed into the treatment of Christine, for she did use as source the huge, very early fourteenth-century verse work which did not see print until the twentieth century. Its close cousin, Bersuire's Latin prose handbook of interpreted Ovidian stories, was much printed and known, and the illustrated Mansion-Vérard prose Ovid, familiar as *La Bible des poetes*, contributed to the availability of Christian significances. Accessible they were, but established they persistently failed to become; though Christianizations which the fourteenth and earlier fifteenth century would not accept seem to have found favour in the late fifteenth century, Spenser and other English Renaissance Ovidians withdrew into the earlier preference for taking one's Ovid straight.

Interest or charm in the iconography of all these books assisted their longevity and their breadth of distribution, but, though we, too, may be charmed or interested, we largely learn that pictures are helpless before this special kind of imposed allegorical meaning. This fact is also related to our fundamental puzzle: *how* and to whom meanings must be "truly in" an image if we are to read it allegorically with validity and enjoyment. It is cheerful that the validity and the aesthetic success go together. The later history of texts and of single images bears this out; it is not unreasonable that a certain few classical-Christian images became richly significant and quite well known. For reasons exactly similar to those we will notice, typology is still potently alive and needs only be familiar to be aesthetically moving to agnostics as well as Christians, while doctrinally Christianized classical figures are, barring these few successful exceptions, mere dead curiosities. This character was noticed immediately by Christian artists and very soon by Christian piety.

Marot's name is the most estimable one we meet when we set ourselves to examine the impulse to read strict allegory into the already formally allegorical *Roman de la rose* (the original book's structure is that of a continued metaphor). The late date is significant. Moralizing the *Roman* did not recommend itself as a strategy of defense to the clerkly champions of Jean de Meun in the famous *Querelle* around 1401-1402, nor to Jean de Montreuil the provost of Lille or to Gautier Col. They make no attempt to claim that by the Rose "on peult entendre" the state of grace, or "l'estat de sapience" or the Virgin, or the glory of eternal beatitude. All these are noted as its sens allegoric by Clément Marot in the six or seven pages of "Exposition moralle" prefixed to editions of his prose redaction (1529, '31, '37).[5]

[5] This is printed in Méon's old edition of the *Roman de la rose*. Marot's first edition, 1526 (?), I have not seen, and it apparently had not the preface we read later. All four are described in F. W. Bourdillon's *Early Editions of the Roman de la rose*, Illustr. monograph No. 14 of the Bibliographical Society (London, 1906) (hereafter "Bourdillon"), and that used here, 1537, is his

The rose that wise Solomon chose from those the queen of Sheba offered him, and the white "virginalle rose" of Jericho, come in for remark; so do the vices which keep us out of, and the virtues which let us into, the vergier d'infinie lyesse. This cannot but cause some flutters of worry in those who recall *who* let the Lover in—Oiseuse who claims she gives all her time to diversion and to combing her hair, and carries a mirror to admire the results. To be sure, Prudence as well as Venus looks in a mirror. And to be sure, the Lover is to receive many tokens of "grace" from that Bel Accueil whose pliancy (when warmed by Venus) encouraged him to seize the kiss. And he is to receive instruction that advances him to a state one could call wisdom, especially from the knowledgeable old duenna. And beatitude is what he would say he anticipates from possession of the Rose. This might do very well if we had lost the work itself with all the details which its author put into his descriptions of the graces and the wisdom and the beatitude.

This then is the first safeguarding principle: if large portions of a work have to be covered with blotting paper while we read our meaning in what is left, we are abusing instead of using the images. Not all the pleasure we have learned to take in ambiguous suggestions (present in most good allegory), not all our habituation to erotic imagery spiritually understood, can avail to make Idleness's conversation that of Heavenly Contemplation who has such different reasons for not being busy, or to take the self-seeking craftiness out of the "wise" hints of the Lover's counsellors. Marot felt a similar discomfort, for he claims only that it could be that the author bent his mind not merely to the literal sense but to the allegorical (he would not say "he did," but "il peult").

Having made it clear that although we need not read thus, we shall find great profit if we do, Marot is free to embark on an unexceptionable summary of the poetics justifying the figurative reading of fables. As with the eagle in Ezekiel which got at the mouelle of the Lebanon cedar, so too if we stop at literal mean-

---

edition S. See comments pp. 157ff. on authorship, provenance of text, and Marot's probable attitude toward his potboiler.

On the text later quoted and stressed (the *Ovide moralisé*) see the quite indispensable article by F. Ghisalberti, "L' 'Ovidius moralizatus' di Pierre Bersuire," *Studi Romanzi*, vol. 23 (1933).

lings, l'escorce, we shall come away "sans obtenir le singulier proffit de la mouelle neupmaticque, c'est assavoir, venant par l'inspiration du St Esperit quant a l'intelligence moralle." This is most certainly true. What is missing is any attempt to face the problem of what we are meant to do with the contradictory portions into which the Holy Spirit has clearly *not* tried to breathe anything more than their original thoroughly immoral meanings —the cynical tricks of La Vieille, the gold-digging tactics of the advising "Friend." And what Marot says next is clearly untrue and does not characterize any good allegory we can point to. He says that even if the principal drift is sensual, we will derive much profit from interpreting morally such "bons incidens" as will admit of it.

We arrive at a second principle: the principal drift *governs* the meanings attributable to the incidents borne upon the stream; the latter cannot take their own moral direction as they choose. If we ignore the stream's main direction of flow, and embark on incidents which travel counter to or unrelated to it, arriving at special separable meanings for such incidents, we shall presently drown farcically, amid the laughter of the characters, who sit on the bank well protected in the natures the author gave them, only waiting their chance to push us in. In practice it is actually easy to distinguish this from something it may seem to resemble—the intermittently allegorical reading I have earlier supported. Also, Marot's frank offers of several readings from which we may freely choose as we fancy seems at first an engaging recognition of the fact that images are multi-valent, and we may think it could be a refreshing importation into modern criticism, which so often proffers us "the true reading" on the point of a sword much as Tamburlaine fed Bajazeth his bits of meat. But when we accept the invitation and read the text assuming any of these symbolic intentions to be there, and find that each is made at the cost of the work itself, Marot's hospitality to profitable significancy becomes only comic. Nothing, not even blinkers, could prevent Marot himself from knowing that by reading in this manner we should *not* thus see more deeply into the doulceurs of grace or the experience of the beatific vision of the essence of deity. We can call the rosier in the text an image of this vision, as Marot invites us to do on grounds of its superlative beauty, but the image presented in the text can tell us nothing about such visions; it can only dumbly receive the appliqués we plaster upon it from notions we already have about beatific visions. This speechlessness is a fatal betrayal. Symbols never appear thus uselessly; they are present because they are needed.

This offer of meanings which "one may understand" is a common element in the poetical theory of these early interpreters; their phrasings prove that they do not claim that the author really meant this and that the images at bottom really signify that. When this represents a willingness to talk about imported meanings just because they are usually thought profitable, the results are as trifling as the theory is untenable. Except in a very few witless readers (a sort of may-fly which breeds in every time and is no more nourished upon allegory than other fruits), I do not believe this offer was motivated by the desire to excuse a work or make it palatable to the pious-minded.[6] Piety is offended by these useless equations long before other minds have felt anything but amusement. The motivation is probably much closer to the modern analogue: spotting meanings that just might be there, for the fun of the thing.

Something more serious apparently lies behind some of Christine de Pisan's similar phrasings and perhaps was not uncommon: a belief that the images can truly carry, though they were not intended to, the imposed significance, and that if we assume this experimentally and read on, we may learn something new about *the subject onto which* we have artificially grafted the image (not the author's subject). Such images have a good chance of life. It is part of the reason why a Hercules-Christ image lived on; men seemed to learn something about Christ's fortitude from Hercules'. The interpreters probably noted also the operation of a phenomenon recognized in modern criticism: subterranean meanings not present to the conscious mind of an author, but so truly related to what he is endeavoring to express that his imagery travels beyond the mark he shot at and thus conveys

[6] These are Bourdillon's phrases (*op.cit.* in n. 5), commenting on Molinet, p. 164; I now take up the latter, and the date of composition (pp. 160-62), data on editions, manuscript authority for texts, quality of translation, illustrations, etc. may be found nearby in Bourdillon's volume. Perhaps we should rather more frequently be skeptical of the ascribed motive of making things acceptable to the pious; noticeable extremes of this ascription in "moralized Ovid-researches" (especially in other countries than England, like Spain) have only made allegory seem foolish. The motive is almost always simply assumed by modern students.

them. Such recognitions are not the basis for reading the *Roman* allegorically. Marot has no such ill-founded hope. Jean de Meun was firmly interested in the relation of eternal beatitude to heavenly and earthly love, but the riotous gallop of his ironies shows that while the blasphemously "loyal" Lover can be deceived into thinking his plucked Rose will teach him something about a paradise other than an earthly one with a serpent in it, Jean de Meun is not so deceived; and he is using every device of writing to make us notice the Lover's deception with amusement.

Neither subtle attempts to reconcile original with imposed meaning nor stirrings of conscience lest the imposition falsify the original, disturbed Jean Molinet, who wrote the complete allegorization, the *Romant de la rose moralisie cler et net* printed by Vérard in 1500, reappearing in Lyons (1503) and Paris (1521). It was composed earlier than these dates indicate, perhaps *ca.* 1482. We begin to suspect, and may bear it in mind as we watch the fortunes of the moralized Ovid, a little pocket of late fifteenth-century taste that enjoyed this peculiarly strenuous kind of allegorical reading—whether for the wit and as tour de force, or for the piety, one is unsure.

Molinet also offers variant readings of images and personages. But his frequent bland announcements that "moralité est ma principale queste" and his refraining from "sentence et glose" when he finds arguments that already "tournent a salut" show he is attending only to the necessity of laying his hand upon good doctrine, salvaging it when it is stated (no matter by whom) or putting it in when it is not, with equal indifference. This is particularly apparent when he comments on Lady Reason's forceful speeches dissuading the Lover from fol amour (as Reason sees the God of Love in the garden). Since these speeches are already on the side of heavenly love against fol amour, Molinet says he will leave them in the condition in which he finds them, and does so, attempting no interpretation. Yet his own interpretation reads the God of Love as Our Lord seeking his spouse Anima (the Lover), and Reason therefore must be taken as a fallacious counsellor trying to "extirper" in Anima the flames kindled by the Divine Lover.[7] Evidently, if fallacious

---

[7] This example, and the general declarations cited in this paragraph, are in Molinet, ff. 36v, 38v, 42v. The example next given is from ff. 77v-78v, and the still later references to Jupiter and to Reason are at ff. 38v-39, 39v-40.

counsellors state what Molinet would ticket as "moral," the whole design may be ignored, and we may attend to their wisdom without suspicion.

Similar remarks accompany Molinet's escape from the difficulty he finds himself in when he, not unnaturally, wishes to castigate Faux Semblant, who is a naughty character in a half-dozen obvious respects, to Molinet not least in his attack on friars. Yet alas, he is the sworn vassal of the character Molinet has identified with Divine Love, and is about to strike the first real blow in Anima's fight to achieve the Rose of espousal with a heavenly lover (by killing the enemy Malebouche). Molinet simply takes time out for a lengthy diatribe "a maniere de satiricque" against a character who thus vacillates from champion to enemy. A page later, Faux Semblant is among those read as "good," for when Malebouche's throat is cut, we hear comparisons to Judith's deed, to Christ and the Virgin destroying the enemy, to man's soul and body combining to achieve success as the Lover of the heavenly rose.

We observe one of the danger signs that indicates an invalid imposition of meanings. These dodges and shifts are typical. They have to be indulged in not only to accommodate stubborn patches of the original author's discourse, but to make some sort of coherent sense of the interpreter's own design. Both necessities are frequently illustrated in Molinet's twists and contradictions. Jupiter is read as Our Blessed Saviour when the tyrant-giants story comes in, but shortly thereafter must exemplify covetous snatching of power as the son who cut off his father's genitals; strict allegory that was unplanned by the author has bumped into ordinary moral reading. Reason, because keeping decorum she naturally talks reasonably, must be praised for a clear demonstration of the truth that "justice" is made necessary because love is not directing men's acts—while we are meanwhile supposedly reading her whole discourse as the false talk of the enemy deflecting the "bon champion catholique" (the Lover) from embracing heavenly Love.

These are not ambiguities, but untenably contradictory meanings tossed about to alight where they can find a foothold in the text. They differ fundamentally from the exploratory ambiguities natural to allegory, through which we watch a meaning gradually emerge in an image and take tangible shape, or in which an object or personage may be host to several similar identifications and we need not choose (as Bel Accueil Christianized could acceptably be grace, the Holy Spirit, or one of the Gifts like debonnaireté). Proper allegorical ambiguity is superbly illustrated in Jean de Meun's own Rose, which is played upon by the shifting lights of first one character's conception of her, then another. She is vulgarized by Dangier, shrunk down to one equation by Honte and Peur (worse than death), idealized (with sly reservations from Auctor) by the Dieu d'Amor, cynically identified with no further nonsense by Amis, similarly understood but quite differently experienced by La Vieille, flatly shown with the fires all lit by Venus, but appears as something cooler to Richesse who drives bargains on roses; and through it all, the Lover stands gazing through the thicket of ideas at a Flower. There we stand also, like him—and I would propose, like Jean de Meun—engrossed in discovering what manner of thing Love really is. We have the advantage of being the sole spectators who detect through the author's ironies the mirthful cracks he points out in each succeeding definition of the Rose. Molinet solemnly gives it all up to inform us that heaven with its bliss is beautiful, hard to get into, but attainable if wooed.

It is wise to realize that it is not some lack of plain sense in Molinet's identifications which makes them suspect. This is a result, not a cause, of his insufficiencies and desperate dodges.[8] There is nothing unacceptable about his major figurative conceptions, which are the familiar and meaningful ones of the soul as spouse of a Saviour who woos her by any and all means (97v and *passim*), a heavenly Venus who is ardent and flaming caritas

---

[8] It is only fair to Molinet to remind ourselves that this book was done by request, that he was aware of its tour-de-force character, and writes often as if he deliberately abandoned himself to ingenuity for the gaiety of it, playing on words and piling Pelion on Ossa. He belies the solemn stupidity of some interpretations by occasional lighthearted jokes; I will point to one, in the rolling boil of mock-serious observations on Amis's reference to good women being fewer than phoenixes (f. 57v). He thinks Jean, as a good Catholic, could have refrained from such comment, that though in the year he wrote there may have been scarce yields of fruits, nuts and *preudefemmes*, still God in pity for *preudehommes* would in a real dearth have created a few extra of the last. He then counts the number of 500-year periods (500 per phoenix) in the 6,000 years of the world; this makes 12, so "fewer" good women would be only half a dozen sown about the universe; one might pray for rather more.

(104v), indigent man who can only enter the Garden if his poverty, since the Fall, is remedied by riches given freely by his only faithful Friend (53v). These ideas are just as interesting as the course of sensual love and they assuredly were thought so up through the sixteenth century. If they were only truly present in the images of the piece, they could be portrayed in a moving structure that could show us what it is like to fall in love with Heavenly Love; and through quite fitting images, the rose and the garden and the storming of the heart, the barons who assist and the fire and the consummate bliss—all are familiar *spiritualiter*, and not foolish but descriptive and just. But it is typical of a set of meanings *not in the matter* that they are not only useless (as we saw) but that an initial false identification lands the interpreter in all manner of inconsistencies and dilemmas; these open the whole false erection to ridicule. Critics usually scoff as if the allegories were inherently ridiculous, which of course is inaccurate.

Molinet got himself deeply into such difficulties when he made *this* God of Love "nostre Seigneur." He has not one of the qualifications for the role, save that of desiring the unswerving allegiance of the creature he loves—an excessively common state of mind. It is insufficient to make the text support the imposed identification. Molinet's later troubles warn us to look very narrowly at the basis for the first decisive step taken in an allegorical reading; in this case we would notice that the God of Love is not shown as loving L'Amant (Anima)—a fatal omission. On the other hand, that it should appeal to us as a natural or sensible parallel is not essential; this criterion is an unsafe one in any allegory, and the old strictures about strained and "far-fetched allegories" will not serve for making distinctions. Contradictions between images and recalcitrant details that require ingenious stunts of interpretation are far surer signs of an untenable symbolic interpretation.[9] These are particularly costly if the text's

---

[9] Examples are countless; they are lengthy, but nothing else is clear, and I take space for one from the description of Nature. Molinet blandly demolishes his central point, only that he may tuck in the moral profit of "significances" for the five naked damsels whom Zeuxis used as models and even then could not by Art make a worthy portrait for the temple of Nature. Jean is modestly disclaiming his power to portray this marvelous character, God's chambrière and the great fabricator of all living creatures. Since she is beautiful beyond all competition, Molinet must ask us to read her as the Virgin, and the five models include

own deeper meanings are sacrificed. The instance outlined in the note well exemplifies this; Molinet's anxious ingenuity in attributing the egregious praise of Natura to the Virgin Mary cuts out Jean's own witty showing up of the merely natural. We quite miss the comedy of seeing this incomparable and superior being, Natura, made morose to the point of distraction by the perversity of her chief work, man, yet stolidly hammering away at her immemorial cure—more examples of him; she has no leave from the head office to stop doing so, and her confusion of mind induces such melancholy that it is no wonder Genius proceeds to treat her with extreme condescension as a hypochondriac female.

Molinet's greatest difficulties arise when his allegory forces him to get both Amis and La Vieille "on the right side," since both instruct the Lover in how to secure the Rose, and "the Rose" is no longer problematical or being defined (as Jean's was) but axiomatically a good. The difficulties are again instructive, for they show us objectively distinguishable signs that characterize an interpretation that will prove untenable—not because it is imposed, but because it is unimposable without transgressing the commonest of literary laws. Molinet's allegory differs from Jean's in that the latter identifies no one with the right side; thus he makes use of allegory's power to examine and reveal. Spenser is another master at this "examining," but he is much less daring about concealing his hand than is Jean de Meun, who elicits more laughter because he is more consistently ironic, and quite willingly risks our missing his point because he has wrapped it up in some bland contradiction that no one on the scene recognizes as an outrage, though we are expected to. An example is Amis's delightfully precise continuation of the Golden-Age cliché; it was a shining time before man's covetousness spoiled all sharing of beauties and goods, and we were free of the self-aggrandizing acquisitive man with his passion for keeping things for himself,

---

(f. 107r) Eve (with the flaw of a gluttonous throat), Duna (with a roving eye), Miriam (with murmuring tongue), Rebecca and Rachel. The function of this image was to claim that the natural is incomparably beautiful; yet now we have the beauty given to one who by supernatural intervention provided a remedy for the flaws of the natural. And the logic of the image had to show an artist with flawless models still unable to match nature; now the flaws in the models allow the creation to outdo them. Distinctions between God, Art, Natura are put into a chaos.

the accursed low villain—and onward flows Amis's advice showing exactly how to grab and retain one's charming Beauty for
one's sole use. How to keep two Beauties without its being known,
how to swear without scruple as long as that is possible, and how
to put on a good repentance scene when it is not, how to give a
bijou and get full value back, how to invent a dream of having
her in one's arms, or to make love at the moment it will pay off,
or a dozen neat ways to make her think she is free—which is all
that is necessary. The Lover opines, as Jean reports with a
straight face and no comment, that it seemed to him Amis knew
a good deal more than Reason.

The Lover is shown as falling for one after another insufficient
or damaging definition of the Rose, and we are never unaware
of the large element of truth or attractiveness each contains, nor
of the interesting fact that people always have so fallen; one's own
memory of how true the definitions sometime seemed is an ironic
note struck. Jean shows some gaping hole in every definer's equip-
ment, and his methods for uncovering holes have the widest comic
variety. In sum, of course both Amis and La Vieille are thoroughly
disreputable characters; and their conversations are strewn with
indubitable and fully specific proofs. These are distinguishable
signs of the resistance a work will make if its current of meaning is too stubbornly reversed or deflected. Hence Molinet's utter folly in reading Amis as the confessor the Lover needed in
his attempt to make Heavenly Love his own possession, and in
reading La Vieille as the sage and experienced mediatrix helping
the mind of inexpert man to get access to heaven's grace (Bel
Accueil in her tower), to know what chaplets of flowers to offer,
what door to try as being unguarded by enemies to his spiritual
quest. These are sensible enough ideas, and we easily read the
inner drama they could figuratively portray—but for the fact
that the two personages have no chance of carrying us toward
these ideas, for they were created (and it is the only existence
they have) to take us in quite another direction. It transgresses
the plainest law of literary coherence to expect parts of the whole
to go against the main stream of meaning when we are delineating a stream and not the struggle of currents. It is even too
much to ask that La Vieille be read as man's mediatrix the Blessed
Virgin. We cannot perform these moral somersaults, and find
the contradictions merely comic.

But Molinet's wildest infelicities are the fruit of disregarding literary decorum, and this is typical of bad allegory. It is not a matter of characters' morals but of clear communication. Literature could not exist if authors created anew the evaluations communicated by suggestions, associations, acts done, ideas espoused; we bring these, learned from a shared language, to the work. All the tiny arrows of Jean's epithets, details of appearance and behavior and tone of voice, point as loudly as actions and credos in one direction to denigrate the two characters. This is not rhetorical persuasion, but the mere action of language, based on innumerable common evaluations of experience. If in our verbal meetings with Amis and La Vieille the whole host of tiny assents and rejections direct their lances one way, no mere announcement of the characters' meaning can reverse them. Earlier poetics *named* this phenomenon. Words, images, details, cannot but "diminish" or "magnify," and if a Molinet wishes those which were specifically used to diminish a character, to have instead the operation of magnifying it, he will be disappointed.

These judgments are not chiefly moral, any more than our constant approvals, rejections, choices, as we live. Obviously La Vieille is an immoral sensual old woman, but Jean chiefly ridicules this sensuality masquerading as a full definition of Love, by the vulgarity of her expression of it: the small egoisms, the vanity and the low cheats, the loud-voiced red-faced grab she makes at pleasure and power, the tiny mind's delight at coming out on top. Her identification between lasciviousness and love, and her appetite for anyone who can serve as instrument to her pleasure, offends our taste more than our moral sense; we would not alter a line in the drawing, but it would be dreadful to be Bel Accueil and have her for company. That she has the keys is of course part of Jean's devastating observation.

Certainly he uses moral point plentifully as well. La Vieille's definition of "freedom" and her small notion of "the natural" is meant to be shocking, but her frank nouns are not so understood (and elsewhere the Lover's silliness on this score does not go unmocked by Jean; it is not undeliberate that Reason is the first one to furnish the fake-delicate Lover with this verbal shock). The character of the things she is "wise to" is Jean's ironic means of commenting on what Wisdom is, if a perverted mind were not distorting both Wisdom and Love. She knows how to wisely leave an appetizing few inches by a well-managed décolleté, how to weep for the occasion, eat "refined," manage disadvantages like bad breath or heavy breasts, how a wait sharpens enjoyment—if not too long—how to come to the point together, how to promise roses to one only while providing for open distribution. Her more general declarations are chosen for their contradiction of universally familiar characterizations of the nature of Love. Above all things, avoid largesse, rather sell dear (get a grip, beforehand, on the price); giving is to be adjusted to whether one gains largely by it; in sum, deceive the deceiver—and that covers all the lot of them. Although her reduction of anyone and everyone to instruments she can use to serve her desires ("freedom") is brilliantly satirized, and the admixture of enjoyment of power is as clear as are the low, neat tricks to get and keep it, and both are shown as immoral, it is the vulgar smallness and smelly squalor of her mental furniture that we mind. Venus's brandon seems a nice clean fire by comparison.

Amis's advice to the Lover has a similar mixture of immorality, which astonishes, and blatant (though more polished) vulgarity, which repels, conveyed by detail which refuses to operate other than pejoratively. The juxtapositions are far more subtle and ebulliently ironic. We are presented with high scorn for insincere friends with their sordid respect for riches, placed next to the advice on cheap presents and urbane acknowledgment of the utter impossibility of a tolerable life without money; eloquent disdain for low minds and vulgar hearts with their readiness to serve power and to judge by externals, is juxtaposed with the outline of exact methods for courting each rascally porter; cool advice on the moment to use force when one is picking roses is surrounded by the current best phrases about purity of intention and devotion to the courtly God of Love. The inclusion of the Jealous Husband's long discourse obviously has another function besides satirizing how faithless a woman will act if the proud fool thinks she has not the "mastery" when it is placed next to unabashed, complete instructions on how the male partner may at all costs retain the "mastery." The speaker tells just how to satisfy one's normal desires (one's infidelities, for example) without giving up a jot of one's freedom. The laments for the unfortunate entrance of Fraud, of driven bargains and tricky women's hypocritical deceptions into love affairs are placed in a discourse framed of nothing but frauds and deceptions. It is typical that the Lover is shocked at being expected to be hypocritically friendly to the villains, yet swallows Amis whole—the incarnation of that conception of Friendship and whose very name is an irony—adding thanks to him for his help. The accusations of women are loud; Jean makes them accurate enough, meanwhile making fools of the accusers. "Le Jaloux" provides us with yet another definition of roses, as conceived by one who has paid more than the going price and thought to have one conveniently at his disposal, and now finds himself frustratingly defrauded of it—but who should understand such flowers if not their owners? Yet Molinet can ask us to read him as the "jealous" Heavenly Lover who has to discipline the recalcitrant Anima, bound (as is true enough) to turn her love in another direction.

In other words, Molinet, by allegorizing a startling but moral work, makes of it a grossly immoral book. We have no right to hold this against him perhaps, but he has also destroyed a meaningful work and substituted an unconvincing tangle of confusions. Time and again the differences between the two authors indicate to us the differences between a good and a bad allegory. For Jean de Meun had a just sense of the peculiar possibilities of allegory as a figure, and his book is one of the few extant demonstrations that it is possible to have a secular allegory in the strict mediaeval sense, extending its explorations beyond moral interests to consider beliefs. Jean does use images to discuss ultimate destinies of souls (questions usually put in terms of man's reason for being), but they are so capacious—like Nature, or Pygmalion—that a reader ignores the direction taken for the nearer interest of the journey. Jean avoids labels; the use of named abstractions so frequent in good allegory is something else. But he talks about going to heaven more cogently than his moralizers; the Heavenly Lover and the celestial Garden are in his book more truly than in Molinet's, and it is only characteristic of what is possible in this mode that he presents no certified truths as Auctor's final word on the matter. We get a half-crooked, half-straight image of the different garden of another love, through the mind and speech of a personage who egregiously distorts both the nature of the place and the route to it (Genius). Jean never drops his method of sustained irony; we are shown only indirect paths, with guides being satirized as we meet them, and must discover what he thinks to be the relation between man's ultimate end and this ambiguous flower. By the conditions of his nature, man must turn it into an object of quest, a necessity and an indulgence, a devilish tool and a definition of the nature of divinity, a creative force and a destroyer, patently part of man-in-Nature and persistently conceived by him as a way of transcending it.

It is not, however, for his definition of Love or his general conception of the nature of the allegorical mode that Jean is outstanding, for many books are more profound. It is in his mastery of allegory's literary methods that he is brilliant and his late interpreters and imitators deficient. Indirection is formally and by definition a trait of the figure of allegory, hence the common praises of the power of such a continued metaphor to illumine matters dazzlingly, as the enigmatic enclosed meaning explodes in a firework of suddenly grasped metaphorical relations. It must, for this reason, be quite sure to go off. The great danger of imposed allegories such as we have examined is that they do not explode, hence the uselessness complained of. This will be found to serve very well as a test, for example, of modern interpretations of Spenser or Shakespeare; unless the imposed allegory picks up and lights many other details in the text as it proceeds, the identification will remain a mere statement, and never do a metaphor's work of opening out meanings through relations.) Irony is native to the figure—one reason for its long-recognized usefulness in satire—for it is an enacted dialectic and the author must convey his *sic* or *non* by covert indications.

These points describe the structure and method of Jean de Meun's part of the *Roman de la rose* very precisely. They also point to the reason why his extraordinary skill in using details and phrasings which bend all in one direction was of such importance; we catch his unvoiced comment as we would see a wind blow over grass, bent stem by stem to east or west. In this particular skill Spenser almost matches him. Although Spenser is far less daring about leaving his own attitude ambiguous, critics of his overplain moralizing are misled by the power of details into thinking the author has preached in plain statements. It is not the statements that make us conceive Hellenore's end to be repellent, Radegund's infatuation narcissistic, Error to have something of hellish ugliness, or everything about Acrasia to be untrustworthy. Jean shows better than any later allegory-writer that eloquence is less necessary than the restraint which waits while meanings arise and, by slowly coagulating into visible form, show surely for what they are. Yet an unerring sense of which tone and dynamics of voice to use contributes what we call eloquence to one after another of his brilliantly invented demonstrations of some position or point of view. The players who dance out this intellectual ballet must remain sufficiently generalized for the masque not to become confused with a drama.

In this connection we should notice that it is a pity, because it wastes one of allegory's peculiar powers, to overemphasize the second part of the *Roman* as a fiction. What is sometimes called "psychological allegory" has a character which suits Guillaume de Lorris' portion better, and we would not like to be deprived of the thoroughly pleasing work which resulted from his gifts (though, to me, much slenderer). He had a flair for most delicate observation, and for grace, and had a talent for minute dramas of motive or impulse, which were staged with tact and led to realistic insight into human behavior. That Spenser too had these talents, and that they had great literary merit, no one realized sufficiently until Professor Lewis's book displayed them to us like a new country. But it is important not to let Lewis's "country" usurp the title of "good" allegory, as have many of his followers, for it does not use the figure to its full power.

Metaphor's great peculiarity is that its particulars are like seeds, very proper "flowers" for all their display of purposeless beauty; they are Cyrus's to make more Cyrus's, in Sidney's useful phrase. Not didacticism but permanent relevance is stressed here, the opposite of singularity. Amis in the poem is not to be described as a marvelous portrait of a roué, an entirely self-occupied man-about-town with a shrewd sense of what will pay and a respect for good incomes, female flesh, and intelligence (as certified by success in getting what you want and never being stuck with what you do not). Although he is such a person, in the poem he is "The Friend." He is his own advice, personified. And he must remain enough of a "general" so that he can suggest what it involves to have such a character constitute one's experience of philia—even supposing a different era, different circumstances, different sex; he must show us the dire results of taking the position that he presents—that such is the nature of Friendship. He need not declare, for he acts out, the idea that what friends do is to "put you wise"; it is ludicrously unrelated to the Love of which it has always been such a famous species. He has, that is, a structural position, as have all the other "characters," in the whole examination of what Love is, for who ever heard of a discussion of Love that did not take up philia?

The portraits of the *Roman* are so famous, and praise of them and of the work's psychological niceties so nearly constitutes the only favorable criticism one finds of it, that it will do no harm to recall the limitations of allegory in these respects. Granted, Faux Semblant portrays those hypocrites who keep the veils drawn over the fact that "*constrained* abstinence" is nothing but a harlot underneath, with a harlot's attitude toward abstinence. But overattention to staying "always in sight of the fictional situation," "the fictional interest of the love-affair itself,"[10] gives us only an extra smile or two at the Lady's fluctuating states of mind, or the lovers' dodges for getting scandal put down (it took Faux Semblant and his lady to kill Malebouche). We purchase these trifles of fiction at the too dear cost of meditations on the ludicrous idea presented: in order to win his fortress, Amor has to take on, as a liege no less, this disreputable old fake whose existence and relation to abstinence show his adherence to the lowest possible definition of Love. The comical notions stimulated by this confession of failure and dependence on Amor's part are much more rich and interesting than the single fictional situation it can shadow.

Of course, it shadows also a real situation of the mid-thirteenth century. Faux Semblant is an embodied argument, on Guillaume

---

[10] I use the phraseology of a particular article not for its singularity of view but to escape the charge of vagueness. These phrases are used (p. 1180) by Charles Muscatine, in "The Emergence of Psychological Allegory in Old French Romance," *PMLA*, vol. 68 (1953), 1160-82, as are a few others used shortly hereafter in discussing allegory's usefulness in portraying the single or individual action or psyche (praised on pp. 1161-63, 1165n). But the points of view indicated by the phrases are so common as almost to represent the current definition of allegory's function. They are often either assumed, or stated generally as accepted truths, with none of the analysis, such as that relating the monologue to the development of inner dialogue, which Muscatine contributes. In any case, this substitution of psychological naturalism for metaphorical action is an unfortunate narrowing, influenced by the combined overimportance of the novel and of psychological description. The *Roman de la rose* is a vastly larger work than any novel could be, under definitions of the genre so far developed.

de St. Amour's side, in the quarrel against contemporary evils in the mendicant orders. Precise knowledge of how this topical satire fitted in clarifies the different strands in the allegory.[11] Yet overattention to the fictional-psychological situations operates exactly as does overattention to the topical applicability of allegory; by taking the story out of the metaphorical sphere, it leaves us with the mere singular particulars of history. It does not much matter if, in turning figurative discourse into history, we turn it into history which happened or a story which did not happen. The loss is exactly the same in both cases. We may see some very neat and amusing disguises for portraying historical events, or we may see some subtle mind-movements within a consciousness under the stress of emotion, but we have not seen the broad sweep of ideas in action, exploring problems of any time and any place, which allegory provides for us when metaphorically read.

This Machiavellian plan for getting scandals assassinated by the best people (for example, those who hold the contract for the friars) shows as nothing else would that Jean wishes us to see through the suspect preciosity of some highfalutin protestations made by Amor. The public answers to those who spoke ill of

[11] Gérard M. Paré, *Les idées et les lettres au XIII*ᵉ *siècle* (Montreal, 1947) and *Le Roman de la Rose et la scolastique courtoise* (Ottowa, 1941). It is profitable to read the *Roman de la rose* with the heavy annotation of a most particular description of the thirteenth-century controversy, for, as often in Spenser, knowledge of exact historical particulars which the story once shadowed to its readers seems to increase our power to see it as a metaphor for our own sets of particulars, and paradoxically enough, to bring it from the past into our present. Such information has long been easily accessible in Langlois' notes, even in Mary's note to section X (André Mary, *Le roman de la rose mis en français moderne,* Paris, 1949); or in Paré's two books, though these, the most informative, are slanted and show our special modern weakness: reading as "Jean de Meun's opinion" extracted hunks of text, without regard to speaker, situation, ironic force or author's attitude toward the speaker. I need not take space for a bibliography of *Roman de la rose* scholarship, readily to hand in the proper places, and fairly recent in Alan Gunn, *The Mirror of Love* (Lubbock, Texas, 1952). The weakness noted exacerbates the pronounced determination of most nineteenth- and twentieth-century writers to see Jean de Meun as an early "naturalist" and freethinker; Alan Gunn, an enthusiast for "natural" generation as a "philosophy of love," is especially liable to tendentious readings on this score. All tools have been used in determining a reading of the allegory (studies of sources, of manuscripts and editions, of background and philosophical milieu, illustrations, analyses).

Love (Malebouche) were a little different from the private arrangements made. There were family connections on which stress
could be laid; Platonic ideas were cousins, though no nearer than
some Christian ones. Jean's introduction of the falsity and hypocrisy of contemporary mendicant orders shows indubitably that
we are to think of how special a travesty their conceptions of
Love and their thoroughly loveless behavior were in the advo-
cates of a religion whose God is defined as Love and which exalts
caritas (agape) above all virtues whatsoever. It had not been a
Holy War until this note was touched. But now the credibility
of the whole new Christian dispensation, the "new" testament
as a true inheritance or as fakery and deception, becomes part of
what is on trial. If we overlocalize (in some single psyche) or
overindividualize the action of the allegory, we may come out
with a very clever way of telling a love-story, but we miss the
wittiness and daring of this final expedient alliance, and Amor's
entrance into it with his eyes open. It is a pity to give up the
ideas of a man in Jean's position on just what alliances *are* necessary if Love is both what Christians say and the possessing of
roses—and all in order to see two or three more little movements-
of-the-minds of individuals.

Too determined a conviction that allegory portrays psychological events is also likely to blind that roving eye which sees with
mirth how this same rascally liege is, precisely now and precisely here, still a chief support of a suzerain who calls himself
by this same name. To be sure, constrained non-abstinence is
more respectable in our times, but it comes to much the same thing,
and idolizes much the same rose, with a different set of local
wise-men to bring the definition into good repute. It makes a
good rule of thumb for detecting suspect interpretations to watch
whether we waste the author's jokes, and twentieth-century psy-
chologizing of meanings turns the most laughable works into
such dutiful case-histories that it may be our form of Molinet
in a modern alb and stole. When Amor tosses off the observation
that Venus his mother has taken many fortresses "in his absence," some very expensively built, it is quite simply a richer
entertainment to turn the mind free to speculate on that distinction
and on Venus and "her son" throughout the book, than it is to
consider how this may help to delineate the fictional situation of
Dreamer and Lady, where they pay allegiance, or how either
psyche is reacting to the other; we hope Jean does not intend

us to read thus. Amor is too interesting and complicated to turn him into steps in a drama in some single mind.

Neither do we wish to give up swift little sparks of wit that are gratuitous extras in the satire; there is Franchise's shield, that covers her so well as she advances in the siege against Dangier—Franchise the frank, the free, the generous, chivalry's noble opposite of a Faux Semblant. But the shield that proves so effective is one solid amalgam of easy promises, engagements, oaths, well-colored assurances, trimmed with pictures of Clasped Hands—one would think Largesse had made it. Jean is not the only one who knows a treatise or two among the many that handle *"vrai franchise"* (he later pulls in her twin "vrai noblesse"). The quick-moving currents of meanings that make this battle a comedy of the first order would have to yield to much grosser strokes if every detail, every trait of an abstraction, had to pay its way psychologically as part of an analysis of a particular mind, carefully kept to the then and there of its single situation. There is richer comedy in the thoughts thus set off about Franchise. There is no literary law against allowing subtlety to be in the things authors say, instead of residing only in the detected plural motives and self-deceptions we ferret out in despite of what they say; not all irony need be dramatic irony, and there can be wittier comedy in what authors notice than in what characters do not. The battle as described did take place in the Lady's mind, but we see it fought in many other places and times, and the satire bites sharpest when we notice where we are fighting in it.

Very often in satire the notions themselves provoke unreflective laughter—as with jokes, dependent on some suddenly seen relation or true sizing-up. It then muffles the humor and blunts the satirical point if we dare not look straight at the idea, but must confine our interest in it to the fictional mental act it is "behind." Even unallegorical mediaeval narrative has a more unabashed and immediate relation to the general than this. It is amusing to have maidenly Honte put to flight (and perhaps the bachelier's own; one need not be exactly sure which character one is "in") not alone by Volupté, which certainly happens, but by good old safe Bien-Celer—very practical. There is not much doubt that when Scandal's tongue has been excised, Bel Accueil will be "free" to smile; there is not a character whose conception of freedom is not satirized. That Love thought it sensible to stop the gossip with a little plain hypocrisy and unashamed false front, when he might have called upon Honour, Simplesse, Generosity, Courtesy (already among his soldiers), lets us see something about Jean's ideas of Love, not the characters'.

The frequent ironies and author's jokes we might miss are not the important reason why we should re-examine our tendency to give allegorical books first place insofar as they portray psychological processes. More important is the fact that this achievement bypasses some of the profoundest powers of good allegory. Concentration on achieving this may even be one of the limitations of Guillaume de Lorris, compared with the completer and riskier use of allegorical techniques which makes the second part so prodigal. One wonders if it would not shock an earlier writer to hear of Guillaume's "organization around individual character" and the "vicissitudes of a completely individual . . . action," "representation of a single female psyche." The major strength of allegory is its brilliant resolution of the problem of the relation of particulars and the general or universal, in works of art. The accolade awarded ("Guillaume's is a species which nearly resembles modern psychological fiction") is one given to a genre which has little use for such a strength.[12]

Moral allegory is the simplest form which that relation takes. A first disservice done by fastening our own conceptions of what is supremely interesting upon this earlier figurative artistry is that a divorce action is brought to separate moral from psychological allegory. The distinction is defined by a difference in the locus of the action: psychic or cosmic. But an extraordinary merit of allegory surely is that it does not part these. The extension of significance which gives great allegories their moving and permanent power to tell us something about man's relation to all

---

[12] Surely it is a twentieth-century literary idol we see described in this characterization applied to the *Roman de la rose*: "the analysis of an individual psyche, with its course strictly regulated by the conditions in which that psyche happens to be placed and by the combination of traits peculiar to it" (p. 1,179 Muscatine, *op.cit.* in n. 10 above). Hard to imagine as a statement of *literary* aims in any earlier century, that century which *has* so narrowed them includes neither the 1230's and 1270's nor yet the reading public of 1590. Allegorical writings may have been delivered from one strangling set of time-bound prescriptions, when Professor Lewis's book let them out of the dungeon of qualifying as realistic yarns with "real" characters, only to fall through the open grating into a deeper cell, where our later generation keeps *its* liberated persons to protect their freedom.

else we call real depends directly on the power of allegory to get the psychic stage and the cosmic relevance of what happens there into one figure. Even in the simple form, pure moral allegory, these are brought together. All the moral allegories we have considered, Guillaume de Deguileville, the images of the *Somme le roi*, vices-and-virtues literature try (in their several authors' capacities) to present the interaction between a mind's experiences and its responses, and precisely upon this depends their authors' hope that the presentation could not help but "fashion" a reader in virtuous discipline; Spenser certainly thinks of this presentation as *one process with* his displaying of the mind's workings. None of these writers of allegory would have understood setting forth psychic experiences if these meant nothing but themselves. That particulars "signify" is what gives them their absolute primary status in literature—which of course occupies itself constantly with presenting them, thereby refusing as stubbornly to be confused with philosophy as with psychology.

It is because its particulars may at any moment be seen for their metaphorical meaning that allegory could keep them so transparently tied to universals (not to concepts necessarily). Jean de Meun is very skillful in making humourous use of this double view, whereby ordinary sensed details mingle with meanings walking about in ordinary clothing. He likes to startle us with a reminder that we are living within a figure of speech. The quiddities we have been following as if they were simply acting, thinking persons will slip into phrasings that mean nothing except with reference to the metaphor we had half-forgotten they are part of; we are delighted when Amis vilifies lovers who are too meekly imploring or too prodigal with presents, because they "raise the price of roses"; or when Dangier explodes with wrathful scorn at the Lover's ingenious idea that he should be thrown into the dungeon with Bel Accueil and share his incarceration forever: "Metre Renart o les gelines! . . . Pour le beau rei celestre!" Bel Accueil deserves death, "Par lui pert l'en toutes les roses!" Jean seems to give us these little shocks of reminders that no detail is only what it seems especially when he wants us to watch out for some acute point in an unstated position, perhaps one of his own being conveyed solely through an irony.[13]

---

[13] This is the case with the double or triple satire in the passage where Reason

FIGURE 93*

We come to prefer these gambols of an omniscient author, fully admitting that fiction is a tissue of conventions, to the realist's guarded "point of view," his masks, narrators, or other devices for blurring the line between actuality and art. We enjoy his sly schemes to awaken us to his own more sophisticated interpretations of the rose, and to puzzle us as to whether he has them, when he underlines the special grossness and physiological literalness of what the metaphor means to characters like False Shame or Cowardly Fear of Detection—the tone is comic throughout their sober description of the awful consequences, in case some wind blows pollen where it ought not to be, in the fearful case that the leaves fall away and disclose le bouton, a disaster. No novel with narrative's ordinary pretenses to preserve could afford the mirthful passage where the God of Love calls his barons together and supplicates them with joined hands to come to his

* Please see the List of Illustrations and Sources following the text.

---

discusses what's in a name, and juggles with the names *relics, cullions, thistles, roses*. Or when, by making Amis the mouthpiece for the glowing description of simple unacquisitive life and shared women in the Golden Age, he throws suspicion on both the "freedom" and "Love" of the relations Amis finds so enviably irresponsible.

Figure 93, with its pair in the pastoral Golden Age-garden modeled nearly after the illustrations of the sin of Luxury, shows that at least the illustrator of MS. Douce 195 (fifteenth century) would have smiled as he spoke of "free" love. As in Tasso, prelapsarian "freedoms" are selected, admired and praised for the most grossly wrong and postlapsarian reasons, even supposing a quite sophisticated reading of the Golden Age-garden imagery.

aid for the sake of his loyal servitor Guillaume de Lorris, over-
taken by death in the midst of his services or at least for the sake
of that better servant Jean Clopinel who is to be born at Meun
sur Loire. He is at a loss for counselors, with Tibullus and Catul-
lus and Ovid all dead and rotten, and Guillaume embalmed in
myrrh and aloes, and Jean not yet born (though he will be the
champion of them all, for he will have the intelligence to turn
down Reason's treacherous advice out of hand, lns. 10560-670).

The self-revelation through which some abstraction draws its
own lively portrait (in which we have already followed Guillaume de Deguileville applying the lessons learned from the
Roman de la rose) is a natural allegorical device for much the
same reason. It too is treasured, despite its proving an awkward
method for a storyteller, an outright violation of the conventions
of non-allegorical narrative, which is bent on showing what is
psychologically true without endangering our belief in characters
as psychologically credible individuals. For such self-revelation,
by Faux Semblant for example, is not the unrealized self-betrayal
novelists use to make fine points about rationalization or projec-
tion, nor is it the introspection which dramatists use in soliloquies
supposedly unheard, nor the novelist's device of allowing the
flow of consciousness to be observed. Faux Semblant must instead
be incredibly false—that is just what is true about him; we are
meeting essential quiddities, and they are themselves unbelievably
"in character," beyond belief. The ordinary dramas and puzzles
of life are caused by mixtures, whereas here we have the constant
sensation of not believing our ears as Faux Semblant, *pure* falsity,
and other characters, exulting in their identity, deliver themselves
with bravado and gusto in brash and gloating monologues such
as we quoted from de Guileville. This exposing of essential identity is part of the mode.

Richesse is one of many smaller examples. She disdains the
Lover as small pickings but also makes no secret of how he will
repent that he ever followed her path of Folle Largesse once
poverty gets hold of him at the exit. We are not to ask why do
these golddiggers gives themselves away? Psychological truth
is the goal, but it is not the kind revealed in personalities credible
because they seem to have mixed natures like all men. Such ones
must hide their nature and motivations to remain acceptable in
human society; but we are seeing hypocrisy and self-seeking and
wealth, who remain in it because they are valued *for what they*

are. Constrained Abstinence does not put on the airs of Abstinence; she travels with a useful second who obviates the need
to pretend. Her sermon to Malebouche on temperance of the
tongue is alive with ironies, but it is her crony Faux Semblant,
and not abstinence of any sort, who has the kind of merits needed
for acting as the unlicensed confessor of the victim. Amis and
La Veille are a little different in being bundles-of-qualities as
well as abstractions impersonated, but they make themselves completely known, not by mistake, but in full sight of the fact that
A Friend (this brand) and A Doorkeeper (this variety) are useful to servants of the God of "Love." Or so Jean is claiming.

It is a cunning stroke, not an anomaly, that Faux Semblant
is the mouthpiece for an open acknowledgment of the valid stand
of Guillaume d'Amour, whose damning criticisms of the mendicant orders were supported with vigor by Jean de Meun. A less
skillful allegorist would have made this rascally abstraction an
enemy. But why should the declared hypocrite "friar," Faux
Semblant, mind the accusations? Their truth is not disagreeable
to *him*; his conscience gives him no trouble; rather, he is pleased
with himself at having brought off these little victories. As everyone knows, the accusations are the usual ones touching usurpation
of the functions of the secular priests and the duties of university
theologians, as well as the charges of hypocrisy, feigned humility
and poverty covering actual ambition, avarice and pride, the
lucrative confessions and easy pardons, the catering to the rich
and powerful and the breaches of the rules, hypocritically em-
braced, of chastity and poverty.[14]

We are surely not meant to forget all these typical references
when toward the end, Genius, Nature's confessor, is provided by
Amor with the right *clothing* to sit and issue pardons in (this

---

[14] See n. 11 above. Jean himself proclaims the connection, and the ideas of
the book are illuminated by familiarity with such matters as the steps in the long
quarrel, the books published by each side, Guillaume's unexecuted sentence of
banishment, etc. The fact that a large section from Guillaume's condemned
treatise is incorporated into Faux Semblant's speech (vv. 10900-11926), as
noted by Paré in *Le Roman de la rose et la scolastique courtoise* (Publications,
Institut d'études mediévale d'Ottawa [1941], pp. 165ff.), does not point to
relaxed artistry. It was a very bold stroke, and stands out in the new context as
an object-lesson in allegory's power to impose new meanings on borrowed materials.

FIGURE 94

FIGURE 96

Comme nature se confessa
il Dieux q de beautez habonde
Quat il tresbeaux fut ce beau mõde

FIGURE 95

seems to make them as legal as need be);[15] he lightly tosses off an
excommunication or so, on grounds that appeal to him and his

[15] The famous illuminated MS.Harl.4425 (fifteenth century) has him togged
out as a bishop; see Fig. 94. The kegs on which his temporary platform is
supported, and the character of his auditory, are enough to tell us whether this
illustrator thought Genius's sermon and pardon in the text was to read as a
serious revelation of the nature of love according to divine intentions. We see
very clearly from the altar where Genius does his offices what the illustrators
of MSS. Douce 364 and Douce 195, thought of the Divinity taught by these
two characters, and whether the "Religion of Love" was being seriously regarded
by the text's author. The naked figurines (Figs. 95 and 96) are the regular convention for portraying a pagan altar; placing them where the tabernacle stands
which did contain "love itself" and referred to the sacrifice made by Love, for
love of men, is a most outright and shocking blasphemy certainly, to any mediaeval eye. Genius's bourgeois clothing and Nature's look and actions are not unrelated to what she and Genius really worship.

penitent. He then issues a pardon so absolutely inspired that Love's barons cry "Amen! Amen! Fiat! Fiat!" with holy joy. It gives a masterly breadth to the whole satire on what "Love" means to men, that the epitome—Faux Semblant—of all the wrenched values and false dealings which Guillaume d'Amour's accusations exposed, should be the character who without a qualm accepts the charges leveled at the friars as true; there is general agreement that the qualities are equally expedient for any servant of the "God of Love" who wishes to succeed. This is not cynicism on Jean de Meun's part, but by playing on "the God of Love" and on the ambiguities of "love" (the subject of the book), he is able to show men how sadly far they have strayed from the fundamental principle they have perverted, once the ground of virtue and an attribute in the divine as well as the best human nature. "A servant of the God of Love" should describe a friar. It does.

But in this garden, the Love that has been deified himself admits falsity to partnership and contracts the allegiances with hypocritical self-serving—the very charges made by St. Amour and other critics against the friars. Suppose, as a less subtle allegory-writer might have had it, the endorsement of Guillaume de St. Amour as an accurate authority had been made by Reason, or by some "reasonable" character standing with him on what Jean de Meun thought was the good side. No such advocacy could have supported Guillaume's strictures as does this open acceptance of the friars' deceptions put in the mouth of the abstract quality which, in them, made their conduct possible and, in others, made it successful. This damning acknowledgment is only possible because allegory can allow the self-revelations that other narrative would find disturbing to credibility.

Faux Semblant can declare outright that Guillaume's picture of his mother Hypocrisy, in his book, was so accurate that it has brought about her exile, and can laugh openly at the fool for expecting him, dissimulation itself, to prefer work to begging; and he can also pour salt in all the cuts Guillaume makes about friars—not by being a bad one (finding a bad one proves nothing) but by showing the real decay that makes falsity the only tool their sort of "loving" service can depend on. One can't get anywhere *au siècle* (two illegalities already, for a friar, who has nowhere to "get" and is not of the "world") on that old super-

stition about fearing God; let John the Baptist have his sojourns
in deserts to himself, for see how well it works to go on living in
the world and simply say you've left it; he'll go where something
can be got and let other shoulders ask for burdens, which are not
his forte. Faux Semblant's explosions of blunt "honesty" and
"realism" are a usual form for that illusion and should be read
with double meanings. We refer them in the first instance to the
corrupt among the friars and are shown in each outrageous misdefinition what a travesty it makes of Love for it to need Falsehood as its servant. But we see simultaneously exposed in Faux
Semblant the pretentious servants of *fin amors* who serve only
themselves and have no notion of what "pure" love is. Jean does
not tire of ridiculing lovers who are too good for nature, but he
does it in the voice of those who understand neither agape or
eros. Yet one cannot be unaware that the pure Love the friars
are supposed to be serving is more truly drawn through the
ironies of Jean than through the blasphemous "misequations" of
a Molinet.

Jean's method is very risky, as is amply clear from the obloquy
he has received from critics who speak of his paraded learning,
his large undigested chunks of interpolated encyclopaedic materials, his digressions. This is an unhappy and undeserved fate for
an author who shows such extreme subtlety in using juxtapositions
for ironic point, in making the arrows of his satiric points all face
in the same direction, or in choosing just such details for his long
monologues as will nail the speaker to a monstrous inadequacy,
and pierce through him to nail his interlocutor to an equally monstrous acceptance. But he has been read time and again as if he
were writing straightforwardly, and not in allegories at all, or
as if his use of the figure consisted of his putting the names of
abstractions upon persons. Even our slow return to a sympathetic
reading of allegory had to wait upon changes—not primarily
literary—in interests and in the kinds of questions which could
be hospitably entertained by serious readers; it is no great wonder
that a complicated, vast web like Jean's should have suffered
longer than other works from the last century's impatience with
"dark" figures and with didactic point, and from our own century's impatience with past authors who seem not to speak of
our concerns in our language or who make fun of our idols. Nevertheless it seems to me undoubted that Jean had every expectation

of being understood when he uses his oblique method of long-sustained irony and definition by unacceptable misdefinitions held up to scorn.

When the Dreamer replies to Reason that he intends to serve not her but only the master he has chosen, that he intends to have the rose and has made himself over to Amor whether it means hell or not, his wilfulness carries without comment the shock of idolatrous, wrong allegiance. That Reason's precious friend Socrates is not worth three chick-peas and he wishes to hear no more of him, or that he declines to take off into the clouds, assaulting paradise like a modern version of the old giants, in pursuit of this wild "heavenly" love which even Reason admits isn't found here below, are two from an army of details showing Jean's characteristic tone when he is banging the head of one of his stubborn characters against a wall and wishes the stubbornness to appear absurd. The reader does not miss the fact that the moment Amis has concluded his remarks on the fatal entrance of acquisitiveness into men's affairs, the Lover makes off for the path of big-presents and gives up Richesse's help only because a man out of pocket is no man for her and she drives him off. We are to observe, even though the Lover does not, since it is part of the point that he is too obsessed to see anything, that Amis is the very pattern of the passion to "get"—without paying, in any coin whatsoever. Jean does not seem to think it necessary that any character on the scene should *remark* (and whom could he draft for such a role without spoiling his figure?) how all the elegant idealists of fin amors hasten to apply the somewhat gross hints they get from the rascally "honest" realists; silently repeated throughout the piece, this grows comic.

Jean has suffered as much for his reticence as Spenser for his great moral plainness, though perhaps from better readers; this would amuse him if he knows it. The parody of required elements of the faith (see Ch. Two above), when the Lover reels off the Ten Commandments on demand, and the catechist goes on to the Three Consolations, mocks not only the dévots with their Ladders of Humility and Pomanders of Penitence, but equally the elegant amorist with his cover-up jargon and his pathetic triviality. The author's setpieces are the great known images, abused or just twisted askew by their users, i.e. by the natures they are seen through, as the exempla of Lucrece or

Hercules are distorted when viewed by the frustrated husband, the Golden Age by Amis, Mars and Venus and the net by La Veille. Though no one in the piece can be safely read and believed, Jean de Meun is serious about the meanings of love, all love, and the degeneration of them, as Molinet is not. Jean allows every liar and slave to misdefine freedom, but not because he thinks there is no such thing. By letting those who are ignorant of freedom define its nature, he shows the nature of each enslavement; all are familiar examples of it, especially Amis's to self-interest and La Veille's to sensuality. The Lover is pliant in all hands but Reason's; of her discourse he hears only some frank words that offend his courtier's taste, and chooses only to argue hotly some old stereotype like the notion that Reason is counseling him to hate all the world since he is to avoid fol amour.

Amitié, or love of one's neighbor as one's self, and the large image of Fortune (from Alain de Lille) are given what comes closest to an untendentious presentation in Reason's voice. But the mantle sits loosely on her shoulders too. Off our guard, we think Jean careless not to make her wooing of the Lover such a thing as might charm and find assent; but it dawns upon us that he means that irony too. She does not understand her subject. Few of her best defenders have ever claimed that she could.

It might be claimed, and I do not know the answer, that Jean fully intended as one of his points the one great and shocking omission from his book: any character who loves anyone. It would be very like this writer, and whether or not it was meant to satirize men's excesses and misapprehensions, it surely does so. The world of the *Roman* is quite loveless, lacking markedly its multitudinous common forms of disinterested affection, kindness, generosity, kept faith, good will. Self-love and self-interest are anatomized time and again. There is no attempt whatsoever to portray caritas. This was certainly glaringly apparent to any mediaeval reader. He was accustomed to at least lip-service to a sacramental view of marriage, and to a New Dispensation whose displacement of Synagoga was founded on the new testament of "love." The omission of her heavenly form agape, and of caritas within relations, and the few cold words given by Reason to love-of-all-men, certainly does not argue that Jean did not admit their existence, and need not argue that he saw no relation possible between these and men's usual loves; nor does it point to the fact that he was skeptical about all that he and his readers knew from the scores of treatises and literary works that handled his subject.

We find ourselves building a definition for love by negatives, as we progress through the ironic presentation of unrelieved inadequacies and deceptions and rationalizations and errors. Genius and Nature for example are not being condemned (intentionally at any rate) for evil ideas but shown as laughably dominated by inadequate ones. The stifling lack, and real untruth to experience, felt at the omission in question may point to its being deliberate. The author does convey by it a deep (though never mirthless) disillusion with men's capacity to solve the immemorial riddle of how to relate their natures to their destiny and raison d'être. If Jean thought it possible to convey thus without statement the appalling contrast between love as it is possible and has appeared in men, and the titillating indulgence to which they have narrowed the word, we would no longer be puzzled by the brilliant physiological tour de force which forms his closing image. It is chiefly puzzling in its audaciousness, that is, in that its manifestly intended salaciousness is never "answered" by other definitions of the rose, elsewhere suggested. It is a brilliant satire on the basic pretenses of "courtly" love, and the choice of Pygmalion who *worships* the stone body for comparison with the Lover's own worship of the sanctuary is a masterstroke which has not gone unnoticed by illustrators.[16]

[16] Pygmalion was as famous as Narcissus as a cliché for vain self-love and idolatry. Illustrators not only touch off a little flame of condemnation in showing him so clearly idolatrous (usually kneeling in adoration) but the humourously portrayed chipping process as he brings his stone lady into a receptive state makes sport of the *folly* of his misdirected love; it seems to me sure that this idolatrous deification of another human being was recognized as the real sin behind "courtly" love. We are familiar with both strictures, the idolatry and the folly, even late as in Bacon (*Of Love*). See Figs. 97 and 98, from edition *C* as listed in Bourdillon, Douce 194 sgg. S8r, v. The inner sanctum-and-sanctuary imagery of the passages following baffles the illustrators, when they try to suggest the obvious lascivious meanings (see later illustrations for some efforts); Jean was surely quite aware that it might have the effects feared by the shocked Christine de Pisan, yet there is no doubt that it stresses the aspect of idolatry, already touched in the exaggeration of the Genius-priest image borrowed from Alanus (his vestments, altar, fake remedium, pardon, promises).

This entire section, like the commentary on the Pygmalion and other images, and on illustrations, was written before the appearance of D. W. Robertson's

FIGURE 97   FIGURE 98

Yet Molinet had the truly shocking taste—for he knew what
he was doing, and so did readers—to advise that this image be
read without "lubricity" as a vision of deduit spirituel. By every
principle we have noted, this is an unprincipled imposition of
allegory. Molinet's disregard of responsible allegorical reading in
favor of mere equations with what he would like to have the
piece mean, has been exactly matched by modern determination
to rescue the author from aesthetic condemnation only at the price
of reading *its* favorite gospel (and especially "naturalism") into
his work, again ignoring the author's own allegory. It is hearten-

Preface to Chaucer (Princeton, 1963). Similar emphases (*Preface*, pp. 195ff.)
were quite independently arrived at—the warning against limiting the narrative as subject, the characters and functions of Raison, Amis, Genius, and
special suspicions aroused by the last named, the illustrators as witnesses, the
quite devastating relevance of Faux Semblant's allegiance to Amor—through
mere care to read the piece with attention to its aesthetic and formal nature
and especially to the allocation of speeches. The critical remarks referred to
(see esp. pp. 99ff., where Pygmalion is most specifically treated) stand almost
alone among modern interpretations in remembering that the piece is a
literary one, with personages speaking and acting in character not as exponents
of the ideas of Jean de Meun, with tone an indication of meaning and author's
attitude a relevant problem to be faced. Though I am not sure of the continuation of points into influence on Chaucer's *Knight's Tale*, and of the *Sir Orfeo*
points, because of yet other literary indications, and am less willing to limit
meanings so strenuously, concurrence with the general drift of interpretation of
the *Roman de la rose* has the added element of relief for unjust strictures against
Jean de Meun set right.

ing to see how stubbornly the allegory, the figure born with the piece and part of it, refuses either imposition. Evidently, we cannot impose a reversed stream of meaning, or an irrelevant and tangential one.

One thinks it true, however, that Jean de Meun wished us to be uncertain of the tone of voice in which he says "the Lover got the Rose," and I waked up out of my dream.

Powerful as this last image is, it is not as audacious a literary device or as magnificently controlled as his great five-thousand-line image of Nature.

Whatever the English Renaissance may have learned about allegory from this much-published book, they did not learn that daring which silently entrusts meanings to ironies hundreds of lines in length, or that insouciance which allows readers to make what they will of an image and impose a meaning if they find it not. We can wish that wordier later writers had copied the daring; the insouciance is a more doubtful virtue, as it leaves the presumptuous and the faithful reader equally in danger of impositions which in the end turn out to be creatures of our own fashions and personal predilections. Despite every attempt to stick to Jean's text, I would not dare to claim exemption from this danger—the inescapable hazard of a metaphorical figure. But there is this great reason for taking the risk, that the image of Nature has been read without apology as expository writing, not allegorically; friend and foe alike have lifted the large section free of complicating relations, design and function, and with a bow to Alanus, read a discourse as if by his familiar character.

The claim has already been made here that but for the vast and many-sided earlier mediaeval development of religious allegory—in its stricter sense of a second significance pointing to matters of creed and Christian dogma—the very few greatest literary exponents of allegory could not have achieved works of such profundity and philosophical importance. This is obvious enough with Dante; it is less clear, but nonetheless valid, touching *Piers Plowman*.[17] It may seem quite untrue regarding Jean de

---

[17] *Piers Plowman* should have had place in this study but for difficulties of language and no convenient unimpeded text for quotation, for paraphrase will not do in analysis of allegorical writings. Perhaps a more important reason is that it is hard to be satisfied concerning the form in which the sixteenth century knew the work, or how well they knew the later sections where ways

Meun, and the claim may seem like plain special pleading in the nearly allied case of Spenser—Protestant, very late, no theologian, in addition to being preoccupied with Jean-like themes such as love, nature, power. A truly severe problem faced the artist who wished to make use of those habits of seeing multiple significances which had been developed in readers by the centuries of allegorical reading of religious writings, to use the methods of indirection, and fictions hiding-dark-conceit, which had high renown in poetics, who also wished to handle problems not triflingly and yet not with the pre-decision they would have if they appeared in a religious formulation. Moreover, such an artist quite often neither wished to nor could write as if Christianity did not exist, and he within it. We can call this problem the secularization of allegory.

A similar phenomenon may look to be opposite. When the material given more serious significance by the familiar method of allegory was not only worldly but classical, a fairly direct solution was found to unify the two heritages; classical gods and images were read outright as figuring forth the truths of Christian belief —they merely Christianized a classical invention for giving seriousness to old fables of the gods. We have seen this in Christine de Pisan, and the example par excellence is the *Ovide moralisé*. Molinet's unsuccessful translation of the *Roman de la Rose* into a potpourri of images with Christological meanings is an attempt to work this transformation upon non-classical secular matter. He does not study morals; instead, he reads everywhere one great figure of allegory—Christ's loving pursuit and final salvation of the human soul. A plain imposition of Christian

---

of reading must keep pace with the broadening of the significances and it becomes apparent that the author is not simply writing moral allegory and social satire. The author's prestige as a "reformer" draws a red herring across our path, in judging how he was read, although in general we are too nervous about English Renaissance readers avoiding Catholic associations, for they recognized common Christian inheritances better than we. When more has been gathered regarding editions, ownership of manuscripts, contemporary reference, and kinds of modernization (of concepts too) judged expedient for Elizabethan readers, the large hole left by neglect of *Piers Plowman* in our understanding of sixteenth-century use of our mediaeval past, can be mended. I am frankly uncertain of how sixteenth-century Protestants of this vintage and that would read the great figure of the Tree of Charity, for example. The problem is a problem of fact, not of critical opinion, and there are several kinds of evidence to seek.

doctrinal meaning upon a secular fiction was a radical solution which Spenser scrupulously avoids (in my judgment). Jean de Meun had avoided it before him.

However, Jean de Meun had marked success in secularizing allegory, without making it trivial. For once, it appears to me, we see in literary history the results of the right choice between two paths. Spenser seems to me to have learned from observation *what* not to do, but also, and this probably from Jean, *how* to use large images in a huge design, philosophically profound if allegorically read. It is hard to be so certain about other individual writers, but our gratitude for Spenser's fortunate choice would be enough. Jean is first (and sometimes alone) in showing certain merits which were later eminent in Spenser and almost singular in him. His work is certainly moral, as Christianity understands morals. The question of whether it has "a relish of salvation in't," or disregards that matter, is more complicated. There is no relish in't of the kind of fake typology that Molinet allows, or that imitated and extended typology forced to include pagan figures (that "mean" Christian dogmas) used by Christine. He gives the appearance of simply not discussing the kind of love which redeems man's soul, as reflected in his behavior to his fellows or his conceptions of love in marriage and the generation of offspring. But he makes contrast apparent by juxtaposing non-religious problems or informing ancient ideas and figures (like Natura) with the philosophical ideas of Christianity, based ultimately and visibly on acceptance of allegiance to a divine creator; he draws thence a definition of love from that misdefined and misdirected love—the self-regarding passion that seems "natural" to men.

That Jean shows a sad series, each one comic, of misdirected "loves" is sure enough. But he cannot so much as broach ultimate questions arising in minds like those portrayed in Amis and La Vieille, in his possessive Husband and willful Dreamer. What he can do is indicate self-aggrandizement and self-indulgence as the roots of error. He treats the pertinent matters of wrongly conceived freedom and misdefined purity. The whole piece is an organization of a few images, each occupying hundreds of lines, and some of his other largest images are less busily taken up with moral and institutional satire, and evoke strong associations with their archetypal or conventional originals. He exhibits to us an erotic garden which is far from paradisiacal, a picture

of unrest, where distinctly postlapsarian inhabitants make traves-
ties of the paradise-images (the Golden Age, the happy marriage,
the rose, love itself); nevertheless, I would argue it to be accident
that his La Vieille is a degenerate Eve and his Amis a Cain, and
that there is no Abel. We have a God of false Love with a satirized
trivial Tables of the Law, false Consolations of the Spirit, and
a set of false barons who (again haphazardly, a gratuitous joke)
bear five of the seven names of the Gifts of the Holy Ghost;
and the "God" employs two representations of faked purity with
cynical admission of his need for them. The extended image of
Reason, daughter of God who woos the human Lover, includes
more than one suggestion that the Lover has made an idol of
"Love," though that is something continually in the process of
being defined throughout the work; irony is used to prevent a
reader from finding in Reason an easy answer to the total problem—it would not be a Christian answer. But the longest image
in the work is that of Nature, which includes that of the priest
Genius, which in turn encloses that of the Garden of the Lamb,
and these knit the whole fiction into a unity by reaching a climax
in the taking of the fortress with Venus's help.

It will repay the student of allegory to look at some of the
minutiae in Jean's presentation of the vast image of Nature, for
no literary virtue is clearer throughout his book than his care
and skill to bend all these in a perceptible single direction conveying some point of view, all but tacitly. Venus and Amor have
just led the barons in the taking of their oath—sworn on their
darts, their arrows and their firebrands, as true as Trinity, since
these they "will never abjure" (nothing is more sure; all are
phallic synonyms; of course, a deliberately shocking oath, with
this indication of the intrinsically holy). All men must do Amor's
works, and all women put castitas out at door. Here Nature enters
the action—she who occupies herself with all things, "under the
heavens," at least, says Jean significantly. She is seen re-entering
her forge, for her assignment is to keep anvil and hammer so
continuously busy that a never-ending stream of individual beings
appears to step into the places of those Death destroys. We hear
that she is profoundly depressed; though she enjoys her work
(ln. 16,151) and the oath solaces her greatly (ln. 16,250) because it will mean full-steam forward, we learn that she is of a
mind to stop off her forge-work entirely if she could get leave
(ln. 16,161).

Like her priest Genius, we assign this inconsistent resolve to her temperament, for indeed, despite her conviction that the product (or the major line of it) is deplorable, the sole solution she and Genius have for any ill, at any point, is to heat up the forge furiously and wield the hammers with renewed fervor, and her every complaint turns around the necessity of keeping production up. The heart of the long planctus, as everyone knows (remembering Alanus as well), is her suspicion that man is a mistake; everything is wrong with him, from pride down through every vice and subvice. But for his sins, she leaves those to God to punish (ln. 19,325); her own action in the matter will be to increase the number produced. Her chief concern is with man's failure to do his part in continuing her work with anvil and hammer; what use to furnish him with her tools, when he has become slack about paying her her tribute (lns. 19,331-334); and mournfully she forges a few more hundred. Her laments are piteous; where to find troth kept any more (*feiz*)? Has she been wasting her labor? Frantically she pounds out a new series. Her very amiability is her undoing ("ma debonaireté m'afole," ln. 16,271).

The three hundred-line gap (apparent from my numbers) between phrasings of Nature's despair over the unnatural behavior of her top-ranking creature is taken up by two motifs, as everyone also remembers: she does not appeal to her avowed master but to Genius her priest, in an extended "confession" which has little to do with guilt or penance, but amounts to an encyclopaedic survey telling why she lodges no complaint against planets, elements, plants, animals—no one but man, the one with free will. Her chaplain is distinctly *her* priest; he is celebrating mass nearby, "en leu d'autre messe, Devant Nature la deesse" (ln. 16,277). It is no new office and consists simply of displaying in a loud voice the natural forms of existing things, which he copied in his book as Nature delivered them to him (for satire of his "altar" see Figs. 95 and 96).

The confession-complaint is no more curious than the central sacrifice in admiration of the natural they have set up in this church; and it would be strange if any thirteenth-century reader missed what we notice, the complete absence of any deity but Natura in the "church," the office, the absolution, or the agreeable penance ("avenant e bone," ln. 19,416). Even we mark the special absence of the idea that nature and all living things cannot but glorify their Maker—which is ubiquitously the emphasis in such contexts, and the one we fully expect. The break with borrowings from Alanus is abrupt and noticeable, for his Natura is firmly a dependent, though of great dignity. Jean has various sotto voce indications of the ersatz character of the whole religion. Genius takes down Nature's dictated instructions, which are such as would be issued by a supreme religious power, and goes off by wing, changing into less encumbering worldly clothes; each flatters the other as supreme authority (he master of things, she queen of the world); he is dispatched with full power to excommunicate all their lax adversaries and to give those who will keep the forges going full blast a pardon not for a few mere years but for all the evil they ever might do. The motif of priestly clothing donned and doffed at will comes in again when the God of Love fits him out with the necessary chasuble, ring and mitre, and Venus lends him a taper (not of virgin wax, but no matter).[18]

Of course these crafty innuendoes about confessions and pardons and borrowed clothes have also their relevance to Jean's satire on the mendicant orders, but taken thus they simply make the same point about what gods are really being served and what kind of notions of man's duties and proper allegiances are being allowed to pose as religion. The comedy is not parodic, with love-religion details, but witty or ironic, touching intellectual positions; the tone is kept comic by making Genius a blandly condescending male, and Nature a poor faulty female, not overbright. The confessor, with the comfort of many unflattering examples, charitably makes allowance for a sex which is given to emotional disturbances, easy tears, and quick angers; he cheers his lady penitent by adding to this theme the equally apropos second theme of the unwisdom of telling your secrets to anyone; keep them to yourself. Granted, the superb picture of the married man who has no more sense than to confess to his wife does not cover situations like that of the moment, where a Man is the trusted vessel for secrets. Genius vouchsafes the graceful addition that Scripture says his particular

---

[18] Of course, the love-religion details are an entirely conventional device by now, and it is normal that they are entirely profane. There is no blasphemy in such jokes, of which we have elaborate early examples (as in works by Bad-quin and Jean de Condé). A difference lies in the fact that such witty works are not occupying themselves with the philosophical questions which are here the issue, but are descriptions of love, pretending only to treat erotic subjects and merely using the language of another "devotion"; Jean de Meun, on the other hand, loses no opportunity to make us take the image of Nature as stating (directly or ironically) a position on the nature and duty of man.

lady penitent is "sage senz fin" (ln. 16,706). "Genius ainsinc la conforte," says Jean ironically after four hundred lines on "fuiez fuiez fuiez la fame," and la fame Nature is immediately on her knees. She is fully conscious of her feminine infirmities, chiefly of ladies' prolixity (she has progressed some sixteen hundred lines, and has another thousand to go). "Fame sui, si ne me puis taire . . . vueil . . . tout reveler"—as Genius had charged (ln. 19,218).

But her confession is not prolix. It is an interesting example of Jean's selection of commonplace material, which he then compels to imply something it does not usually imply, and thus evoke our judgment on the speaker. Nature shows none of the ordinary forms of hybris in erecting the only law she knows into the sole and entire end of all things—work unceasingly according to your nature, which for planets is "turn," for elements "mix," for plants "grow," for men "reproduce"; for all things, quite simply "live; process is all." She reels off a few of the usual acknowledgments to God who started things, but His place in her discourse soon becomes just that of the form of words proper to swear with. He commanded her to see that "the forms continue," and she advances this cycle of generation as the reason *why* everything in the universe exists, with reiterations which become quite comic—in effect, whatever the intention. All values, for all creatures, center in this final end of hammers and anvils kept busy. She has become the Goddess, and constant forge-work the way to worship her, for we never hear more of the role of chambrière, with its modesty concerning final causes. This is not presented as condemnation, but appears as a particularly vivid way of saying that nature sees only natural functions and laws, and does not know about, certainly does not consider, ends. Her end is to keep plenty of things alive, and if there is beauty in anything, it consists in potent arrangements for keeping things going. The sinners are: suicides, celibates, eunuchs, Empedocles, Origen, and of course Orpheus, and those who abridge their lives by disregarding the rules of hygiene.

She has no great occasion to recognize any possible order of reality other than her own (creation seems to call for decidedly less admiration than procreation), but when she bumps into some fact from another view, the Incarnation for example, she makes short work of it; it took place without her, she does not know how. She gives numerous passages to ironic comment on supposedly supernatural phenomena—meaningful dreams, inescapable destinies, resurrections, demons with claws (not worth two radishes as causers of disasters; strong winds are more likely). Lazarus, said to have been resurrected, is a special case. But the miracles she finds fascinating are those of technology. Here, as more subtly earlier (especially in those portions where the life of the senses is erected into the end of human existence), we are plunged into laughter at the aptness of the satire for our own age and its special idols; it is hard to believe Jean did not foresee us. Nature is most humourously held up to the satirical eye in her earnest solemnity about the hammers and anvils; but we see a simpler aspect of the future coming as she proclaims the true miracles—such as burning-glasses, optical illusions, distorting mirrors, or the kind of mirror-microscopes Mars and Venus should have had. We have speculations on how they might have detected the net, which she submits to Genius; Vulcan could not then have proved their adultery. Very useful, for they could easily then have gone elsewhere, says her confessor. The point of view is *natural* enough, for adultery carries on the species quite as well as marriage; and these various little departures from the unalloyed praise we have come to expect are typical of Jean's gradual portrayal of an inadequate set of purely "natural" criteria for evaluation.

There are occasional larger shocks which often take the form of some blandly inadequate statement on a familiar problem. Some intensified passages portray the relentless pursuit of all things by Death, and their terrified running from his black face, ten years, twenty, forty—a flight entirely and without exception hopeless (lns. 15,890, 15,915ff.). The image is picked up in Genius's address (lns. 19,753ff.), and the bizarre and dreadful passage on the Fates and the ravages of Atropos is one of the few in which Jean shows that power of poetic imagination we are accustomed to meet in the greatest poets; the image of Cerberus at the three breasts of Atropos is inventive, frightful and frightening. When Genius tells us we have but one enemy, one danger to guard against (lns. 19,757, "un seul nuisement"), we are startled, but the whole heavy push of these passages rolls like an avalanche toward that impressive statement. Then we realize what Jean has said, that to Nature and Genius the cessation of physical existence is the supreme, the only, danger, and that both believe entirely in Nature's hammer and anvil as a *remedy* for Death, his sole and his sufficient defeat. Our only enemy! The implicit definition of Life is surely being deliberately pointed out. We may be certain of this when we watch Jean sandwich the powerful passages of Genius's speech in between his calculatedly incendiary and vividly physiological adjurations: "drive the plows! lift the hammers! to work! no cooling of the engines, no resting, to work!" We are aware of what crowd he addresses, and hover between laughter and astonishment, for Genius's oratorical flights are irresistibly comical, and need only to be crowned with the report that when he finished his "bon sarmon" (ln. 20,686) and threw his sacred taper to start the conflagration, the lieges of Amor shouted "Amen" in joy. "Si grant pardon" they never had heard.

The power of images is subtly misused, by a logical sleight of hand, and this will be found to be a typical method of Jean's in all speeches. Here, though indeed the death of the species is circumvented by Genius's command, "put your mind upon multiplying," this "death" is not what their minds are engaged with; death is not thus conceived, and circumventing it does not avert the Death so fearsomely pictured. These are the tricks of rhetorical persuasion at any time. But few contemporary readers can have missed the satirical fact that Genius has done what Guillaume de St. Amour accused the friar-confessors of doing— given free rein to irresponsible and self-indulgent human desires under the cloak of divinely sanctioned purposes.

At first we may not notice the absence of all recognition of man as a spirit, or of any of his spiritual capacities (even that for intellectual development; we hear no nonsense here about an immortality secured through a sonnet); but the confinement at length becomes stifling. This effect is simply one strand within Jean's determined exclusion from his book of all presentation of Love as positive goodness of will, caritas, agape, beneficence, affection, misericorde, sympathy. These omissions were certainly not unremarked. He treats a subject which was handled in treatises by every important theologian and moralist, and all the puzzles he introduces for our consideration are ancient, common ones; so also Nature's encyclopaedic review skirts the ideas and the problems of supremacy and relationship made famous in a score of expositions. But unlike those, it takes care of them all with one simple notion—the one we notice every spring when a thousand fertilized blossoms ensure the dozen apples of the autumn. But this is Nature speaking; Jean himself is aware that the traditional naturalistic definitions and "solution" are no more than a part of the problem. He is careful that all its complexities arise in our minds; he then has either vicious or inadequate persons confront them. We feel the dull thud of anti-climax in Genius's speeches especially, when an "answer" is produced. Yet this is a moment which is almost always made humourous.

However, the constantly humourous texture is rather a result of the scores of tiny absurdities or niaiseries which decorate the long discourses of speakers who are being shown up. It is not enough that Amis is not author of one single friendly utterance; his speeches betray an avaricious, sensual vulgarity even when he borrows them. Details are minute distortions or illogicalities of the order of Nature's complacent recognition of the animals' ignorance of their power as an evidence of "natural order" (monkeys can use their hands, and if they took up literature, men would have to look to their laurels); or her remark that she cannot go into the scientific explanation of distorting mirrors, as the "laity" make sense of nothing which goes beyond general propositions. The author is careful to make Nature not wrong but incomplete on numerous issues.

The idea that even Nature is being seen as exponent of an inadequate view may be unwelcome to those who take deep satisfaction in her defense of free will and her definition of noblesse as Nature's gift at man's birth, a gift unaffected by his lineage. The latter, a stock subject for discussion, glaringly omits the stock grounds for every man's equal opportunity to achieve nobility— his spiritual heritage as son of a divine Father (we saw the point made in the *Somme le roi* and Guillaume). Hence her argument is full of ironic inconsistencies, which show as unavoidable if the grounds are to be naturalistic. She defends the nobility of those who till the soil—telling aspirants to devote themselves to the noble pursuit of arms; she supports the cause of noblesse based on "bon courage" and "bonte de cueur" by the unsmiling claim that clerks are all noble since they can read the books and see on good authority what to avoid.

As in many of the speeches, but Nature's especially, we could not hope to put a finger exactly on where Jean starts and stops believing what he has his creatures say in this tissue of ironies and sincerities, truths and monstrosities. It can scarcely be accident, however, that the pictures of reasonless chaos, of floods, storms, destroyed streets and towers, followed by calms and rainbows, are an "order" supposed to contrast with man's willed disorders but instead resembling them. The aimless fertility which sends the fishes swimming among the drowned temples or produces ants or insects in dangerous millions to challenge man's power provides the vividest visual images in this presentation of ceaseless procreation as the cure-all. The representative of natural, naked truth free of illusions is openly fascinated by the illusory and delusive appearances which natural phenomena can produce, her new "miracles"; the picture supposed to show up man's disharmonies and unnatural vices is that of an "orderly" universe of creatures at each other's throats—birds to peck men's eyes out, wolves and lions to devour anything defenseless, and so on.

At any rate, it is apparent throughout the clearly tendentious handling of familiar materials that Jean has been too carelessly charged with throwing in great gobbets of borrowed "information" unaccommodated to his own purposes and the whole subject. Molinet failed in his pretense that such accommodations and purposes could simply be blandly ignored or shouted down, and another purpose substituted; but modern interpreters have followed the same course in the opposite direction. For it must be suggested that those who have accepted Jean as an out-and-out exponent of naturalism—whether in dismay or (as is now more frequent) in delight at finding a thirteenth-century defender of nice, clean, honest, healthy generative functions as a definition of Love—have not sufficiently considered contexts and speakers, audiences and startling conclusions to arguments. Early pious critics (like a Gerson) feared the partial reader,[19] with justice as

[19] The famous quarrel over the *Roman de la rose* of about 1400 (whose jeu d'esprit quality we have inadequately noticed) shows the point of view of pious censors rather than serious unconscious misreading. Gerson has an eye to the morals of his flock, Christine to the prestige of her sex. Of course, I find it plausible that Jean knew and enjoyed the fact that the surface of his piece was lascivious in effect while, in sum, images ridiculed or exposed the purely sensual as incomplete. Chas. F. Ward's old partial treatment of the quarrel (1911) needs to be superseded; references to it and other early work are in Robert Bossuat's *Manuel bibliographique de la littérature française du moyen âge* (Milan, 1951), #5385ff. But later work not directly so focussed is sometimes as

the event has shown, but also we have become even more unaccustomed than the readers of 1400 to figures which stretch over hundreds of lines, or ironies which are maintained through half a book and never labeled save through the stupidity or exaggeration of some final reductio.[20]

Nature's simple confusions are mild compared with those Genius provides for us. The pre-eminent example furnishes one of the few incontrovertibly deliberate "shockers," for Jean usually prefers the indeterminate and ambiguous effect of leaving us a loophole for believing the outrageous things we hear. It is Genius who is allowed to describe the lovely parc des brebiers, the true Paradise of the white Lamb who shepherds the sheep, with its olive tree and its fountain of life. It is most familiar to us in another art than literature, and we are accustomed to the necessary translation of all its details into symbols, for all are known and common ones. The quality of this image has received much notice, its function far less. One of the main objects in its introduction is to allow the ludicrous assumption by Nature's priest Genius that entrance into the Heavenly Jerusalem is in *his* gift: you shall drink of this fountain, you shall go into the field of delight, following the Lamb's steps, you shall sing eternally under the olive, the Lamb awaits you (lns. 20,267-650). You shall not be prevented from entering, "selonc mon dit e mon acort." The consent and the opened door depend upon the one condition we now expect but still find startling as well as deliberately ridiculous

informative, for example, Alfred Coville, *Gautier et Piene Col et l'humainisme en France au temps de Charles VI* (Paris, 1934); I find myself in sympathy with the witty if somewhat exasperated oppositions in A. Combes, *J. de Montreuil et le Chancelier Gerson* (Paris, 1942), taking previous students to task for their oversolemn building up of pseudo-animosities, their parrotting of each others' "evidence" in the name of a doctrinaire "humanism."

[20] Those who are familiar with *Roman de la rose* interpretations and literature of recent decades will recognize that the complaints of this paragraph are not general laments but specific references to the extant books and treatments. We have been well served by the attempts to clarify the thirteenth-century matrix of thought, less well by the direct criticism. What is not so directly attached is often equally illuminating and less tendentious; I would mention work on Alain's (and contemporaries') conceptions of Nature (as in G. Raynaud de Lage, *Alain de Lille*, Montreal and Paris, 1951) though Jean corrects or deserts Alain as he pleases. Or some work and some citations under the topic "The Goddess Natura" in E. Curtius, *European Literature and Latin Middle Ages*, pp. 107-27. See n. 11 above.

when it is flatly stated: the lieges of Amor must vigorously perform Nature's forge-work; they are to admonish those who are
laggard with their hammers, and to make their own acts accord
with their admonitions. The barons are only too happy to comply.
Genius's understanding of the abundant life is laughed at from
the start, for these matters are introduced by the injunction,
"pensez de mener bone vie." To our interest, this is immediately
continued by the dazzling elaboration "Aut chascuns embracier
s'amie. . . . E baise e festeie e soulace" (lns. 19,885-888).[21] The
irony is broad.

Genius has already proclaimed, by pronouncing the excommunication and by offering the pardon, that the power to say who
shall be admitted to this other Paradise, of other Love, rests in
his hands. But Jean makes this wild usurpation, by *Nature's*
priest, evident to the least attentive reader by the audacious use
of the most famous of anagogical images and by tightly locking
Genius's *promise* (!) of Christ's eternal redemption to that
narrowed definition of doing Nature's works which has been fixed
in our heads by continual vivid reiteration. If at first we were
surprised by the seeming interruption of the Paradise image by
digression on the special wickedness of castration, or by discussion
along the way of jovial Jupiter's instituting of division and strife
(in the name of Pleasure and Appetite) and our descent thereby
into the age of iron, we soon perceive that as usual Jean intended
all the relations he introduces.

Jean does not stop short of using all the traditional anagogical
symbols, despite the closeness to blasphemous distortion; he is
not the speaker. The olive-tree "Qui porte le fruit de salu" (ln.
20,523), the Tree in the Heavenly Eden, is both Christ and
cross as is usual; from it flows the fountain of living water, whose
three streams unified in one though triple, whose three-faceted

---

[21] The slightly veiled, ostensibly moral injunctions which enclose the promise
of salvation (be loyal, be piteus, mixed in with "serve-Nature" by inscribing
tirelessly with the stylus provided, hammer away at the forge) are punctured
by inserting such anticlimactic thuds as a command to return the funds you bor-
row, and if you've spent all, then resolve to do so when next you have extra.
Such parodies of the commonplace that repentance includes restitution were obviously intended as such, and the definitions of penance are of a piece with the
bathetic injunctions on the Good Life (besides satirizing friars). Similar tactics
make clear what Genius means by a "black" sheep, unfit for the garden, offering chances also for jokes on whether angels wear white wool or hair shirts,
and double-talk about the orders as well as getting in on one's clothes.

FIGURE 99

stone, radiant and indivisible though three, with facets separate but inseparable, openly points to the Trinity. Some illustrators attempt to make the same sort of lascivious transformation of the imagery which is represented by Genius's naturalistic misreading of the whole image of the Garden of Heavenly Love.[22] The wrench thus given to the relation between text and picture is comparable to that we feel in watching Genius pervert the known images. Yet also his hypocrisy in contrasting the two Gardens, his taunts about the "pin" and remarks on Deduit's doomed dancers, is felt as justly grounded denigration of the pseudo-spirituality and elegant cover-ups of Amor's courtly feigning. It

[22] See Fig. 99. There is no chance that the illustrator does not know what he is doing, when he mis-portrays the flowing of waters of grace from the Trinity by translating the imagery (into conceptions such as Genius might have had on how to enter "heaven"). For the text illustrated is the part about the Three seen often to be One, but never adding to a Four; ostensible references are entirely clear. Though this manuscript, Douce #195, is from the fifteenth century, it shows care about the allegory, keeping Bel Accueil a man, not mistakenly the Lady (I do not understand his marked look of maturity), and portraying an embrace when the Lover takes the rose, though with no attempt to represent a scene. When early on he is allowed the kiss, he kneels beside flower, not girl; minor "characters" are, on the other hand, ably represented as persons; Nature hammers out "kinds" (even a bird) rather than merely babies to fill cradles, and the Golden-Age picture shows the same attempt to weave in an ambiguity (see Fig. 93), though the sanctuary imagery was beyond his skill. There are attempts to stress Nature as God's vicegerent through commonplace religious images, and to portray the horror of death. The castle-on-fire is quite amusingly a proper fire-outbreak-scene, and is allegorically more sophisticated than pointing at its meaning.

FIGURE 100

is not the habit of this author to allow us the easy assumption, this is a "bad" character and we are for whatever he is against, though this is a common device. We have to watch the decorum of the details and of the whole. Moreover, the Eternal Garden is not mocked; it should seem like Heaven and it does, as we compare it with the unrest and pretense of Amor's. These and many other distinctions are not laborious; the decorum comes effortlessly from Jean's clear-reigning ideas and the intelligence with which he practices the literary virtues and devices for indicating drift which we distinguished earlier. He has fully prepared us for the accompanying criticism of Amor and *his* Garden, and has made it in other ways.

The Pygmalion setpiece that follows picks up this mockery of affairs with the stone Lady who can receive worship but is too cold and too fin for the affair to be consummated in sexual relations. Much else is mocked. Pygmalion as a current counter for lechery and idolatry is not dissociated from the image, nor are the idolatrous aspects of a misdirected love unemphasized (idolatrous and fond not because it is physical but because latria is given to a creature; see Figs. 97 and 98 and note 16 above). The long image is allowed to seem as if it were casually brought in on the wing of a comparison of statues, but it both mocks pretended delicacy and slyly joins the nearby image of luxurious Venus's part (disguised, or not) in taking the fortress, all the fortresses.

All this supports the deliberately lascivious purport of related passages, like the culmination of Genius's sermon, but especially the image of Venus's target for her direct hit, the sanctuary with its statue. Illustrators may make matters quite clear by a naked statue with genitalia aflame, which Venus shoots at (see Fig. 100);[23] others may handle images in ways which might have seemed to Jean like the hypocritical pretenses he mocks—e.g. MS. Douce 195 shows the Lover regarding the "sanctuary" as a gallant kneeling by an amply dressed Lady. The words and images Jean himself put in underscore the fatal perversion of a divine conception much as does Spenser's eucharistic image used of the "love" of Hellenore and Paridell in the *Faerie Queene* (III.ix.30).

Perhaps the most daring instance of Jean's willingness to rest all on the allegorical method, with its indeterminate conclusions and veiled presentation of the Author's point of view, is found in his "conclusion" with the frankly sensual, or rather lustful, final metaphor. But by now we have seen satire playing upon a good many of the Lover's deceived acceptances of half-sufficient definitions of what Love-the-rose is. We have followed every step in the taking of the fortress, had every chance to see what Auctor thinks of the Lover for identifying these two, and in the clear light of the systematic development of the large Genius image, which makes it lead to the grand conflagration, there is not much chance for us to take the final brilliant tour de force as a defense of honest, healthy, generative "Love" with Nature and Venus as twin presiding goddesses. Jean takes care to make the image exceedingly narrow; there is very little "love" in it, especially in the sense the writers of the Middle Ages used that complicated word. We are intended to have a hard time finding even Venus as a cosmological principle lurking in any image.

The mere exercise of reading allegorically, maintained through so long and so complicated a work as the *Roman*, was bound to

[23] This manuscript, Bodl. e.Mus.65, is early (second half of the fourteenth century, written in England); but even later illustrators usually understand the allegorical mode too well to introduce the Lady in person (of course, she could be said to be in the picture). This manuscript pictures lovers in bed at a major "forge" passage, but the fully figurative portrayal (Natura pounding like a smith) is completely typical of both manuscripts and editions; of course, it was understood as phallic, and emphasis on its crassness points Jean's jests.

teach a craftsman much, for both its authors are highly skilled, and the second so brilliantly intelligent that his mastery of arts peculiarly important to allegory is uncannily adept. Spenser at least was sufficiently a reader with needs, and a devotee, to notice such arts with sympathy and profit; I think he learned most, as we do, from pleasure in Jean's wit. Men of Spenser's century, I am sure read, the *Roman* not as a text annotated by a Langlois, but in modernized French prose or verse re-doings;[24] luckily Jean's talents, narrow in some ways, chiefly produced effects which do not vanish in prose redactions—the large controlled structure, the way to make details "signify" and the special decorum with which they must be controlled, the way abstractions are presented and the special understanding of "characters," the ironic wit, the tone not depending Romantically on associations but on other factors (sometimes visible in eighteenth-century poets). Certainly the existence of a sample of the *Roman de la rose*, by Chaucer,[25] insured its being read by Englishmen. Spenser's predilections, and concerns as a writer, argue an interest that would soon find these fragments insufficient, and a man with Natura agitating his mind as a subject does not omit the most famous poem about her since their common source. Granted, it must not be too hard to get; but here, to hand in several editions, lay something Spenser, at least, knew was unusual—a good example of secularized allegory.

This is so rare as even to be "experimental," but still we should beware of claiming exact lines of descent, for which proper evidence is irreparably lost. Methods are those common in good allegorical writing, but good allegorical writers are not common.

[24] The editions available to sixteenth-century readers in French can be more spaciously described where they are the subject, and a good idea of the woodcut tradition is also obtained from F. W. Bourdillon's *Early Editions of the Roman de la rose* (1906). He speaks of some twenty-one in forty years, and when names like Marot's were attached (even to hackwork), or Chaucer's and Alanus's, interested readers did not neglect works so related to their own. Even Molinet's several appearances are explicably popular by the fact of his straightforward modernization. These readers did read something a little other than the poem we read, and unfortunately, such relations are (in work after work) part of the unexplored territory students have not chosen to explore. The aesthetic validity of our criticism much depends on such knowledge.

[25] Printed as his since Thynne in 1532; no sixteenth-century reader had any inkling of three parts and authorship problems. Easiest to consult are E. Hammond's lists (*Chaucer, A Bibliographic Manual*, New York, 1933) in her section v and *passim*.

Jean de Meun and Spenser belong in the still more select company which shows that allegory severely and knowledgeably defined could be the key to right reading of secular works as well; it seems sensible for the later man to have learned some of his rarities from the famous accessible earlier one. It is folly to consider the "influence" of such works upon each other in the usual terms of story motif, similar ideas, concepts and definitions and attitudes. Virtues that make allegory successful are quite locatable technical merits.

They are likely to be large, broad literary virtues. Some things are observed rather than learned; for example, a poetic skill so universally essential as managing the decorum of details. All poets learn this, but it is true that it is peculiarly necessary, if one expects to be allegorically or ironically read, to watch cunningly over the natural power of details to magnify or diminish a subject. Important to any poet and possessed by them all, this can be, in allegory, the sole instrument for communicating evaluations and ideas. Jean de Meun's details are those of indicated tone of voice, exempla used or misused, phrasings that demonstrate quirks in speakers' minds or underline some idée fixe, states of mind made apparent as characters, usually minor, that explicate or espouse points of view. The consistency with which all these arrows are made to point in one direction is subtle but does not result from meticulous planning; Spenser's host of details in his storytelling is similarly single in direction, but their variety is staggeringly greater.

The two poets are not at all similar in texture or quality of detail, the most striking addition being Spenser's plethora of visible detail; it is not always pictorial, but I do not think the reasons for its suitability are very recherché, as they are not in the other storyteller. We have only to think of scenes wherein tone of speeches, attitudes of mind, or irony are meant to be pre-eminent, like Braggadochio's meeting with Belphoebe (II.iii.), to remember how natural it is to Spenser to let us know also how things looked (on a sunny bank, the wood, the scarecrow). He seems instinctively to allow the significancy of images to be underscored by our inner sight of them—the fowl that comes out and shakes itself, the peacock with tail feathers. His characters' talk is full of visibilia ("kisse my stirrup," "dead dog," "foure quarters of a man"). Each bears its tiny load of opprobrium or magnification ("roses in a bed of lillies," "many Graces," honey, music, stars), little pushes toward an inner judgment; they have this not as a gift from the author but from the meanings inherent in the language of men's ordinary experience. The ridicule is transported in different vessels in the *Roman*; only when we look back upon a tract of it do we realize that we are never told how anyone looks or is dressed, how they mounted a horse or lifted a weapon—but an attentive reader (Spenser, for one) with his own allegory to write, must have noticed how unimaged particulars can be made to do that very work of magnification or diminution. This poetic virtue and this skill, common to good poets, does not set these two men together, but its relation to allegory does. A continuous exploitation of this aspect of language is so useful to an enigmatic figure like allegory (just as with irony) that men generally learned it by seeing it successfully used by others. Spenser possibly all the more readily watched and followed Jean in making certain larger decisions.

That Jean de Meun does not himself allegorize by reading Christ as actor and the events of Christian story in an ostensibly unreligious action, may be claimed provable. It is also apparent as we read Molinet that Jean gives no foothold for those who would impose such interpretations upon his large images. When we claim that it is impossible to think these (of course unstated) meanings present in his piece, we are on solid ground, not simply contributing an opinion; we have noted objective reasons why the images "will not read" in this way. The same kind of reason will apply to any poet (like Shakespeare or Spenser or Chrétien) where similar imposition is now attempted. But that is not because the imposed reading in all these cases is religious; absence of religious meaning is not at the heart of our grouping Spenser and Jean together as writers of secular allegory.

Neither author wishes to accept and substitute the values of saeculum where once those of religion took precedence (by such a definition both periods in England would show singularly little "secular literature," and this would be grossly untrue). But religious values are not directly the subject, as they are in the church's holy books, in liturgy or allegorical devotional literature. When Jean uses Genius to expose the folly and untruth with which Natural Man presumes to deal out salvation, or uses the figure of Nature to build slowly in us a realization of nature's limitations, we are meeting ideas no less religious than when

Molinet tries to get in Christ wooing the soul and securing her love. It is not in being religious that Molinet's kind of reading belies the nature of the work he plasters it upon.

But it is one thing to discuss, through presenting a religion as subject, the ways in which man is a spiritual being with a spiritual destiny, and another to show man leading his life in the world and discovering ideas which are in that religion. It is of the greatest importance to know which of these subjects the author is treating. They do not differ simply, distinguishable, for example, as we distinguish doctrine from morals. It is Christian doctrine not Christian morals that we are brought to consider by trying out the stances in Jean's dialectic of images of love, or Spenser's.[26] We are not only concerned with philosophical questions; we are concerned with them as they are metaphysical rather than ethical. These themselves are not the subject; their coming to life allegorically as persons is not the subject; but, this trying out of stances raises all such questions and leads us to believe or reject answers.

We may not impose upon poems subjects their authors did not choose. This is a basic problem in modern criticism and is the real reason why Molinet's allegorizing was unimpos*able*. In Molinet we were presented with an easy case, which helps clarify the matter where modern attempts at imposition of meanings seem to fall nearer the border line of possible truth—meanings imposed on Shakespeare, on Chrétien, on Spenser. Subjects, unlike the often enigmatic meanings of images, must be not just implied, but *there*.[27] The author's position on such matters is not always

[26] The brevity of the life of secular allegory is a foregone conclusion—a fundamentally religious figure erected on such presuppositions as God seen as the architect of history and of the universe. The unobstructed flow of narrative onward to solutions bodying forth the truth of Christian doctrines held only while readers were a small homogeneous group seeing the truth of the Christian revelation in all history, in previous writing, in natural phenomena. It could not long survive even the jolt of the Reformation, though antipathy to the figure is overstated because of misunderstanding of terms (especially of "literal" meanings, in the arguments of Tyndale and others); this and related complexities vitiate the often-cited article "On the Meaning and Function of Allegory" by J. McClennen, in *University of Michigan Contributions in Modern Philology*, vol. 6 (1947).

[27] This demand that the seemingly imposed subject be truly *in* the original work, though terms, images, incidents may receive an imposition of meaning from us, is to be distinguished from the familiar claim of "unconscious meanings" discovered in a work. These are admittedly different (even ironically

easy to find, but it is not entirely hidden, and it is up to us to look responsibly. He may, for example, deal with a subject without realizing the full meanings of his terms, as in psychological discoveries made before the development of depth psychology. The principles which were found to govern imposition of meaning and warn us of unimposable, nonexistent inventions of our own, will hold. We saw them pretty well subsumed under the grand heading that the decorum of the whole piece must not be violated. Statements about that matter regard substitution of subject, though the phrase is never used, and the craftsman's problems, not the reader's problems, engross men's interest. But there exists no Elizabethan or Stuart rebel against established poetics in this regard.

Of course these complexities are not new to the discussion of Christian allegorical meanings given to classical images.[28] Only a few classical images, artificially made into Christian symbols carrying meanings and thence poetic subjects which Christian symbols more naturally carry, achieved this status successfully; only a few carry potently the meanings imposed. For example, Christine de Pisan uses, with the unusual addition of explicit theoretical comment on her own method, materials which had not been read allegorically, or even read "morally," to convey points of Christian dogma; if we look carefully at some of her attempts, we may observe whether there are any reasons for success and failure. The attempt was a widespread habit which influenced the functions of classical images in authors who did not practice it (as I think Spenser and Milton did not) and varied with authors

opposed to) the author's ostensible and intended meanings; they betray unrealized contradictions, and confute rather than complete or fulfill his interpretations.

[28] Complexities have been most apparent to students of the visual arts, and the distinction between "classical themes" and "classical motifs" in Panofsky's *Studies in Iconology* is the best known attempt to isolate the problem. If its most sophisticated complications seem to be here disregarded, this is partly because verbal evidence is so rare, lesser artists like Christine do not give us clear evidence on subtler matters, and partly because I wish to keep to explicitly declared intentions, and so on. Of course, the literature germane to this question is quite impossible to cite; see n. 2 above and later notes on the *Ovide moralisé* (touching which there are selected later citations in Panofsky's *Renaissance and Renascences*, pp. 75ff. and notes, referring e.g. to Lavin's bibliography in *JWCI* for 1954).

and with times. Since the examples are diffused in numerous
fifteenth- and sixteenth-century works, an examination of the one
most explicit text, the *Ovide moralisé*, will lead us only to outstanding principles, to be applied with qualifications to other practitioners. But Christine, who declares what she is doing, was popular and unforgotten, was read, was available in print in illustrated editions, and was translated.[29] The combination is under-
standably unique, for theory and practice are usually separated,
but sixteenth-century availability confirms its value for our purposes.

Christine, like many allegorizing readers, embarks on a far
simpler endeavor than did Molinet. She will escape his most
dreadful flaw, of shattering into fragments the unified work being allegorized, because she had no great work to shatter. It will
be recalled that she takes up one hundred separate figures, selected from the general stock of classical myth and story, and
also that contrary to the title later given her, "Cent histoires,"
she does not tell one hundred stories but interprets one hundred
personages or story-moments. That keeping of decorum, at which
Molinet failed so lugubriously, and which is so fundamental in
making material carry an imposed meaning, is hence a simpler
task; there is seldom a whole stubborn fiction to be read through
the glass of a new symbolical import in the personage. More than
this, her book takes its basic structure from elsewhere, a familiar

[29] We study no obscure fifteenth-century text in Christine's *Épître d'Othéa*.
P. G. C. Campbell's study with that name (Paris, 1924) lists thirty-six manuscripts and additions have been made; several are famous for their pictures,
and early became so. This is true of the editions (also listed); Pigouchet's
first printing, *ca.* 1490, had one hundred cuts, and there were editions in
1522, *ca.* 1518, *ca.* 1521, 1519, two others; see Saxl, *Cat. of Astrol.* . . . MSS.
III. The three English translations (one made and printed *ca.* 1540) are noted,
as well as a corrected manuscript list, and studies, in Curt Bühler's "Sir John
Fastolf's Manuscripts of the . . . *Othéa* and S. Scrope's Translation . . . ,"
Scriptorium, vol. 3 (1949), 123-28; Scrope's was edited by Sir Geo. Warner
for the Roxburghe Club in 1904 (see his Introduction) and will be re-edited
by Bühler, from the three extant manuscripts. I cite other work where relevant
and necessary, but the literature on this well-known author is large; since the
French *Othéa* seems unlikely to be in print, see for some points on her work
and on the manuscript most used here (Laud misc. 570) and its iconography,
the two-part article by the present author in *JWCI*, I used for the *Ovide
moralisé* Vérard's *Bible des poètes*, 1493 (*et seq.*), a virtual reproduction of
Colard Mansion's 1484 *Ovide*, leaving citations for later notes.

Christian organization shared for historical reasons with many other works. It has been noticed, but the aesthetic significance thereof not to my knowledge pointed out, that she handles the Seven Virtues, Twelve Articles of the Faith, Ten Commandments, sins and so on, giving us a classical image which may be read as signifying each. Her *Othéa* thus joins the large group of earlier *sommes* which were produced and were popular for the reasons given in Chapter Two; it is an ingenious little classical *Somme le roi* with adornments.

It has therefore an ordo and purpose which give to its artificially created symbols a kind of witty usefulness and point which is fulfilled with an unexpected success. Its purpose is only half-seriously a mnemonic one, for the book was ostensibly written for a boy of fifteen, possibly Christine's son, possibly the young Prince; and were it not a mediaeval work, we would attend more to these facts of audience and narrator. This "Hector" knew his creed by this time, and the book is no confession manual except as those too attempted to remind one of all the unnoticed ways one could commit the sins and forget the faith. But it is a revealing demonstration of the fact that authors were not deceived about the didactic force of such images to go through any of these well-known sets of Christian essentials, making the mind concentrate upon the new relations that accrue with the new images. Suppose we follow Christine's lead and think simultaneously about Ceres' significances and the Second Article, "Jesus Christ his only Son Our Lord," about Isis and the Virgin's conception, Midas' false judgment and Pontius Pilate's, Hercules' descent into hell and the Harrowing—and the rest of the Twelve. Despite their alien birth, they not only come remarkably near becoming symbols, but also accomplish what this kind of image-making had as a purpose: they deepen and extend our grasp of the mystery supposedly "symbolized." The difference is immediately apparent to us when, with Fable 45, we leave the most common sevens and twelves and go on to sets not so readily recognized. I think it extremely likely that it was recognized by early readers; Christine ought to continue either with the Seven Gifts and their virtues and elaborations or with some order related to the familiar branches of sins.[30] The sense *we* have that the work

[30] Though I might indicate some "clumps" that resemble other series (as around Fable 48 we note topics treated by the *Somme le roi* under the gift

is going to pieces, that it is becoming the mere series of little frit-
ters of haphazard didacticism—as it usually is treated—may not
have been felt by readers who found themselves unexpectedly
rehearsing the old lessons by setting them to all these gay new
tunes.

It will be remembered that Christine differentiates allegorie
from glose by a distinction which quite clearly descends from the
well-worn definitions of religious exegesis.[31] Roughly and over-
simply, the second interpretation persistently conceives of man
as a soul to be saved, and as always in strict allegory, the singleness and simplicity of the redemptive doctrine which is usually
signified made a few great symbolic images the recurrent ones:
the soul as spouse, wooed or nuptially united with or ravished by
evil or rescued from it; the pilgrim; the castle besieged or delivered; humankind liberated from an enemy, or the recipient of
some inexpressible beneficence, symbolically expressed.[32] As she
turns from Glose to Allegorie, she seems simply to have thought,
"How does this touch man in his relation to the Deity?" Temperance (Fable 2) is to be loved and reasons are given, but in the
allegorie, Temperance restrains that *basic* Concupiscentia (Augustine is quoted) which makes us faithless to God's new covenant
with us. The pursuit of riches, of which Juno is goddess (Fable

---

of Dread, allegorized in 48, Corinis; around Fable 52 some traces of *consilium*),
I have not attempted to study out Christine's system of organization after she
finishes the most ordinary sets. What touches our purpose here, of studying
"imposition," is to notice how a difference to the *artistic* effect results from
our being aware of an imposed structure directing the stream of symbolized
ideas (notably suggestions and mnemonics). These effects are totally absent
when we pursue lists of Christine's images and "meanings"; her equations do
not constitute images, least of all allegories. Campbell, p. 171, saw a source
for the structure in the *égide* of Pallas described in *Ovide moralisé*, v, with its
several Sevens (Gifts, sacraments, virtues). But this, too, is just another evidence
of the popularity and spread of the tradition treated in ch. 2 above.

[31] See n. 20 above and pp. 45 ff.

[32] This limitation of vehicle makes for comic effects in bad or forced or
merely sketched-out allegories. Abuses were obvious in Molinet, while in the
collection of hastily noted illustrative stories (like a speaker's jest-manual) of
the *Gesta romanorum*, we learn to dread another ravished innocent and fly
from all marriage-stories. Though published in the sixteenth century, the latter's influence on allegorical habits was negligible (useless for secular materials),
and the tangle of the texts encourages us therefore to ignore it. Its unwavering
use of strict allegory reinforced the definition.

29), will turn a young knight from Honour; but in the allegorie, the son of Adam, not seeing that riches are neither "vraies ne vostres," loses the kingdom of heaven. As we proceed through the one hundred fables, this constant turn from the temporal world to the eternal one silently builds up a quite spacious definition of the chevalier Jesus Christ whom Christine's allegories instruct.

One other principle differentiates her two interpretations. It may be stressed because it is of considerable help in apprehending the quality of Spenser's obscurely felt difference from authors who simply moralize images. When both her interpretations enjoin some virtue, an attempt is made in the Allegorie to present the virtue simply as an adornment of the bon esprit which is Christ's knight. This beauty of the spirit suiting with its heavenly destination and origin is indicated as the reason for allegory's concern with the virtues (in Christine's Prologue to the Allegory);[33] and images displaying it will be different in effect from those portraying the strenuous battle to conquer vices and achieve heaven.

Christine tries valiantly to make her interpretations show this distinction, usually by some quick attempt to see the thing discussed sub specie aeternitatis through an anagogical reference. Warnings that greedy ambitions may lead one to death (Fable 85; Hector was killed as he stooped to seize Patroclus' fair arms) are diverted to concern "la mort espirituelle" (cf. Fable 92); or from the advice not to trust Fortune's promises (Fable 74), the allegorie turns to a differentiation between her false delights and eternal felicity. Christine has not Spenser's genius to persuade

---

[33] Before her first Allegorie; this is a passage in which Christine verbally parallels the *Livre de sagesse* (see above ch. 1, n. 19 and pp. 41ff., where this point has been already touched upon). We recall the commonplace from Isidore, quoted in the popular *Dialogus creaturarum*. It shows a proper understanding, surely not uncommon, of virtues as strict allegory is concerned with them. The very notion that there should be such a distinction, vague but nevertheless kept alive, is another inheritance from the operation of allegory in religious exegesis, where the figure does not focus on moral injunction like tropology, but reminds man of the beliefs which make possible his "imitation" of Christ and his divine destiny. It goes without saying that during these several centuries there should be currents which made first one then another of these seem most important, and these may be followed through the citations of B. Smalley, *Study of the Bible in the Middle Ages*, e.g. pp. 176, 198-202, 209.

us through the very beauty of virtue seen and the ugliness of vice, but her attempts, even though they fall short, often teach us as much about the way an allegory ought to work as if they had succeeded; and she obviously tried consistently to turn from the good knight's struggle to achieve virtue, to virtue as a divine condition or a beauty which man as chevalier Jesus Christ approximates here and enjoys hereafter.

The laurel crown in the Daphne story (Fable 87) is that New Testament crown which those who attempt the highest virtue will wear, perseverantia (named) understood as we read of it in the *Somme le roi*, Christ's virtue.[34] The basic distinction between the two chivalries, in her piece as in others, involves these two motivations to virtuous conduct. She makes outright reference to the militancy of the faithful, here below, and their state when victorious; "la vie presente et appelle guerriant," when perfected, "appelle triumphant." She does not explicitly use Dante's terms of the two allegories, the poet's and the theologian's, used in the *Convivio* and so much discussed, but seems at any rate to differentiate between the pagan or Christian grammarian's figurative explanation of a fiction, and the allegorist's portrayal of types fulfilled or things in their essence, beautiful to contemplate. She does, however, constantly refer to her glosses as the poets' explanations, and a curious, long preface in MS. Harl. 838, also in Scrope's version, speaks of the three interpretations of "poetrie, philosophye, & theologye" (stanza 18), the third excelling all the others in its furnishing us with "gostely sustenaunce."[35] We

[34] Christine's sketches for symbolic images are often left for the young reader she addresses to think out. The idea of God's strength made available to man through grace is in this figure of Daphne, and the initial fiction of Phebus' pursuit would have to be transformed if it were fully presented. I think Christine does not intend to present total old stories as amenable to a total new series of meanings; of course, it is a weakness of the whole attempt that the newly made symbol will not detach itself from its known story, and the abstracted Texte, "pursue Daphne persistently," cannot be abstracted and made to carry a burden dissimilar to its original one. The *Ovide moralisé*, 1.3065ff., which does take on the whole story, but attempts to make Daphne the Blessed Virgin Mary (1.3215ff.), shows up the weakness.

[35] See James Gordon (ed.), *The Epistle of Othea to Hector* (Philadelphia, 1942), for the preface described (discussed p. xxxviii); the source is unknown. A recent discussion of Dante's two "allegories" that brings out many points relevant to our own will be found in Chas. Singleton's *Dante Studies I: Commedia* (Cambridge, 1954). The Augustinian distinction between *use* and *fruition* is especially relevant to the two conceptions of virtue.

attempt at least what we seem to experience in greater writers, and it is explicitly described as an intended differentia; we see good and evil pure as the blessed "enjoy" God in heaven, seeing with the eyes of the *intellectus* like the angels.

Spenser is far more successful in making us experience this distinction between a virtue seen militantly struggling against vice, and the beauty of a virtue contemplated. We do not resolve to emulate Britomart in Books III and V, but rather simply feel the beauty of her generosities when seen against the rasping ugliness of the surrounding crowd of self-seeking small natures. This is constant, showing especially in the portrayal of vices in the Malbecco story as more outrageously and fantastically ugly than as the source of conflict; perhaps still more striking is the way Radegund's "love" does not impress us as reprehensible or wrong but renders that beautiful warrior ugly with the familiar ugliness of the small ungenerous nature capable only of an entirely self-directed infatuation. We take rest, as at an oasis, in the loveliness of good actions, pre-eminently in Arthur's acts full of love and grace, but also in Una's and Britomart's, after the thirsty deserts of hypocrisy, discord and quarrelsomeness, and self-seeking expediency which have been laid open to our view in other characters' actions. The overt moral statements for which Spenser is so much dispraised are not, as they are so often charged to be declarations of what his images mean, which *good allegory never tells* in so many words. (It would then be supererogatory.) They are parallel statements in another form of discourse, that give us hints of what path to take to a meaning.[36] Spenser is usually satisfied, for response to his allegorical images, with our heartfelt sense of the complete loveliness of virtue and shocking ugliness of vice, displayed before us, "imaged."

One reason for Christine's lesser success in obtaining our sympathetic concurrence as to where lie moral beauty and ugliness,

---

[36] I know of only one place where this extremely important point about Spenser's narrative and allegory is made: the discussion on the "reader's response" in Paul Alpers, "Narrative and Rhetoric in the *Faerie Queene*," *Studies in English Literature: The Renaissance*, vol. 2 (1962), 27-46, first read as an MLA paper in 1960. Relation to my point about the decorum of magnification and diminution, is clear, and connections are made with the relevant and very puzzling matter of Spenser's characteristically "intermittent" allegory.

FIGURE 101

is in her ineptitudes touching a literary quality which we extoled in Jean de Meun: careful government of the decorum of details. Instead of magnifications or diminutions tending unobtrusively but irresistibly in one direction, our approval or rejection of a figure will depend all on some one intellectually grasped attribute which we must be instructed to select. We are entirely prepared to find Cassandra a diminishing figure because of her faithful worship in their pagan *loy* (Fable 32), when behold she is magnified for "haunting the temple" as the knight should do; she figures to us that article of the Creed which binds our faith to the Holy Catholic Church, the Communion of Saints. The pictured Cassandra is highly ambiguous, and quite purposelessly so (Fig. 101), though it is acute of the illustrator to picture her worshipped gods as idols, and to praise not her true religion but her faithfulness to such a *loy* as she knew. Such similitudes are in truth "forced," and must expect failure as impositions.

I am certainly not interested in drawing any lines of source-relation between Spenser and Christine on this matter of an inherited differentiation between moral and allegorical reading, or between virtues in conflict in a psychomachia, and virtues as ineffably beautiful universals or ideas, seen fully only by the perfected citizens of the Heavenly City when they shall have returned home after their exile. Christine's book is proof that the inheritance was not forgotten; if we overmoralize Spenser it is partly because we have forgotten it.[37] References here and there show that this truly allegorical way of reading, spiritualiter or mystice, became lodged in common notions of figurative speech; even Milton's four uses of images read mystically show the distinction, and it is perfectly clear in Harington's *Brief Apology* where the reading of Perseus "morally" is distinguished from "more high and heavenly Allegorie" touching matters that are cosmological and theological. Christine needed no special source either for her threefold pattern. She was acquainted with the common habit of providing a texte with a glose, texte . . . glose, texte . . . glose, in her own adaptation of the pseudo-Seneca-Four-Virtues treatise; it was the ordinary procedure there as in the glossed *City of God*, the glossed Boethius. Many explanations of Christine's method have been given;[38] even the best students of

[37] I think the moral allegories (and hence moral suasion) were introduced into Spenser where none such were intended. Yet it is no service to revive and apply allegorical inheritances in their strictest theological form (the fourfold interpretation), for Spenser only loses by the over-Christianizing of his images; and Christine reminds us of some of the ways he chose to *refrain* from such explicit allusion. Expectations and habits changed as they came down into secular vernacular literature, meeting the other stream of Christianized classical allegory with its lesser respect for literal meanings, its greater tolerance for equations and for substituted figurative senses, and its inability to "figure" in types the later revelation of a New Testament and thus achieve the profundity of symbol. But we should make room for distinctions of *aesthetic* importance in either tradition, like this differentiation between moral adjuration and allegorical "image" (reflection). The Harington examples may be found in Gregory Smith, *Elizabethan Critical Essays*, ii, 202, and similar points on poets who "glose on a trifling text" in Lodge (i, 65; producing satire); pseudo-Seneca was treated in ch. 2 above.

[38] An interesting text, *Los doze trabajos de ercules* by Enrique de Villena (Burgos, 1499) shows a variant attempted secularization of the inherited schemes (reproduced in facs. Madrid, 1879). The historia nuda (the fiction, told) is followed by a declaracion, pre-eminently a moral reading, often touching the

the *Othéa* do not make the connection between it and the ancient distinctions of religious exegesis. Accordingly and as always, much criticism at her expense derives from expecting her to do what she is not doing. She glosses her *texte*, not the full ancient story; she is providing ways to read, not substitutions, and they are sketches of illuminating extensions, not ways to get rid of the pagan story by whitewashing it.

This is not to claim that her figures are truly potent. Many glosses draw forced morals tangential to the person's story. The allegories may not even hope for success unless underlying them is that assumption so difficult with pagan material (tenable for Orpheus, Ceres, Hercules) but endlessly reiterated by contemporary and later theorists of religious allegory: that the plain historical meaning, in scriptural allegory the Old Testament narrative itself, in classical and other fables the story with its temporarily credible marvels, was not erased or invalidated but "fulfilled," when later deeper metaphysical interpretation showed the image's kinship with doctrines held true or with archetypes. This fundamental notion is of great assistance in the puzzling problem of deciding whether Spenser is telling a story or declaring an allegorical meaning; he is always doing both. We must allow all allegorists to tell their stories movingly (see n. 36), not forcing them into the limitation of those moral statements which Spenser especially provides as alternative hints of what is thus doubly pointed at: the significance "embodied" in the image and, of course, never satisfactorily enclosed in any *sentence*.

Although Christine shares with Spenser a kind of residue left from the centuries of theological theory and practice, which gave her an idea of how allegory's deeper reach ought to differ from

---

struggle in us between virtues and vice, sometimes quoting Fulgentius as authority; thereupon *verdad* is usually a rationalized or quasi-historical demythologizing, and an *aplicacion* brings the point directly into connection with present society. Scraps of information on the development of similar ways of treating a text may be found in B. Smalley, *Study of the Bible in MA* (*passim*, e.g. pp. 93, 176ff., 198-202, 209). Properly allegorical meanings are ignored—though familiar opportunities arise in Hercules materials—the author perhaps, like Conti, having little taste for them; the occasional use of the word in the *declaracion* or *verdad* readings underlines the warning that we cannot find the terminology accurately preserved even when the distinction remains (see ch. 1, p. 35). The *Ovide moralisé* and Molinet's *Roman de la rose* are both *allegorized*—though when a moral reading is slipped in, it is seen as a separable kind.

tropology's moral usefulness, we must add to her far inferior imaginative powers the disadvantages of her more direct claim that Christian doctrine informs classical images. Most of her examples in which it is claimed that a classical personage or narrative event can declare the mystery of the Incarnation, the Passion, or the nature of the Christian deity, are taken by her from the *Ovide moralisé*. Campbell has proven that in her frequent allusions to "Ovid," she refers to the metrical *Ovide moralisé* of the first years of the fourteenth century, a rare restriction of dependence even in vernacular belles-lettres.[39] As we noted, she had an easier task than the author she plunders, in that the structure of her book as an ingenious little *Somme* of Christian rudiments gave a kind of rationale to her parallels; thus she had no need to embark on the transformation of whole stories still in their context in a total narrative work, the *Metamorphoses*. When in 1484 Colard Mansion did just this, allegorizing copiously with the use of her sources and others, the difficulties proved insuperable, like Molinet's, as we may notice in enough instances to show the same principles at work. Although many of her newly created symbols are sterile and never caught on, Christine does not produce the effect of wild absurdity and irresponsible imposition of equations which leads us to wonder why Mansion was more than once reprinted.

[39] See ch. IV of Campbell's book cited in n. 29. I do not think the poem can have had much currency in the Renaissance, though there remain to us some twenty manuscripts, some impressively (rather than interestingly) illustrated; it was first put in print by C. de Boer and J.van't Sant in 5 vols., *Ovide moralisé* (Kon.Akad. Amsterdam, 1915-38). I therefore prefer sixteenth-century texts showing its influence, and use Vérard's *Bible des poètes* (1493), which virtually reproduces Mansion's 1484 *Ovide Methamorphose*, re-introducing materials from the early poem and from Bersuire. Vérard's book was reprinted in 1507(?), 1523, 1531, and again this whole group of books was important among illustrated *Ovides*. The remaining text of importance is that by Bersuire (Petrus Berchorius), a fourteenth-century Latin commentary forming Book XV of his *Reductorium morale*, but appearing by itself both in manuscripts and in print. The textual history and iconography of these redactions, interdependent in odd and complicated ways, I do not make quite plain here, counting upon the very important and clear article by F. Ghisalberti, " 'L'Ovidius Moralizatus' di Pierre Bersuire," *Studi romanzi*, vol. 23 (1933), 5-32. Bersuire's frequency in manuscript (see Ghisalberti's list, pp. 52ff.) was supported by the early printings (1509, '11, '15, '21). Modern citations are brought more nearly up to date by Lain and by Panofsky (see n. 29).

FIGURE 102

Christine's success or failure, like that of other Christianizers of classical images (in literature at least), seems to depend on the *truth of the underlying similarity of import* which has led her to offer a classical figure as capable of symbolizing the mystery or doctrine for which we usually use a Christian symbol or name. Only if the same drift of meaning, a similar burden of feeling, is already *that which seeks signification* through the Christian symbol, does the offered classical synonym really succeed in providing a new usable symbol for us: Orpheus has become an acceptable Good Shepherd, for example, while for all the implications held within the words "the Baptism," only the familiar pictured Christian event suffices, to my knowledge. I will exemplify, after we look at some half-successes.

If there chances to be something of real moment in a classical figure's story which admits, say, of parabolic likeness to Christ's acts, the image will have some chances of Christian life. It is told of Hercules in *Othéa* (Fable 27) that he went down into Hades to rescue Pirotheus and Theseus, his friends; this sufficiently resembles in import Christ's descent into Limbo to deliver his lieges and supporters, the patriarchs and prophets and faithful precursors, that it can take on the mystical import of the Christian event: divine power conquering Death (Cerberus), eternal faithfulness between lord and subject, the quality of love braving the abyss of destruction and evil so as to save, and so on. We might come to see, quite unconsciously and effortlessly, in the valiant and courteous deliverer pictured in the Laud misc.570 Hercules, the very qualities and lovelinesses which make the faithful action of the Christian Hercules so fair (see Fig. 102).

The picture of Busiris, worshipping his abominable idols by the sacrilegious offering of violated and destroyed life, figured in the bleeding heads of his victims on the blasphemous altar, does indeed have something of the awesome pure Evil of Busyrane's (and Satan's) substitution of hate for love and destructiveness for creativity. We cease to consider Christine thoughtless for attaching Busiris and his story[40] to the Commandment against stealing rather than to that forbidding us to kill, for we see that rapine, injustice, usurpation of another's rightful place, stubborn hybristic idolatry, worship stolen to give where it is not due, are the deeper implications. It is these implications in Busiris' action, *that which is signified* by the symbol, not the body of it, which horrify us in Busiris and in Busyrane. The purport *of what is signified*, is assisted by the image of Busiris to wake in us the same unreasoned terror of a "monstrous enmity" which strikes us speechless when we read of it in the *Faerie Queene*, described in that masterful ambiguity—"so we a God invade" (III.xi.22; *Othéa*, Fable 41; see Fig. 103).

When Penthesilea (Fable 15), out of pure loving admiration for Hector, seeks him out and grieves finding him dead and revenges his death, she becomes, with no sense of dislocation or strain, a figure for Christian caritas. But the similarity lies too completely in the mere exemplification of a quality to form a sufficient basis for Penthesilea to become a symbol carrying the meanings of Love's descent in the Incarnation to rescue man from death. And revenge does not rescue. Thus, it seems to be necessary that meanings coincide in true identity if the image of one is to bear the symbolic burden of the other.

Whole groups of images offered as symbols newly endowed with Christian meaning have this basis of a typified quality which the chevalier celestien is to wonder at and set his thoughts upon "mire")—an adornment of the questing soul. "Les proprietez des vii. planets" (f.35r) were so well known that all of this

---

[40] I am released from the necessity of further discussion of Busiris-as-inherited-figure by the admirably perceptive treatment in T. P. Roche, *The Kindly Flame* (Princeton, 1964), pp. 80ff.; I should welcome a circumstantial presentation utilizing, e.g. the rich and complex Ovidian suggestions. Roche's method is so sound that his conclusions demand belief; but I wonder if a study of Busiris and his victim, along Roche's own indicated lines, would not evade my sole objection (to a heroine "fearful" of physical aspects of sex in a nineteenth- not a sixteenth-century way).

FIGURE 103

group already had symbolic power, and Christine leans much on convention, not least on the commonplaces of astrology. With only one, Mars, does she attempt the sort of artificial typology which results from emptying out the old symbolic force and putting in new: "le bon esprit doie . . . suivir son bon pere Jesus Christ et batailler contre les vices." She does this by thinking of the "mars" in one's soul as being the Christ within us who is god of the only battle she admits into these allegorical interpretations—that against Satan, fought by Christ literally and also *in* the Christian spirit as it achieves the supreme victory, self-conquest (Fable 11). Despite a certain thought-provoking in-

FIGURE 104

geniousness, such an image has no chance of permanence; we can imagine no literary work centered on the new symbolic Mars; and Spenser did well to make his champion, the exponent of Christian grace who makes the soul's last stand in every battle, a mediaeval knight. With the other six planets, Christine merely gives Christian force to the planetary properties of conditions: pité or misericorde (Jove), light or truth (Apollo), gravity (Saturn), slowness in judging, for judgment is God's, and so on. The grace and benignity of Jupiter's action as he sprinkles balm upon his needy followers easily translates into the grateful sense of grace received from a Christian deity from whom we prayerfully ask it (in Fable 3; see Fig. 104). Indeed, pité and misericorde are the very names of the Fifth and Second Gifts of the

Holy Ghost. Christine uses symbolic deepening that is already half-conventional for her most successful translations. Venus and Phebe are pejorative (inordinate love and changeableness), but they do not become the Great Adversary; nor do the sins, when we come to that group. Nor do they become before our shocked eyes evil in essence, but simply sum up conditions of spirit. Christine had no space to create a Mammon or an Acrasia, who go beyond this to become embodiments of satanic force able to inhabit and possess the human spirit and turn it into itself; neither does she point to this extension of significance. She at least attempts in both glose and allegorie to keep her distinction between the bon chevalier's struggle against these personified single vices and the bon esprit's heavenly destiny when, "perfect" in virtue like a Christ, he fights only as a god fights and is victor over the source of evil as well as its manifestations the vices. She invents no symbols as Spenser does; at most she strengthens the symbolic power of old images by attaching them to Christian truth.

There is a difference between a basis found in some salient quality or story-motif, as in these partial successes, and a more lasting basis found in similarity between the full meaning of some classical story and the full meaning of some Christian dogma or act of Christ. (Inability to re-state full meanings, despite the experience all men have that symbols do somehow convey them, is responsible for our inadequate phrases for referring to that which is signified, the meaning behind the symbol, presented by it.) When a true similarity resides in this, the classical figure baptised into Christianity works movingly, and lasts. Orpheus is the best example. All important pastoral metaphors are so based; *Lycidas* is movingly filled with the many figures which adumbrate harmony, concord, love. Christine's best novel symbol for Christ's gift to men is Ceres, and the translation is based on the similarity seen in their free gift of "a life more abundant"; their largesse was "abandoned," complete, and motivated by love not merit in the recipient. It is this, the condition of Ceres which the bon esprit is to resemble; Christine ties it to the Second Article of the Creed ("and in Jesus Christ his Son"), and the connection with Ceres who discovered an art to sow in ploughed ground calls on other ancient metaphors (both the sower and the buried seed). The spiritualization of the meanings is effortless, not obstructed.

Of course it is not novel in that it is original, and indeed Christine found it in *Ovid moralisé* (v), where its power is marred by a determination to equate every detail of the Ceres-Proserpina-Triptolemus stories with something profitable.[41] The relevant parallel in significancy between Ceres' loving search and delivery of her daughter and Christ's deliverance of anima whom another King of Hell had ravished is an image which also has the seeds of permanence. But in the *Ovide* it is weakened and made indecorous by attempts to subdivide anima and by eagerness to take care of every detail with an equivalent. Spenser's restraint in not using these fairly well-known Christian significances in Proserpina's Garden in Book II warns us not to obtrude them into his image. He rests content with the vague shadows left upon the image by its history—associations that merge Hades with Hell, that make Mammon-Pluto a satanic *figura*, that integrate Garden and Cave to give the whole relevance and depth. Guyon is surely looking at damnation, not at a moral lesson about the golden mean, touching love of money. But still, if Spenser had wished us to find a Ceres figuring redemptive love toward this Proserpina, and abundance-as-against-sterility, we would have known of it from him directly.

Another image which might have lived but for other stronger moral significances (Midas's love of gold) is based on the similarities seen in the judgment allegedly made by Midas when he deemed the God Phebus unequal as musician to Pan with his pipes, and the judgment made by Pontius Pilate (Fable 26; introduced where the relevant article from the Creed occurs). A God, *pur sans tache*, was doomed, and it was that god who as Light and Sun was amenable to the identification with Christ; it is interesting that Scrope's translation puts in the image, familiar from other sources, of Christ "streyned as a harpe" upon the Cross to make the music of Love.[42] But given some confusions (common)

[41] I am using the late fifteenth-century prose in Vérard's *Bible des poètes*, ff. 55v-59r (see above n. 39); we could quote Bersuire in manuscript or print, or go back to the metrical *Ovide moralisé* (v, 2882ff.).

[42] Not in the French. G. F. Warner edited Scrope's translation in 1904 (forthcoming edition by C. Bühler); but the English versions are seldom used here because their currency is doubtful, and their ineptitude would have sent an interested sixteenth-century reader back to the French version, probably equally accessible and printed with full illustration by Pigouchet. The attractive "Harmonia" turn to the image which condemns Midas and Pilate alike be-

on Christine's part—the firm entrenchment of Pilate as sermon-cliché for the False Judge and of Midas as avaricious, and perhaps the contradiction inherent in the fact that the other party to the judgment, Pan, was often connected with Christ—it is no wonder that we never hear more of "Pilate, a mere Midas," false judges both in choosing the wrong allegiance.

Another figure for the Christian deity's supreme love of mankind, in Bellerophon (Fable 35), has the qualifications of a translatable symbol, and his later history as an image[43] may indicate that something of symbolic power clung to him. But though Christine's allegory is firmly directed toward the praise of "troth" or true faith rather than to the warning against lechery (thus fitting the First Commandment, in her scheme), she uses a Hippolytus-like element in Bellerophon's story which is not in Ovid, but which, from the *Ovide moralisé* (iv), probably came on to later mythographers like Comes; she does not use the blindness, the hybris or the famous mount that attracted later poets. Despite a parallel drift of meaning, the obvious recalcitrance of parts of the anti-infidelity story, and the use of the figure both for faulty man and for faultless Christ "plain de toute loyaute," show us why Christine's "Follow Bellerophon" never became a cliché as a way of enjoining us to keep the First Commandment, as "Flee from Venus" became a clear way to say the Fifth.

This modest sheaf is surely not the full harvest of pleasure-giving images that kept alive in the *Othéa* notions of how to read allegorically. But they help to show several general points touching a special method of Christianizing classical imagery which

---

cause of their inability to understand divine love and ally themselves rightly (if the whole had any currency), has left upon Pilate-Midas enough taint of that intemperance which substitutes false values for true, to make it reasonable instead of puzzling that he appears with Tantalus in ii.vii. On Christine's errors see Campbell, p. 127 (but not all unfortunate, or peculiar to her; some perhaps by choice).

[43] Bellerophon "peut notter le dieu de Paradis," for he faced wild beasts sooner than accord love to his stepmother; *latria* is due to God alone. Milton's use (vii.18), though quite differently based, is a figure for the audacious poet and is quite as clearly symbolic, though perhaps turned to his own purposes. See M. M. Lascelles, "The Rider on the Winged Horse" in *Elizabethan and Jacobean Studies for F. P. Wilson* (Oxford, 1959). It is a weakness of these translated images that so often the *whole* of a story-figure cannot be accommodated to the new interpretation.

never established itself in imaginative literature, although it had two centuries (the fourteenth and the fifteenth) of especially insistent support. It died without gaining adherents in the great English Renaissance poets, did not (for good reason) inform the dramas with secondary meaning, and is deliberately absent from the two long poems (the *Faerie Queene* and *Paradise Lost*) of the age. It seems to me that we should be similarly restrained in our willingness to claim that Spenser's and Milton's classical images may be read with a symbolical force, making them hospitable to direct Christianizing (even in the cases where this new meaning is "traditional"), unless we detect with sureness some of the multifarious ways authors have of indicating that we are to read symbolically. Occasionally later baroque images show their kinship with these habits of the fifteenth century; it is commonest to find the Christological parallels overtly pointed out.

The whole attempt is outstandingly different from serious religious exegesis, which is concerned to find and read the meanings indubitably *in* the history read; it would only be hampered by this multiplication of vessels to carry the same meaning in different and clever ways, pleasing for their wit and because added terms brought in another range of associations. Though I think the habits established by religious allegory, especially the expectation that images should function to declare the deepest mysteries, were influential, the resulting allegories are very far removed from those of exegetical commentary—though in a way the attempt could be characterized as an effort to turn the whole classical past into another Old Testament, allegorically revealing the New. The figures are almost inevitably less capable of lasting symbolic power. Yet it is clear that the factors which prophesy failure are neither a ridiculous or blasphemous mingling of associations, nor radical distance between vehicle and tenor (Ceres' and Christ's redemptive gifts are radically unlike). It is not likeness between vehicle and tenor but likeness between two *tenors* conveyed by a single image which counts. The other factor is indifferent. The pleasure taken in occult resemblances between unlike things is there, but it is minor compared with the intended pleasure in seeing into the far corners and obscure pathways in that which is signified—by the help of the unexpected linkage.

Christine's bad or weak images do not result inescapably from her poetic theory (a chief difficulty with the *Ovide moralisé*),

which is coherent and clear. She is as impressed as all her fellows
with the necessity of looking under "lescorce" for more important meanings; though she explains that "la matiere damours"
[the usual husk] "est plus delictable a ouir *que* autre" (Fable
82), she does not try to throw out all such idle meanings for
profitable ones. In this I think her to have represented a common attitude based on a real acceptance of multiple meanings
as the author's own—often stated in ways very congenial to the
modern critical welcoming of all the images possible, except for
the more careful protection of the last point, now not so regarded.
Thus she speaks of the loy of the pagans without condescension
as the frame of reference necessarily of their interpretations
(Fable 33); it is neither pitied nor ridiculed. She constantly recognizes the fact that images can be understood "en plusieurs
manieres" and often herself gives "maintes exposicions"; her
commonest words are "*povons* entendre" or "*peut* notter."[44]
That is, she knows allegory is a way of *reading* significances in
materials, not an author's stunt in which he can say the same thing
two ways by cleverly stringing variant sets of equivalents together in parallel order. Although she is not entirely clear on what
kind of truth an allegory has, she never claims that it alone was
the author's real meaning, or substitutes it for his ostensible meanings.

When Christine talks of poets speaking "en maniere de fable"
or "soubz couverture," this generally precedes some rationalization of a figure, euhemeristic or cosmological. In other words, she
thinks of the moral glose as the poet's type of figure, but she
does not explicitly mention Dante's "allegory of the theologians,"
though the distinction she laboriously attempts to maintain is
based on the difference in aim in these two groups.[45] She explains
to her young Hector the sense in which all knights are sons of
Minerva, though he knows his mother was Hecuba; that is, just
as the illuminations are briefly explained, so also an elementary
explanation of how universals can be in particulars, in figurative

[44] See Fable 72 (Atalanta), Fable 82 (Hermaphrodite). Some wordings are
revealing: "peuent estre *entendues et mises* diverses expositions" (Fable 56,
Venus and Mars); "peuent estre *prins* plusieurs entendemens" (Fable 62,
Semele). "Et pour *ramener les articles* de la foy *a nostre propos . . . prendrons
pour Dyane* dieu de paradis" (Fable 23).

[45] See n. 35 above; the translation Gordon edits does not follow through the
promisingly accurate distinction, each allegory indeed being labeled "moralyte."

language, is embarked on; just so Faith, another arms-bestower, is "mere au bon esperit" (Fable 13).

Though Christine is often solemnly pious, the small amount of prudery in these texts should remind us that there is little to support the idea, frequently still stated, that this sort of imagery results from a kind of clerkly movement to bowdlerize the classics and thus to save them. That at least is no part of the meaning of the debated phrase, "the allegory of the theologians"; I incline to accept Christine's own insecurely kept but accurate differentiation. Certainly these Christianizers were not (as commentators have loosely said) trying to get naughtiness out of the classics so they could be safely read—but trying to make them more meaningful and more contemporaneous. In fact, Molinet is the best example of this seemingly well-based conclusion, for he makes no attempt whatsoever at bowdlerization, despite his observed temper and aim. He translates the text completely and baldly, and the most lascivious passages appear uncloaked; meanwhile the ensuing "moralite" may include Christological allegorizing interpretations of the most extreme kind. The Pygmalion image and the long final physiological metaphor are reproduced without shuffling, and in the arguments about "coillons" Molinet is forthright, at one point remarking as Jean means us all to do, that he does not know how the Lover can afford to be so scornful about something without which he cannot, after all, pick the Rose (f. 49r). One is convinced that Molinet's straightforward prose, which modernizes the archaisms and is effortless to read, sold the three editions of this work,[46] rather than interest in his imposed meanings.

Molinet's phrasings, like his practice, reveal no constructed poetic and do not repay quotation; in one he gives himself quite away, "Pour *reduire* a sens moral l'hystoire precedente . . ." (f. 93v). Elsewhere he argues the equally unfortunate notion that Jean's long sensual figures are not metaphors for physical union, and in both cases he obviously intends a substitution not an interpretation of meaning. But neither Christine's pedantic

---

[46] He did it at the request of Philippe de Clèves, and though publication dates are in the 1500's, Bourdillon (pp. 160ff.; see nn. 5 and 6 above) dates its composition around 1482, just the period when Mansion was doing his eclectic redaction of *Ovide moralisé*—putting back in the doctrinal allegories which we find excised from some prose versions in manuscript and also adding from Bersuire.

care, nor Molinet's redeeming willingness to reproduce honestly his frank original, characterize the literary theory underlying the *Ovide moralisé*, whether we read the fourteenth-century metrical work or the fifteenth- and sixteenth-century vernacular editions in their imposing folios. These redactors regard neither the decorum of the Ovidian story nor the decorum of the meaning imposed—drifts or slants widely at variance with one another, and the latter often includes self-contradictions preventing us from reading even it as a unit. The new "meaning" is irresponsibly fixed upon Ovid the author; a glose will state, "Il semble par ceste fable qu'Ovide entende la creacion de Adam" (Bk. I; Vérard f. 2v); or under sens moral we hear, "nostre acteur ouide entende par ceste fable l'histoire de la confusion . . . de la tour Babylonne" (Vérard f. 5r). More interesting still, Actaeon (Bk. III), who in his "sens alegorique" is read as Christ attacked by his own (he turns and says the *Popule meus* to them, but is pursued by the mockers with nails and crown, and the fourth "dog" pierces his side), provokes the observation: "Certes ie croy que le saint esperit inspira nostre acteur Ovide de mettre par poesie et par fiction la vrays histoire de nostre redempcion. Combien de son temps ne fust advenue. Mais elle estoit prochaine a venir" (Vérard f. 27r). Hospitality to the idea, that a poet could write better than he knows, could go no further than to give to Ovid this generous gift of being able to see around the coming corner.

Large numbers of unrelated separate significances are hustled in, but there appears to be no considered theoretical basis for this, such as choice of a deeper functioning of the image (if figuratively complicated). These writers of mythographical Christian-doctrinal allegories for classical figures do indeed seem to regard allegory as a series of equivalents, as the modern accusation declares, and since this is a truly remarkable definition among writers of the least degree of taste or imagination, before the seventeenth century, it demands remark. It became the commonest understanding in the nineteenth century, especially where Bunyan was allowed to typify the form. Questions of specialized audience and the purpose of a book (as in Christine's *Othéa*) will lead us to make a few qualifications, but in general, these writers stand out from others by virtue of the fact that they blandly and baldly offer strings of elaborate "profitable" substituted-significances for details and whole images, with very little attention to how the profit should accrue. The major flaw in all this procedure lies in the fact that such images, and their details, have ceased to *convey* meaning at all; the Christian doctrines said to be pointed at do not impress even their author with their urgency and truth; no basis in a likeness between original and new *signification* of the translated image has been sought—neither the ancient nor the Christian significance being seriously regarded, rather only the forced or even contradictory cleverness with which some superficial likeness can be claimed. The power of the Christian doctrines asserted is no whit assisted or broadened, for that is not the objective, and since those *meanings* are not the literary subject, there is no interest in seeing the classical shadows as prefiguring the later fuller light. The images do no useful work, but remain dead statements of parallels merely said to obtain, for no reason. This is unusual, except in very minor bad allegories (bound to exist, like bad writing in any mode or period, but often blithely used for drawing up the rules, by us late-comers with no allegories of our own). This is no matter of taste erecting categories which allegories may not enter if they are good; it allows of any of the word's definitions, which uniformly concern function not quality.

It is important to look briefly at a few differences which make the images in this body of material so singularly fruitless and inoperative, since the fault is usually laid at the door of the *kind* of image—the doctrinal interpretation or strictly allegorical reading given to a classical figure—and since all Christianizing of non-religious images has been lumped together to receive the obloquy which these proponents of it truly deserve (in my judgment). The few imaginatively powerful images which survived (like Orpheus and Hercules and Proserpina) were based on very different conceptions of what constitutes meaningful similarity. But there are several smaller, easily detectable differences which prevented the horde of Christian parallels in these materials from having any further history.

When Christine's images are weak and dead, the reasons lie in her having chosen a Texte with no clear salient point, or in the bad logic of her application, or in there being no true link between the classical story and the announced Christian significance—as when Pasiphae is "taken" as the penitent soul returning to God, seemingly for no reason except her superlative dissoluteness,[47]

[47] Fable 45; other examples are Fable 78, where moral advice not to regard

though that reason is theologically inadmissible. Christine shares this flaw with the *Ovide moralisé* searchers for parallels, but she does not egregiously multiply its paralyzing effects by introducing crowds of tiny equations for inessential accompanying details, each weak and thoughtless at its link—as when the metamorphosis of Cygnus is to encourage us to cover ourselves by confession with the plumes of chaste conversation, to have the black feet of humility and the long neck of discretion (Vérard, f. 14v).

Obviously, of course, when the useful functioning of images is being so disregarded, the careful distinction we noticed between a moral figure's adjurations to struggle for virtue and an allegorical figure's contemplation of virtue as a lovely adornment has been largely lost; the *Ovide*'s allegories are merely hortatory, and seldom does one display a mystery for our wonder. Very like the thoughtless multiplication of glib parallels is another suspect habit—the admission of Christian parallels that have become commonplace, without attending to local suitability. Both these are flaws shared by poor allegorists of any date, for these do not attend to the chief result in both cases—impotent images, which are powerless to do anything in an action if they merely stray in through some open door. Christ seen as a white stag, for instance, occupies the beaten path so comfortably that Actaeon must perforce be Christ, sent to hunt the devil in this miserable world. Yet encased in the story of Actaeon seeing Diana, this signification must remain helpless and inert (Bk. III; Vérard f. 27). All loves are likely to be *l'âme humaine* wooed by Christ; Calisto is the human soul (Bk. II; Vérard f. 16v), "siringle" is *l'âme pecheresse & obstinee* (Bk. I; Vérard f. 10r), and Yo is the soul and *amie* (Bk. I; Vérard f. 10v) led by Jupiter-Christ to the Nile of Baptism.

This last is one of Molinet's most striking pitfalls, for it illus-

---

Morpheus' dreams overmuch is allegorized to remind us that tribulations must not be overweighed by those who expect God's heavenly inheritance; or Fable 37, where Laomedon's churlish treatment of Jason is related to not honoring the Sabbath, on the ground that both spring from outrecuidance. So much does. We are to remember that Christine is allegorizing *her texte* not *our myth* as the used name or incident suggests wholes to us; thus we may not carelessly scorn her severely narrowed significances. Such failures contrast with the simple but just linkage in (Fable 32) Cassandra's haunting of the temple, truly comparable to those believers in the "communion of saints" of the 10th Article in that both are "devote en *leur* loy."

trates the same lack of care to preserve the drift of thought, the parallel decorum of the two interpretations. Molinet, typical in this of fundamentally unserious allegory, uses images which cannot adumbrate any Christian idea profoundly because they are mere hasty applications, taken for granted (Virginia is daughter of God in that she is *anima*, yet must be beheaded by her helpless father if he is to keep her from the World); or because when Christianized the images get the author into disastrous contradictions (as when Christ must be Vulcan because he is the Spouse, in the Mars-Venus story, f. 89v); or because they turn morals upside down if accommodated within the original text (the Lover is advised to get all the funds he can out of some unsuspicious Friend, which must equate with Christ's giving all to poor indigent Man, simply because Molinet cannot resist the cliché of Christ as par excellence the Friend). These absurdities do not represent the natural results of imposition of alien meanings in a forced type of parallel and an injudicious mode of figurative thinking, but show the misuse of allegory by writers insufficiently intellectually endowed. They exhibit a bad and foolish theory, not the proper traditional theory on which allegory is based. It is worth noting that Christine, with all her faults and though of a date to promote them, sufficiently avoids this one. She uses ancient commonplaces when they suit (in Narcissus' idolatrous pride, which transforms the figure into a true vision of man's littleness, or in her Actaeon, who as *cerf* figures the true penitent and is moving in his suffering). But she shows restraint in keeping free of familiar identifications when they would have such results as we have noted. This is a principle as applicable in reading allegorically as it is in writing allegory; as critics, we are to notice and follow authors in their tacit demands for restraint in the extension of meanings.

One of the strengths of allegory is thus seen to be one of its dangers. Criticism of the present day just happens to be faced with a similarly delicate situation, caused by our hypersensitivity to the power of images to point to some large archetypal significance, universally applicable and timeless. Since strict allegorical figures are always urging the one great basic significance—the mystery of the soul's victory—this mode is content with a few large metaphors such as ravishment and rescue, the garden, loving pursuit and wooing of the soul, the Old Law and the New. It is entirely natural that these should be the staples sought for by the *Ovide moralisé* redactors; what leads to their monotony and sterility is their acceptance, without experiencing them figuratively, of the truth of the significances being conveyed; they neither need nor care to let stories reveal that truth in figure, they accepted it long ago. We have demonstrated a similar willingness (indeed, enthusiasm) to substitute a few large paraphrasable indications of archetypal meaning as "the basic meaning" of great works of literature, for images which function to bring these meanings before us. We have a similar readiness to accept the truth of an archetypal significance without the long experience of discovering it. It is this reduction, this substitution of declarations of meaning for revelatory working figures, rather than the much complained of wrenching of unsuitable vehicles to a desired meaning, which produces the strain and the lifelessness.

The fault of the Ovidian allegorizers lay not in making wild connections,[48] but in failing to make any. All the inadequacies we have noted, working toward this nullification of figurative sense in the supposed figure, result from mistaking a mere statement of a likeness seen for the "translation" of meaning. One who accepts Christ's double nature without second thought, or who thinks it unimportant, has no use for an image of Tiresius' serpents or of the centaur Chiron interpreted as figures for it (Bks. III and II). Our comparable readiness to admit archetypal sug-

---

[48] We are undeniably more surprised to find Io serving as a symbol of the Ascension than we are illuminated about aspects of the latter which we had missed (Fable 29; article seven of the creed; one fears ignobly that the fact that both went up outweighs Io's currency as patron of contemplative wisdom). Nor are we wrong in finding more mirth than merit in an Allegorie (of Fable 56, Venus-Mars-Vulcan) which quotes as climax, "Sobrii estote et vigilate" but refers it to vigilance in escaping nets. We are unsatisfied with the glibly adventitious bases of similarity which Christine sometimes clutches upon only so far as we are unrelaxed in our determination to perceive the things signified more truly through them. Usually mere likenesses help us to no insight. This remains true in the modern analogue, where I refer especially to the unsupported parallels common in incidental criticism, classroom exegesis, and stray articles; all readers are familiar with the tendency to see the Fall in every work and Eden in all gardens, with a few likenesses offered as evidence that the extension of meaning is proper, while bread, wine, underground rivers, lambs, fathers, mountains, mothers and caves can with difficulty achieve phenomenal existence. Bells are papish, as Ananias exclaimed.

gestions as profound offers the same risk of glib parallel-making, and a desolate monotony in the "basic" meanings of literary works. We shall not cure matters by requests for more reasonable metaphors, or more sensible relations between vehicle and tenor, for again it is the *relation* between things signified which is claimed but unrealized. All the vehicles in allegorical images are in a way unsuitable; they are grossly disproportionately trivial to carry their great tenor, and an inescapable radical distance characterizes the relations between terms. This observation does not turn the surprises in Christine or *Ovide* into valuable literary achievements, but it is well to recognize time and again that it is not the bizarrerie or lack of common sense in the relations seen which is the factor deserving rebuke. This remains, irrevocably, the uselessness of the figure, its failure to function and hence to live.

It is easier in a simpler type of image to see the figurative uselessness of mere likeness-pointing (often deemed sufficient to define an image as allegorical, among those who regard the houses of alma and purple islands of literature eminently "allegorical"). Christine is singularly unfortunate with the rationalizations which utilize physics or cosmology as explanations. Comes and Sandys liked to incorporate them, and seem not to object to the monotony with which all stories can turn into variants of "heat encountering moisture results in generation." The *Ovide* allegorizers, like all those who show Stoic influence, find such images congenial, and any trivial noted likeness allows the interpretation, which again shows the same uselessness, since no reader has the least intention of regarding the physics as serious. Erichthonius, son of Vulcan and Pallas, was feigned to have serpent's feet because he invented chariots of war (Bk. II; Vérard f. 18; smooth rapid transport?); historically Daphne was daughter of an important man Peneus, living on a river where were many laurel trees because of the humidity, and Phebus the sun multiplied them (Bk. I; Vérard f. 8v); Argus had a castle on the river Ynacus (called a god because it never dried up), with a hundred towers (eyes, f. 10v). A prose redaction in B.M. MS. Royal 17 E iv which admits none of the Christian-doctrine transformations, nonetheless permits scores like these. It would show greater respect for the poetic original to re-mythologize the images by reading Christian myth into them—yet, as we saw, the Mansion-Vérard texts applying this method wholesale to Ovid have left us no living figurative counters. Christine also willingly includes rationalizing explanations of this historical character which come closer to silliness than any of her Christian translations do, for these at least attempt to seize upon serious parallels in *meaning*, not upon information of no consequence. Of all the many kinds of interpretations that are somewhat uncomfortably sheltered under the term "allegorizing," it is no wonder that this had least importance for later imagery—despite Bacon's and Boccaccio's and Comes' additions to it. I know no example of a highly imaginative and powerful image in any later poet using this basis of rationalizing a myth.

There is one reservation which it is only fair to keep in mind in making these strictures. Bersuire is criticized for giving a mere semi-synopsis of the original stories and bending all efforts toward the elaboration of many moralizations; we accuse both predecessors and followers of untenable interpretations irresponsibly suggested. Modern writers, using the works to help characterize "the mediaeval mind," seem to assume that Bersuire thought to displace Ovid's text, and that the new meanings, with almost no story, were to constitute the *Metamorphoses*. But Bersuire's audience *had* Ovid, and those who read his Latin expositions read with equal ease Ovid's original, entirely accessible, Latin text. The printed editions of Bersuire, from the press of Badius Ascensius, have very much the look of his other handbooks of commentary and annotation, whether on ancient Latin poets, modern Latin writers, or the sequences of the church or Christian "classics." If these redactors and printers were getting out manuals of study, suggestions for possible interpretations of the classic being studied, a quite different light falls on their handling of images. Annotations include suggestions, rather than full espoused interpretations of the kind Molinet attempted, and it is impossible, perhaps even inadvisable, to maintain completely the decorum of the original piece. Some of this invitation to meditate upon analogues, not claimed to be the same but comparable, may have entered as motivation in the case of some *Ovide moralisé* materials. If so, the same hospitality as we accord to the similar enrichment of modern images through association should be extended to these sixteenth-century tries at serious readings.

Another frequently heard modern claim equally disregards the question of audience—that by Christianization the classics were saved, made palatable, turned into acceptable books. These were scarcely clerics' books, or substitutes for real Ovids in pious centers and austere monasteries where no real Naso must appear. This denies all we know about the actual copyists, readers, composers, of such materials, yet it is tirelessly urged by present-day critics as a reason why the works exist. As well assign the yearly crop of freshman essay books to the inability of top-level critics to possess censored copies of volumes of social criticism.

It is dangerous in any case to assume that we get much true insight into "the mediaeval mind" or its Renaissance analogue from considering likely motives or from reading the books—familiar as we are with the traits usually deduced, of fondness for parallels, fierce intent to turn all things to Christian uses, inattention to literal meanings and the like. One is convinced that, for example, in Molinet we have met not the mind of the 1480's but the single mind of one bewitched moralizer, a mind ready to obey commands but not sharp enough for the task taken on. This may be the case with the single-version fourteenth-century metrical *Ovide* and its author, while Bersuire's preoccupation with such inadequate definitions of figurative language, shown in other works, may put him in an only slightly more estimable category. The more imaginative uses of allegory currently being practiced argue the existence of a scornful as well as an accepting public that watched experiments of this type.

The possible exception to these remarks is Colard Mansion. He composed in the vernacular, and the character of the large, opulently illustrated volumes which he and his imitators put out in the late fifteenth and early sixteenth centuries argues for audiences that may not have known much of Ovid, save what they found in books like these attractive, deluxe popularizations. Mansion's version, reproduced outright in succeeding years by Vérard, is a rare phenomenon, for he does not transliterate or simply modernize a mediaeval text; he evidently worked with several sources to hand and eclectically wove into the fiction itself all the moralizations and allegories he found and liked. He is especially fond of the Christian-doctrine type of figure we have been examining, and adds them from Bersuire or from the Old French metrical version, without (it seems to me) asking that they be convincingly parallel in significance, but only that some habitual Christian metaphor may be claimed and some profitable equation may be indicated on grounds of some trivial similarity of detail.

Except for cherished clichés, one feels obliged in fact to see the mediaeval mind quite as typically at work behind such redactions, as the insufficiently examined fifteenth-century manuscripts, fr. 137 in Paris and the B.M. MS. Royal 17 E iv. Earlier statements claiming close connection or identity with the prose version we find in Mansion must be qualified, for though all these are late enough to show up traits by exaggeration, it becomes clear that not all late fifteenth-century audiences liked an allegorical Ovid as well as Colard Mansion, who may just as easily be the untypical one. Relations between the two manuscripts need study, but reading the text of Royal discloses an author who gives the plain tale first emphasis, puts in some of the morals to be deduced (making no distinction in terms from allegoric) and admits a few natural-philosophy or historical interpretations rationalizing Ovid's oddities, but rigidly and systematically excises Christian-doctrine translations of the sort here considered, cutting them out consistently where they appear in the version followed. When one thinks of the dates of the Bersuire reprintings, of the dates of Mansion and Vérard editions juxtaposed with those of Molinet's work and publication, and of Christine and her like and of their translations and editions, one sees some room for a theory that there existed in the very late fifteenth and early sixteenth centuries a little pocket of taste, a smallish public which asked for these "profitable" ingenuities and equations. The distinction (though not the terms) is kept between mere moral interpretations and what I have described consistently as strict allegory, but disfavor is brought upon the whole endeavor by the laxity of poetic taste in this group; it was of little importance in the sum of things and did not much affect the sixteenth-century developments in poetic imagery. If such a fashion truly held sway, say for twenty to forty years, we cannot tell how influential it was—but such readers were catered to by a quite small number of refurbishers. Such a strand within the reading public is a phenomenon that would much remind us of our own day, in which there is a limited but coterie-lively and seemingly insatiable public hospitable to ingenious "readings" of the imagery of well-known poems. Similar latitude concerning serious functioning of images and concerning the rights of original authors to their own intended meanings, characterizes the modern analogue to these fifteenth-century devotees of their own kinds of profit in images, though profit is now seen in a different area and kind of equation—archetypal, Freudian, mythic, as well as religious.

These fifteenth-century tastes were not to have much influence on major developments of imagery in the great English Renaissance poets. The giants (Spenser, Shakespeare, Milton) are not in this line. The "influence" of materials includes also influencing later men as to what to avoid, and some such effect may have been felt by Spenser, nearest in date to these developments. Surely he made classical figures and great images based on this heritage permanent denizens of English poetry, and we have only to imagine him rubbed from the list of English poets to realize our attachment to Continental habits in images, through him alone. I have argued that his habits in writing images, especially his Christianization of their outer detail and inner sense, at a very deep level of fundamental serious signification, was affected by the same inheritance of strict allegory which produced these Christian translations. But the bald and overt form of this conversion of old myths he carefully avoids, nor have we anything resembling the obverse, like the young Milton's rejection of the classical pantheon for a truer Deity, in the Hymn and in Book I of *Paradise Lost*.

Spenser's preoccupations were such that we cannot imagine him ignorant of these manuals, and the gain is perhaps largely in seriousness, when we compare a Fradubio metamorphosis with changes like Io's or Actaeon's. Though we have no poet showing likeness to Jean de Meun in the texture of his poetry, Spenser does exhibit a likeness quite as fundamental, and perhaps learned: the way he employs allegory to make huge, lengthy images speak to us on puzzling philosophical or metaphysical questions. Answers are often only tacitly given (say, to the question—in all of the *Roman de la rose* or in Bks. III and IV of the *Faerie Queene*—of what is the nature of "Love"). Images are dramatic as a masque, not as a play or a débat, is dramatic; and more likenesses than we would think are owed to the simple fact that both men are serious about the issues their allegories present and therefore use narrative images similarly. Certainly this fact is responsible for many of the differences we have noted in these other

Christian allegorizers. Where others have reprimanded a Bersuire for letting Christian seriousness engulf Ovid, and the common complaint against all these writers is that they were dévots, I would propose the opposite accusation—that they took so little care to convey Christian ideas and mysteries that serious educated Christians could not stomach them, and the others had not enough Ovid to catch even the witty shocks which displaced serious imaging of Christian beliefs.

One other pleasure men took in these materials is one we too still take in them. All three clusters of texts commented upon in this chapter are famous iconographically. Pictures did much to keep the *Othéa* alive, though in its printed forms it does little more than satisfy our curiosity. The *Roman de la rose* produced enormous numbers of illustrated books; as Bourdillon confesses (p. 74), the several series in the profusely illustrated printed editions afforded no first-rate woodcuts, and so too, the well-known tradition in illumination is charming rather than beautiful, and has much of monotony and superficiality. Contradictory as it may sound, the moralized Ovid is basically an unillustrated text, though its existence is responsible for many opulent books and famous pictures. It is convenient to take up these riddles in their relation to allegorical imagery together, and to take up first this last set of books, which cannot even be safely neglected by the art historian.

Those who later made synthetic books out of the old materials are chiefly responsible for this artistic importance. The two authors who were prime sources of the allegorized materials produced texts in which illustration was of little importance and singularly uncontributory when attempted. Of Bersuire's book, of course, the small, utilitarian printed editions (1509, 1511, 1515) are unillustrated, and the largish number of manuscripts shows nothing we could call a tradition of illumination.[49] The fourteenth-century metrical version, with twenty manuscripts,

---

[49] On manuscripts, see Ghisalberti (*op.cit.*, n. 5), pp. 52-66. The manuscripts are nowhere described completely as a group, but those one sees or can study are the expected pedestrian copies useful for glossing. The several B.Mus. copies are unillustrated, as are the various scattered copies in English libraries; the text is not well represented in the Bodleian and I have not attempted to identify partial copies. Manuscripts containing Bersuire include no interesting illustrated books, and several copies are in college collections, as one would expect.

occurs most frequently unillustrated;[50] huge, archaic, and never existing as a unified text modernized or prosified for early printing, one doubts its Renaissance currency. How and where was it read? However, one outstanding exemplar of the metrical text (MS. Thott 399-folio in Copenhagen), is impressively decorated with pictures which have immediate and narrow relations to the woodcut series that began its life with Mansion's book in 1484. These relations (forming a connection between the two original allegorized texts) are complicated, but the problems belong to the art historian interested in the transmission of graphic conventions, for the character of the illustrations offers us no light on the kind of problems touched here. They are entirely disconnected from the allegorical interpretations offered for Ovid's figures and stories; none gives us any inkling of what a designer, deliberately indicating allegorical or moral meaning in the visual images, would seize upon as a method. They illustrate Ovid's gods and Ovid's narratives, not the literary phenomenon we know as Ovid *moralisé*. The Thott Manuscript has been amply discussed, and the woodcut series in the Mansion and Vérard editions fully described or reproduced, and therefore we will not examine the matter in detail here, but rest content with the reader's easy access to reproductions showing the nature of these late and purely narrative illustrations.[51]

[50] Again there is no study of manuscripts as a group with special regard to their illustration. There are *dessins ombrés* in fr.373, colored designs in fr.871 (both late fourteenth century), illustrations in the Geneva manuscript and in Brussels Bibl.roy.9639; the pictures are interesting to the historian of artistic styles and of ateliers, but examination of illustrations mentioned in our discussion, and of the quite conventional pictures in Vatican MS.Reg.lat.1480 (at beginnings of Books), and of samples from MS.Geneva 176 (fourteenth century) showed no hint of a pictorial tradition peculiarly suited to a *moralized* Ovid. Hence I have not pursued this unrewarding line of study in manuscripts none of which are first rate or well known.

[51] Two works by M. D. Henkel handle these questions, with full series of reproductions: *De Houtsneden van Mansion's Ovide Moralisé* (Amsterdam, 1922); and "Illustrierte Ausgaben von Ovid's *Metamorphosen* im xv., xvi. und xvii. Jrh.," Bibliothek Warburg, Hamburg, vi (1926-27), 58-144 and plates. Since these, J. van't Sant has studied MS.Thott 399-fol. and edited Book vii from it, in *Le Commentaire de Copenhague de l'Ovide moralisé* (Amsterdam, 1929). Since this does not give information on the extremely copious small and large illustrations in the manuscript, I mention the narrative character of these where pertinent.

Two additional points should be made regarding this Ovidian tradition (quite possibly overemphasized) of imposed allegorical meanings, and the illustrations developed for the texts which transmitted it. The two manuscripts so frequently cited (Bibl. Nat. f. fr. 137 and B.M. Royal 17 E iv), are both illustrated and contain a prose redaction of uncertain provenance, late fifteenth century but closely related to the narrative parts of Mansion's printed prose version; I have already noted Royal's striking difference therefrom, in that it never includes any of the doctrinal identifications and interpretations[52] which Mansion inserts so consistently, confident apparently of pleasing some audience of the '80's, and copied in the early sixteenth century by Vérard. Again, the Royal Manuscript's pictures[53] reveal nothing to our purpose; these purely narrative or representational miniatures, of Saturn, of Phaeton and his father, of Pyramus, or Arachne, shed no light on the problem here studied, of how moralized and Christianized force, claimed to be carried by classical figures and stories, can be indicated. They have neither. I give the Mansion picture of Phaeton's request (the fatal chariot seen on the right) as Fig. 105, to exemplify this point, juxtaposing as Fig. 106 the merely king-like father and his son from the Royal Manuscript. Though

[52] Evidently like fr.137 in this; see Ghisalberti, *op.cit.*, pp. 75-76. The miniatures of this important manuscript are described in part, p. 75n., and apparently keep to story-telling purposes like so many others we mention. But they are said by Henkel (pp. 8ff., 37ff., of his later work; cited in n. 52 above) to have been used for some Mansion cuts and have been dated 1460-75, and conjectured to be by the artist of Brussels Bibl.roy.9305 (Henkel p. 8). A similarly relaxed attitude toward the moralizations resulting in similar omissions in what is probably a nonce-version of the 1460's warns us against generalizations about "intellectual climate" (for Mansion was soon to begin his different work); de Boer's edition in the early 1920's of this 1460's *L'Ovide moralisé en prose* presents a version that is disregarded here since it is extant only in Vatican MS.Reg.1686. It is the less interesting to us since it progressively omits more and more of the moralizations, by direction of the patron who had it made, though its existence shows how single persons of pious tastes could keep a text alive.

[53] The subjects of the pictures in MS.Royal 17 E iv can be read in the catalogue description; the subjects are comparable with those in fr.137 and in the woodcut tradition. But the Royal pictures are not at all similar in design and disposition to Thott-Mansion-Vérard pictures of the same subjects. No doubt the manuscripts did as usual establish conventional choices as to which figures or story-moments should be portrayed, a separate point from the manifest imitations traceable in cases mentioned above.

FIGURE 105   FIGURE 106

an occasional detail can be interpreted if the story is known as
exemplum, there is really nothing but narrative significance here,
even in Mansion who would do his text any violence to secure
"profitable" readings, and though the two first-mentioned subjects (Saturn, Phaeton) had been moralized and allegorized time
out of mind in many types of materials. In sum, the evidence
seems to point to the fact that illustrators of Ovidian materials
either could not suggest the extensions of meaning provided by
interpreters, or did not wish to.

The second complicating fact is the existence of a preface describing the nature of the gods, which is responsible for many,
and the most impressive, of the pictures. It turns out to go back
to Bersuire and (Petrarch), to have close relations with the famous
Libellus, and to be the source of numerous well-known details;
it appears, e.g. in MS. Thott-399-fol., of the *metrical* text—a
factor of its history which is of interest mainly to the historian
of art, since again its illustrations do not attempt to portray the
allegorizations and Christian translations which interest us. It is
of much importance in the transmission of visual images of the
pagan gods now best known. But it assisted transmission of information about classical myth, not transmission of mediaevalized
Christianizing of myth.

We must beware, then, of the overeasy assumption that there
was current a corpus of traditional Ovidian allegorized interpretations, cliché-substitutes for the original Ovidian meanings. The sit-

uation is not the same as with other similar bodies of converted material. The moralized Ovid remains a body of materials always to be consulted because it may explain a puzzling peculiar detail in some writer's or artist's handling of an Ovidian or other subject;[54] we cannot know which persons were temperamentally attracted to these translations and parallels, and the material, in varying forms of unequal attractiveness, was kept available and was not allowed to be forgotten as times changed fashions. But when some sixteenth-century image is referred back to "tradition" because it appears thus or is so interpreted "in the *Ovide moralisé*"—our question must always be "in which *Ovide moralisé*?" and just what was the author reading or seeing? For we have seen that the texts differ greatly and may not be counted on to include at expected dates this or that extension of the imagery, that they in all probability did not displace the original, and were not justly translated into visual terms exhibiting the same new characteristics as the verbal forms. This is in the widest degree untrue regarding other traditions we have examined, like those touching the cardinal virtues, of the seven gifts related to virtues and to vices. The Ovidian conversions and translations could not seep into men's common conceptions and be taken up in book after book to thus influence all later literary and graphic treatments; nor could they leave the vestiges of their distinctions upon later pictures and phrasings.

The proof of this claim lies in the fact that from this wealth of material only a very few images established themselves as commonplaces. I doubt this would be true if it did not also appear that the inability of visual images to portray this kind of metaphorical dimension is another striking fact we observe.[55] Jason's

---

[54] See, e.g. I. Lavin, "Cephalus and Procris," *JWCI*, vol. 17 (1954), 260-87. It is typical that even as early as Caxton's *Six Bookes of Metamorphoses*, a few rationalizations and "natural" interpretations are included, but doctrinal figures are given short shrift. Caxton's book has been neglected here because it had no currency, seeing print first in 1819 (ed. G. Hibbert for the Roxburghe Club, from a unique manuscript). Caxton may have used some manuscript more like Royal 17 E iv, with its characteristic omissions, than like the Mansion text his editor conjectures to be a source.

[55] The most deeply dyed of allegorical readers cannot extend this element into their illustrations; cf. Fig. 105, and Marot, with his predilection for moralized meanings and his contribution to the edition of 1556 (*Les trois premieurs livres*). The preface uses the familiar figure of *escorce* and *moëlle* and *noyau*, and many morals and natural-philosophy meanings for the gods are given,

pride can be distinguished as the pride *of Lucifer*, the fundamental ingratitude, only through literary means; the eye can no more tell kinds of pride apart than it can see that Narcissus's self-love is *idolatrous* as he gazes at his image in the fountain.

These remarks are not intended to countermand all that we have said concerning the importance of some of the Ovidian figures and of men's attempts to portray them to the eye, or to discard (for literature) this whole newly opened terrain wherein the mythographers and others have fruitfully replanted "the allegory of poets." This may have been a commoner phrase than we suspect to separate off this kind of allegory from "the allegory of theologians," and shows vague but important effects of the centuries of exegetical use and of belief in the truth of both readings. We may be glad that Spenser came in time to feel the importance of the latter, without giving up the kind of enrichment which the high Renaissance secured for some classical figures. An image-manual or handbook, like Christine's, had fewer difficulties to face than did stories in narrative form; advantage accrues if an attempt to catch the new-interpreted significance can show in some details of the iconography, a known picture will be read metaphorically (as Orpheus the good shepherd was) for what it cannot really display to the eye; partial abstraction into mood or quality—as with the planets and their typical natures—will allow symbol to arise from narrative. But even so, and even with known figures, there is something we must *know* rather than see before Andromeda will look like a soul, not a maiden (Harington's *Preface* shows the commonness of this figure), before Isis will be transformed from the simple indication of fruitfulness and abundant life that we catch in the portrayal of graffing, to

---

but no "doctrinal" ones, while the pictures are narrative. Marot's translation of Book 1 does not undergo at all the same treatment as those discussed here; what is evidently the presentation copy (to King Francis I) is Bodl. MS.Douce 117. The pictures are narrative except for the first (f. 3v in which Christ blessing stands in a Paradise of Peaceful Animals, with Chaos like a towering gray boulder nearby—oddly like *Ovidio met* . . . (Venice, 1497), with each fable given its alegoria, by Bonsignore (not doctrinal but moral, natural or rationalizing). See Henkel, *op.cit.*, n. 52, "Ill. Ausg.," 65ff., and E. Krause, *Die Mythen-Darstellungen in der venez. Ovidausgabe* . . . (Würzburg, 1926); also cf. B.Mus. IB 23185, cut for the Creation of the World in the Venetian Bible. It is not unusual to translate Ovid's story of the reconciliation of the elements (by "God") into the Christian story of creation.

the complex logical parallelisms of double natures joined and marvelous abundance secured through the Blessed *Virgin's* special "graft" of divinity upon humanity. Evidently, not only is language the carrier of evaluation in its very tissue, making us respond with tiny impulses of repulsion or attraction to the language alone, but the kinds of meanings allegory sees, leading as they do to what we shall *believe*, are unavoidably couched in the conceptual medium of words, unless our private prior knowledge makes these unnecessary.[56]

The third group of books enabling us to study successful and unsuccessful imposition of allegorical meanings, those which perpetuated the *Roman de la rose* in various forms, shows also a well-established iconographical tradition. It was early, firmly fixed and extremely popular, for the *Roman* both in print and in manuscript is one of the longest-lived picture-books we have.[57] It will exemplify some curious new points, but in sum we learn the same lesson—that allegorical imagery is obstinately difficult to translate into visual terms unless we ourselves know enough

[56] Images in Christine's one hundred stories which show elements such as those noted, in their *formal* character lend themselves to allegorical reading even in the most makeshift illustrations; an example is MS.Bodl. 421. Moral meanings can be quickly indicated by ingenious artists; Bodl. 421 has for Bacchus (Fable 21) the usual feast, but the two drunk gallants on the floor are swine from the waist up. However, though Cassandra (Fable 32) is a "devoted worshipper" and Busiris (Fable 41) is a type of sacrilegious rapine, the visual images of their two pagan altars cannot themselves direct us toward the approval we are to have for Cassandra and the condemnation for Busiris; and in Aglauros' story (Fable 18), the seated goddess-like Envy in the sky aflame must chew serpents before we rank her where she belongs. Contrast this helplessness with the unobtrusive deftness with which evaluations are embedded in the very medium of language. Allegorical subtleties offer precisely the same difficulty—e.g. that Latona's enemies (Fable 20) warn us against the unending cupidity of Avarice, not the naturalistically portrayed sin of Envy. More careful attention is given to minutiae in the Christine manuscripts in an article by the present author cited in n. 5 above.

[57] On the latter, see Langlois, *Les Manuscrites du Roman de la rose* (Paris, 1910); on the former, we have the good fortune to possess the classifications and ordering of Bourdillon's study cited in n. 5 above. No attempt is made to reproduce schemes of related cuts or lists so easy of access. The number of manuscripts is enormously large, but illustration in the twenty or so editions melts down to a few interdependent series, and the principles and points that interest us can be exemplified from any smallish group of the two main forms of the text.

to provide the "literary" key. We see it here with a double demonstration, for not only the imposed allegory but the author's original allegory asked to be visually apprehensible, and in neither case could the difficulties be surmounted.

The choices of when to illustrate seem to bear no relation to allegorical intent and were virtually fixed, as is so usual, in the manuscripts, and came down thence into the cuts for printed editions. We could ourselves have conjectured that the large groupings chosen would be: the dreamer asleep, going to the garden, the vices outside the walls, the garden-pictures with the god and his companions, the action when Reason, when Bel Acceuil, when Amis, when Faux Semblant enter it, chosen exempla from the speeches, the Natura and Genius figures, the taking of the castle. Obviously these different kinds of images offer different problems touching the transmission of allegorical meaning since they possess it in different degrees. As we have noted, images already abstracted from multifold experience find the task easiest, as with the set of vices; Guillaume de Lorris' Hate and Villainy and Avarice have meanings generalized by some familiar attribute or expression or act (Avarice's chest, Tristesse stabbing herself). The exemplum pictures are in a similar though not identical category (Seneca dying in his bath, Dalila shearing Samson). The *Roman de la rose* series contains a few stereotypes meant to convey allegorically with power some idea-cluster difficult of statement—an occasional Fortune's wheel, Golden Age pictures "significant" rather than narrative (one reproduced as Fig. 93). The garden pictures are frankly representational, but one would like to know whether the ubiquitous final appearance of the Lover plucking the rose was really "seen" as figurative; there is no suggestion of a psychological or physiological conquest, except when very occasionally in some manuscript a picture of two human beings is substituted for the usual flowerbush scene.

A first simple test of whether one is reading both text and pictures allegorically comes in the portrayal of Bel Acceuil, who is, of course, masculine in the text. But to the eye, he is usually presented not as the psychological abstraction he is, but rather as the Lover's lady, pure and simple. We see that this simplification and descent into outright naturalism would destroy the text's subtleties, removing the very reason for Guillaume's choice of allegory as a mode. Though he is addressed as "beaufils," he is a young woman leaning from a turret (Bodl. MSS. Douce 332, f. 119v, xv; Selden supra 57, f. 106r, xiv) or receiving the chaplet from La Vieille (e. Mus. 65, f. 99v; Bibl. nat. fr. 380, f. 84, xiv), flattening the point of that incident most extremely.[58] This obfuscation of the psychological allegory, precluding ironic implications or universalized meaning, is carried over into the woodcuts. In the important series which Bourdillon calls Lyon ii, responsible for many editions' cuts (e.g. C or F or Molinet 1503) a lady who is referred to as *le* throughout is consoled by La Vieille (also true in the woodcut series called V ii and P vi and in series L i—see sg. o 5 of Bourdillon's edition Λ). It is especially odd when "he" becomes both sexes, appearing in the good miniatures of Douce 364, for example, as a gowned man talking to the Lover, becoming a lady in the tower, a man again later (ff. 23r, 28r, 95r, xv; there is some vacillation also in woodcut set L ii; see Bourdillon's list nos. 73-5, 30). Occasionally he appears throughout, properly, as the masculine abstraction (Egerton 881, ff. 23v, and with garland 96v; Royal 19 B 13, f. 31v, xiv, only one picture; Douce 371, xv; Douce 195, xv, unaccountably old and with a perceptible corporation, though in a careful manuscript). There is an effective series of fights between states-of-mind in this good manuscript, ff. 109v-111v; Pitié fights Dangier, Franchise, Peur, etc., and the fights need rubrics, but in reading the pictures we absorb psychological allegory effortlessly and enjoyably. We grasp the mode far more readily when we see *him*, Bel Acceuil, taking off over the stone wall when Dangier appears (Douce 195, f. 21v). But he is usually the Lady—placed therefore in unaccountable narrative situations, and mingling straight narrative with allegory disagreeably.

This is a simple failure in transmitting the narrative sense of a text, to be compared with illustrators' ineptitudes far more

[58] Or even, still more "narrative" though very elegant, clinging to her Dreamer-Lover, Douce 188, ff. 21r, 25r, xv. I give only samples, to avoid the frustration of unexemplified general claims; points made are typical, though I adduce chiefly manuscripts in England. We must bear in mind that these pictures were most often turned out by workers following models or rubrics, not by artists reading a text to be "illuminated." One would not dare suppose a designer deliberately, tongue in cheek, placing a ploughboy picture where it stands by Genius's excommunication passage exhorting Love's servants, "Arez, pour dieu barons arez / Et vos lignages reparez" (series v, ii, in edition H, Vérard's quarto; not uncommon because it depends on a verse title).

FIGURE 107

FIGURE 108

fundamentally inconsistent with the purpose of a text. The first important puzzle is Nature. One representation of her at her work, creating individuals to keep the species alive, is universally popular: she stands by an anvil, shaping upon it, with hammer uplifted, a baby (or homunculus), and beside her the pictured forge shows its flames, see Figs. 107 and 108 which are typical of a vast number of both miniatures and cuts. No reader misses the physiological symbolism so repeatedly emphasized in the text, and part of this picture's popularity came perhaps from its being read metaphorically. But we cannot really tell to what extent this picture was read as indicating the act of generation, throughout the universe, in relation to the definition of "love" being attempted. Or had Nature become the almost fully abstract personage Natura with a conceptually clear set of "works," an image almost divorced from the complexities which flicker across this text—natural love, our nature, animal nature, natural man's viewpoints, created nature including him opposed to the Creator, marriage natural and sacramental, divine love reflected in nature, chastity, fidelity or virginity natural or forced, and the like. It is not really possible to tell how much of the *text's* figure of Nature was read in this visual image, unliterally though it must be read; but at any rate she became a stereotype, and one doubts if her portrayals carried any but the most conventionalized symbolic force, unmediated and unelaborated. Sometimes Nature shapes a bird or animal (MS. Douce 195, f. 114v, xv); sometimes merely a stick of iron (Douce 188, f. 122v, xv), but the usual figure as exemplified is found both early and later in edition after edition (having the same elements in the much-copied series L ii and PV 1).

FIGURE 109

That Natura has none of the majesty we habitually attach to her image, brought up on Chaucer, Spenser and Alanus, and living in the century we do, is not astonishing, but quite proper, for Jean demonstrably avoids giving her this expected character. Despite the passage he calmly lifts from Alanus, and his obvious general borrowing (including the very motif of her *complaint*) and grand survey of her powers, the tone of the long image is too frequently punctured by ironies, and Nature's talk and behavior too often allowed to approach inconsequentiality and feminine smallness, for us to see her as we do the great shadowy half-divine beings created by these other poets. The unprepossessing busy old dame of the illustrators is no travesty.

In one fourteenth-century manuscript (Bodleian MS. e.Mus. 65), the text-break (f. 98v) where Nature is introduced busily working at her forge is illustrated by an elaborately drawn picture of man and woman naked in bed,[59] and this translation has the same effect upon a reader who is pursuing with interest the nearby text as it does in the editions when beside the long verbal image of the castle being taken there stand two naked combatants fighting with their shields and weapons (see Fig. 109). We feel

[59] There is a marriage picture at this break (Bourdillon's verse title no. 94) in woodcut series v i (edition E)—but this edition borrows cuts with abandon, and nothing is probably intended; the B.Mus. illuminated copy of it (IB 41225) substitutes the old Nature-baby-forge picture, sg. O 8v. The naked figures are not in MS.Harl.4425, despite its use of verse-titles from the editions, already appearing; no. 111 which evoked this illustration ends "Dont aulcuns jousterent tous nuz," and comes just as the brand is being thrown and they issue from the castle.

the same sudden universalization of the "Natura generatrix" figure and the same spanning of the gap between literal vehicles and full meaning. An unelaborated chance line in a verse-title produced this last picture—No. 111; these are found only in the printed editions and are studied by Bourdillon. But if instead one reads the castle-siege figure while giving it the accompaniment of Fig. 110, the attacking knight sometimes pictured, one sees how necessary it is for a visual image that is metaphorical in nature to evoke proper associations and convey concepts by giving away some of the secret hidden by the metaphor. These suggestions can be evoked unobtrusively by language, but we generally put them in ourselves, reading some long metaphor whose signification, earlier lodged in our minds (as Nature's is), controls the otherwise unrevealing words and seen objects and makes them betray hidden meaning. It is clear that even this early the castle inhabitants were not read entirely as a psychological allegory. The poor illustration of the knight from Molinet is used to show also how little the moralizing rubric fits. In the text we thus miss two allegories; what we see is only a knight shooting in a siege.

It is instructive to watch the attempts made to follow pictorially the text's metaphors of castle-siege, Venus's thrown brand, etc., and simultaneously to convey the lasciviousness which inflames the verbal images. The "sanctuary," when pictured, is meaningless; a lover worships a fully dressed lady in a pavilion (Douce 195, f. 155r). The *meurtrière*, impossibly difficult, but often attempted, best approximates the effects of the text when freely drawn with much architectural license, but given lascivious suggestions by frank departures from the written image (see Fig. 100, MS. e.Mus. 65, from the latter half of the fourteenth century). In all these cases we have merely observed how difficult it was to suggest visually the simplest allegorical intent of the author, his psychological and physiological double meanings couched in metaphor. Except in Natura, we have not touched upon the greater difficulties of indicating Jean's favorite function for allegorical figures—the dialectic dramatically presented by his acting and speaking "abstract" *personae* (Amor, Amis, Faux Semblant, Genius, Nature, a Lover). The stage beyond even this—visual suggestion of the imposed doctrinal allegories Molinet or Marot sought to repose in these images—is attempted

FIGURE 110

by no one. But indeed, it did not seriously enter men's understanding of the true possible content of the *Roman*. Even so, one knows of no comparable analogous attempt or success.

Irony is Jean's chief instrument to indicate (as he constantly does) what is fallacious or absurdly inadequate about positions taken by the *personae*, or exactly where he himself stands on a question, though this is left ambiguous quite through the end of the piece. Ironic qualifications are almost impossible of portrayal. We may be as glad that Faux Semblant receives little illustration (and that little in his disguise) as we are that no one tries to portray Hellenore and Prisdell, or Malbecco's transformation. We are now upon the ground where we see why the *Faerie Queene* has never been satisfactorily illustrated—for Spenser's favorite and usual function for allegorical images is precisely Jean's enacted dialectic which "opens" some large philosophical question to the view.

Such complexities were beyond the designers of cuts for the printed *Roman*, but some manuscript illuminators do attempt to convey evaluations of the so-called characters which puncture their false claims or otherwise show up their true affiliations. There is something of this in the frequent pictures of Genius being togged out as a bishop by that unlikely sacristan, the God Amor. Any reader realizes anew that he is a fake as a dispenser of pardons. A surer example, since not supported by text, is the attempt to show Genius as an unfit confessor and to call attention to the absurdity of a naturalist confessor; strong suggestions I

have seen are embodied in miniatures where Genius openly of-
ficiates at a pagan altar with the usual naked figurines indicating
false god (see Figs. 95 and 96 from Bodl. MSS. Douce 364,
195).[60] That both Nature and Genius have made something less
than God into their god is after all plentifully clear in the text,
and no illustrations try to make them the sacred messengers of
God's Own Simple Plan, which some modern commentary sees
them as; but many visual indications of their insufficiency as philosophers of Love are less striking than these—for example, the
emphatically and restrictedly secular appearance of both Genius
the Priest and Nature the divinely appointed.

Perhaps it is a mere chance effect of this denigration through
images that we feel when, reading the Pygmalion-images near
the end, we see him chiseling away at an obvious lay-figure, and
within small space find him kneeling in worship before his cold
naked goddess. Figures 97 and 98 perhaps sufficiently suggest
the effect; verbally, the long image not only mocks the courtly
lover's idolatrous folly in worshipping what he himself has made,
but counts upon the common signification of Pygmalion as luxurious sensualist. In the literary work it forms part of Jean's
final reduction of "love" to pure sexual desire and completely
self-indulgent physical titillation and satisfaction which ends the
poem. Jean's view of this is not stated outright, but certainly he
has shown it as a glaring reduction. Whether or not "a blasphemous reduction" is harder to say; but the shocking circumstances
which surround the one declaration that "God *is* Love" (in the
parc-image) make this stricter use of allegory fairly probable. A
definition of love that omitted all concern with Heavenly Love
was scarcely possible to this audience.

One of the most curious examples of an artist's attempt to show
ambiguity of meaning that is clear in the verbal allegory may be
mentioned again here because it exemplifies the shifts to which
illustrators are put when allegorical subtleties are to be visually

---

[60] This is all the clearer if mitre and alb are being deftly substituted for a
pair of peacock-feather wings (as in MS.Douce 195, f. 139r). The satirical
import is felt in the Genius-preaching pictures of Harl.4425 and other manuscripts; it is as clearly a travesty of a properly devoted sermon as the pardoner's,
and this is the source of the humour of the text. Later manuscripts especially
are not to be thought of as showing us individually conceived "illustrations,"
but were decorated by persons who had not read the text.

presented. The image of the *parc* of the White Lamb (*Roman de la rose*, lns. 19,931-20,031, 20,243-596) shows Jean using the allegorical mode most subtly and powerfully. It is an un-mixed straight Christian symbolical image of the Heavenly Par-adise, deliberately traditional, to be read *mystice*, an anagogical figure in the direct stream of Christian religious allegory; it is solely its use in the piece that provides the ambiguity and the irony. We recall that Genius is the speaker to whom the descrip-tion is given; part of his false pardon is that he gives "Love's barons" promise of entry therein. The ironic reverberations are rich and manifold, not excluding references to the St. Amour con-troversy, and friars—as well as other barons of Love who are devotees of poverty—being given special right to enter heaven. We have been made alert to greater ironies to come by the shifti-ness of Genius's action and speech, but the pictorial image itself is kept clear of this irony—that he will thus reward those who go unremittingly about the physical business of procreation, or rather of uninhibited sexual satisfaction, for there is little thought of progeny when he tosses the burning taper, certainly none of multiplying life to glorify the Creator of life. But our full real-ization of this comes later, and our shocked turning away from Genius has very little of moral condemnation even in its over-tones.

If we are reading about the heavenly *parc*, and the Fountain of Grace which wells from all three Persons of the Trinity, in the manuscript from which Fig. 99 above comes, we meet that picture at ln. 20,465, just as the three life-giving streams are described, and the *olivete* which grew in the waters of Grace, the Tree that was to bear the fruit of salvation. If this designer was reading the text (unusual for the date but surely not un-known), then he was trying to show the reduction and perversion of the fountain of eternal life and abundance, turned into a lascivious image—which is the very thing Genius does, but *only* allegorically. It has a startling effect, to see visibly, not what is in Genius's mind (any cinema does this) but to see the real great symbol as well as the perverted replica of it as it is being *mis*understood. We see Genius's incapacity to understand his traditional figure and his use of it simultaneously with appre-hending the enormous gap between that and the reality of the figure; the latter disappears even as Genius is that moment picturing it and we see the two figures only for an instant, then are left with his. This is a complicated idea virtually *seen*; it is comprehended in a flash if we are reading the book.

All the examples, introduced for whatever reason from whatever text, show in sum how various and how complex were the pleasures to be taken in allegorical figurative presentation; the more complex, the more enjoyable, but these were enjoyments best offered by images in verbal form, perhaps not possible in other forms. We have seen how difficult a task was taken on by those who sought to find in or impose upon classical images any profoundly allegorical significance, and that success attended their efforts only if certain principles were observed with an artist's unrelaxing care for decorum, and then (especially if the bridge must be crossed to a different religion) only when they chose images of a suitable formal, not contentual, character to translate. The imposing of allegory upon an already extant artistic fiction, whether of different religion or not, apparently involved such difficulties that the only hope of success occurred when a fundamental similarity in meaning or drift of thought allowed the old decorum in details to suit the new interpretation. In this situation, which we know in a few images like Orpheus as good shepherd or Circe as luxury, when the seemingly new Christianized meaning was really already "in" the images, the allegory is found rather than imposed. But even then we discovered no examples where a new Christian interpretation could be grasped visually; it had to be declared and made to inhabit the ancient image. This was verbally possible, and enjoyable, enriching both the symbols and the new Christian matter they pointed to.

But imposed allegories even thus liberally defined as already in the old images, though not known in our new terms to the authors, required literary subtlety and meditative thought; iconographically the images stubbornly refused translation. Even typology, the far-distant parent of this successful finding of new beliefs in old story, relied upon juxtaposition as a method of indicating identity of significance in Old Testament and New Testament figures—the Manna is *placed beside* the Last Supper. The illustrated *Othéa* texts merely juxtapose the pictured old symbol on the verbal new-thing-symbolized; the Ovid text declined the task and merely pictured the old-thing-symbolized.

Examining the *Roman de la rose*, we observe that this difficulty is related not to the gap between Christianity and Classical thought but to the gap between what concretions (unaided by any knowledge we have inherited from their traditional use) are able to indicate and what allegory asks them to indicate. Jean's allegory, let alone Molinet's could not be indicated. The same far-distant parent, strictly religious allegory, was perhaps responsible for a habit of looking for pleasure in figurative expression of profound beliefs and presuppositions (now a very uncommon expectation). This was usually extended expression wherein details progressively opened up new bases of similarity and new alleys and pathways within the general drift of the ideas, while double readings flickered across the surface, now seen and now unseen. It is this motion of progressive unfolding and this continual possibility of dubiety which gives literary expression of an image, moving through time, one advantage over pictorial presentation that must choose a moment and arrest it, with its meaning in its countenance. But the chief factor is a concretion's capacity to signify many things at once, some of them irrelevant. The fact that the reader does so much of the unfolding, and yet must follow his author conscientiously as to relevant significances, makes such figures harder to tie down.

I am convinced that this was the major enjoyment felt in the mode of allegory in these periods, little as the poorer examples can achieve it. Pleasure in ingenuity surely enters, and pleasure in recognition (both of imagery and concept) was a stronger element still. We can test this by noticing how spontaneously we share it; Christine's book gives this pleasure, and the *Ovide* texts largely fail of it because they are so greedy (to claim many significances) and so helter-skelter. It is true also that men do not weary of meeting, especially in interesting disguise, ideas and beliefs that they hold with real firmness. We shall have little sympathetic understanding of this mediaeval and Renaissance taste in imagery unless we can conceive of readers who thought deliverance from hell to heaven was extraordinarily interesting good news. Recognition of the statement of it and descriptions of it, in unexpected contexts, was a pleasure in itself. The developments in secular allegory, which were confined rather than numerous, retained these emphases upon the importance of what-was-symbolized; this interest seems to me to have outvied interests more typically Continental—in ingenious fancy or in associations gathered around the vehicles of images.

Moral allegory has not this stirring importance, to the degree that is natural even in later and diffused forms taken by allegory more strictly defined. Moral conflict is always interesting, to the present sensibility enthralling; but it is not engrossing to the degree that ideas touching the meaning of life and its ultimate ends, are interesting. This is a reason why one is concerned to urge a reading of Spenser which sees his "allegories" as well as his "morals," for his work eminently fits all the statements of the last two paragraphs touching pleasures in *allegory*; his peculiar quality and effects are far from satisfactorily accounted for by descriptions of psychomachia and moral exhortation. He does not separate the two in practice; perhaps no poet could. Even by Christine's time the rigid separation was forced. But images function differently, largely considered, with these different ends, and his are deepened and lit up by observing both uses and both kinds of effect.

The terminology we cannot retain, it seems to me. It had been lost to common use even before the era of the works we have discussed. Christine retains it, and if so typical a cultivated common reader tries consistently not to misuse the terms, and tries successfully not to confound the two functions, then others too still understood these matters. But if one reads the *Ovide* texts popular late in the century with special attention to terminology (moralement, allegorie, etc.), one finds Sponsa-Christi figures frequently referred to as interpreting moralement, "historial" alone keep clearly for its supposedly proper use, and an occasional use of the word "allegorie" to mean topical reference, showing that this loose modern use (as in "Spenser's historical allegory") was already current.[61] It no longer bids fair to engulf

[61] The word "moral" for doctrinal interpretations can be noted in Bk. I (Syrinx, Io), Bk. II (Callisto), Bk. III (Tiresias), Bk. IV (Atlas, Perseus). But in Bks. IV and V, Perseus as Christ is also called an "allegory," which it is by most definitions, and there are other examples of carefully correct use. Examples of the breakdown of the terminology could be vastly multiplied; see n. 45 above, the titles of works, and such phenomena as the innumerable "moralizations" of song-words in the sixteenth century, many of them "allegorical" by most earlier definitions. See the present author's "Sacred 'Parody' of Love Poetry, and Herbert," *Studies in the Renaissance*, vol. 8 (1961), 249-90. A "historical" allegory that is a topical satire is in Bk. II (Phaeton), and Abr.

the older and more valuable uses. But it would be an advantage to the reading of Renaissance authors other than Spenser if, without squabbling over keeping the term "allegory" for figures with some relation to mediaeval religious uses, we could yet maintain the distinctions in *functioning* which were so fruitful, let them be called what they will. Of all authors, Spenser is done the most harm by translating all "allegories" into "moralizations."

Fleming in his little book translating Virgil's *Eclogues* in 1575, 1589, means solely and simply this when he says "the matter or drift of the poet is meere allegoricall" and explains the matters of state pointed at.

CHAPTER FIVE

Romances

THE relationships spoken of in this chapter are clear and interesting only if they are tasted and experienced. It is therefore addressed to those readers of Spenser who are willing to embark upon (or who know) a body of romance readings: a considerable portion of the French so-called "Vulgate" Arthurian Cycle—perhaps a third of the *Lancelot*, besides the *Queste del Saint Graal* and the *Mort Artu*, the *Perlesvaus*, certain long-lived noncycle pieces like *Huon de Bordeaux* and *Bevis of Hamtoun*, a respectable number of small detached romances (of *lais* such as those of Marie de France, or the very different type as in *Gamelyn*), and naturally all of Malory, and Chaucer's romances. Connections are none the less real because they are deeply pervasive effects rather than precise borrowings of items, but the lines must not be drawn too taut; to counter this necessity of generalizing, Spenser primarily will be cited for types of relationships. It must be remembered that the special interest of this book is in inheritances that touch allegory, although such points must be presented here in a wider context, given the non-allegorical nature of most of the materials and much of their influence.

We fix our attention upon certain likenesses with the realization that they will make large differences all the more impressive. The poem Spenser wrote would have been totally impossible to a mediaeval writer. This is true also of genres formally closer, of Sidney's and Lodge's pastoral romances, of Drayton's verse-tales if not of his *Nymphidia*, that delightful single success in rivaling Chaucer's doggerel mock—the minstrel-romance. Nevertheless, we see in the relation under review an especially outstanding example of a phenomenon that begins to look characteristic of the Renaissance in England as compared with other countries: that the refusal to give up mediaeval forms and habits resulted in a forced marriage between those and new forms, motifs, stuffs, imagery, which, though an unnatural union, was a fertile one. Qualities of the offspring cannot be neatly separated into distinguishable inheritances from separate parents. In qualities, inclusions and altered purposes the combination differs from either source, seeming to owe its life to them both but its typical character to neither.

Various studies that search the romances for specific influences have made the whole relationship appear trivial. The bane of studies relating Spenser to romances has been the hunt for borrowed story-motifs. These connections seem largely illusory—and all but completely unimportant; meanwhile, far too much has been argued from their absence. I shall neglect such borrowings entirely. The important connections are persistently of another kind, important to the aesthetic judgments we make, but hard to isolate and seldom securely provable; the points to be made are incorrigibly large, vague and loosely drawn, and will be falsified if not allowed to remain so. In sum, they have enough relevance to what was learned about symbolic and non-symbolic fictional writing from mediaeval reading to belong in this book.

That we withdraw from precise source study and deny the importance of plot comparisons does not make the central fact any less true and important—that "mediaeval romance" is what is responsible for the character the *Faerie Queene* has as a narrative. We ought occasionally to think of what an unimaginably different poem we should have had if Spenser had written Christian history like the Fletchers, du Bartas, Milton; if Spenser had kept to secular historical narrative like Drayton in his Legends and his two heroic poems on Mortimer, or had written of the Irish and Belgian conflicts as Daniel did of the Civil Wars; or if Spenser had written "classical" historical epics like a Petrarch or a Ronsard, or mythicized pseudo-classical narratives like a Jean Lemaire de Belges; or if he had confined himself to (instead of merely using) Italianized, Platonized mythological poetry of the kind found in his temples of Venus or Isis or revolt of Mutability. Spenser finds use for all these kinds of narratives, but it has an extraordinary effect upon their durability and their absence of preciosity that they are set in a matrix of the most ordinary kind of storytelling in Europe for four centuries: the straightforward tale of chivalric romance.

Certain presuppositions, all now suspect, have governed criticism when it has touched upon Spenser and romance; two general observations with their sub-points may illustrate this. The relation of the *Faerie Queene* to mediaeval chivalric romances is seldom mentioned without a stated or hidden assumption that this provided "escape." Yet a major influence of this body of stories upon Spenser was that they taught him their flair for ordinary realism in its simplest sense: for situations drawn from daily life, natural rather than contrived or stilted conversation, unadorned reportage of a matter-of-fact presentation of what we instead isolate and call "the marvelous,"[1] credible and unelaborated motivations, modified by a few large accepted conventions like inviolable "customs," or the granting of quests or boons. This can be supported presently, but one might claim with justice that the romance-like portions of the *Faerie Queene* are the portions where we retire comfortably from the exotic and the thoroughly incredible into the plain affairs of serious but ordinary daily life. Feudal life was of course just as daily and just as ordinary as ours or Spenser's, and Malory's influence especially we would expect to be toward plain narrative of plain events, the romantic

[1] In this connection, all discussions of Spenser and romances would profit by renewed reference to Dorothy Everett's classic correction of familiarly accepted ideas, "A Characterization of the Engl. Med. Romances," in *Essays and Studies of the English Association,* xv (1929), and in her posthumous volume of *Essays on Middle English Literature* (Oxford, 1955). Such emphases in the present chapter are part of an approach so different from that of a closely related book, John Arthos' *On the Poetry of Spenser and the Form of Romances* (London, 1956), that I have decided not to cross-reference some natural similarities we show. Though we both mention a few points (romance settings, the pathlessness and the chance meetings, etc.), quite other points are here stressed than Professor Arthos' basic themes—such as Spenser the-poet-"complaining," self-conscious formation of the personality in romances, the romantic dream, or quest of innocence, and so on. A narrow look will show some of these general differences not unrelated to facts brought forward by the historian J. H. Hexter in his "Myth of the Middle Class in England," last appearing in *Reappraisals in History* (London, 1961) (and others cited). It may be unfortunate that so many of the same romances are mentioned by us both, but generous space given to the Italians, e.g. by Arthos and by an informative recent book more like the present one, G. Hough's *A Preface to the Faerie Queene* (London, 1962), enabled me to give place rather to the less worked-over mediaeval materials (largely ignoring Tasso for example). The present studies, begun with an article on Auberon and Huon in *PMLA*, Vol. 44 (1929), 706-714, long antedate recent published work.

See above, ch. 4, n. 4, for a disclaimer of any intention to enter the present-day controversies regarding "allegorical" interpretation of literary pieces—most often tropological, occasionally allegorical in its strict sense. I have cited outright those who seem to me to err grossly through imposition of "allegorical" meaning on mediaeval works, if the error is pertinent; oblique references or innuendoes are disclaimed.

"remoteness" of armor, moats, castles and jousts being still two centuries off.

Two side points are as little recognized as is the firm grasp of most mediaeval romance-writing upon actuality and the habitual use of that element as the ground of these fictions. One is that whereas it is naturally assumed that romances markedly influenced Spenser in his use of the supernatural, we notice rather that his most important large images portraying places and times beyond the natural, and actions beyond human nature, are not fundamentally romance-like. Mammon's otherworld is Dantesque and classical, the House of Pride is like a setpiece of Christian didactic literature, the Gardens of Adonis and Nature's realm in Mutability are influenced by cosmological myth of a Platonic cast, Isis' temple by Plutarchian late-classical lore, Acrasia's Bower by mediaevalized classical moral imagery.

These wonders, however, are set in a solid framework of chivalric story—real tournaments fought in visitable places (unlocated but less fanciful than the meetings and combats in Ariosto to which we are brought by a specified routing through the right countries and across the right borders). Nights are spent and wounds cured in ordinary castles; giants and monsters combatted as often as the conventional lions and bears, but as a mere variation of the inhabitants, and usually vanquished by valor not magic; the day's adventures, duties and hazards lived through without deliberate fostering of "romantic mediaeval atmosphere." In the prose *Lancelot*—romance par excellence, and natural source of habits and commonplaces because of its scope, frequent publication[2] and famed hero—supernatural marvels are largely clustered

---

[2] In the group presented as a unit: *Lancelot*, the *Queste* and *Mort Artu*. See below nn. 54-56 for data on publication of this most venerable and constant part of the Vulgate Cycle. The *Estoire del Graal* (on the early history of the Grail), prefixed later, as now seems pretty well agreed, and the *Merlin* ("Estoire de Merlin," or "Vulgate Merlin") form the two first sections of the five that make up the cycle, though both are later productions. This characteristic development of a narrative structure by accretion, in early sections, is not unlike some of Spenser's procedures, like furnishing a pre-history for Braggadochio, later but attached forward; what occurs haphazardly in most fiction is systematized as a principle for building a romance. We are accustomed to read the five in the order of their *events'* chronology, in the still indispensable H. O. Sommer edition, *The Vulgate Version of the Arthurian Romances*, Carnegie Institute of Washington (8 vols.; 1908-16). But they were not so met by the Elizabethan

around the acts and habitat of the character whose extra-human powers are meaningful: the Lady of the Lake, once no doubt a fairy mistress but now a benevolent otherworld patroness. Elsewhere large tracts of the story proceed as straightforward recounting of knightly prowess, avengings, promises, battles, mishaps, wounds, love affairs, the proving of character under stress and the relations and feelings of persons.

Spenser's use of the admittedly marvelous is roughly similar, and his significantly isolated otherworldly places or supernatural characters are set in a natural matrix which is that of the ordinary mediaeval world. Powers beyond the natural have true spiritual significance and are possessed by those meant to have such roles, while the communication or traffic between this world and the super-humanly evil or good worlds is always open but always important. These comparable narrative procedures are contrasted with, for example, Ariosto's lightheartedly fanciful and unrestrained use of the magical—of trance-inducing irresistible shields and incredibly convenient wishing-rings, of enchanted palaces that spring up and disappear as needed, psychological powers that exchange appearance and reality in the minds of "natural" characters, conjuring-books, recognition-charms, hippogriffs guided or unguided and the like machinery. All late romances, especially other Charlemagne-romances with enlargements, lie *Huon de Bordeaux*, similarly multiply machinery to advance plot, but most retain some shred of the important spiritual significance of the otherworldly elements, later so inventively developed in Spenser and integrated with Christian allegorical and symbolic meanings. There are good reasonable grounds for the effects recounted of Arthur's bright diamond shield, the unearthly landscape of the island where Venus's temple is found, Phaedria's boat that skims without power across the Idle Lake when "only she turn'd a pin." Since I think we may safely say Spenser learned to use the mediaeval milieu from those who lived in it, it has not the suggestions (of nostalgia, of daydream, of sentimental en-

reader, even in Malory's compilation and highly selective re-organization. Easily accessibly descriptions of the relations of different parts, with citations to data in studies, may be found in the several pertinent essays in R. S. Loomis, *Arthurian Literature in the Middle Ages* (Oxford, 1959) (esp. Frappier's on the Vulgate Cycle), or see E. Vinaver's several introductions in his Commentary, vol. III of *The Works of Sir Thos. Malory* (Oxford, 1947), e.g. see p. 1,265.

thusiasm) which would threaten that serious involvement with actual life which he desires and achieves. This is a kind of realism which is unchallenged by what Mrs. Bennett calls the *Faerie Queene*'s "unflagging unreality."[3] There is a sense in which this phrase points to Spenser's poetic creed, and it indicates a kind of distance from life neither produced by the use of romance milieux and motifs, nor challenged by it.

Like the use of the supernatural, a second side point touches accepted stereotypes of what romances are. We should ask "to *whom* are chivalric tales a nostalgic re-creation of what is lost, a harking back and wishful return to a vanished past"? Possibly only to us late-comers, prepared by *The Boys' King Arthur* for the stronger adolescent dose of *Idylls of the King*. We know considerably more than we did about the Tudor revival of Arthurian history for serious political ends, and about fifteenth-sixteenth- and seventeenth-century English attitudes toward chivalry. From the time of Greenlaw's early suggestive inquiries, Spenser students have been aware of the topicality and political seriousness given to Arthurian materials by two facts: the Celtic or British origins and Arthurian connections of the house of Tudor, combined with the legend of Arthur's prophesied return from Avalon to bring Britain again to her ancient glory. Charles Bowie Millican's carefully circumstantial book long ago (1932) made more obvious the inaccuracy of attaching usual connotations of "romantic" or "imitation-mediaeval" to Elizabethan use of Arthurian materials; special areas of new information were: the number and scope of serious references relating such history to Henry VII's Welsh lineage, the specific parallels (like Henry's exile in Brittany, like Arthur's purging the land of false religion, i.e. "Saracens"), the connections with interests of men like Dee and Daniel Rogers, the Polydore-Vergil controversy, the scope and importance of antiquarian interests and their tie to contemporary ideals, the organization of societies, the use of Arthurian "patrons," support of customs, sports or manners connected with

---

[3] In a spirited defense of the *Faerie Queene* against the charge of escapism in "Genre, Milieu, and the 'Epic-Romance,'" *English Institute Essays* (New York, 1951), p. 119. Mrs. Bennett argues against the influence of Arthurian romances on Spenser, but her reasons have nothing to do with the supposed escapism, but deal rather with the absence of plot influences (e.g. p. 108, the "avoidance" of Arthur's "legend" as told by Malory).

Arthurian romances, not for their quaint remoteness but for their current interest in a time of vigorous chivalric revival.

In the detailed study of this revival by Arthur Ferguson (*The Indian Summer of Chivalry*, 1960), it is impossible not to observe how completely Spenser's tone and handling fits the earlier English developments outlined. Often in some portion of the *Faerie Queene* where Ariosto is the undoubted immediate source, of plot motif or character, Spenser's altered tone and different narrative impulse show how the very changes of his source fit him into the mosaic of this English development. We watch this development from the time when Caxton and early printers found a motive for printing romances in the desire to enhance England's prestige and revitalize her institutions, down to the high tide of Arthurian interest in the 1580's. The *Faerie Queene* no longer stands so alone, as we consider plentiful evidence that the obsolescence of chivalry as an institution was far from obvious to a still partly feudal society, or evidence for the aristocracy's attempt to revitalize as well as to take refuge in the traditional ways of living and thinking, or as we observe the many other manifestations of close relations between chivalry and developing concepts of the commonwealth, of national pride, courtiership, or the ideals of other classes. Many of these points of view have been obscured by our interest in satire directed against quite limited aspects of the ancient institution.[4]

These very numerous evidences of interests and motives held

[4] More knowledge has diminished the impact of famous remarks like Ascham's about the "manslaughter and bold bawdry" of the *Morte Darthur*; a more discriminating understanding of what widely different works come under "romances" has affected similarly Nashe's famous slur on the style of *Bevis*; only the careless observer still sees in the *Knight of the Burning Pestle* a satire on knightly romances, where even its first audiences saw satire of callow city apprentices and their notions of chivalry (just so Drayton in *Nymphidia* satirized "the romances" no more than Chaucer had in *Sir Thopas*, though both mock the writers of doggerel trash fobbed off on minstrels' audiences). The very excellence and completeness for its early time of R. S. Crane's pioneering *The Vogue of Mediaeval Chivalric Romance during the English Renaissance* (Menasha, 1919), and of Furnivall's study of the famous list of Captain Cox, perhaps left us for too long emphasizing the chapbook kind of romance-reading (see the preface to the edition of *Robert Laneham's Letter*, London, 1907, orig. for Ballad Society, 1871). The information on early diffusion of romances, like that in Warton's *Observations on the* "Faerie Queene," is only partly superseded by the more recent books cited in n. 6.

in common with contemporaries call our attention to the possibility that Spenser's choice of mediaeval romance settings, characters and conventions is to be seen as a choice of fashionable
"modern" idiom, the choice of a genre with a fillip of topical
contemporary interest, not nostalgic return. To be sure, romances
were a genre that portrayed life idealistically, but on the assumption that it was a realistic portrayal of life.[5] Setting "a romance"
over *against* "real life" is a late habit, and we run the risk of
confusing an opposition that is irrelevant here—the opposition
between idealistic and *un*visionary—with a different distinction,
between the fictive imaginary world and the world of daily life.
Spenser is unabashedly idealistic about chivalry, as Malory and
the author of the Vulgate Cycle and of all the major romances
had been, and as many living Elizabethans were, but that does
not remove his portrayal into some dream-world. An example
of idealization very like the Spenserian sort in tone and point
is the long discourse to Lancelot by the Damsel of the Lake on
chivalric origins, virtues and symbolically interpreted accoutrements. This last has a long history, and the virtues are almost the
same list as the Gifts of the Holy Ghost, "courtly" though we
might think them (largesse, debonnairté, fortitude, sagesse and
so on). Spenser's chivalric world is archaic rather than sentimental-
ly nostalgic, and it is the archaism of an admired old-fashioned
worth, not of the unreal and remote; Pléiade theories on the use
of old words for the strong life that is in them bear relation to
this form of archaism too.

Like the whole matter of Spenser's relation to "real life"
through, rather than despite, his romance genre, yet another point

---

[5] An article of some scope by J. Frappier, "Le Graal et la chevalerie," *Rom.*,
vol. 75 (1954), 165-210, shows how interestingly parallel were motivations
for earlier French development of Arthurian chivalric romance, with characteristically greater glorification of chivalry's responsibilities toward the Church,
and of the chevalerie celestienne. The reference to the *Lancelot* is to Sommer,
III, 113-17. We are reminded of the familiar English time lag; for we meet
early in France the familiar Spenserian ideas and motives of a much later century, very different from Ariosto's but very like certain predecessors'. Mrs.
Bennett traces the fluctuating "Reputation of Arthur" over late decades, in ch.
6 of *The Evolution of the Faerie Queene* (Chicago, 1942), showing how the
1580's stand out. The special Tudor development was of course not due to
time lag, and, similarly, most special Spenserian developments are due to many
factors besides his "personality differences" from the Italians he copied.

suggests that our commonplace stereotypes about Arthurian romances may be more mid-nineteenth century than accurate, and our conception of romance influences on sixteenth-century writers thence mistaken. The familiar assumption dies hard, that Spenser's structure, influenced by the haphazard movement of romance plots and by their Gothic wildness and multiplicity of motive, is something well passed over with charitable speed, though its oddities as evidence of changing plans have been examined of late years with a beneficial increase of both sympathy and understanding.

But modern research and criticism in fields other than Renaissance and Spenser have brought us to a quite different view of romance form. It is not only seen as an artistic design, far from haphazard, but as a form able to provide narrative excellences and subtleties which other structures cannot provide. It may be that we should be closer to the mark if we were found talking about Spenser's deliberate and wise choice of the romance structure, responsible for the *Faerie Queene*'s controlled and suitable complications of pattern, sanctioning Spenser's skilfull use of the basic romance device of entrelacement, and protecting him from the error of forcing the different logic of epic design upon materials and purposes unsuited to it. There will be time later to condemn such a galloping swing of the pendulum, as this represents, away from our current acceptance of Spenser's undisguised shifts and excusable unsuccess as a designer. At least, our discussion should consider what characteristics of *structure* would present themselves *for imitation*, to a reader who surely added numerous earlier romances to his Ariosto and his Tasso, his Homer and his Virgil.

Such structural relationships are, as I have said, large and vague, and many are perhaps unamenable to satisfactory proof. The last points are important because such presuppositions direct the kind of reading we give to literary works. But they will not serve to handcuff two works together in a "source relationship," and proper evidence isolating the romance that was influential from other pieces is usually unobtainable. The only entrance of iron into a discussion of such aggravating ties comes with the question of accessibility. This chapter is resolutely closed against all consideration of materials which were not demonstrably *to hand*; the conception of "mediaeval romance" must be that which could be formed by an Elizabethan. This means a narrower conception than that of our day, with our Early English Text Societies and our Societés des anciens textes français; romances were not studied but merely modernized with indifferent care and put out as good if rather old fiction.

If we are to judge of relations like style and tone, instead of plot motifs, we must know the texts in the form our sixteenth-century predecessors had at their disposal. The present state of studies in this area makes this extraordinarily difficult.[6] It is, however, absolutely necessary. The kind of looseness the present study has will, at least, not be the sort which conjectures interesting possible relations between Spenser and a mediaeval piece he could not have read. If he read it in a different linguistic form, a differently abbreviated or expanded text, those differences in detail may be the very ones relevant to some relation we think we see in thematic implications or suggested double meaning. Men learn artistic lessons by way of specific detail, and the only "tradition" from the romances that could influence the Renaissance writers was that carried down in the details of the books they could lay hand upon and read.

However, this precision touching accessibility will be a gross disadvantage if we extend it to kinds of relations looked for. The

[6] A large number of studies is needed in this area. Even though there may be a good modern edition of a piece and a manuscript tradition that has been extensively worked over, one must time and again stop to do the pioneer investigation of slow comparison between early printed versions and manuscripts, often differently divided, or without rubrics or foliation. Modern editions do not always find it part of their obligation to list early printings, and the nature of redaction and translations goes unremarked. The tasks to be done are minute but truly critical, for one's constant concern must be with those artistic minutiae which determine literary effect. The valuable handbooks have been Arundell Esdaile's *List of English Tales and Prose Romances, Printed before 1740* (London, 1912), and the extraordinarily useful Handlists of de Worde's publications and of Translations 1475-1560 in H. S. Bennett's *English Books and Readers 1475-1577* (Cambridge, 1952). These have made it possible to know something of the English sixteenth-century field (cf. the well-reported fifteenth century), other than by the slow pursuit of data on single text by single text. Since 1954 we have had the benefit of gathered data on the French works in Brian Woledge's *Bibliographie des romans et nouvelles en prose française antérieurs a 1500* (Geneva, 1954) (*Soc. de publ. romanes et françaises*, 42). Of course, one cannot distinguish versions, or character of adaptations made, from such listings. I have always sampled texts available to readers in the sixteenth century before making points about romances which are now read in "correcter" forms.

effects of plentiful romance reading upon a Spenser, like its
effects upon us, are important but rather indistinct. Two categories
first come to mind. Certain large expectations are pre-determined
for the critic, as before him for the teller of the romance. One
set has to do with plan and structure. Also, the whole outward
garb of a narrative, its furniture and its image in our minds, is
pre-determined. This last embraces some motifs so important
that though they cannot be called plot motifs, they are the data,
the unjudged conventions, the données, upon which the story
is built; these range all the way from manners and notions of
honor and thence of character, to such a familiar instrument for
producing incident as the "customs" of castles.

We mention first the sort of expectation that concerns the
plan and conduct of a work. The fundamental element of design
—a quest structure—is too obvious to discuss, i.e. not just chivalry
but knight-errantry supplies a pattern; if Spenser, like his immediate predecessors, had failed to seize it and had written a
Charlemagne romance rather than an Arthurian romance, we
would soon notice how little of the *Faerie Queene* we could keep
without this structural convention. We need not decide just when
each element was introduced by Spenser to realize that a very
early stage included a knight on a quest, whether pursuing the
enemies of Chastity of (the usual quest) searching out the true
nature of something, as one "achieved" the Grail not by fighting
for possession of it or protection of it but by trying to understand
what it meant.

A less obvious point is the fact that the role of Arthur in the
Faerie Queene is directly in line with what a reader of earlier
Arthurian romances expects. In the creation of Arthur, Spenser
has been superbly inventive and original, but still obedient to what
his predecessors made inevitable. Arthur's role came to him with
an important and very ancient meaning, long his meaning as a
fictional hero. Fresh from (for instance) the Vulgate Cycle, we
do not expect Arthur to have more part in the action of the
Faerie Queene than he has, or even a different part. Against this
or a similar background of story, an Arthur pursuing "his" adventures like the other errant knights, or "central" in the usual
way of epic heroes, or given a Book of his own, would be a
monstrous alteration of function, though Spenserians have often
been known to ask for it.[7]

[7] The dissatisfaction aroused by the supposed insufficiency of Arthur's role has

Arthur is pre-eminent in Arthurian romances for other reasons than those which touch logical structure, and he has a traditional and predictable role, which Spenser both uses and transcends—after the habit of true artists making use of inherited elements. Given Spenser's accessory purpose of shadowing Elizabeth's own majesty and her court, he must naturally choose to portray Arthur Prince not Arthur King, and we need think up no excuses of scruple or taste to account for a choice so sensible and even necessary. But Prince Arthur has next to no "legend," and none at all if we read our Arthur in the great famous reprinted French fictions.[8] The *Merlin* texts, from which Malory extracted the little he tells, were printed; but the fact remains that Arthur's traditional role in the great ancient tales is something much closer to the meanings with which Spenser invests him.

Despite the moment's enthusiasm for historical allegory with

---

been constant. Mrs. Bennett handles the objection in chs. 5 and 6 (*Evolution of the Faerie Queene*), and several of the earlier objectors are there quoted. W. J. B. Owen, in "The Structure of the *Faerie Queene*," *PMLA*, vol. 68 (1953), 1,079-1,100, touches upon it on pp. 1,087-88; he does not tax Spenser with this as a flaw, but does think of Spenser's introduction of Arthur as a conscious late attempt to impose unity on a series of "repetitive structures" (as in Books I and II), and to subordinate the minor motifs offered by separate patrons of each Book's virtue. The presuppositions of both discussions are those of epic structure, not romance structure.

[8] The complaint that Spenser does not tell the expected stories about Arthur is so commonly put forward as puzzle or surprise, that we should keep on remarking that legends for Prince Arthur are not part of the ancient and canonized tradition; the later Merlin redactions for which they were compiled were published alone but not with the great popular Vulgate prose works (*Lancelot, Queste, Mort Artu*). Spenser could have gone back to Geoffrey—but what use had he for either a Marvelous-Birth story or the young king's harrying of other tribes to refill his depleted treasury? He undoubtedly read Merlin materials, as well as Malory's compilations from the *Suite du Merlin* and the alliterative *Morte Arthure* (see Vinaver, *op.cit.*, III, 1266, 1361), or probably late and untraditional romances like *Arthur of Little Britain*; but he certainly resembles most in tone and texture the great traditional Arthurian productions. See below, and n. 10. One critic even considers Spenser's possible puritan objections to tales of bawdry and aggression (presumably only puritans like Elizabeth's tutor Ascham objected to these) in trying to imagine what can have deflected Spenser from telling the usual tales of Arthur. How could a public of 1580-90 read of a Faeryland that was (among other things) real and ideal England—with a King upon its throne, and its Queen upon hers only by right of her marriage? We must even be so skilfully kept (in the *Faerie Queene*) in the short pre-Guenevere epoch, that we can be betrayed into forgetting her importance and her absence.

its overemphasis on personified equivalents, even Greenlaw saw
early that Arthur may shadow this courtier in one place, that one
in another, and need not always figure *any*. The Faery Queen
holds that role of shadowy but great importance, the Sovereignty
itself, in a sense "the realm"—to be shared with Arthur King,
whether she marries any consort or not, for this is not the only
way she is made one with all Arthur's meanings. A symbol can
be but lamely explained. But a ruler was still the incarnation of
kingship; kingship, though more obscurely symbolical in
Elizabethan than mediaeval writings, had still the shreds of ancient meaning about it. The identification of ruler with realm
and "the sovereignty" was felt, even if the old belief had
weakened in the intimate tie between the king's health and the
commonwealth's, an Arthurian commonplace. The ancient role
of donor of gifts and "boons," donor of quests or adventures, is
more important to a romance than to a *Beowulf*.

The ancient Celtic historical realities touching the king's function as sworn granter of *dons*, realities which are argued by many
scholars to be vaguely present in the romances though not understood by French tellers, may have been no more clearly understood by a Spenser than by us. But he understood just as well
as those who he says asked boons because "the manner then was"
that his was an *obligatory* royal function "which during that feast
she might not refuse" (as he says of the Faery Queen in the
Letter to Ralegh). This tabu-like, sworn-oath forcing of the
king's will, the Jephthah motif, is of course frequently important
to start off the plot of a romance. During the stories, other evidences of the traditional centrality of the court and sovereign
whom the quester-hero serves also show up. Some are: the
sending back of captives who owned defeat to report to King
Arthur or to Guenevere, like a kind of trophy presented where
it is due (a parallel is the sending of "captiu'd Acrasia" to present
herself to the Faery Queen in III.i.2); the fact that Red Crosse,
to whom Gloriana "gave" (I.i.3) his "great adventure," is
Gloriana's knight and remains so; she gave it for the reasons
Arthur passes on quests as *dons* (for the King's "grace," and the
Knight's own "worship," as he "learnes" his "new force," or becomes competent in his new fortitude). He is Gloriana's knight
though and even *because* he is Una's own knight, in love with
her and with her affairs. As in Arthurian situations, the two fidel-
ities do not collide.

This is felt to be true because strength yet remained in the idea that through these granted and assumed loyalties, the Knights accomplish for their King his obligatory responsibilities—impossibly hazardous test-tasks, strokes of destiny to be met, "rash boons" granted as in honor bound to Messenger Damsels, otherworld taxes as it were, tabu-like irrational unfathomable trials of worthiness to be entrusted with the sovereignty. The royal person, who looks passive to our eyes, most certainly acts, but does so through his fellowship as through an extended self. In the prose *Lancelot*, the sleights through which Lancelot obtains even his sword from Guenevere and is her knight, not the king's, symbolize a cleavage that is also symbolized by their adulterous relation; and moral explanations of the decline of the Round Table on grounds of their simple unchastity have the same oversimplicity as do modern complaints about the "small" role of the court, of Gloriana, or of Arthur-the-perfected-form of each virtue, who intervene in extremity.

All err by ignoring the spiritual relations of the members of this fellowship, with its otherworldly sanctions; some of the oversimplifications were made in mediaeval times, and the fact that Spenser was able to return, largely unconsciously, to a *sens* closer to early origins, shows the trustworthiness of metaphorical understandings. The knights *owe*, as duties, as fealty, their performance of these task-like "adventures,"[9] but to their King not

[9] This emphasis upon allegiance to virtue as a thing not admitting of choice or deserving of compliment is much stressed, and Spenser or romance-writers often find very similar words for it: "I have nothyng done but that me ought for to do" says Lancelot (Vinaver, I, 274), and Red Crosse, "all I did, I did but as I ought" (ii.i.33), or "Suffise, that I have done my dew in place" (ii. viii.56), which is Arthur). All the writers naturally attach these attitudes to Christian humility, and to the allegiance to God that transcends even chivalric codes. It is less an attitude of humility than of chivalric noblesse defined and claimed, and seems on occasion proud; I would attach to this conventional attitude (toward the perils to be faced) Guyon's comforting himself with thought of his own strengths and his deeds so far that have been worth praise (ii.vii.2), which would be much more overtly indicated as "guilty" if we were meant to infer from it a vital flaw in Guyon (as Berger thinks, *op.cit.*, see pp. 29, 15). No profound meaning in the *Faerie Queene* depends on an unheralded and unconfirmed interpretation of some phrase or speech which we think "must" involve the moral judgment we find most natural. Spenser does not leave the recognition of his heroes' sins to our chance reading of Augustine or Thomas; he points to their mistakes with visible finger.

to their Christian caritas or the sufferer's common humanity, or
to principle, and the sovereign is the one who gives them guerdon
("she" in 1.x.59; granting "glorie . . . to them for guerdon,"
"*For she is heavenly borne*"). This last phrase shows the connection ultimately responsible for the royal person's curious kind
of centrality, possessed not achieved. He holds it at great risk,
and loss is always imminent, so that the mutual obligations of king
and fellowship are most profound; in a Christian translation of
these ideas, we would incline to the phrase that he keeps his role
by the grace of God, though virtues assist him to perform it.
Spenser's transformation of ancient symbolisms was aided by their
gradual metamorphosis during the centuries when they formed
the ground for Christian romances, or didactic materials that were
occasionally even allegorized.

All this is somewhat obscured to modern English readers who
isolate and give pre-eminence to Malory's versions, for he gives
an outstanding place (the commencement) to the story of Arthur's
birth, augmented by the wars fought soon after his coronation
("interlaced" as usual with other men's "tales"). He thereupon
inserts the unusual section (Bk. V), Arthur and the Emperor
Lucius, a prose redaction of a separate English romance, the
alliterative *Morte Arthure*. He had to extract these few stories
about Arthur the prince and the young king from a form of the
Suite du Merlin usually referred to as the "Huth *Merlin*" and
one in a Cambridge manuscript that shows relations to the Vulgate
Merlin.[10] Thus the legends of Arthur, which Spenser is so often
alleged to neglect, were not such expectable commonplaces after
all, and neither very extensive nor traditionally attached. The
extraction, highlighting and placing of these events is unusual in
Malory, whose sources were not widely distributed and were very
different in effect from his nonce-version. The well-known three
parts so often printed as an entity were the *Lancelot*, *Queste*,
Mort Artu; the Merlin texts were composed to fill in preliminaries
thereto and never had the same popularity or circulation. Of

---

[10] The last, ed. in Sommer's vol. II, is the only one said to be early printed;
Sommer, I, xxviii, cites 1498, 1516, 1528. Tucked away between the conception of Arthur (p. 68) and his coronation (p. 80) we find some parallel stories
to the manuscript Merlins (there is a modern edition of the "Huth *Merlin*," ed.
G. Paris and J. Ulrich, 2 vols. in *Soc. anc. t. fr.*, and Malory reveals something of
the character of his sources; Vinaver's commentary can be consulted, vol. III,
I, 265-82 and *passim* through 1,397).

course Spenser read Malory. But he must have read so much else
which his writing resembles more, structurally, that he surely
needed to feel no discomfort about preserving the traditional role
of Arthur; that is preserved (more than if he had copied Malory's
incidents) in Arthur as a combined figure for the dynasty, the
all-inclusive virtue, the spouse-to-be of the personified realm, the
royal house through whom divine power flowed into country and
people.

Whatever its origins, and whether or not it was historically
connected with potlatch and with geis—questions of fact which
luckily do not make a substantial difference to us—this truly
central role has been Arthur's throughout so many romances that
we seldom think behind it to explanations and causes,[11] and have
ourselves accepted the irrationalities it brings (chiefly into our
judgments of Arthur's character). Modern complaints get confused with those which stem rather from the ancient antipathies
to the structure of romance rather than of epic, but Arthur seems
inactive and minor only if we are unable to realize and allow
the romance conventions which gave his role its longevity. That
in the *Faerie Queene* it takes two personages to fill the functions
gives no trouble, except to those who want allegory to provide
us with fixed equations; it is obviously prudent, given the sex of
the occupant on the throne of the returning-British-Arthur's kingdom, but also this metaphor of a marriage is the only way to state
all the meanings at once, a marriage in which the Faery Queen
is to be made one with all Arthur symbolizes, including establish-
ment of the true faith, by God's grace. Arthur is given no double

[11] Of numerous possible references treating this matter of historical origins,
I give one which cites important earlier ones: Jean Marx, *La légende arthurienne
et le Graal* (Paris, 1952), pp. 45-107. He attacks the problem of historical
fact, but though ours is the simpler task of observing what we find portrayed in the Arthurs Spenser read about, it is proper to note that some
Celticists do question the assumed relation between historical usages and romance
conventions; they have trouble with the geis as an explanation, and find proofs
of its real nature insufficient; see Kenneth Jackson, "Les sources celtiques du
roman du Graal," *Les romans du Graal* . . . (Paris, 1956) (*Colloques inter-
nationaux*, Strasbourg, 1954), pp. 213-27. It must be constantly recalled that
origins are not what Spenser knew about or treated, just as full and realized
pagan significance for the Grail had vanished long before the prose Vulgate;
when we know about them, however, anomalies thus bequeathed do not lead
us to wrong conclusions.

fidelity to correspond to Artegall's and Red Crosse's; and it is made clear in Book after Book—in this case fortunately we need not know their order of composition—that Arthur is uniquely related to the queen of the "faeries," uniquely related to the questers or to the virtues they seek and find, and that as Magnificence he retains, divinely elected and strengthened, the kingly functions tradition gave to him. He has transcended the role of his historical kingship; but the way to the transcendent role he has in the *Faerie Queene* was pointed to by his primitive one. The mystery of Arthur's supernatural election and the question of his fitness as chief of such a fellowship is felt even in the prose romances; moderns are not the first who would prefer an epic hero with clear merits, and Malory tried to make him one.

Various notions responsible for King Arthur's traditional role merge somewhat hazily together, and have done so in any literary treatment. Spenser makes no important use of the motif of a land waste through a wound given the ruler, which is the form of a clear identification between King's and country's health most common in Arthurian romances. But Spenser's way of allegorizing the human pursuit of a fée, commonest of all plot motifs of romance, does convey something of the symbolical relation which we meet in another element we are told is more thoroughly "Celtic" and primitive—a feminine embodiment, in a real otherworld being, of the realm. The image is familiar to us in modern form because of Yeats' fondness for the old idea (of a Kathleen ni Houlihan). But the ordinary way for these images of a kingdom and its health to appear is that used by Spenser and by romance after Arthurian romance—the royal court as the place where the one in whom the "sovereignty" of the land inheres is faced with tests and demands, and "gives" to a fellowship of knights the various adventures on which health and permanence depends. Much is said of the last-minute addition of the Letter to Ralegh, but a reader of Arthurian romance all but supplies its framework scene to the action before reading the Letter; we would invent something very like the annual feast if it were not provided by Spenser.[12] Though once primitive, the situation had become a firmly

[12] Such a statement does not basically question the careful researches that have been made into the date of a specific design for his poem as revealed in the Letter to Ralegh, the puzzling divergences, etc.; what is controverted is not that Spenser's plans shifted and developed. But we must recognize how con-

expected part of knight-errant romances, and the donation of
such trials of the realm's health to members of it, both a responsibility and a test of the sovereign, was expected too. It explains why
errant knights are errant and puts a proper light upon the notion
that these benefits are being secured to the realm or fellowship.
That the virtues sought in the quests are secured to the commonwealth is part of the inherited design, and the Books are not separate. But an Arthur as a protagonist, parallel to and a peer with
others, or as one of the questers seeking *a* virtue, would be to a
habitual romance-reader a most unwelcome change in an established character whose traditional meaning is essential to the very
existence, health and functioning of a "fellowship."

Spenser's combination of this element which survived into the
Arthurian romances with a theologically sophisticated and subtle
presentation of Christian grace in his Arthur is one of the superlative examples of his genius for creative amalgamation.[13] Divinely
endowed Fortitude takes over as the knights approach the end
of their natural powers and "Magnificently" perseveres in a
virtue, attaining a perfected and triumphant form of it. For
kingship primitively understood, not personifying but *symbolic*

---

ventional and unfortuitous his design is, and how likely it is that such a framework was assumed long before the precise statement of it.

[13] This is a true piece of invention on Spenser's part. I hasten to add that
it does not make Arthur a Christ-figure. Nor would the most Christianized of
the romances encourage him in such a figura. It makes Arthur (the lover and in
a way the "regiment" or ruling house that could save the realm, which is one
thing imaged in the Faerie Queen) the channel for divine Christ-like power—
as every man can be, with grace, but as kings and dynasties must be or rightly
lose their kingdoms. This was a common enough understanding as late as the
Spenserian discussions of kingship and divine justice.

Arthur seeks the Faerie Queen—this is not to be understood too simply as
just another love story in the tangle of pairs seeking each other. His quest of
Magnificence is not conceivable as a thirteenth virtue-hunt (see ch. 2 above).
He is seen demonstrating its nature, achieving his quest of it, in Book after
Book, just as Spenser says: in each Book appear "the deedes of Arthure applyable
to that vertue, which I write of in that booke." "Arthur seeks his love Gloriana"
is the same statement, if I read allegorically. Of course, nothing will stand up
to iniquitous abuses like "Arthur (Leicester) wishes to marry the Faerie Queen
(Elizabeth)," or "Arthur (Grace) loving Gloriana (Protestant England) is
irresponsibly chasing Florimell (Chaste Beauty)." The repeated lesson of all
earlier good allegory is that relations, being symbolic, will not translate into
equations.

of the realm and its health, did provide (it was thought) just such open channels to divine power. And even this late, Elizabeth the historical queen as defensor fidei is to be seen as one with, indissolubly united to, the instrument of God's grace for her realm, quite aside from the more particular significances of an Arthur as royal spouse, which history was *not* to see emerge. Allegorically this is a trifle; the queen of this golden England is loved by, is wooed, is married to, all the unphraseable great things Arthur symbolizes, and the multiple appearance of some of them, in shifting but perfectly real literal historical personages, reminds us that we must not suffocate an allegory with the tightly drawn noose of inflexible equations, but allow meanings to flow into and inhabit the literal so that it is symbolic also. These various ways of being real do not lend their excitement to the Arthur of earlier story, but the role which there gave continuity to his sporadic appearances seems to me retained and transmuted to give a similar continuity to his functions in the *Faerie Queene*. Such conceptions of course develop during writing, and what Arthur became in the *Faerie Queene* is to be sought in no romance.

The traditional romance role for Arthur thus differs sharply from that of a hero whose importance is gained through accomplishment of deeds of epic valor, and Spenser's would certainly be an oddity among Arthurian romances if he had done what some apologists suggest he intended—if he had made Arthur the "chief hero" in unwritten later Books. The different way in which the traditional role sets Arthur apart from other knights is all the more apparent in romances where the old conception betrays itself in some unclear plot motif (in the *Perlesvaus*) or in some puzzling treatment of character (the sinfulness of Arthur in the first part of the *Lancelot*). In both these romances, Arthur's guilt and sorrow over lost powers or mysterious inadequacy is a poignant motif; it is rationalized, but nevertheless we recognize the more primitive conception of a loss of sovereignty or unexpected decline of power through causes that cannot be countered in natural ways, by heroic virtue or meritorious valor.

In the incident in *Lancelot* of Arthur's strange dream of losing all honor terriene unless his rescue is effected according to a riddling prophecy, by the "lion in the water" and through the "counsel of the flower," the rationalization is elaborated: Arthur has destroyed what he should have guarded, he has not watched over the rights of the poor, nor sustained orphans and the weak.[14] The hermit to whom is given the long and bitter accusation of the King also condemns him on the ground that he was born in adultery, but this supposed revelation is here passed over rapidly. The logical charge that he has failed in his duty to his vassal, Lancelot's dead father King Ban, so long unavenged, is also made here and at earlier points. But the abject humiliation which the King is made to undergo, the profundity and mystery of his guilt, the constant warnings that even his wisest clerks (brought in to advise and later to receive his expiating penance) do not pierce the secrets of the celestial message conveying God's will for him and God's reasons for the fact "quil te voloit oster de ta signorie" —all these far outweigh the attempted rational explanation, that he has not been a good king to the commons. We have not heard about these insufficiencies, and they are not seriously used in the later characterization of Arthur. His inadequacies really have more to do with the confusing of earthly honor with heavenly, the misunderstanding of the "celestiens" by the "terriens," and he can only be cleansed by the mystical Lion, Christ, through the counsel of the flower of flowers, his Mother. This little flurry of Christian allegory is not pervasive; these interpretations and explanations are awkward but they do underscore for us some sense of deep human inadequacy which must be expiated even though it is not understood. We catch a sense of man pitted against circumstances beyond his size, when even the best are found wanting, though assistance from God, from offended divine powers, from the otherworld, may equally inexplicably save a man in the nick of time.

No proper use, for plot or for character development, is made of these poignant admissions of Arthur's sin. Occasional references fasten upon Arthur's laxity in the matter of King Ban as his great flaw; he is powerfully affected by the thought of this guilt, weeps, so that his tears fall upon the table where he sits. Or he is accused by a former knight turned friar of one sole lack tarnishing his right to be seen as the best king, foremost in "maintaining chivalry in honor"—that he forgets those (e.g. Ban) who have loyally

---

[14] The important passages on the interpretation of the dreams and the penance of Arthur are in Sommer, III, 215-23, 199-200 (op.cit. in n. 2 above); for some earlier accusations, endured with shame and passive grief, see pp. 109-10, 45-47. The humiliation of Lancelot in the Queste is sometimes comparable.

adventured, and lost, their lands and their lives in his service. The basic notion conveyed by these emphases, rationalized though they are, is a mysterious and sad inability of the King to keep his kingly powers. The lamentable results always accrue through the weakening of his *fellowship*, and we get little sense of personal danger or personal courage that could counter the decay; he repents deeply, and revived largesse and the "medicine" he can secure from the divine Physician are of some avail—but we feel the presence of unexplained tragedy and the mutability of all human affairs. Most powerful of all intermediaries, a King can keep a human society erect for a time. But the painful lack and taint shows up at length in him too—imperfection, mortality, the implacable secret; contrive and exalt as we will, we are not divine. It would take too long and detailed an analysis to discuss the talented ways in which various authors made use of these original notions to create moving and tragic stories of the final decline of the Round Table, and the mort Artu; the rationale of the tragedy of course varies, and under some hands becomes almost unconnected with the earlier stratum of ideas.

Before leaving the Vulgate Cycle, we may merely notice the way in which these ideas of human inadequacy and guilt and sources of redeeming power became thoroughly Christianized in the quest, a word which does not quite fit Spenser's imaginative extensions and graftings in the *Faerie Queene*, since he did not follow the *Queste*'s invitation to write an allegory we must read as Christological. Though the *Faerie Queene* is too long and too complicated a poem for any motif to be consistently suited by one interpretation, it seems true that Fairyland and the Faery Queen Prince Arthur seeks are truly allegorical, in that we must not think we cover the question by reading them as "England" of "Elizabeth," or even as "the good society" and "the ruler." This is one of the literal meanings we take in through the allegory. But they point also to an England (and a society of men) which never was on sea or land, and never will be, since they adumbrate the *perfection* of some virtues Spenser wishes for England and for fallible man.

Arthur comes into most of the Books as an earthly completion or a superlative extension of whatever virtue we are seeking in its knight's company; he is a "magnificent" manifestation of it. Every instance in which Arthur, empowered by heavenly grace or indeed its instrument, goes beyond what the knight himself can do toward perfecting the virtue in question, is part of his quest of the Faery Queen. This quest is not forgotten or neglected, but is in all the Books. An Arthur distinguishing and following after true "glory" (not to be mistranslated into "secular fame," which Spenser openly discredits) is in each Book or unit (III-IV) in the form the Letter claims, "the deeds of Arthure applyable to *that* vertue...." One romance, the *Queste*, had read spiritualiter (that is, strictly allegorized it) the knightly quest for virtue before Spenser. Many had moralized it, but the *Queste* had distinguished between the quest of moral excellence and the actual attempt to unite with perfection itself. Arthur does not present this in the *Queste*. Only Galahad views perfected virtue, and he leaves this world for a place where such sights (the Grail) belong; we watch him—in his complete achievement of or union with perfection—take on a shape which Spenser's Arthur, and no other romance Arthur, ever does: he becomes a *type* of Christ, though in after-history and in a man-made allegory.

Arthur's court in the *Queste* is the apex of the chevalerie terriene; he quite properly goes on no grail-adventure himself, but is the shadowy figure from whose court Lancelot, Bohort, Gawain, Perceval, Galahad, all these kinds of souls, go forth. Its glory and his fellowship will fade after the fashion of all earthly power, which he sees and mourns with an inconsolable grief that would be reasonless but for the deeper double meaning and the nobility of that which is so fragile. What is interesting is that Spenser, fired by an idealized patriotism and a zeal for true religion which brought him close to the ideal Chivalry that defended Honor and Ecclesia, is able to use a knight-errant-romance form so that we grasp not only man's struggle for attainable excellence but see an image of his quest for unattainable perfection. Largely because it freely leaves this world for another, the mediaeval piece is clearer in its portrayal, but that it was possible in the 1590's and in a secular work is extraordinary. Here I consider Spenser's choice of genre a masterly stroke.

The grief and shame over realized powerlessness is even more striking in the Arthur of *Perlesvaus* than in the "sinner" of the *Lancelot*. Especially long and striking is the episode in Branch I of the King's chagrin at his unexplained falling "from honour to shame," his expiatory journey to St. Augustine's chapel, his reviling and humiliation, the prophecy by the voice in the forest that he may again be one who helps to exalt and establish the Law which is renovelee par la mort (crucifiement) of Christ.[15] This incident is completely Christianized by weaving into it the familiar motif of a eucharistic miracle, but again the guilt of the king for his failing realm is accepted though imperfectly rationalized, and a connection is made with the other failed test in which the grail question was not asked and disaster and war ensued. Attitudes and events do not seem intended to be psychologically reasonable; for example, the author apparently does not intend the damage to Arthur's character which would ensue if we read the conversations with Guenevere, the laments over "feebleness of heart" and loss of "volonté de fere largesce" and the acknowledgments of failure, without sensing a primitive background wherein Arthur's situation and passivity had causes that were amoral, fated and implacable. Details combine to emphasize the uniqueness of his relation to the health of the whole fellowship—Guenevere's secret weeping, the violence of the humiliation Arthur must endure from mysteriously informed underlings who all know his shame, knights who defy him and must quench flaming swordpoints in his drawn blood, damsels who mock "the worst king in the world" and his patient and mild and humorous suffering of it, as well as the phrases about "slackness in welldoing" and then the restored "talent de bien fere," oneur, and largesce.[16]

---

[15] Le Haut Livre du Graal, Perlesvaus, ed. Nitze and Jenkins (2 vols.; Chicago, 1932-37), references to line numbers (in vol. 1), 349 and 88. I shall commonly refer to and even quote the translation by Sebastian Evans, High History of the Holy Grail (London, 1910) (here pp. 13, 4), always checked, but more convenient than the 1516 and 1523 editions to which we ought to refer. For remarks on studies, and relations of the early editions to our manuscript-based texts, see n. 40 below; in Woledge, No. 114, No. 81 (op.cit. in n. 5 above).

[16] See the texts cited in n. 15; Evans, pp. 14-20 and Nitze, lns. 519-65. Certain peculiar traits of the Perlesvaus author, like his light, swift, living flow of conversation, his use of images of light and his portrayal of pensive or emotionally heightened states of mind are shown well in these scenes in which Arthur faces the meaning of some of these events. We are reminded of the later scene when Arthur, unable to sleep, rises and watches the calm sea from the windows of the hall, and sees the marvelous ship rushing silently toward him, bright with a light like a candle (Evans, pp. 148-51; Nitze, 4,075ff.); again he forgets a promise (the question for Perceval's sister) and again is obscurely guilty, but his pivotal position is never questioned, despite the frank emphasis on the visitor's being "the best knight."

Arthur's traditional importance is obviously quite different from that of the epic hero, the strongest warrior or the wisest leader.

These observations suggest that Arthur's role in the *Faerie Queene* being an inventive adaptation and spiritualization of his usual fundamental but not dominating role, is much more truly essential than has been allowed, though no larger. His importance is not the intelligible dominance of the epic hero who accomplishes the most important adventure with greatest glory. He is not the "best knight in the world," Lancelot is; he is not the most courteous knight, Gawain is; he is not the holiest, Galahad is; nor born to achieve the greatest of all the adventures, Perceval is. Arthur in the high period of Arthurian romances is similarly essential, but there, too, he is far from being the most active of the knights, or most heroic.

Spenser's Arthur has to be fundamental in a somewhat different way, but the meaning of his role has been retained and spiritualized (even somewhat theologized). Others seek, fight for, or learn how to embody this or that special virtue, but royal Arthur perseveres to the degree of Magnificence in that virtus or fortitude which is to be had by tapping the reservoir of divine strength, not by superb human gifts. Guyon can be shown the nature of intemperance and look upon yet not desire this or that form of it; but Arthur conquers that very propensity to evil which makes intemperance an indwelling enemy—the root itself, which we may call original sin, our mortal condition, or Maleger, as we choose. Arthur can demonstrate the offices of Friendship where others wear out or must give in; Arthur is, as it were, an extension of the active Knight of Justice, set to confront In-Iustitia in essence in Gerioneo and the Beast. As Arthur's primitive kingship and symbolic embodiment of the fellowship of the Round Table did not make him actually a dominant character in the Arthurian romances but simply more basic, so Spenser's transformed Arthur, a piece of great originality in the *Faerie Queene*, is more important to structure and design than to the flow of the narrative.[17] Nor

---

[17] I do not understand the comment on Arthur's lack of a "sustaining thread of continuity" (remarked by J. W. Bennett as evidence for Arthur as a late addition, *op.cit.* in n. 5). The notion that there is less "connection between Arthur's different appearances" than between Orlando's seems to depend on a definition of "a continued action" which does not allow meanings of events, but rather incident-sequences, to provide coherence.

is the notion of influence to be interpreted too literally, and one doubts if Spenser was conscious of imitation. His is a natural development of earlier Arthurs, but to have made an epic hero of him would certainly not be so. Occasional romances try. I do not imply here that there was anything thought mystically significant, or messianic, or symbolic of Christianity, about Arthur's kingship, as some interpreters of romances have claimed. Remnants of older notions helped establish a role which later writers kept to without special thought.

Thus in addition to the useful inheritance of mediaeval realism, we have noticed some expectations aroused by the conventions of the genre which affect notably our judgments of structure and design. But by far the most striking element of structure which Spenser has caught from much attention to romances is the principle of entrelacement. Intermittently defended from the time of the first imitators of these fictions, this was most clearly isolated and discussed as a principle of design by Ferdinand Lot in his *Étude sur le Lancelot en prose* (in 1918; ch. 2), but it has been brought back to special notice recently by Vinaver's discussions of Malory's structure.[18] Likenesses to a similar principle in Ariostan structure are apparent; the commonly used metaphor of the web, Ariosto's own figure in 1381, best describes both Arthurian romances and Ariosto's late Charlemagne romance. Yet students of the two eras for the most part walk separate paths, each praising his own epoch's weaving. One would like to see more serious examination of the assumption that all which preceded the great master was merely "episodic," and more serious comparison with romances of the great period, before the vast compilations of the decline. The relevant tie with Sidney's *Arcadia* has been noted.[19] The wider ramifications of the sub-

[18] Lot's book is Fasc. 226 of *Bibliothèque de l'École des Hautes Études*. See I, xlviii ff. and III, 1,266ff. and *passim*, in Vinaver's *Works of Malory*. Lot's ideas are extended in Frappier's *Étude sur la Mort le roi Artu* (Paris, 1961), esp. ch. 6, although with the departure from a quest-organization, the interlaced structure is naturally less marked. Though Frappier says (p. 348n.) it is this technique which Ariosto brought to perfection in *Orlando Furioso*, it seems to me that there it is a little different in effect and intention.

[19] In an interesting article by Freda L. Townsend, "Sidney and Ariosto," *PMLA*, vol. 61 (1946), 97-108, though not concerned to enter the Old French field where Lot's and Frappier's studies center. It was done before the bulk of the Vinaver work, but might even so view earlier works like Malory's with a

ject, structural likenesses between Elizabethan romances and tales and the first redoings into prose of the great mediaeval fictions, have not been studied.

No doubt it is this characteristically "interrupted" and interwoven structure which is referred to when W. J. B. Owen distinguishes the typical "Ariostan structure" of Books III and IV of the *Faerie Queene* from the contrasted "repetitive structure" of Books I and II; Spenser is thought to have failed to accommodate these structures to each other when he conceived the idea of a "super-epic," in which each Book should be a little epic or miniature *Aeneid*, with its separate hero, as in Books I and II.[20] However, typical romance entrelacement, a thoroughly mediaeval development though altered by Ariosto for more suspense and variety, seems to me to characterize all Spenser's designs—those of the books written early, and later (though Books III and IV appear as less skillful; they seem to me also, as Mrs. Bennett and later writers have taught us, to contain the earliest and most Ariostan writing). The well-organized Books I and II are not little epics with separate heroes, but parts of a whole, connected as the parts of cyclical romances are ordinarily connected, and in fact showing extreme likeness to the way the different quests of the *Queste* are connected. The separate Books exhibit, as units and as parts of

---

clearer eye; the judgments made are ironically reminiscent of those made on Ariosto by his more hostile contemporary readers.

[20] Owen, *op.cit.*, in n. 7 above; see also "In These XII Books. . . ," *ELH*, vol. 19 (1952), 165-72. Matters like the evolving structure of the *Faerie Queene*, the betrayal of other plans by its author for its design, etc., taken up in these articles and in Mrs. Bennett's *Evolution of the Faerie Queene* (n. 5 above), have been thought out with such competence and presented with such persuasion that I make no attempt to treat on such a level of complexity points which are side issues in a chapter like this. In any case, reminders like mine change an emphasis here and there, rather than challenge basic theses, and most wasteful of results would be a flurry of arguments touching a "new position." I do not have a position. I merely think that our conceptions of the artistic fitness of Spenser's structure and plan would be subtly affected by serious attention to the principles we observe in romance structures. I would suggest that the vocabulary used for discussions of epic often does not fit, that the conception of "subordination" as a main principle of organization is only sporadically relevant, and that other clichés which may seem to us similarly part and parcel of all organizing do not suit the way the best romances are organized (such as providing unity through a major character, distinguishing parallelisms; e.g. the juxtaposed questers in the *Queste* are not "parallel").

the unfinished whole, a romance's kind of coherence. It is unlike, even opposed to, that epic coherence which was most palatable to the eighteenth and nineteenth centuries, and which was all the more attractive to the nineteenth century if the piece got its unity from an epic hero more visibly than from an epic action.

These oppositions actually received most articulate statement in still a different century—Spenser's own. For the modern objections to Spenser's structure are often almost humorously those we hear repeated time and again in the famous quarrel over the structure of Ariosto and later, of Tasso—the structure "dei romanzi."[21] It seems to me more likely than not that Spenser's poem, written and published when controversial treatments on one side or the other were coming off the press regularly, constitutes a stand taken on the matter—for of course he blithely adopts a "romance" structure and in the Letter to Ralegh cites as virtues the very disputed characteristics of the accused genre. Conditions of his life perhaps precluded his following all steps of the quarrel, but after warm squabbles in the '50's, it broke out with voluble fervor sustained right through the '80's. What we know of Spenser's friends, his interests, and his advocacy of Ariosto in the direct form of declared emulation, disposes us to believe him not naïve about contemporary poetics.

Of course, I do not wish to deny the plain fact that Spenser knew and deliberately emulated epic structure and epic conventions. But the *Faerie Queene* stands like a demonstration to prove that it was possible still to avoid the misunderstanding of romance *virtues* which turns up so stubbornly in the theorists nourished on Aristotle and chained to "his" definitions of unity, of an action, of superiority of epic, and the like. It does not seem possible that Spenser could have emphasized so neatly the "new" merits pointed to as native to the romance form, praised them on similar principles, and relinquished contradictory "epic" merits in their favor, if he had been quite unaware that he was taking a well-known stand on a famous question. It is sufficient for our point to recognize in the repeatedly stressed flaws for which Ariosto and romance-writers were belabored those structural flaws with which *Spenser* has been charged, from the 1700's through to the

---

[21] The steps in the long-continued quarrel of the mid- to end-1500's can be followed in B. Weinberg chapters in *A History of Literary Criticism in the Italian Renaissance* (Chicago, 1961), II, 954-1,073.

present. The "flaws" are indeed departures from epic structure, but they are characteristic and deliberately followed principles of romance composition.

The most important complaint is that against a multiple action with multiple actors. The principle of entrelacement deliberately and inextricably attached thereto is condemned as interruption; objectors are quite oblivious to the narrative virtues of this structural device and denigrate it in phrases very reminiscent of modern comments on the structure of mediaeval romances. "Variety" as the principle most stressed in defense is not only mentioned (as in the *Letter* and in treatments both by enemies and friends) but enormously developed as a chief literary pleasure, applicable to characters, supplying the place of unity, the major lesson learned by Ariosto from the romances. We seem to meet well-known friends in the condemnatory remarks about episodic structure, digression and the objection that even supposedly important characters do not stand out as "main" or "chief." There is also much discussion of the suspicious importance of marvels in the action, and of their fantastic nature. The great mediaeval development of the romance form was in French, and it makes an interesting point that whereas some of these eminent critics launched their objections with an eye primarily upon extreme developments of the mediaeval principles in Ariosto later, Spenser somehow managed to return to more restrained application of some of the heretical conceptions. I believe this was possible because he read widely in the corpus of Arthurian romances, to which he intended a sophisticated contribution, but which developed chiefly in the great high period. It is astonishing to observe how like virtues some of Spenser's presumed lacks or inattentions look if we see how such traits are regarded in theories of *romance* design.

One must distinguish entrelacement from the mere practice, ubiquitous in narrative, of taking one character through a series of actions, then deserting him temporarily—often with the object of introducing suspense—while another character is given primary attention, then returning to the first, and so on. This is a simple device to get around the fact that the medium of words cannot recount events happening simultaneously to different persons living through the same time; though we cannot play on several strings simultaneously, we accept the convention that we can show the polyphonic nature of what we have to tell by juxtaposing separable persons' stories. But events connected by entrelacement are not juxtaposed; they are interlaced, and when we get back to our first character he is not where we left him as we finished his episode, but in the place of psychological state or condition of meaningfulness to which he has been pulled by the events occurring in following episodes written about some one else. Moreover, though the intervening episode will look like a digression from the line previously followed, it will transpire that that line could not go on without something furnished in the seemingly unrelated second line of narrative, the "digression." Or, if the digression has rather the character of a flashback or an elaboration or a supplying of background, it will turn out to carry onward some second "new" theme as well as the first one which needed the background; and from that in turn we digress, or seem to, and then come back, not to precisely what we left but to something we understand differently because of what we have since seen.

All this is, of course, extraordinarily well suited to a narrative organized as a quest, but not all romances making use of such principles of structure are romances of knight-errantry. Moreover, some romance-authors have genius and wit, but some only succeed in showing up the natural weaknesses of their chosen form; late prose romances so abuse this principle that they degenerate into haphazard aggregations of adventures.

Specific analysis of successful use has chiefly touched on the *Lancelot* and the *Mort Artu*; but the *Queste*, which appeared between these in the cycle, exemplifies many of the narrative advantages of this structural habit. We take in quickly the significance of Bohort's rapidly presented dilemmas and choices, because we have accompanied Lancelot slowly in the pain and pathos of his recurrent failures, and with guileless Perceval have learned when to suspect machinations of the same enemy whose disguises bring Bohort to such anguished indecisions. One character's dream may assist us to see through another character's experiences the moral double meanings that are hard for himself to see. Minor characters like Meliant demonstrate motives, or minor incidents (this damsel helped or that castle rescued from siege) may harp upon consequences, which enable us to see that there are implications in the innocent-looking behavior of,

say, Gawain, or Hector, or the uninstructed early Lancelot—
though the stories are seemingly unrelated. We should never
understand the purport of Galahad's actions or take in the quality
of his single-minded fidelity, if we did not come to it by way
of the several varied and flawed forms of devotion which the
other questers exhibit. And in all this I do not mention the in-
tensifying of meanings through their reappearance—never identical, never repeated, but like enough to illuminate some difficult
conception that later comes close to showing as the "theme" (as
intervening tales of the searches of the others help us to take in
what *is* Galahad's "achievement of the Grail").

This is not truly a repetitive structure, which we see exemplified, e.g. in the repeated conquests of a Tamburlaine, though the
quest-organization in romances or in Spenser makes the not-truly-
parallel encounters look repetitive or purely episodic—as it makes
the frequent necessary transitions easy and deceptively naïve. It
has always been noticed that Spenser looks at his chosen abstraction or virtue through the perspectives of several incidents, as
in Book V we look at aspects of Justice and In-Justice or unrighteous tyranny through one after another token incident or
fable. We therefore approach with clarified sight the real unveil-
ing, or the climactic joining of the issue if the terms are those of
a conflict, near the middle and near the end. This structure also
is incorrectly termed episodic or repetitive or parallel, for the
subtler effects and advantages here noted as typical of interlaced,
not parallel, happenings will be seen to characterize any Book
the reader cares to examine closely.

This web-structure has special possibilities of gradually dis-
cernible meaning as the woven pattern shows it *is* a pattern and
takes shape. Hence it was a superbly invented instrument for conveying not only what we called the polyphonic nature of what
is happening, but that which interested Spenser supremely, the
fact that to human minds what happens "means" something, is
significant. We may seem to digress from the pursuit of Florimell,
and flash back to the Merlin's cave episode to know why Britomart is on that road and meets the others; we also experience,
however, the way the "love" we condemned in Castle Joyous
in iii.i, now retroacts to complicate the love that seizes the heroine in iii.ii, for we perceive likenesses as well as differences. We
see that the Florimell-pursuit is going to have meanings which
the Artegall-pursuit will clarify, that the genealogical prophecies

had been given significance (before we knew we were meeting them) by the British emphases of Book II. No matter which was written first, the Braggadochio-False Florimell section or the Braggadochio-Belphoebe of Book II, the "patchiness" with which a later-appearing character is just lightly drawn in for an episode in a Book we read first, merely *seems* patchy. For both appearances are needed, in the contexts they are in, to fill out the presentation of the Bad Knight—as he lacks understanding of chaste love, and as he lacks understanding of temperance. The presentation will be properly continued in the episode in Book V where Braggadochio is the Bad Knight since he lacks that virtue which gives "to each man his own," or in Book IV where he is the Bad Knight incapable of Friendship, a knight sought out and preferred by falsity.

The Marinell of III.iv would not be capable of conceiving the love he is later to give Florimell, nor have we quite distinguished it ourselves before it occurs (or is patently missing) in incidents involving others. Florimell must remain in the straits we leave her in in III.viii until those happenings occur which bring the characters and the readers through the changes that make us (and Cymoent and Marinell) consent to the marriage in Book IV. The romance convention of enfances furnished for Amoret and Belphoebe in III.vi throws light backward upon Belphoebe's actions toward Timias and the "love" therein portrayed III.v. 36), just as canto vi also prevents us from suspecting Spenser of oversimplification when we confront sexual love as it is portrayed in the seemingly unrelated episodes of Paridell and Hellenore or the tapestries of Busyrane's house.

Meanwhile, while the real principle of unity lies in "meanings" of happenings, *which inform what happened* and are not separable from the story, the events can be made to happen without pinning all importance upon psychological motivation. In any romance, the story can be easily advanced by such conventions as "customs" of castles, quarrelsome knights provoking battle, stops for lodging, knights-errant who merely "meet" adventure, enquiry into lignage and enfances, or climactic meaning concentrated in some otherworldly or symbolic *place*. It is this use of significances as the cohering factor, not the fancifulness of romance, which enables us to move in and out of symbols like the "real" places they are.

This mode of making separate incidents cohere in a unity is

even easier to see in Books where a single hero achieves some aim or learns some great definition. The series of happenings chosen by Spenser is not the sequential series natural to a biography-of-hero principle of organization; we deal with a different structural conception from that which would give us an epic action toward which every event builds, or an epic hero whom every action ultimately exalts. In a "well-organized" single-hero Book (II), Braggadochio looks like a digression, from the Bloody Babe story or the Medina section. But we are dealing with a design wherein pattern slowly *takes* shape rather than with a design wherein a theme is stated and variants develop it. The Braggadochio episode is neither a digression from Medina nor a continuation of her theme—it is the constant problem presented in a different frame of reference. He is intemperate in every way the Knight may not be and maintain "chivalry" by definition based on fidelity to good. He is fearful, vainglorious, advises expedient cunning not prudence or wisdom, responds to beauty with lascivious desire rather than love or wonder. In a word, his allegiance is to "the world," and the climax is his sensuality and his vulgar advice to Belphoebe to go where she can make the most of her charms.

But for the notion that the episode ought to mean Aristotle's middle way between foolhardiness and cowardice and thus attach to canto ii, we would have noticed that foolhardiness is absent, that the character does not err by excess but by confusing vainglory with fortitude, and shows not wrong balance but wrong aims (just as prodigality is not there to answer to avarice, and as *any* traffic with Acrasia, not *too much* traffic with her, is intemperate). Having brought us to think of aspects of the problem connected with temperance defined as the mean, Spenser half-leaves this conception to illustrate temperance as defined by that element of right allegiance which Christian thought gave to it down through the centuries to Milton's *Comus* (fidelity to "the right loves" is the emphasis we persistently meet from Augustine onward, preventing the excesses of enslavement to Mammon or to Acrasia).

Similarly the opening up of the nature of Temperance is continued in the Guyon-Furor encounter which happens during this Braggadochio passage. So too does the Squire's Hero-and-Claudio story seem to be a digression from Guyon-and-Furor, just adventitiously attached in that Furor maltreats its teller the Squire; actually, however, it opens Temperance's nature to our view by showing how a faked "Occasion" roused "Furor" in the Squire. Thus the supposedly separable episode really enacts the meanings of the very characters it seems to desert capriciously.

In this interwoven structure, then, that which seems to follow (or precede) by chance is in fact discovered to be related, necessary where and when it occurs, and part of a hidden time-scheme; this is typical both of Spenser's early and later Books and of the great Arthurian romances in their best known French and English forms. Touching the French material, this has been amply demonstrated by the careful analyses of Lot and Frappier, especially of the hidden chronology; I do not think it is worthwhile to work out Spenser's timing of events,[22] made less important and less deliberate by his request to be allegorically read.

[22] It is true, however, that if we stop to analyze, as Lot and Frappier did, we realize that Guyon might fight Pyrochles (II.v.3) before the provocation Atin uses (II.v.36) can make Cymochles call for his arms and seek out a fight (II.vi) which enables Phaedria and the Idle Lake to be introduced. These things must happen between the time that Guyon fights, and Pyrochles frees, Furor (v.14), so that the hasty plunge of the burning Pyrochles into the Idle Lake (vi.42) can be understood to be the completion of Guyon's binding of Furor (II.iv.15). Cymochles and Pyrochles have to be left, from canto vi to viii, until we get the exhausted Guyon to where they can be dangers to him. Guyon's overthrow by Britomart and Marinell's overthrow by Britomart (III) help make important Artegall's and Britomart's overthrow of each other (IV); we cannot proceed with the Florimell tale until Marinell has the things happen to him which bring him to the sea cave and make psychologically possible the action for which Florimell has been brought there much earlier (III.viii)—but not by an uninterrupted telling of her flight (III.i), but in a third picking-up of it (III.viii) after we have met Marinell and heard of his parentage and prophecy (III.iv.25; which we did not know was being fulfilled when we met him, iv.12). This second Florimell stretch had to be interrupted by the Argante-Squire portion so that the Beast who is responsible for the girdle-complication can bring about the rumor of death that leads to a False Florimell's creation, and which reaches Paridell in viii.50. Often occurrences cannot be told "in order" because we have not arrived at the time they will happen.

These may seem to be the normal complications of a planned fiction; to a certain extent—because mediaeval practice carried on through Elizabethan prose has affected prose fiction more than we have realized—these have become familiar conventions of timing management. The deliberate reasonableness of the "interruptions" should be noted as a factor in entrelacement. However, we should notice the reasons other than timing, which made mediaeval writers prefer such structures, and which are seldom deliberately sought by any modern authors we could analyze similarly.

But one aesthetic result is outstanding, and makes Spenser's inheritance of structural entrelacement a piece of real good fortune. He did not inherit this as an advantage, but made it one by the all but new turn he gave to the form. We change from character to character but never leave Temperance. We cannot keep straight what happened next to Artegall but we watch each canto add lines to the drawing of a just knight. We find no hero at all to embody it, but we do not misunderstand the nature of Friendship or its opposite; we are discontent with the portrayal of the Courteous Knight, but we find no objections to raise to the portrayal of Courtesy. We shift rapidly from incident to incident and place to place, but we pursue steadfastly and without agitation the question of the nature of Chastity. Especially this last unit will be seen to adhere carefully to the exposing or opening out of its subject, once we define Chastity with its traditional Christian overtones of total fidelity, love purified of idolatry, lust and self-indulgence.[23] Incident after incident and character after character build up the inquiry into the part played by a right love in man's life—what draws him to it, its opposites, perversions, faked appearances, striking examples where it shines out, its relation to "natural" love and generation as cosmological principles since it alone is creative and its great opposites are destructive principles opposed to it in their *direction* which is toward possession and self-aggrandizement, the self-idolatrous ends of sterile and indulgent lust. It is wanton quarrelsomeness to point to such observations as evidence that Spenser was interested first in the ideas, for in the piece itself there is no separating idea from story (absurd notion); it is we late-comers who phrase these summaries. For a writer with Sidneyan poetics, the mediaeval structure which promoted ever-fresh but never repeated "actions" and thus allowed these meanings to re-state themselves, was a fortunate gift of time.

[23] So purified if all creatures are loved "in God," the theologians said; virginity is this faithfulness when the love is man's love of God. But the absolutely traditional virtue of castitas which opposed luxuria, is not confused with virginitas but includes it. See my article "Notes on the Vices and Virtues," in *JWCI*, vols. 26, 27 (1963, 1964). As usual, Spenser is not drawn into portraying these elements of Christian doctrine and definition. The distinctions are observed and the accurate meanings of words depended upon, but the kind of help we get from knowing Christian doctrine is general and unmeticulous, for Spenser does not shape his allegories to convey Christian mysteries directly.

The real reason for entrelacement is not necessity but choice; it is more interesting and suits the importance of the piece. As we pursue such analyses, we see that the plans of romances are not visibly dictated by that principle of subordination which governs our notions of plot, of how to outline a schema, or of how the members of a structure are articulated. Dominance, of a character especially, does not appear in the usual forms; the main line may not come first, and the most meaningful character may not get most space. The *Queste* dwells but shortly upon the chief quester before going on to the adventures of others, but this does not subordinate Galahad. More time and attention are given to Lancelot's failure than to Galahad's success, yet these failures are not the theme nor Lancelot the pre-eminent character. The web is uncuttable, the delayed continuations necessary for enrichment of themes; the seeming elaborations are essential parts after all, as Lot stressed long ago for other romances. In the best pieces the *sens* is constantly felt, giving unity. In others, as in some of the longer non-cyclical romances with single heroes, like *Bevis* or *Huon*, unity in any subtle sense is sacrificed, though some pervasive ideal provides the coherence rather than the hero's developing character; the loss is not grave under mediaeval conditions of hearing or reading.

Spenser's usual structure is this complex interweaving of seemingly unrelated parts that unobtrusively take shape as a pattern. Unity is not provided by a hero's series of exploits, even when it looks so, nor by a single mind's development (like an assumed growth of Guyon in Book II), nor by a conflict. An opposition defined, fought out, concluded in triumph, is the structure of I.xi, but not of Book I, of III.xii, but not of Book III. The sought virtue is the unifying factor in *every* Book. This is usual enough in romance (the *Lancelot* with its attempt to combine presentation of the ideal knightly code and the ideal knightly lover is a complex example); also, Spenser seems to have fallen into it and then realized that his earliest portions (now embedded in Books III and IV) really do consider what it is man seeks under the name of "true love," and that he had looked at aspect after aspect of a quiddity whose Christian name was Chastity—for neither Caritas nor Agape, Eros nor Love, will convey the meanings we are shown. When he then chose as the design of other Books the seeking and realizing of a virtue, his fidelity to the romance structure was wise, since it fits his quest-organization and his narrative texture, which are conventional, as well as his allegorical use of them, which is unusual and original. Allegorical reading is very well served by this opportunity to realize, re-realize, and realize again, the full import of something we can only lamely point to by its abstract name.

I think it should be noticed as a by-point whenever chance brings it up, that through this inheritance of a structure that was neither episodic nor articulated like an epic action, Spenser could heighten the presentation of reigning themes to produce actual allegory, and yet evade the problem which teases moderns, whether and when the story is subordinate to the allegory.

I am convinced that this is a nonexistent problem which did not worry Spenser and only makes us misread when it worries us. The reason is much the same as with the point above touching "happening and interpretation," event and meaning. The story is *read* allegorically. If I am asked to write down the notes which constitute a tune or to write down a tune, the same demand is made of me; "the Book is Red Crosse's story" is the same statement as "the Book is the discovery of Holiness," for there exists no man "Red Crosse" whose story would be different if the author did not have the claims of allegorical Holiness modifying his intents. The unifying principle is not the *history* of a particular or an individual; the action is not a biography, a life, but an action. However varied the definitions of allegory, they are at one in raising to an extreme Sidney's remark about poetry, that it deals with things "in their universal consideration" so that we view abstractions themselves interacting. It was brilliant of Spenser to realize that a structure which weaves a tapestry before us is particularly well suited to allegory, where pattern must steal upon us. He was also supremely successful at this secret conveying of unparaphrasable meaning, and we should not obscure the success by re-writing his stories into their allegories, but resolutely claim whole images with all their depicted feelings as the sole true statements of his allegorical meanings.

To observe how well these structural conventions suit Spenser's enlarged purposes gives marked pleasure. Enhancement of pleasure in a simpler form is perhaps the only result of another, and the most obvious, of the resemblances he has to romances—the *Faerie Queene*'s use throughout of the world of objects and circumstances, the adjuncts or things or furniture of mediaeval story. Spenser writes something that is not overplentiful once the great period passed—an *interesting* romance. The *Orlando Furioso* is not "an interesting romance"; it is Ariosto that is so interesting. His twists, his turns, his ways of picking things up captivate us even when we choke upon his invention, and the sense of his presence is exhilaratingly constant. But Spenser is anonymous in the manner of the old tales. A striking point is that the *Faerie Queene* is so much more like the interesting stories of the early development than like the late and dull compilations supposed to be so influential. It is vastly more similar to the prose *Lancelot* than to a *Perceforest* or an *Amadis*,[24] and resembles Hawes so little in all that makes us enjoy reading that all the parallels in the studies have been unable to tie the two men together in an important way.

Spenser received the interestingness with the genre, when he chose it, and when he thus decided once and for all the whole wavering question of what should be the external garb of his story, the world of sights and sounds and particulars we are given to live in, the conditions and the scene-settings and the undescribed circumstances that surround his people. Spenser is the

[24] Only the grim length of these decadent pieces, which quite properly prevents them from being read, seems to me to keep in circulation the notion of their great influence. An occasional resemblance in a plot motif is as naught when compared with similarities like those found between the *Faerie Queene* and the attitude toward chivalry in the Vulgate Cycle, or the conversations and encounters in *Huon* or in Malory, or the tone and use of otherworldly elements in lais or in any version of the *Mort Artu*. The late works mentioned will be found to differ vastly from earlier romances and from Spenser in literary quality, a difference as visible to him as to us; and though he doubtless nibbled these current fictions and picked up, as Drayton did, the little Wynken de Worde reprints of minstrel pieces or charming trifles, he is no more likely than we to have read the poor and neglected the good. A dull, late piece like *Perceforest* is not at all a typical romance. But serious studies are needed that are sympathetic enough to understand Sidney's respectful reference "even" to *Amadis de Gaule* (God knows no "perfect poesy"). However, these studies should attend to more literary elements than merely story motifs; this would then enable scholars to evaluate the real dependence on these sixteenth-century publications. The reference which allowed the later claim that *Amadis* had "allegorical" meaning, in the prologue to the Book usually styled xi (or xv or vii) in the French version, turns out upon hunting down to be a thoroughly general and conventionalized claim, and mean very little.

most successful of any Elizabethan in portraying his imagined characters living in a milieu. Though it appears as a consistent seamless tissue, unselfconsciously recorded as by one living in it, it was not the milieu of an Elizabethan and could not have been portrayed unlearned; he borrowed it. It is the first thing that interests us about a mediaeval romance, this quiet, constant flow past us of all the accidents, the whole superficies, of life in the chivalric world. Romance plots are not outstandingly competent, characters rise infrequently to the height of great creations, but the minutiae of a life that seems to us lived under interesting conditions quite simply engrosses the attention.

This is not because such details are outré or fanciful; neither is it because they have a cachet of strangeness, being alien to our prosaic present world; and I do not here refer to what is often called the machinery of romance, i.e. any and all fantastic elements. The prose *Lancelot* is as good an example as any. From the first page, we are placed in the midst of situations which would repeat themselves endlessly if we possessed or looked at detailed actual records: the smouldering feud, the besieged castle, the decision to seek the help of the liege lord, the attempt to get away by a secret postern, the underling one could not trust, King Ban who looks back at his land and sees the flames take his castle, his faint, his fall, the hill where he dies (the very grass of which he takes three blades to signify the Trinity and hallow his unexpected death), the heritageless child, only the riderless horse to reveal what has happened to the frightened young widowed queen. The supernatural is used with marked restraint, confined to one element—the Lady of the Lake and her beneficent and often magical assistances to the infant Lancelot whom she steals and brings up. We go on to an otherwise quite straightforward story of youthful heirs kept from rightful inheritances, the meticulously delineated sympathetic villain Claudas, exhibitions of the knightly society which are plainly simple "recording," though details have the immediacy of imagined fiction.

It is true that the author makes use, as we read two hundred pages or so into the story, of what we are accustomed to call the machinery of romance and note as a Spenserian borrowing therefrom. There is an enfances for the hero, unaware of his identity, as protégé of otherworldly guardians, their agent, a helpful

Damsel who assists escapes by changing of the children into grey-hounds to avoid capture, an enchanted ring, copper automata who are tests of Lancelot's valor, silent castles, horns whose blowing brings enemies, breaks enchantments or causes wonders, forces from the world of unnatural evil betrayed by stench, by awful cold, by fire that surrounds protective swords or makes entrances impenetrable. Moreover, these marvels are given the same matter-of-fact narration as the natural incidents and details—a literary characteristic to be expected in romances, and equally characteristic of Spenser, giving to his stories of Orgoglio's Monstrous Birth, Satyrane's enfances in the wilds, or the hornblowing at the silent castle, the same combination of dreamy vividness and ordinary credibility which we feel in *Sir Orfeo* or *Lancelot* or *Sir Isenbras*. Yet mediaeval authors would be abashed at Ariosto's easy invention of supernatural rings and shields and escapes.

We have overemphasized the marvelous as characteristic of romances, for its overuse was a late abuse, and it is more typical of the earlier pieces to introduce superhuman powers chiefly where they have a meaningful origin or "reading," as Spenser does. Even where his source shows pure love of the marvelous, Spenser may restore such a meaningful reading. He may have got the horn of Bk. I.viii from that in *Orlando Furioso*. xv, which straightway sends all hearers scurrying, but it has taken on the character of romance horns, objects sacredly imbued with powers not of this world, such as the basin at the fountain of *Ywain and Gawain*, from which one sprinkled water to set the cycle of enchantments in motion; so a seriously supernatural challenge like Arthur's in the *Faerie Queene* marks the crossing of a threshold between two kinds of reality. Duessa's uncovering may be "from" Ariosto's discovering of Alcina's true ugliness (*Orlando Furioso*. vii), but Duessa's allegorical roles connected with forms of falsity make the truthful naturalness of the image outweigh any sense of supernatural machinery. I do not think occurrence of these more sensational elements is responsible for the firmness of one's interest in either the earlier pieces or in Spenser's.

I do not wish, by stressing the ordinariness of the happenings and giving less importance to the part played by the strangeness of fantasy, to remove all that made these stories "romantically" moving. For it is also true that romances like the *Lancelot* move us, as narratives usually do move one, in that we discover we are undergoing the characters' experiences of grief, longing or joy. Claudas is the enemy, but we are cut by the sharpness of his loss when his one son, unadmirable though he is, is killed, and we respond sympathetically to the long sorrow of the young queen over the uncertain fate of her baby or to the boyish resentments of the king's two heirs with their mixture of arrogance and nobility. The unending series of simply presented human affections evokes so constant a stream of responses in a reader that we know the *Lancelot* for a great fiction in this respect long before we arrive at the love between Lancelot and Guenevere, of course the major such triumph as Dante's reference to it reminds us. In fact, this true portrayal and rapid evocation of emotional responses is so typical a literary trait in the romances that we may locate therein one chief reason for their interestingness.

It is what primarily kept them alive into the sixteenth century, and the whole crowd of accessible romances should be kept in mind, not just the Arthurian cycle or the large great works. A mere chapbook piece like *Sir Degare* can make us catch the quality of feeling of the knight riding through the forest where no common beast is seen and where the castle with its central fire and silent occupants makes the young man pit his endurance against theirs; the sharp sense we have of Sir Launfal's state of mind, when he sat under the tree thinking how alone he would be in his ruin, is what supports our interest in the fairy-mistress plot that follows and in his exultant largesse, and underscores the vividness of his shock as he stands looking at the naked fée, or his pride in his vindication when she rides silently into Arthur's court so opulently accoutred. A Spenser needed no doggerel *Sir Eglamour* as the source for the visual traits of his great worm, but he might note as we do the realism of the dragon's apparent movement, though it was dead, and how it stank. It is no wonder Drayton mentions *Sir Isenbras*, if he was struck as we are by the many details that sharpen the pathos—the beautiful sterile thorn-blossoms which are all the hungry knight can see, how he is shaken by the vision of his naked children, the little boy who weeps to see his father beaten.[25] In the great romances like the

---

[25] There were three sixteenth-century editions of *Sir Degare* (de Worde, Copland and John King *ca.* 1560, with a copy in Bodley); *Sir Launfol* is men-

first part of the *Lancelot,* the *Perlesvaus,* the *Queste,* the *Mort Artu,* or Malory's versions of the basic stories, the emotional power of whole pieces of work is of course more important, but it is not more noticeable than this continuous felicity in seizing upon small but true human responses to very particular situations.

Contrary to an often-asserted commonplace, it is not the "anatomy of love" that is thus so interestingly and revealingly demonstrated in a typical mediaeval romance. If Spenser really had clear ideas and firm opinions about the mediaeval literary-historical phenomenon that goes by the ambiguous name of courtly love, the romances (except for the *Troilus*) were not eminent as places where he learned them. He would read a great deal about love as that term embraces an endless variety of human affections—the poignancy of the relation between Gawain and Lancelot,[26] the love Galehaut bore Lancelot, sudden ungovernable

tioned in the Cox list; fragments of two editions in Bodley are printed in Appendix to *Bishop Percy's Folio MS.,* 1, ed. Hales and Furnivall, 1867; *Sir Eglamour* was printed in Edinburgh in 1508, by Copland (Bodl.), by Walley (B.Mus. copy; 1570?). Someone took the trouble in 1564 to copy many of these (including *Degare, Eglamour* and *Isenbras*) in MS.Douce 261; see *Summary Catalogue* 21835 for interesting facts of provenance and related copyings. *Sir Isenbras* was published by Copland (n.d.; fragments of others) and is listed by Captain Cox. I cite these editions, as I cite the details in the text, not to argue that they stood out or were used as sources or even were influential, but as reminders of how much and what varied materials, and problems, lie behind the unexamined statement "Spenser shows little use of the romances."

[26] In a moving page, like Sommer, IV, 137 for instance (*op.cit.* in n. 2 above), when the imprisoned Gawain and Lancelot (who has just killed Carados) recognize each other by their voices; but there is literally no end to exemplification of this peculiarly felicitous and varied emotional portrayal—in Malory as well. Early editions of the French cycle romances mentioned are numerous, and are impressive but not de luxe books. Non-cycle works like *Huon,* and some chansons de geste (those which were "modernized" and printed) deserve mention. But I refrain from citing parts of cycles which the sixteenth century knew in forms less remarkable for literary excellence. The greatest deprivation for a reader of Spenser's time would be the Tristan. Of course there were numerous early editions, for it was extraordinarily popular in the elaborated and deteriorated form of the "prose Tristan" (see Woledge, No. 170). A concentrated session is necessary with Vinaver's *Études sur le Tristan en prose* (Paris, 1925), his Malory studies, Loseth's *Le roman en prose de Tristan* (*Bibliothèque de l'École des Hautes Études,* Fasc. 82), and his study of the B.Mus. MSS. *Le Tristan et le Palamide des mss. français du British Museum* (Kristiana, 1905), with exact attention to the contents of particular manuscripts and prints. The matter is

desires or *folies*, consistently faithful devotion, the protective love of powerful beings like the Lady of the Lake, love especially intense between leader and men, especially resilient between brothers, especially tender between parents and children—but the wire-drawn distinctions and paradoxical exaggerations which our definition gives to the phrase "courtly love" are not the mainstay even of a love-romance like the *Lancelot*, Chrétien's influence and the charrette notwithstanding. The fidelity and the secrecy, surely not reserved to courtly love, are of course essential in the *Lancelot* presentation, but the most noticeable parallel element, Lancelot's trance-like loss of himself in Guenevere's presence, has important relations to the problem of tragic doom, and Lancelot's love-frenzy is not shown as the complaint of an Aurelius. It is the theorizing and the phraseology which we miss.

With an occasional exception like the monologues of a *Guy of Warwick* (and even that, like *Ipomedan*, is different), the much reprinted and durable romances and the popular smaller ones would scarcely pass on as a heritage the artifices and sophisticated attitudes we have labeled courtly love, for they do not really present it. Perhaps Spenser did not know much about it either, and would not have talked about Love versus Courtly Love, but about Love versus False Love, Lust or Folly. The love of the court which he criticized did not deserve the name, but he writes about something Elizabeth's court exhibited to him (as we see from "Colin Clouts Come Home Again") not about something chiefly known from what was written at the courts of Marie and Eleanor. One certainly doubts Spenser's familiarity with actual "courts of love" and their progeny of débat and tençon.[27]

---

far too complicated to report on here; I must merely state that the evidence seemed to me sufficient that the forms best known to the sixteenth century were so inferior to the great story as we generally read it, that exemplification from it was unwise. This is an example of the researches needed on *literary relations* of versions.

[27] I believe Italian rather than French sources responsible for what Spenser knew of these matters, and that they were late rather than earlier works (except perhaps for Dante's *Vita nuova*). The Platonic elements which differentiate his conceptions of love from those in mediaeval romances surely show this filiation. He doubtless knew this or that trattato d'amore, and his subtleties and exaltations are those fashionable in his day, contrasting with the Provençal amors or the minne of German texts. The question of the *Troilus*, set apart in this respect from the large body of romances, would need separate examination.

Instead, a primary lesson learned from these old stories was the presentation of these sympathetic quick insights into all manner of feelings. To notice how unusually frequent they are in Spenser, as in earlier romances, we have only to allow ourselves to read him with the free and leisurely interest and pleasure which was a chief reason for writing in the romance genre. Everyone recalls the few famous examples—the delicate perceptiveness in descriptions of Britomart's jealousy, people crowding about the dragon that still seems to move, Una's rejoining of the knight she thinks to be the unjust but deceived Red Crosse, or the comic conversations when false Una or Malecasta climb into bed with startled knights. But this narrative trait is far more constantly present, and without ulterior motive, than criticism is now inclined to notice, bent rather upon detecting an unflagging awareness of significances and upon seeking equivalents in signification for each separate movement in the narrative. Yet that is not the way allegory operates, either, in such romances as use it.

We shall see later that even their hermit-exegetes show us that the surest guide to what is allegorically significant is to notice what captured the imagination in the story one has just read—but *after* that capture. If the whole burden of the feeling in that scene (ii.viii) where the Palmer sees the protective angelic spirit at the exhausted Guyon's head is compassionate love, with stanza after stanza expressing wonder at that divine love which is unfathomable for one sole reason, that it keeps coming to man the enemy and alienated one—then the scene is not functioning as an accusation of Guyon and a warning against an insufficiency that shows him weighed in a balance and found wanting.[28] The

[28] I am referring here to a different interpretation of Guyon's state and reasons for his faint, in H. Berger, *The Allegorical Temper* (New Haven, 1957), where Guyon's faint marks the shift from classical to Christian temperance in the "strangely divided" two pieces of Book ii, and is held to be the result of a blameworthy overdependence on his self-supported virtue. There will be disagreements on meanings of individual scenes in the *Faerie Queene* as long as it is read, and I adduce this one only to make specific enough my plea for remembering that the *Faerie Queene* is a species of romance. I do not believe the complications of the interpretation (e.g. pp. 29-44) to be in the text. But one notices in many other books as well the tendency to treat single lines, small images, or verbal tags almost as magical keys, and the imposition of dubiously applicable theorizing (here cf. the "levels" of Berger, p. 35, absolute definitions

feeling of scenes is never denied and canceled out by meanings. Where we have repeatedly been told that what we look at is that marvel of loving protectiveness which unceasingly enfolds the human creature, out of love alone and whenever he is in danger, we are not to deny the whole because some seeming verbal twist is puzzling. For that is all there is to the fact that "good Guyon" is called God's "wicked foe"; the whole point of introducing right loves and God's ordering love into Christian discussions of temperance lies in the fact that even a good man is God's foe and is wilfully prone to oppose rather than love God, except through the grace whose operations we are about to be shown. This is what defines the marvel, which is not turned on like extra electric power when the load is heavy; the omnipresence and gratuitousness of this love is what makes the sweetness of stanza 8 and stanza 2 so unexpectedly powerful, like an effect of music. The straightforward, free response to directly encountered emotions, indicated without elaboration but quite openly, could well be brought back into the reading of Spenser's allegory, as it had been an expected element in romances from their first development; further, it was conserved in those which are to be read allegorically, and is a guide to their allegorical points.

De Selincourt long ago observed Spenser's gift for seizing upon some simple and natural detail which conveys quality of feeling more rapidly and exactly than analysis. All good narrative writers command this virtue, and we notice it in romances not to discover influences but to recall that sixteenth-century romances were enjoyed by readers for their truth to life as much as for their fantasy. That we are far more alert to the enjoyment of fantasy is

---

of quite modern vintage). Current weaknesses touching what constitutes evidence have left us especially open to the dangers of overreading that accompany image-interpretation when simpler indicated meanings are left behind for possibilities suggested by similar images in other contexts. (E.g. the angel-Cupid simile of Bk. ii.viii. must surely first relate to the iconographical identity of the winged young-man God of Love with the exactly described angel-portrait, with the direction given by the remembrance that angels ministered to Christ also after the Temptation, deliberately alluded to but of course not represented; cf. Berger's discussion of the "world of Cupid," pp. 43-44.) Berger's and other critics' return to some consideration of Christian thought on these matters would be welcome if it were not so doctrinaire. Berger is certainly right in his perceptive distinction between "significations" known to us, or to the character caught in action (p. 36), and in pointing out that those who think Guyon has sunk under the excessive cares of wealth have not read the story (p. 33).

partly due to very much later meanings of "romance" and "romantic."

These late meanings have obscured the reasons for another curious and probably adventitious likeness. In the framework of a presentation of chivalry for the sake of its high code, and in Arthurian stories, the excellence of the characters was an historical *given*, and we are likeliest to be asked to share the feelings of the admirable characters, the most noble, most generous or most honorable. In Malory, in the cycle, in lais, wickedness is presented briefly and without analysis, often without much curiosity. Spenser's dastardly or immoral creatures are described elaborately, but the sudden touches which make us share feelings with imagined characters, usually with an inner rush of credence in their reality, are cases where Spenser evokes pity, generous love, compassion, shared sorrow. This similarity in the emotional tones which are made most of, links Spenser's romance with others, in contrast to most fiction, wherein the sudden jab of shared feeling is likelier to be felt for a character in conflict or one whose fault we share. Certainly, however, this cannot be shown to have been learned by Spenser from predecessors whose tone resembles his for this reason (it is very marked in the prose *Lancelot*). He did learn, I think, the simplest kind of realism both show: the unmistakable and unselfconscious fixing of the narrative in a chivalric social milieu, recorded sparely, with little attempt at description, but in such a way as to unify the fiction and render it credible as a tale of real life.

To a great extent the details so often shared between Spenser and Arthurian romance-writers stem from the initial *datum*: these are tales of knights errant. We may notice now some specific effects of Spenser's choice to join his predecessors in the use of their mediaeval milieu; we have already remarked that it led to certain expectations touching structure and major roles. (See n. 8 above.) Of course knight-errantry is a deciding factor in producing a plot of which the staples are the performance of tasks, rescue of damsels, restoring the dispossessed to their inheritances, sieges, captivities, and meetings leading to love affairs, with incidents simply "met" rather than logically evolved, and constant movement and introduction of new characters. This factor is as decisively important to Spenser's fundamental design as the absence of certain plot motifs is unimportant (famous plot-clichés like Lancelot's swordbridge, an actual grail, tomb-inci-

dents, court feasts, betrayal through bloodstains). More particularly, this initial *datum* brings two incident-producing elements
of a romance in its train: castles with "customs" which the errant
knights must face, and the whole series of results following on
the simple fact that characters are peripatetic and continually
placed in new situations by each night's search for hospitality. But
setting, manner, temper and texture are much more interestingly
affected than plot and incident, for in those invention is far more
important than influence, and Spenser borrowed them oftener
from modern romances like Ariosto's. But we need tell no lies
about his close dependence on Ariosto and Tasso as we notice
Spenser's extreme success in reproducing the superficies of a
mediaeval tale.

He learned (I think through reading) to imagine things as if
they were taking place in a real and ordinary mediaeval world
where chivalry, and the way of living that went with it, was a
common and living institution. There are many knightly romances in the Renaissance, in England, but others do not have the
flavor of ordinary though deeply idealized mediaeval life, moving
with the same tempo and tone as life in the cycle romances or the
lais, among the same landscapes and objects. Things take place
in an England townless and untenanted, where we come upon
people only resting by fountains, or on great horses charging
toward us (always involved with us, never casually passing),
though land is empty and spacious, with meadows and waterways
interrupting the all but ubiquitous forests, or with here and there
a hermitage, or two or three huts of villeins, or the isolated fortified castle. Through the woods (I think more archaic than symbolic) ride the familiar characters, encountering when they should
the intended person, or alternatively experiencing the chance meeting which produces so many unintended battles with unrecognized
friend, brother, or boon companion. We expect characters to
"seek" desired persons simply by setting out into the forest, we
know the conventions of a promised return or a sworn later meeting elsewhere or a promised delivery of oneself as trophy at
court. We accept the last-minute deflections from a first duty into
another met en route, the dungeons where one comes upon half
one's fellowship evilly deterred from their quest, and the libera-
tions; we expect the constant single combats (bringing with them
the customary easy assertions about numbers killed, blood shed,

wounds and cures) which need no elaboration of motive but only a bad "custom" bumped into on the road or a chance-met oppression that needs remedy. We take for granted riddling inscriptions or prophecies, or tournaments universally accepted as a way to decide matters and hence the periodical converging of the whole action upon such a point, as well as constant awarenesss of the code of knightly honor and occasional serious exposition of that code— the oaths, the skills, the accoutrements (sometimes the young knight's initiation, all usually tied to a dominant plot motif, the enfances). To avoid the deceits of memory, this series was written—abstaining from actual plot motifs—with one eye upon the conventions that govern the *manner* of presenting events in the early part of the prose *Lancelot*'s first book,[29] but I could perfectly well be describing the expected circumstances which surround events in a Book of the *Faerie Queene* or a non-cycle romance.

This is a kind of similarity to be distinguished from parallelisms in incident (also from the fantastic elements we call romance machinery). It is felt even when Spenser is deliberately copying a plot motif that would seem out of place in a mediaeval romance, such as the Ovidian metamorphosis of Fradubio, or the Ariostan pursuit of Florimell. It has the realism of well-known actualities much heightened; little needed to be "invented." The actualities may be archaic, but we find the same ones if we pick up next a romance of later date which the reader will recognize: knight and lady, who apparently are in love merely by the same chance which endowed him with her "quest," journey slowly toward their object, stopping to sleep or to carry through the adventures that they evidently are responsible for handling if they are but encountered, through woods and past the dens and caves where action takes place, past crossroads, hermitages, chapels, but nothing else, except the castles that are virtually small courts, down paths which always lead to meaningful encounters. The enemy is consistently "the Saracen," fights are in-

[29] It is always possible to pile up these lists that make likenesses appear so singular and persuasive, just as the new fashion of paraphrasing Spenser, image by image and line by line, can make him seem to have said almost anything that one would like. But I am not looking at peculiarities, made to seem "shared" by my forced phrasing. I notice the ordinary commonplaces of mediaeval stories, which an Elizabethan had to learn somewhere if he makes them his common dress.

stant, combats (extremely specifically described) take place the
moment knights meet, and the accompanying damsels fall to the
victor and join his retinue. Ladies, upon desertion, wander up
hill and down dale but with the hope, always fulfilled, of meeting the one desired lost knight; characters are benighted, trains
of action follow from the mere facts of where and with whom
the travelers take lodging (with sanctimonious deceiver or half-
civilized peasant). Decisions hang upon the outcome of single
combats fought at tournaments where we see the court under its
canopy, the minstrels, the ceremonial drink and trumpet, and
afterward hear of the disarming, the cured wounds, the knight
who escapes by privy postern after coming upon the inevitable
dungeon with the castle's victims. Forests are so uninhabited that
they serve as places for the wild enfances of the naïve bold youth
who manages savage beasts, for dangers met unwittingly, and
tests that must be passed. Chance wayside meetings lead to the
necessary rescues from dungeons, the awakening of silent castles;
religious houses serve the familiar purpose of allowing reproof
and instruction of the characters, the oppressed look over their
tower walls at the victorious fight that ends a captivity with the
marriage of Emperor's daughter to courageous Knight, at nuptials
celebrated through castle and land.

These are not the plot motifs of Book I; they are merely the
unmistakable mediaeval-romance garb in which those motifs are
clothed, so unerringly that it seems folly to say, as Greenlaw did,
that Spenser shows little "use" of Malory, or as many currently
writing searchers have claimed, that the influence of Arthurian
romances is small. Spenser first wandered as a knight-errant
through their well-wooded small lonely mediaeval counties before he knew how to describe life in his own. But though the
influence of knight-errant romances, an extensive genre, is large,
eminent and decisive, we shall never know just which ones "influenced" Spenser. It does not seem sensible to rule out the most
aesthetically satisfying English form, and the most common
cycle—both abounding in cited traits—just because the likenesses
are not shared peculiarities of plot complication.

Yet it is equally important that we not deny the vast differences.
They are readily apparent from noting what has been omitted
in the quick run just completed over the surface of Book I—from
Morpheus in canto i to the utterly unromance-like introduction

of Despair, from the thoroughly unmediaeval satyrs-canto to the
Reformers'-use made of the material from Revelations. An astonishing accomplishment of Spenser's poem is that he makes one
poetic whole for us without losing the intensely felt classical, or
high Renaissance, or mediaeval character of materials so varied;
all is not watered down into one unidentifiable drink like so many
Renaissance fictions drawn from this many old tuns. Splendid
large images from a very different frame of reference—Gardens
of Proserpina or Adonis, marvels of Aesculapius—their classical
reminiscences undisguised, do not threaten unity of tone. This
was possible in part because Spenser did not create tone, milieu,
conventions, from scratch. He chose a genre hospitable to varied
kinds of opulence and reminds us both through our visual imaginations and the constant use of familiar narrative conventions
that we are reading an especially inventive and poetic exemplar of
a genre we know. It was one so firmly set in the mediaeval world
that it could assimilate Renaissance uses of classical detail, just
as earlier it had assimilated Chaucer's and Boccaccio's and remained "chivalric romance." There is no attempt to mediaevalize
the great Renaissance adornments and motifs. It is not necessary.

When the plot and incidents are quite identifiably dependent
upon Ariosto, as they are in Book III, it looks as if the habits
Spenser learned (as I think) from mediaeval romance materials
play quite as much part as plot itself in determining the quality
of the *Faerie Queen*. They seem even partly responsible for the
tone and characteristic temper we denote as "Spenser's." I think
we have been too ready to find Ariosto's manner typically Renaissance; Spenser's revived idealism may have been just as Renaissance, though not so much as a change. Such effects are always
a matter of the slow piling up of numerous details.

Consider the early part of Book III, where Ariostan borrowing is so consistent. We begin, as does any fresh branch or interlaced fresh unit of a cycle, with the two knights taking congé of
the lady at whose castle they recovered strength, and sending the
defeated and captived object of their just-finished adventure back
to the court and to the sovereign who had given them the don.
(Castle Joyeous is almost surely both Rinaldo's and Lancelot's
Joyous Gard.)[30] As we embark on the journey motivated only

---

[30] The descriptions of wall-hangings or paintings is a romance convention
become a Renaissance one. They were famously used as Morgan's means of

by its knight-errant aims, the meeting with a stranger-knight comes immediately to an issue in a combat, described precisely as the early models would teach one. Battle scenes are different in Ariosto, and much more ludicrously extravagant when it comes to the killings, with arms and legs chopped off and rolling, or six victims spitted on a lance like frogs. Similes are outwardly similar, but in the end, Ariosto's heads cut as if *pruning willows*, the steel cleaving flesh *like a cheese*, like *cabbage*, and the irresponsible numbers slain only serve to show up how much more Spenser's animal similes in battles resemble Malory's and all his predecessors'. Spenser exhibits the interest in exact moves of man and mount which makes Malory's combats different from later ones, and he very often includes the romance-like vigorous, rapid, even pert interchange of threat and challenge and defiance. These sets of speeches usually read like a pastiche of Malory's exchanged insults and pat rejoinders (from those with the Sans-brothers right onward, especially the comic interchanges of i.v; or the convention-filled i.ii; or iii.i.20ff.).

While the plot remains largely Ariostan, suggestions of romance genre-conventions, in the story's management, pile up: the "bad custom," as usual involving the foregoing of one's own proper love to exalt the castle-Lady's beauty, a familiar irrational allegiance laid upon mortals by fées; the six fought by one;[31] the characteristically exact portrayal of a familiar romance tête à tête when an unwilling knight is wooed by his Lady-hostess;[32]

---

betraying Lancelot's disloyal love to Arthur in *Mort Artu* (Sommer, VI, 238ff.), for they remained on the walls where Lancelot had painted them when he was Morgan's prisoner (Sommer, V, 218-22).

[31] Whether or not they are accommodated to Lucian's ladder of voluptuousness; see A. H. Gilbert in *MLN* (1941), 594-97.

[32] The quality of conversation and meticulous detail is what likens Spenser's to earlier "chivalric" presentations. To talk of source would be silly, and we could never decide *which* was influential. Like the innumerable battle descriptions, these amorous conversations, and the pert ones, occur very often in Malory; and I only cite one among many in *Lancelot* (Sommer, V, 132-33). Yet this common scene is called "the exact reverse" of Ariosto's Ruggiero-waiting-for-Alcina's-coming, and conclusions are formed about Spenser's "moral gravity." Reversal does seem to change an attempted seduction, especially when failure is also added. But the details are not similar; subtract these, the irony of the disguised sex and the dénouement and what is left? "Woman comes to man in bed"—an odd thing to send us looking for the poet's source. For the

the absolutely proper attempts of all knights-errant to save Florimell, and the perfectly ordinary declaration of their "hope to win
thereby Most goodly meede, the fairest Dame alive."[33] It is not
possible to mention all the examples where clustered conventions,
often of manner or detail, really contribute the temper, though
plot motifs have real sources outside early romance. Very occasionally the stream flows the other way, as when the Miraculous
Birth motif is classicized in a way no mediaeval writer would
present it (see both Marinell's chance conception, and the twins'
generation by the sun). But usually, for example, we meet des-
mesure in the person of the well-known knight unwilling to allow passage through his domain (Marinell looks and acts like a
knight, whatever his sea-deity heritage); or we move, as romances often ask us to do, into the fully "romantic" Castle of
Busyrane, though we have just accompanied our characters
through the spot-scene ordinariness of the errant knight's nightly
search for lodging—the storm, the pigshed, the yelling, the waiting, the other travelers, the courtyard scenes, the drying out, the
supper.

When we take our eyes from summarized plot action and rather
read and imagine whole scenes at the suggestion of such details
as are slipped in by the author, we observe more and more that
the point to be made about the Merlin material is typical. That
Spenser took his use of Merlin in iii.iii from Ariosto's *Orlando
Furioso* III is completely unquestionable. He not only copies
the nature of the incident and the function of the incident, but
the whole intent and purpose of importing such material was
suggested to him. But nothing could be more different in effect
than these two visits to Merlin, and Spenser's is that of a writer
to whose inner eye Merlin is the well-known character of the

---

most part, I have chosen undeniably dependent Ariostan motifs in Spenser, but
we should also take care to notice when dissimilarity in detail casts doubt on
the relation. Cf. Dodge's "Spenser's Imitations of Ariosto," *PMLA*, vol. 12
(1897), 151-204, abstracted in *Variorum Spenser*, iii, 213.

[33] iii.i.18; it is unreasonable or at least unhistorical to boggle at this as a
motive for Arthur and Guyon, as contradictory to their fidelity and their temperance, respectively. This very ordinary phrase refers conventionally to the
common-day work of the knight-errant: to take up any "adventure" without
hesitation, at its conclusion attach the dependents as "meed" to his large retinue,
send the oppressors off to court as trophies, and eventually reinstate in their
rights those under his guard.

earlier Arthurian materials. Instead of the fanciful necromancy of Ariosto's speaking tomb, the handsome subterranean setting with no hint of a real locale, the crowd of demons trumped up by an enchantress impersonating the prophesied descendants, Spenser has the spirit of the earlier tales because he has some of their details and implies others. Suitably to the traditional Merlin, we find this one very strictly localized in Wales (with comfortable advices to stop by when passing through that part), his other works are noted and new events worked in with the known tales of Vivien. The look and talk of this living Merlin, no mere roused spirit but the important character of the passage, show him the person we know very well elsewhere. Ariosto's important "character" is the enchantress who affects plot, and he does not care about presenting a known Merlin; Spenser does. He enters the story, and it leaves him again, but he is that great Merlin whose story we may go elsewhere and read, a part of England's history presented with quite a different aura and through quite other details than Ariosto's Merlin, though the latter is absolutely certainly responsible for his presence. It is an interesting situation, and it is repeated, I think, time and again. Though I would consider it a waste of time to search for the precise source in romances of Spenser's single details, such as those on Merlin, we should realize that we do have to add to Ariosto a further "source" for such characters, and for Spenser's tone and temper in romance situations.

It would be a welcome change from the remarks about Spenser's lack of humor or his serene gravity if we would seek some of the reasons for his differences from Ariosto, so tirelessly noted and often so unfairly judged, in the tone and temper of the predecessors whom he agrees with and therefore resembles and imitates. It would be more knowledgeable of us to look elsewhere than merely at Spenser's personality traits.[34] They have their

[34] The balance is somewhat adjusted by perceptive comments on Ariosto's quality as well as on other Italians and on theory in Graham Hough's *A Preface to the Faerie Queene* (London, 1962), which is an aid in several areas that had been but little examined publicly at the time when this chapter was completed. We notice some of the same things but usually to support different points. The treatment of allegory seems to me overinfluenced by one kind—the grammarians' allegory, familiar in classical studies, with its Italian descendants; Italy did not have the widespread mediaeval development (vernacular espe-

place, but have been asked to explain what is better explicable otherwise. The scene of Malecasta's night visit, wherein dissimilar details function differently from the Ariosto "reversed" scene, which I have questioned as perhaps quite unrelated (in n. 32 above), is used to show how Spenser "reads his own steadfast idealism into the most openly licentious passages of the *Furioso*" (Dodge's phrase, cited in n. 32). Did he do this? Many a such scene, with details more like Ariosto's, used like his to show the fortitude of an admired character, hence like his in tone, was there in earlier materials to be struck by and followed. I would not question his extreme dependence on Ariosto, usually a veritable "source relationship," and it seems to me to have been proven that the earliest and the most deliberately Ariostan work is found in Book III. But his steadfast idealism, an attribute we would all agree in assigning, was a stronger thing with better reasons for flourishing than the kind of sentimentality which reads idealism into licentious passages.

Of course, Spenser is far from having "a mediaeval tone." In fact, in this very Book III, he does what all men of his time do—elaborates old romance motifs and situations with all the sumptuousness a Renaissance imagination could command, colors images or philosophies of love with fashionable Platonism, certainly mediaeval enough but no part of love-in-the-romances. He does a little of that rather decadent literalizing of metaphors which we find in others; the bleeding heart separated from the body is an image of late romance (the mainstay of the plan and of the illustrations of Olivier de la Marche's *Chevalier delibéré*, in famous manuscripts that one would not dare claim Spenser saw, without more evidence). Many of the differences from mediaeval writing are subsumed under one vast one, "He wrote in the high style." As his tone constantly shifts in accordance with decorum, a matter handled with extreme artistry, and one we are barely well enough educated to apprehend, we see the influence of something much more considered than a vague serene idealism. Spenser's attitude toward his chivalric materials, so different from that of a Cervantes or an Ariosto, antedates his definite plans to write a quest of the virtues, and he had it partly by reason of some-

cially) among writers of talent, familiar to us elsewhere, and Dante stands much more alone than Langland or the *Queste* author.

thing so unavoidable as his date. Even an Ariosto would have been less ironic about knighthood and its tasks if he had written in the context of a seriously possible widespread restoration of ancient harmonies and purities with the returning house, and with the hopes for Arthur's kingdom that were agitating the 1570's and 1580's.

There were more reasons than the British blood of an Arthur to explain why Spenser read of his own country and its possible destiny when he read the great prose monuments of Arthurian romance. Even in these late French forms (late thirteenth century), one still heard a tone that was to vanish, of enthusiastic faith in the religious-political ideals of knights who were conscious of their responsibility to the chevalerie celestienne as well as of their active duties in the realm.[35] And this is the tone which Spenser takes on as to the accent born, for use when fitting and necessary. It may have been an accident of history, but Spenser's date, the existence of Malory with his particular attitude toward Arthur and his knights, and Caxton with his, and the momentarily tenable parallel between England's destiny and the Arthurian dream as great artists had presented it, combined with lesser things to make it impossible that Spenser should write like an English Ariosto, even when he is stealing plots from him. The hands are often the hands of Esau, but the voice is the voice of Jacob.

[35] This elevation of a dying institution of chivalry by those who did not know it was dying, its idealization by the remnant of the aristocratic classes who had lived by its code, is well substantiated both for France and England, but at different dates (see notes and text above, nn. 4-6, citing Frappier's article). Ferguson's careful analysis of the English attitudes of the fifteenth and sixteenth centuries is to be set beside Frappier's analysis of the last attempt to join chivalry and religion in a glorification of both, in Arthurian romances of the time of the cycles. Both suit oddly well with Spenser's hopes, his characteristic presentation of the holy state and the ruler divinely guided to the true reformed religion, preserved by God's grace and a strong fellowship of virtuous Christian knights. Points about the importance of "lignage," the mythopoeic developments from a legend that was religious and mystical but not ecclesiastical, have suggestive relations to the *Faerie Queene*. They are not source relations. They are reasons why the re-published romances would be peculiarly congenial reading, with a tone sometimes retained in their late analogue even when he is imitating Ariosto's incidents. We certainly need embark on no quarrels over "influence of Ariosto *or* of the romances"; these influences had the same spring and were flowing in the same direction.

The transposition of whole actions to a credible other time, the chief characteristic which betrays Spenser's wide reading of earlier romances and is peculiar to him, seems remarkably un-selfconscious. Because it is accomplished with the unemphatic un-Romantic tone of one recording the commonplace minutiae of life as it passes, and because anachronisms do not intrude them-selves, we all but accept the unselfconsciousness as if it were a deception and think of knights-errant in an England which by 1570 certainly had no visual memory of them.[36] Spenser's addi-tions to the romance world he pretends to keep us in are so bril-liant and striking that if we avoid the one error, of forgetting that the chivalric world was not his either, we err in the other di-rection and tend to credit him with the total invention, matrix and poetic additions both. But chiefly his chivalry is neither nature nor invention. He got it by contagion; and his unmediaeval ad-ditions do not destroy it. They are seldom the intertwined Eliza-bethan actualities we are accustomed to find in the dramatists when they portray other periods, but are great extensions—clas-sical or mythical fictions which his mediaeval figures enter as agents. This absence of any high threshold to cross, entering the beneficent otherworld or the imagined marvelous, is of course a romance habit too. It is very different from the juxtaposition of the two, with a pretended acceptance of marvels, which points up their irrationality; this is rare in England, and when Spenser "emulates" it as he found it in Ariosto, he only emerges with

[36] We are not deserting a previous point regarding the double relation of Spenser's details both to romance conventions and to the current practices of Elizabeth's court. Compare, e.g. the descriptions of ceremonies at a tourna-ment to the order, imagery and tone of the ceremonial actually maintained at Accession Day tilts; see F. Yates, "Elizabethan Chivalry," *JWCI*, vol. 20 (1957), 4-25. Cf. her citations of others, including Ivan Schulze who long ago com-mented on this double realism and romance touching St. George Day fêtes and Garter ceremonies (in Schulze, "The Maiden and Her Lamb, Faerie Queene, Bk. I," *MLN*, vol. 46 [1931], 379-81; Schulze, "Reflections of Elizabethan Tournaments in *The Faerie Queene*, 4.4 and 5.3," *ELH*, vol. 5 [1938], 278-84; Schulze, "Notes on Elizabethan Chivalry and *The Faerie Queene, SP*, vol. 30 [1933], 148-59); Miss Yates' connection of Lull's book to Aristotle, to Spen-ser, to Caxton, is very important (p. 22). These researches help us to be conscious of the fact that Spenser's customs and conventions are not nostalgically dredged up from the unknown fascinating past; but no one would maintain that in Elizabethan life, chivalry and its characteristic manifestations were the pre-eminent and funda-mental institution which Spenser's poem portrays.

likenesses to earlier models which cancel it out. One does not believe that Spenser cared an iota about presenting an historical period or that he studied correctness; he caught correctness from those who wrote of what was not yet history.

He had a further and more important reason for finding romances congenial. It seems to me that Spenser recognized, from significances given to ancient romance plots in a few great well-known pieces, that romances were a sort of "historicall fiction" naturally amenable to being read as "continued Allegory, or darke conceit," though primarily "historicall" and delighting.[37] One may take quite "au pied de la lettre" his remarks about most men delighting to read such fictions for variety of matter—this is the reason for and chief effect of romance entrelacement, and the connection is made by Ariosto when he talks of his "web"; it is too famous as a rhetorical word and much too controversial a point for Spenser to use innocently. Equally serious are the claims about these stories being profitable for ensample, which was an early recommendation for urging the printing of romances from manuscripts, and modernizers and introductions did not let it die. Also, the connection with allegory is a proper part of his declared reason why he "chose the historye of king Arthure," who was furthest from "suspition of present time" while capable of bearing other than a single significance. The romances chiefly are what is referred to by the phrase, "many mens former workes" that have made Arthur "famous" and suitable because of "the excellency of his person."

The motif of a quest that was yet not precisely a pilgrimage lent itself, as it had before Spenser, to the combination he shows himself interested to produce from the very beginning—multiple meanings to be read in a delightful history. The physical world and furnishings of mediaeval life, within which the fiction takes place, were felt as actual parts of Britain's past, distanced from his "present" not by fancifulness but by time. Thus the satirical point which was expected in allegory would not be made too topical through "daunger of envy." It was also distant enough

---

[37] Of course his word "historicall" has not yet its sense of fiction-based-on-history, nor does it claim history's objective truth; it is closer to the words "narrative" and "story," and related to the "literal" sense, as in the word for that first way of reading ("historialiter") that must form the basis for an allegorical added interpretation.

for a treatment scarcely possible to fictions of contemporary manners: it could be combined with the fashionable newer elements
from the mythographers, the Platonic temper of the decade and
the richness of Renaissance artifice and decoration.

This choice, one may stress again, was a choice exalting the
importance of the *fiction*. It was open to Spenser to write a didactic
allegorical piece of the kind familiar in Hawes, in the *Court of
Sapience*, in *Piers Plowman*, in Lydgate. He chooses instead a
fully fictional kind with definite narrative characteristics. He was
entirely aware that mediaeval romances, and certainly Arthurian
romances, do not as a kind ask for allegorical reading. There was
never a genre that held more stubbornly to the simple object
of telling what people did and said, or directed such hundreds
of pages simply to watching the flow of events and human partici-
pation in them. Spenser not only keeps to the idea that this is
a great desideratum but has caught the knack of doing it successfully; in his success he resembles the old mediaeval models rather
than their duller sixteenth-century imitators. This is great good
fortune for us, since long Elizabethan poetic narratives are not
outstanding for their ability to command our continuous attention
without efforts of will.

In addition, however, Spenser certainly observed that these
delightful historical fictions, if so written as to ask for a double
reading, did not ask the persistent and detailed attention to rather
tight structures of double meaning which one finds in many didactic allegories; rather—as in the *Perlesvaus*—they proclaim some
large general idea (like the Old and New Law) which thereupon
directs the large lines of meaning and enriches or deepens where
it fits, without being by any means constantly mirrored in the narrative. Barring the special case of the *Queste* (where we follow
the author's open leading), romances are too secular to show the
stricter sort of allegory which presents precise aspects of belief
"in figure"; they are more given to moral allegory—but that
invades most serious stories in the same loose general fashion.
Moreover, romances demonstrate, and Spenser must have observed this, the accepted convention of being *intermittently* allegorically significant—and indeed would be unreadable otherwise.
This is surely true also of the *Faerie Queene*. The word "intermittent" does not indicate the stop and go of some mechanical
inner traffic light but rather the greater or less penetration of de-

tails of an incident with metaphorical meaning, the incident as a whole lending itself to a metaphorical as well as literal reading (not a tight translation or paraphrase into equivalences, which precludes the need for metaphor).

Moral allegory has this intermittent appearance by its nature; we so read meanings in life's events as well. Ever since Chrétien's occasional conversion of warring motivations (for example) into named abstractions, we have been accustomed in romances to have our attention called intermittently to the openly universal character of specific situations; we are asked to note how Desire battles with Humility as the knight speaks to his lady in the castle hall, or how Fortitude conquers Fear in a combat. This type of moral allegory, popularized by the Guillaume de Lorris portion of the *Roman de la rose*, became hackneyed through use; Spenser does not use Chrétien's (or, say, Drayton's or Daniel's) precise form of it but shows complete mastery of its virtues and advantages in his stories using named abstractions. It is sometimes distinguished as "psychological allegory," sometimes it is called "personification allegory"—the last a very unfortunate term for any allegory since the creation of a personality is not the important thing and since allegory of all kinds shows ideas acting and interacting. Even this simple form is not very much used in romances proper, and almost never in the high mediaeval Arthurian pieces. Meanwhile, strict allegory, with Christian doctrine to present, is restricted to two or three outstanding texts, despite the early date of Robert de Boron, whose attempt to present the whole body of material as Christian religious history might, one thinks, have encouraged allegorical reading. In these outstanding texts, Grail romances that do invite an allegorical reading, we are no more left in doubt as to how we must read than in the case of the simple moral allegory universalized through naming. The fact that we are to read symbolically is made entirely open and foolproof; hermits enter to tell us what meanings we should have read in the events lived through.

These two general points are of great importance for Spenser specifically and for the technique of later allegories generally: that the presence of allegorical meanings in romances is clearly signposted, and that the story moves in and out of the allegorical dimension as is suitable. It would be curious if, finding himself caught up in writing an allegorical Arthurian romance, Spenser

entirely neglected the two extant such pieces when they were
perfectly accessible, the *Queste* and *Perlesvaus*. The first was even
to hand in a version in his own language, and Malory's English
has the flavor of archaism that Spenser enjoyed, though his abridgment would send anyone interested in allegory to his original.
Symbolical meanings are not left doubtful in either piece, nor are
events left to be argued as "probably conveying" this or that on
the grounds that some object is traditionally a symbol, or that a
prologue or passage enunciates the commonplace claim of poetry
to have deeper meanings. Only in the *Queste* are most of the
events amenable to metaphorical interpretations—which helps us
to see how easy it is to tell when romances do have such consistent
double meaning and keeps us from imposing an unsuitable such
consistency where it does not belong (as in the *Perlesvaus*). Spenser supplies other devices which, like their hermits, instruct readers
in intended significances, and he has mastered admirably the
technique of moving from literal fiction that is purely narrative
to literal fiction understood allegorically also, thence very occasionally into the realm of pure metaphor (e.g. Malbecco) and
without break, back into literal story. This is also the method of
the *Perlesvaus*.

The Didot *Perceval* Christianizes incidents and images, but
does not present them as allegory; I believe it to have been unknown to sixteenth-century readers. I neglect the *Parzival* here,
despite its early date, because it rather moralizes than allegorizes
(even were language no obstacle; late studies cited in Loomis,
The Grail, New York, 1963, esp. Springer in p. 196n., in the
collection cited n. 58 below). Non-allegorical Arthurian romances,
like the *Lancelot* or the *Mort Artu*, like Chrétien's, like the various *Tristans* or most of Malory, are easily distinguished as more
typical of the genre, and prevent us from overreading. The more
one reads, learning from earlier romances how to detect or decline a figurative meaning, the less one is inclined to read Christological or doctrinal meanings into Spenser, or ingenious and systematic doctrinal allegories, except when he asks us to. His predecessors in the genre taught him how to make the demand clear.

The one other important romance suspected of consistent allegorical significance is Chrétien's *Perceval*. The Elizabethans
had access to this, apparently not much refurbished, in the 1530

printing,[38] and genius was as likely then as now to hold readers where mediocrity could not; but still one is unwilling to assume familiarity without more evidence of popularity. We should at least remark here on the possibility, currently so much debated, of Chrétien's romance demanding an allegorical reading, like these two later Grail romances. If it was allegorical, then we must extend our notions of how authors indicate (and readers detect) double meanings in romances, including Spenser's.

The signposts so carefully provided elsewhere are quite absent here; there are no hermits to explain, no Castle of Enquiry as in *Perlesvaus*, no initial indication of some large, loose parallel (like the struggles between Old and New Law), or of symbolic values *established within this text* (like blackness in the *Queste*). The commonplaces of Chrétien's Prologue are like the dozens of other mediaeval claims for poetry as learning and for fables as wisdom in disguise, which precede Renaissance claims of the same kind and which we meet again in romance prologues (to *Amadis*, to Marot's *Roman de la rose*) accompanying thoroughly generalized moral, not doctrinal, meanings. The references in Chrétien's Prologue to caritas in his patron and in the gospel do not at all warrant our finding profound mystical meaning in the work if the author makes no moves within it to point to some, and we do not find contemporary examples of such interpretation of general claims. Certainly I do not think it would have occurred to a Renaissance reader of the 1530 edition that this prologue directed him to look for allegorical meanings in the events of Perceval's life (in Hilka, pp. 501-502).

One of our concerns is the likelihood (or not) of this romance

---

[38] *Tresplaisante et Recreative Hystoire du* . . . *Chevallier Perceval le galloys* . . . (Paris: J.s. Denis and Galliot du pre), colophon 1530. A considerable portion, 47 of the 220 folios, is printed as Appendix in A. Hilka's edition, *Der Perceval roman* (Halle, 1932). Sample checks with a modern text satisfy one that the tone is not materially altered in the sixteenth-century prosifying, though much of our amused pleasure in concision and neat sprightliness is tempered. We have always to subtract the paraphernalia as well as the information of modern scholarship; the sixteenth-century reader knew nothing of "the continuators" of Chrétien, of dates, linguistic changes, nor had the concept of "literary history" been born. *We* can gratefully use the admirable editions of the continuations coming out under the editorship of Wm. Roach, but it is still necessary to use the 1530 edition itself (though the continuation it prints does not invite allegorical interpretation; the crux is Chrétien's own text).

being given a doctrinally allegorical reading in the sixteenth century. This is a problem whose existence would not have been suspected some years ago, for the theory that the piece has deep allegorical meaning is recent, but very strenuously argued, and claims no mere moral or general allegory for it, but the strictest type of doctrinal signification. There is not place in our discussion here for examination of the evidence for and against the currently argued theory; that examination is being carried on in the liveliest possible manner by scholars in the fields concerned[39] and must be approached by consideration of matters much too far from our concerns—the dates of Chrétien's life and works (and those of his patrons), his identity with various other *Chrétiens*, whether he was a converted Jew, the debatable moral-allegorical signifi-

[39] The theory of Judaeo-Christian allegory (with many Christian-iconographical ramifications by the second author) is propounded in book form in Urban Holmes and Sister Amelia Klenke, *Chrétien, Troyes and the Grail* (Chapel Hill, 1959); articles for and against it are for the most part cited there or in the literature of protest, which is large. To the latter there have been important contributions by Nitze, Levy, Loomis, Adolf and others; they adhere closely to this one specific problem of interpretation, though in sum they enable us to judge the very large steps that would be involved touching the use of Christian allegory in secular literature, were we to accept this theory. Citations to the very numerous articles will be fairly well covered if I refer to the recent long review article by J. Frappier, "Le *Conte du Graal* est-il une allegorie judéo-chrétienne?," in *Rom.Phil.*, vol. 16 (1962), 179-213, and that by R. Levy, "The Motivation of *Perceval* and the Authorship of *Philomena*," *PMLA*, vol. 71 (1956), 853-62. Deeper interpretations of Chrétien (especially in Holmes) have been less irresponsibly based, and less irresponsibly accepted by critics, than interpretation of *Perlesvaus*; proponents of all sides have shown the same misunderstandings of the allegorical mode.

Chrétien's poem is read as an allegory of Perceval's learning to set Charity above Prowess by D. N. Fowler in *Prowess and Charity* (Seattle, 1959), but this seems unconvincing as a reading-back into earlier stories of a theme of the *Queste*, wherein feudal chivalry is indeed so attacked (not in these words in either place; they would make a vice out of the Fourth Gift of the Holy Ghost). The grounds for suspicion are similar to those I mention in my text: the paraphrases on caritas are outlined from St. Paul or St. Augustine, which we must see in the romance itself on the bases of some supplied equation (*this* is what his mother's advice imported, *this* constituted his sin). The father-mother conflict seems imported, by making hermit equal father, uncle equal mother; similarly I do not see that Chrétien makes the sword equal Perceval, the winter equal spiritual winter of the soul (see Fowler, pp. 56-57, 48, 39, 44). Certainly the answer must be "no" to our first question of whether Elizabethans would so read it.

cance of Lancelot in the *Charrete*, the central question of the Grail ritual bearing allegorical reference to Synagoga before her conversion by Ecclesia, or the Fisher King's palace as a reference to Solomon's temple, the Fisher King's relation to Jacob, etc. All this needs to be viewed together with notions of Arthur as symbol of Christianity or a messianic figure, and the validity of textual evidence and iconographical or other support, for these and numerous other senefiances. But besides our wishing to determine whether any other available romance (besides the two famous ones mentioned) was allegorically read in such detail, and whether it was able to teach Elizabethans something about allegory in such a genre, there is the additional point that these modern readings supply models of a "tradition" for similar interpretation of Spenser's and Shakespeare's allegory. If we can work out safeguards and principles by observing overreading of mediaeval romances, we may stand on surer ground to counter that phenomenon in Spenser criticism. It will not quite serve to refer the reader to the controversial literature referred to above, where points useful to students of the sixteenth century are engulfed in the extreme complication of the mediaeval materials involved. The seeming simplicity of our points stands to be elaborated by reference to the matters we need not bring in here. They are knottily specialized, and the objectors to the theory never go outside the period to notice more general effects. But perhaps the heat of the argument shows the realization that this is no tempest in a scholarly teacup but involves the entire matter of reading works symbolically in any period.

The great objection to reading the *Perceval* allegorically is its tone, which in all the "significant" parts and in the whole is quite at variance with such a reading. In other tales, when we mistake the depth of meaning through ignorance or lack of alertness, are given a key and go back to observe what we missed, we find that an allegorical reading does not fly in the face of the literary effects, but suits and explains them. We do not find ourselves so embarrassed if we keep to paraphrase; the difficulty comes with the details the author has invented and the way he has chosen to put them. If a damsel sleeping in a pavilion shadows forth Mary-Ecclesia, the early Church persecuted by Saul, what shall we do allegorically with details we should otherwise think were clearly intended to move us to mirth? The familiar "clown-

ish young man" who has already delighted us by thinking first
that armed knights must be devils (so noisy), perhaps rather
angels (so shining), and who now so wildly mis-applies his
mother's injunctions, reduces the damsel to tears, extracts the
kiss, pockets the ring, gobbles the pastry—these were freely invented details, and if the motive were to convey the trials of
the church, what was the hidden decorum of their invention? If
Gawain represents willed-caritas, what can the author have
thought was his purpose in inventing just such incidents, as he
told of Gawain's rude awakening of the wounded knight to ask
news, his boast that he will leave when *he* pleases, his motivations when dared to show off by doing this or that? Allegory is
by definition enigmatic, but it is not a tissue of deceptive—or at
best meaningless—detail.

One has to be warned in all allegorical fictions not to expect
"naturalistic" motivations, psychological verisimilitude and credibility; rather, we must look for conventions, or public meanings,
which point more surely to the reasons why events or details take
a certain form (why knights faint, why they bathe in wells, why
they ride horses well or ill). It is characteristic of such a conventional significance, especially if it was once symbolical, that
there may be a wide gap between what is meant by it and what
we would naturally expect it to mean—and the gap shows especially in tone; the seeming ridiculous may have serious connotations, the trivial may be excruciatingly important. I think this
fact about conventional or "given" detail has confused the interpreters of allegories; it is still an untransgressible rule that
invented details must have been invented for *some* motive. Events
in the story are not to be thrown out; and if their whole temper
and feeling and obvious literary merit quarrels with the "meaning," an explanation must be found for them or we may not have
that "meaning," since it is denied by the form.

This denial is characteristically, indeed almost universally, the
case with the allegorical "meanings" put forth as those intended
by Chrétien (despite the utter unsuitability of his details as he
put them to convey such meanings, and the absence of a public
language of images that might explain the indecorum. Hence, we
must declare it quite impossible that the readers of the sixteenth
century could have read this romance and taken in the allegory
proposed by the modern interpreters. On that score, then, we

have nothing to learn from this supposed mediaeval allegory by following in the footsteps of Renaissance forerunners. There is a more practical point. These and some later examples from romances show up a particularly insidious way in which errors creep into the interpretation of allegorical texts, Spenser's notably among them: the process is reversed, and we begin with "meaning" rather than a work of literature. We insensibly proceed with questions like "what piece of my meaning can this detail signify?" instead of setting off from the detail itself. For we must assume that an author had a reason for his deliberate choices of invention. It is the old error of supposing allegory to be a puzzle-language, when it is a way of conveying meanings. We do not start *with* them; we are thus shown them. If the inescapable conviction beats in upon us that we are being shown all the secret ways charity works in human life, or that the strange adventurous chronicle of the miraculous successes of a persecuted early church is being narrated and is responsible for the odd shape certain events take—*then*, and only then, the meaning having come through to us by means of the details which are its instrument, we may look for just which particulars have been able to convey just which subtleties to us. This reversal, it seems to me, is the greatest single cause of error and overreading in the criticism of sixteenth-century poetry. It is as unnoted in the wave of Christological and doctrinal and Christian-moral interpretations now current as it was in the wave of historical-allegory interpretations to which the abuse is also native.

Because it is an unbreakable rule that we may not assume the presence of a symbolical meaning which makes no use of the literary merits given by the author to his piece, and because tone is so important among these merits, one other confusion should be cleared up. It may seem that in most Christian allegory, unsuitability of tone is a commonplace—how defend the tone of the Song of Songs as befitting pre-eminently a heavenly Love and Lover? And no fitness appears to dissolve the comicalness, especially if seen in picture, of the twelve oxen around Solomon's laver, "signifying" the twelve Apostles.

These similitudes have a totally other basis. If the claimed inner meanings do appear in Chrétien, he invented their outer dress, and he is the author of the connection. One of the great weaknessess is that there is no reason for the meanings to be

brought up, no reason in the tale to portray the church's defenders, no place for a ritual including synagogue and church.
The basis of a typological similitude, on the other hand, is an
inherent real resemblance which God himself put into two historical happenings; the Last Supper fulfills the Manna. That
Isaac carrying his wood is a child makes no difference; a comic or
tragic tone in a tale would make no difference. And the basis of
the Spouse-image in *Canticles* is, as Origen explains, a completely
different order of reality and of love than the order whose tone
we find unfitting; the tone too is translated. Its fervor and its
languor are not only fitting but necessary. No such other order
of the real is shadowed by Chrétien; and only an arithmetic of
unsuitable equivalents is suggested in the interpretation.

Unlike Chrétien's poem, the *Perlesvaus* (a work accessible in
pleasant and dignified form)[40] itself proclaims its allegorical
character, though making this too pervasive may be a modern
error. The work exemplifies especially clearly some points touching allegory in romance which a sixteenth-century reader would
pick up merely from practice in reading. Time and again we are
invited to read a set of incidents or characters as portraying loyalty to the Old Law or the New, or even as related to the historical triumph of the New Law in the Christianizing of peoples,
while the addition of a third group, the Sarrazins with their false

---

[40] The *Perlesvaus* could be read by sixteenth-century men interested in
Arthurian stories in a 1516 or a 1523 edition, the latter almost a word-for-
word reprint (see A. B. Swanson, *A Study of the 1516 and 1523 Editions of
the Perlesvaus*, Chicago, 1934); Nos. 81, 114 in Woledge. I have used both;
they are well-got-up volumes, sufficiently modernized for easy comprehension in
the late sixteenth century, with useful tables, rubrics, etc. The inclusion of the
Estoire (the first, though not the earliest, among the five Vulgate Cycle parts,
ed. Sommer, vol. 1) and an extremely abridged portion of the *Queste* (the
fourth Vulgate Cycle part) made the book more desirable. Sep. t.p. ("Le
second volume du sainct greal," after the *Estoire*), in *L'Hystoire du sainct
greaal* (Paris, du Pré et Lenoir). The authoritative edition is by W. A. Nitze,
Le Haut Livre du Graal, Perlesvaus (2 vols.; Chicago, 1932–37); I refer to and
sometimes use for quotation the translation readers are more likely to own, by
Sebastian Evans, *High History of the Holy Grail* (Everyman edition; references
are to page numbers). I have done sample comparisons of these several texts,
rubrics, etc., and consider it safe to read our texts to follow the sixteenth-century
reader. See Nitze's introduction for the two versions (but a strict outline of plot
is not our concern).

law, rounds out a total view of human society ("Of these three manner of folk is the world stablished, est establiz li mondes"; Nitze, 2,172; Evans, p. 80).[41] This is doctrinal or strict allegory, where the fable or personages teach something about the true faith, not merely about moral conduct, but with subject matter and actions that belong completely to Arthurian romance.

It may also be typical that the romance does not ask for, and really refuses to bear, a reading which translates each incident and character into its equivalent significance, in line with this announced complex of meanings. Yet modern interpretation leans more and more in this direction, and we have finally a full schematic outline turning the whole romance into a Christ-allegory and determining the significance of each scene as portraying Nativity, Crucifixion, and so on.[42] We have again to consider

[41] Of course, the Old versus the New Law is the basic contrast which made Christian apologetics out of the underlying unities that are the concern of typology. It is the theme par excellence of allegory strictly defined and had always been, including as it does the redemption by love. Like other works, the *Faerie Queene* shows the tendency to attach Old Law-New Law contrasts to the Elizabethan religious situation, i.e. to see the true New Law of Protestant reform victorious over a blind Old Law of Catholicism. One can hardly imagine that Elizabethans could resist a situation like *Perlesvaus* (line 5,900) where a Queen is persuaded by Perlesvaus' successful fight with the Dragon's or Devil's Knight to accept "your new Law" and is baptized with the name ELYZA; she then leads a good life, bringing her people likewise to the true Law, and dies a virgin (checked in 1516 edition, Evans, p. 213).

We have no way to determine whether the general idea beneath this story, of the virgin queen Elyza upholding the true faith, did lodge in the mind of the later creator of Una. I prefer not to claim *Perlesvaus* as a "source" for Spenser, though this has been claimed (as usual for shared plot detail; see Edgar Hall, "Spenser and Two *OF* Grail Romances," *PMLA*, vol. 28 [1913], 539-54, emphasized in *Variorum Spenser*, VI, Appendix III. Also *Variorum Spenser*, I, Appendix IV, where various romances are discussed as sources). I do not find convincing (or, if so, important) most arguments for use of romance materials as plot-motif sources. For Spenser, Greenlaw's old definition of the relation as a use of romance situations for spiritual significances, stands up best. Spenser may have recalled some details from the *Perlesvaus* for the beard-story in Book VI; but like the "Perceval-elements in Spenser's Tristram," thought to relate Spenser to the 1530 Chrétien (*Variorum Spenser*, VI, 370), these stories usually occur in too many places for us to be able to isolate a source. Listed synopses of plots so often include points an author could not help inventing (hero meets obstacle; hero though wounded downs opponent).

[42] J. N. Carman, in "The Symbolism of the *Perlesvaus*," *PMLA*, vol. 61 (1946), 42-83, interprets it as "a sort of symbolical New Testament" or "a tissue of

whether this is modern overreading or was characteristic of mediaeval allegorizing of romance materials, and further, whether
the sixteenth-century readers knew it. I have never seen any attempt to spell out what is acceptable procedure, and what is
not, for coming at what we call quite blithely "the mediaeval allegory" in a romance. Most of the elements I shall criticize as
supplied by the exegetes, not the piece, are regularly denominated
as the hallmarks of "mediaeval" allegory. It must be stated that
the romance of itself encourages us rather to that general sense
of a double meaning, that absence of equations which carry
through, that flickering intermittent clarity of the double senses,
which is so much more consonant with the meaning, origin and
development of the mode of allegory.

It is not that we are not invited—or indeed required—to give
the *Perlesvaus* the further dimension of meaning conveyed by
reading allegorically, in those portions where this is asked of us.
But what seems modern in the response to this request, rather
than either a mediaeval or Renaissance way of reading, is first
the extreme detail and rigidity of interpretation; earlier "hermits" and earlier writings find the second meanings (such as Old
and New Law contrasts in *Perlesvaus*) in a far more general and
loosely reined manner. There is also a different understanding
of the relation implied in allegorical reading—later incidents
which recall, rather than *copy*, events which have happened. This
remembering or putting in mind of, re-enacting the meaning of,
earlier historical events (the phraseology is the *Perlesvaus'*
own) is very different in imaginative effect from the identical re-
telling offered as the meaning by modern exegetes. Perlesvaus
"is Christ" in a far more meaningful and better-motivated way
than in the arbitrary parallels of a modern literary game, and
there is a meaning to be seen and conveyed, not a stunt to be
detected.

As important as any point is the fact that such a romance—deliberately allegorical—seems to train one to expect a narrative
that is now symbolical, now flatly relating incident; we find that

---

exempla recalling the New Testament. He cites previous allegorical readings,
less thoroughgoing; his own are cited as if accepted by later writers on the
romance. One should note that the literary method of *Perlesvaus* has still less
to do with exempla, which do not work symbolically, and are only figures in a
different sense from "Perlesvaus as a figura of Christ."

we unconsciously desist from anticipating hidden meanings in every exit and entrance of a chapter, perceiving that it is quite impossible to read the story unless we accept the fact that though a horse may betoken undisciplined impulses in one context, a knight parted from his horse in the next episode may be just a knight parted from his horse. We find that such an announced allegory as the *Perlesvaus*, far from being consistently interpretable on two levels—as if it were written in a language of signs—does not lend itself to the notion of "levels," will not allow us to read the story as if that were shaped and mastered by the allegory, even refuses to be read as if declared parallels could be safely applied in the later appearances of the same characters. In a word, the mode brings its own safeguards with it and points out our errors if we carry "interpretation" too far. This is very useful knowledge, for it was probably learned by others before us, and it becomes yet more practical when we observe that certain modern ways of detecting symbolical meanings, which turn out to be questionable—seen more clearly when we observe how they have been applied to the romance—are also typical ways of approaching Spenser's allegory, with results that have brought discredit upon it. They have also brought an inimical attitude toward the whole matter of symbolism in earlier literature.

A first proof we have that the fiction is in command, and that it is advisable to have the author's own warrant for it before we read other parts of the story as allegory, lies in the fact that identifications outright declared in one place cause absurdities when applied in some others. "Li Noirs Hermites est Lucifers," says an exegete we may trust, the priest at the Castle of Enquiry (Nitze, 2,182; Evans, p. 80). Explaining the 150 sealed heads carried in the damsel's car (Evans, p. 25), those sealed respectively in gold, silver and lead, which "signify" the three Laws, with the King's and Queen's heads referring to Adam and to Eve, he reminds the quester of how Christ became man that he might deliver all good souls from hell (i.e. at the Harrowing of Hell). "And to this doth Joseph [the pretended transmitter of these things from the Holy Ghost] make us allusion by the castle of the Black Hermit [*fet remenbrance du Chastel*], which signifieth hell." Now, the capture of the Black Hermit's castle by Perlesvaus takes place at N. 9960 (Evans, p. 372). If we follow the modern interpreters and *equate* this incident with the Harrowing

of Hell, turning it into a re-telling thereof, we find ourselves en-
cumbered with the most embarrassing meanings—that Christ wins
the allegiance of all hell's devils, that they promise to turn hell
into a hospice for errant knights, and will say Mass there daily,
and the like.

The author had said, through the explaining priest: "ce nos
trete en senefiance li bons hermites por la Novele Loi, en la
quele li plusor ne sont pas bien connoissant, si en volt fere remenbrance par essanples" (Nitze, 2,184). Surely the *allegorical* relation
between the two captured "castles" is *not* that we see presented
in the story "a symbolical Harrowing of Hell," "a portrayal" of
it, with "every element assigned" its symbolic equivalent (I quote
a modern interpreter). Rather, as is usual in allegory, the chief
meaning of the Harrowing of Hell (the delivery of the innocent)
is adumbrated in another event, which thus speaks of it, reminds
men once more of its message of hope or salvation or terror—but
does not portray or represent it. The sense in which the Black
Hermit's castle "senefie enfer" displays a truly allegorical relation
between them, learned from Biblical exegesis: the author has
attempted to establish the almost typological relationship by which
one person or event alludes to another. If we follow modern exegetes and turn this into a relation wherein "the castle *equals*
hell," and make all details of the castle-story fit a Harrowing of
Hell, instead of letting this recall for us that once a good knight
delivered the innocent from a yet more terrible captivity—an
archetypal deliverance mirrored in some sort by all deliverances
since—it is no wonder that we get into difficulties that show our
author did not thus see the relation.

He could not fully succeed, of course, in his attempt to make
a "type" of Christ out of Perlesvaus. Only God, the author of
history, could make a later Person, or events, "fulfill" those in
which earlier Jewish history figured them forth, and of course
there is no attempt in Biblical exegesis to find post-Christ "types."
I am sure that mediaeval writers and exegetes understood this
perfectly. Though Orpheus, or Perceval, are in some sort types
of Christ, they are not in the same relation to Him as Moses or
Abel or Joseph. But never, in this strictly allegorical relation, are
we expected to equate the persons and pair their stories; there is
no attempt to find parallels in Christ's life for the attacks of the
women upon Orpheus, nor do we look for something to parallel

the bush Isaac's ram was caught in, the anguished prayer of Abraham-the-father, the ass they left behind, the fact that the sacrifice was burned. Equation is simply not the character of the allegorical relation.

It is clear that Spenser knew this too. In the same way, Red Crosse "figures" Christ, but is never equated with Him. That Red Crosse or Perceval (whose case is much the same) shadows Christ more than Everyman does or can, is clear, but all are images of Christ in a similar way; perhaps they all learned it from ordinary Christian doctrine, in which Nativity and Passion happen again constantly. Christ is born in each heart, men who redeem other men shadow Christ and even "are" (have put on) Christ. At all events, this is the way in which Arthur "is" heavenly grace, Mercilla "is" Elizabeth's Mercy ("Mercilla is Elizabeth" is careless talk; and Mercy pure and perfected is a heavenly not a queenly trait), Duessa "is" Falsehood and yet does not equal Satan who *is* Falsehood. Though she similarly "is" the corrupt Roman church and the Queen of Scots, she must never be so equated with any of these that their story commands the shape of the *Faerie Queene* character's story. It does not "mean" any incident in the histories of any of these characters that Duessa is turned out into the wilderness; the two renewals of Red Crosse's strength during the dragon fight do not equal the two sacraments but refer to the *meaning* sacraments have in the lifelong struggle of a Christian against evil.

Since the characters do not equate, their stories need not echo each other, but merely meet where meanings touch. There are very many uses in Spenser of the conventional freedom of an allegorical writer to tell the story of *his* character without carrying onward all the allusive double significances his character reflected where double meaning was suitable. Many nonexistent problems have been raised on the assumption that Una equals Truth and so on—about Una mistaking Archimago for Red Crosse, about Britomart's clearly humorous lovesickness or unlovely jealousy, about minor examples of persons doing things out of square with their allegorical significance. Somewhere Spenser learned the nature of this relation of signifying, and he does not make the error. Bad allegorists do, in all eras.

It is sensible to remind ourselves that there is no point in having a romance re-tell the Gospel of Nicodemus. Allegory is not a fancy way to tell history, even divine history, over and over again. It is the meanings that recur. The events of the life of Christ are not the rationale of the structure of *Perlesvaus* (though modern exegesis has begged this question, and sometimes treats similarly the structure of the *Faerie Queene* or a Shake-spearean play). At one point, Meliot of Logres as a child of seven, blithely and safely riding the lion, is connected symbolically with "li Sauverres du monde" who was born under the Old Law, apparently for the suggestion of innocence in harmonious control over the very symbol of strength and power, and because Christ-Leo-Majesty is an ancient association of notions to figure the victorious New Law. But this is no warrant for our trying to make later appearances of Meliot make sense as appearances of Christ; and when to Meliot's great discontent the lion is killed by Clamados, it certainly no longer refers to the world and all its people and creatures (Evans, p. 82) governable by the humble Saviour. By the same token, we cannot approach an allegory knowing what it must mean because the same character in another source (Christ in the gospels, for instance) does thus or so. We are not in the least constrained to suppose (as the modern inter-preter says, by a logic sometimes used to justify events in the *Faerie Queene* also) that the author felt obliged to invent the character Meliot so as to get in Christ-as-child, since he had two adult figures for Christ in Perceval and the Fisher King.

Still less are we being directed by the author, since there is a child-Christ, to seek for an Adoration-of-the-Magi scene retold, with hermit equated to Magi because he shows his joie as he looks on the child's subjection of the lion, and with these other startling resultant equations: the damsels standing by equated with the midwives, the valets with the shepherds, the lion with the ox and ass. It seems obvious that these meanings would never have been thought of but for the pressure, from a separate presentation of the events, of what ought to be included. This is a familiar pres-sure warping Spenser interpretations, where once Aristotle, and now Christian myth, weigh heavily.[43] If we merely follow the

[43] It reveals a quite topsy-turvy conception of how allegory is read or can possibly have been written when we read of *Perlesvaus* (Carman, *op.cit.*, p. 57) that "the episode symbolic of the Crowning with Thorns *should be followed by one equivalent to the Flagellation*." Why? The author's object is not to re-tell Luke. The phrasing shows acceptance without demur of allegory as a stunt,

Perlesvaus author without thus importing from other narratives, we observe that the text does not encourage us to pursue the parallel possible in the joie with which hermit (and wise men?) look on the child—for we notice that the author has not put the *meaning* of a Nativity into his romance at all. Allegory cares about the meanings its images introduce. If there is no place in a work for the *significance* of the Incarnation, we may be sure it is not reflected in the imagery.

The means provided us for making sure of this are quite simple. Dumb beasts who adore without capacity to understand why (the ox and ass) are not *like* majestic power being guided and subjected by weak innocence; being ridden, smit with a whip and got into the den conveys not the worshipful awe of sentient but an irrational nature. However much being a beast likens one to other beasts, nothing can liken this lion to the ox and ass *symbolically*. Their presence at the mystery of God taking flesh is essential to their symbolic meaning; the romance does not present that mystery. It has place for some emphasis on the meaning of Epiphany—the revelation to the outside world of Christ's divine nature and power—but it is best admitted as a hovering suggestion, as though one pointed at an idea to be held in the mind if the romance should at any time refer to it through its action. This loose juxtaposition, as the way for basic Christian doctrines to be signified allegorically, is Spenser's way too. It is far more moving, also, than providing sets of picayune equivalents. Great numbers of guesses at meanings could be ruled out by applying this law that *significance* must be comparable, and meanings needed by the poem, or helpful to it just there.

This requirement does happen to be filled by another meticulous pairing of romance-events in the *Perlesvaus* with events in Christ's life; the taking of the Grail Castle is interpreted as "a symbolical Crucifixion," and the author is said to equate the two. Though the phrase would have seemed a blasphemy to a truly

---

a clever way of putting meaning, already known, into an interesting disguise which we detect and see through. The phrasing and the conception are common in modern Spenser interpretation, being there based on the same misconception of what allegory is. The scene discussed just above in my text, of Meliot as child, is at Nitze, 1,570ff. and Evans, p. 58ff., the interpretation Nitze, 2,230 and Evans, p. 82; later incidents which will not allow of continuing assigned significances for child or lion occur at Nitze, 3,330ff. and Evans, pp. 113-15.

allegorical writer, we do indeed find the romance concerned here
with "a signal victory over evil," with the conditions of the
enemy's powerlessness, the need of the "vertu de Deu" or more
than nature's own strength. But aside from the unlikelihood of
an author writing in the 1200's presenting the Crucifixion symbolically without overt notice of it by one of the interpreting
clerics put in for such purposes, one must disclaim all faith in
an interpretation which identifies each of the nine bridges into
the castle with a particular incident of Christ's journey from Pilate
to His death. The idea of allegory behind this is common—that
it portrays a series of known events or facts in a form which is
rendered interestingly obscure by using a language in which
one thing stands for another. It is particularly strong in handbooks
on Spenser, as in ordinary readers' or classroom readers' understanding of him, and is usually assisted by outlining "what he
meant" on these different "levels"—as here in *Perlesvaus* each
incident on the story level is made to parallel its twin up above
on the Christian allegory level.

We may omit mention of the fact that this attempt to make a
story re-tell a story elsewhere told would be an endeavor without
point, and note first that it is not the kind of reading we or the
Elizabethans could learn from our mediaeval text. For every
illegality of method is necessary to fasten such a series of equated
events upon our writer: choosing matters that must be the subjects included, from a source outside the romance, instead of reading the romance to find out the subjects; assigning symbolical
meaning to every object and occurrence, which results in a complexity of parallels very difficult to take in; pairing Objects with
their Meanings according to some property or accident instead of
according to their use in an action; tightly applying a significance
(such as the declaration that when accompanied by mule and
pennon Perlesvaus will be facing his enemies armed with "la
vertu de Deu") so that the reader finds himself forced to decide
which event of Christ's Passion he is reading about, at which
bridge, by deciding which of His trials necessitated Christ's
calling upon his divine nature and which did not (from our
vantage point!). A revealing case of basing symbolical significance
upon a purely adventitious similarity is the explanation that the
mule which Perlesvaus mounts when divine strength is needed,
simply exemplifies the substitution of "a more common hybrid"

for the hybrid steed the Church may ride upon, formed from the four evangelist-beasts.[44] It would be hard to think of anything more impertinent to the symbolism of the four evangelist-beasts, writing their gospels as we are accustomed to see them, than the notion that they are hybrids.

So far, then, when we look at the allegorical reading given to romances (whether with warrant from the author as in *Perlesvaus*, or without it as in Chrétien's *Perceval*), we find the tight relations and complex networks of equivalents to be characteristics of modern interpretation but *not* of mediaeval presentation; this is not, therefore, what we expect a sixteenth-century reader to have learned about the mode from its earlier practitioners. Historically, the vast development of allegory was concerned to let story point to doctrine, not to make story re-tell Christ's history. It is doubtful if the conquest of the King of Castle Mortal figures forth the narrative of the Crucifixion, except as all crucial battles with evil seem to a Christian reader or author to reflect some of its meanings. At any rate, what we observe in the text itself is not a re-telling through a code of equivalents but instead, a loose juxtaposition that makes us connect the story we read with significances more universal because we see that it shadows a greater story in general drift of meaning, and its hero is the image of the divine hero of a different action, to a degree not usually possible to earthly men. Similarly, we observe suggestions of familiar doctrines about divine help through grace, and observe suggested ambiguities in the name "Castle Mortal" which make the self-destruction of the evil king very interesting—and numerous such provocative openings of-

---

[44] Carman cites one miniature in Mâle "from a thirteenth-century Book of Hours" (p. 45); editions and paginations differ, but he describes the figure (#101) reproduced from the *Hortus deliciarum*, not the *Horae*. The episode being discussed is in Nitze, 6,060 to 6,260 and Evans pp. 220-29. We cannot hold that iconographical detail sheds any light on what the *Perlesvaus* means, unless accessibility or at least wide diffusion is supported, but even more crucial is the necessity to show that the same symbol is being used. The hero mounting a mule is simply not the same image as crowned Ecclesia upon a beast with the head of the four evangelists' symbols; moreover, the meaning of this latter image is not useful in the context. All three difficulties make the uses of iconography in part II of the book on Chrétien's allegory very suspect (cited above n. 39). A burning need in English studies generally is some consideration of the conditions required for iconographical detail to be used as evidence.

fered to the imagination. Usually the imagination is provoked simply to powerful realization once again of large and familiar ideas.

As we learn to suspect the complex networks of parallels and regard them as danger signs, so do we suspect sources outside the pieces as models for what they may mean—whether such sources are other narratives, as of Christ's life, or what "the exegetes say" or "the iconography shows us."[45] Even if we can come close to proof that the author knew *that* exegete, or could see *that* picture or one like it, we have yet to make the demand that there should be place in the work for the *meaning* of the image said to be symbolic. It is true that we can fall only too easily into our old and opposite error of being so inhospitable to meanings that we do not see the symbols. One does not know which is worse, the re-shaping without warrant or Bruce's bland tossing away of the same episode as a mere capture of a castle "with no mystical elements," making the "magical *motif* hardly worth inventing."[46]

It is very reassuring that a truly allegorical piece like the *Perlesvaus*, which does use romance situations to allude to the great deeds or images from Christ's life and thereby to Christian doctrines, is all the more convincing and moving in its allegorical "reference" when we do not fasten too precise or doctrinaire a reading upon the situations. For these caveats regard the similar doctrinaire procedures which have damaged Spenser so appreciably, being defended as his intended meaning since he was writing "mediaeval" allegory. The ways of overreading a romance which

[45] This use of a narrated history as the "real story" whose events we are to search for in the romance's story, leads to another illegal procedure not uncommon, exemplified in Carman, p. 46: if the postulated point-by-point retelling presents us with detail that will not fit, if one of the bridges, say, in the story supposed to re-tell the events before Calvary, presents us with a red lion and a white one that do not seem to equal anything—we cannot get out of the double difficulty by declaring that the white lion represents the good thief who argues with the bad thief (tears to pieces the red lion). The white lion is not simply white—i.e. good; he assists Perlesvaus with unobtrusive but miraculously understood directions and warnings. No writer, even supposing he were deliberately trying to accommodate "givens," in the form of uncomprehended Celtic magic details, to a Christian meaning, would expect us to understand good thief by describing that as his relation to Christ. Resemblances must extend to meaning when symbolizing is in question (not necessarily logical meanings, if conventional—as with stars and stripes).

[46] *Evolution of Arthurian Romance*, II, 19.

we have been exemplifying are not asked for by the good allegories of the great period (though some poor writing does seem
to demand this schematic translation into notions and re-told
stories), and Spenser has produced a work which, showing the
virtues of the tradition at its best, requires a reading in the best
tradition. I would remark again that these understandings were
short-lived and special; the influence upon secular literature of
the long and careful religious allegorical tradition could not
continue very long and was congenial only in certain kinds and
to certain authors. Already, a Spenser moves away from the
direct references to Old and New Law of a *Perlesvaus*; but he
seems to me to have learned from these or similar materials upon
which his century was still nourished the ability these writers had
to invest the interesting literal tale with a powerful further significance, going beyond time by its attachment to truths of religion. The *Perlesvaus* does this by overt reference to Christ's
victory over our enemy, to events of the narrative of divine
redemption—not re-told, but alluded to in that shadow of them
which the literal tale provides. But the connection is not pulled
taut. A meaningfulness which takes away their triviality hovers
over the romance fights and sieges, and whenever it is possible,
we are reminded to see in these triumphs of fortitude or of
willing sacrifice the real and pure triumph of the "New Law"
of love as it once historically triumphed. Spenser avoids these
overt parallels with Biblical events, but he, too, does what is
so truly allegorical in the *Perlesvaus*: he conveys the doctrine
which the Biblical event taught. The combats of Book I and
even of Book II are thus appreciably like the combats Perlesvaus
enters into. But the doctrines of the nature of Justice, of philia,
or of chaste fidelity, are conveyed by modes influenced by
much else than religious allegory, and there remains chiefly the
persistent attempt to see Christian chivalry as a way of achieving
man's metaphysical destiny. Here, too, we are well served by
what we have learned about keeping the basic allegorical parallel
firmly in mind and then riding with a loose rein.

I think it appears from Spenser's practice that he could still
read mediaeval allegorical romances allegorically without stumbling into these pitfalls, as an interpreter; hence, he does not
make similar pitfalls for us by writing an allegorical romance
with such abuses of allegory written into it. One is led likewise

to the conviction that he and his contemporaries had not yet fallen into a worse but common error—the misjudgment of the whole purpose of the mode. This is the most serious of all modern troubles with allegorical reading. It may be that the reason lies deeper than any lack of skill or habit, perhaps may be found in our inability to read the symbols to learn "what to believe." This is the end which defined allegory proper, and it clung to serious uses of it like those discussed here. It is not the same as "reading the symbols to learn what propositions are true." But the raison d'être of symbolical images, the motive for borrowing them, or inventing them, or catching them up and using them, is that they can convey that which they symbolize—usually more safely and always more fully than discursive language. Hence, if we know these meanings already and come furnished with our list and ready to tick off which detail conveys which meaning, then either the piece is not symbolical at all but merely written in a code, or we are reading wrongly. In a mode whose end is the uncovering or revealing of meaning through similitude, it makes utter folly of the whole procedure if the reader brings the discoveries, ready to be appliquéd where the outline of the puzzle-piece shows upon the pattern. No great known story or myth is "signified" or imaged in a later allegory merely to let us recognize it, and certify that its parts are there.[47] In topical satire or "historical allegory" part of the amusement

[47] It is necessary every so often to append a note admitting that everything evil is done at one time or another in stupid and bad allegories. These are not as numerous as reputed, but I would put forward many of the imposed interpretations of the *Ovide moralisé* or Bersuire as in the category. I believe sixteenth-century readers were not as misled as we are by deceptively mechanical parallels seen in dictionaries, pious treatises, or allegories like Guillaume's, or Caxton's version of the *Somme le roi* (to use examples which can be referred to in this book). It was clearer, while there was still some unselfconscious use of religious allegory, that figures in their places worked in a profounder way than the lists indicated (often meant for study). Poorer allegories, unknown to the Renaissance, have been dug up by modern scholarship. As interpreters, we may have contributed much of the mechanical aridity; it would be difficult to find mediaeval writers so glib as to levels, equations, the four senses, dismissing of the literal meaning, etc. as we. There would be fewer uses of the easy phrase "a purely medieval allegory" (as used of the Castle of Alma) if it were used only with full knowledge of the warnings and safeguards directed to *readers* of allegory, so familiar in mediaeval writing on the subject and quoted from many sources—for instance in H. de Lubac's *Exegèse mediévale*.

is using the key to read the puzzle, but none of Spenser's great classical images open with such keys, and to avoid this abuse may have been one of his reasons for withdrawing from Christological allegories.

Paradoxically perhaps, this freedom from imported schemes or series directs authors to emphasis on the fiction, and especially relieves them of the necessity of making every detail of it conceptually significant. A common misconception is related to this. We are accustomed to phrases that assume a sort of competition between the demands of the story and of the allegory, and that one or the other is primary. This makes no sense except under a deteriorated definition of allegory. Definitions differ very much, but not in the basic assumption that the story is one with its meaning. The romance writers who claim to convey allegorical significances obviously have no notion of this competition. It is as though we thought van Gogh must have had much ado deciding whether to make a sunflower look like a sunflower, or, to paint it yellow.

However, an author has the right to choose the subject his story concerns. I believe we have developed a presupposition that a story is by nature a transcription of actuality as the ordinary man experiences it, and that this is a really quite recent obstacle. Do we think that, were it not for "his allegory's demands," Spenser, describing the old porter Ignaro, would portray for us an old man who had no more trouble walking straight ahead than old men usually do? But Spenser's subject is not Old Men. We may assume this to be a "natural" subject for a story, but to Spenser the nature of Ignorance was quite as proper a subject; and that it cannot look forward though its feet are advancing is an undistorted, accurate detail. It is part of the story, without any supposition that the author's allegory forced him into oddities. Spenser chooses to write of Fury and of seizing occasions for wrath; there is no relinquished tale he would like to have told in which old ladies' hair grew naturally and their sons could be wounded in the usual way (by putting swords through them) instead of, like Furor, being strengthened by such treatment.

Because the meaning is the story, the author may not be denied details which the meaning can shine out of, but equally, he must not be coerced into telling monstrosities wherein each detail must be at the mercy of some meaning. We do not thus take in the

significance of experience, in life or in fiction. Much is said of
Florimell, or of Furor, which is only there to make us take
notice, or to so transport us into the situation that we are agitated,
afraid, charmed; otherwise, not taking in the story, we do not see
the meaning.[48] Furor's iron teeth do not mean anything; they are
there to grind one into bits. Whenever a character leaves or enters
the scene, we are not to examine whether the hero lost his Shame-
fastness, or met Accidia. Neither Spenser nor, for example, the
author of *Perlesvaus* temporarily departs from a primary purpose
of instruction in order to clutch at another purpose—to delight—
thereby moving from level to level in a multiple meaning divided
into several separable stories or floors. The meaning is one, and
the story is saying it, but an author must be permitted to tell
stories, and not draw up schemes. The notion of levels, unfortunately now a critical cliché, has served us very ill, for the connection is always open between the literal and the shadowed deeper
meaning. The apprehension of both is simultaneous, and the
movement should be vertically free—if we must make do with
a spatial image. The relation is that of a metaphor, continued
into a whole story; it is not the relation of a thing above with
another below it. "Every likeness hobbles," as Milton and dozens
of other logicians say; the aspects of a similitude that are impertinent to the likeness seen are parts of the story-telling that
must be allowed in if it is to get told.

An important reason for our rejection of the crowds of hobbled
equivalents which oversubtle exegesis fixes upon Spenser, as
upon other allegorical romance-writers, is that poets with such
plans are impossible to conceive. Stories are imagined events taking place in time, and the imagination does not work in these
ingenious dichotomies and well-contrived doublets, which we are
to decode into an Idea. It is hard to conceive of the state of mind
of a writer who would try to convey that one attendant damsel
with the Damsel of the Cart meant Historical Record, while her
companion meant History in General (Carman, 52 n.). What

---

[48] The most direct and helpful approach to this point that I know is in the
work of P. Alpers, in a forthcoming book and in *Studies in English Literature*
(1962). By analysis of Spenser's scenes (rather than as here by attention to
allegory as it had historically developed), he seems to me to take the strength
out of this old bugbear of the sacrifice of story-to-allegory and vice versa. See
n. 1 above.

experience shook him into a realization of this distinction, and supposing it struck him as vitally worth conveyance, would he have undertaken through a story in a romance to make this difference spring out upon us as the real and significant meaning? Open to the same objection, that it is all but impossible to imagine and write a story thus, is criticism which draws the noose of an implied scheme of moral (rather than doctrinal) meanings extremely tight. Some recent explanations of scenes in Spenser require page upon multiplied page of re-phrased argument, re-written conversations, unwritten soliloquies added to make complicated motives seem plausible, supposed ejaculations, speeches translated into the tone necessary for the claimed meaning to be there—in short, the use of paraphrase to a degree never before attempted in any criticism.[49] We are often presented with entire sections that are re-worded—a substitute version of the *Faerie Queene* that shows us what it means as the original could not.

To be sure, the original has not presented readers with an absolutely clear meaning, or so it may seem as we observe the confusion of three or four incompatible interpretations in a given year for some puzzling incident, such as Amoret tortured by Busyrane. Some are moved to repine that Spenser did not use

[49] It is ironic that this critical method has overgrown the poem, like a sort of carpet of succulents, as an outcome of the appeal to regard the "poem as poem." With the best will in the world, writers convinced of a meaning will paraphrase agreeably to their interpretation, and one's first objection is to the labor involved in ceaseless check of these "real readings" over against actual text. The book by Berger (see n. 28 above), and A. C. Hamilton's *Structure of Allegory in the Faerie Queene* (Oxford, 1961)—to say nothing of numerous recent articles up and down the field—seem to me to make Spenser's understanding of his own poem laborious beyond what is credible, and to err in some of the ways noted in this chapter. Hamilton leans toward a more churchly Spenser, but both books (it seems to me) over-Christianize Spenser. We are grateful to Hamilton for insisting that readers not throw out the literal sense and substitute the allegory (an insistence characterizing mediaeval allegorical theory since Augustine). But we find less than sufficient warrant for many meanings supposedly conveyed: the Dragon battle of Book 1 as "imitating" the Harrowing of Hell; the vision of false Una as parodying Arthur's vision of the Faerie Queen; Fradubio's story as a "classical" version of the Fall; squared bricks (Bk.i.iv) reminding us of Egypt, mortar of Ezekiel; Aesculapius a false Christ, Arthur as a true Aesculapius, a sort of Christ; Red Crosse in the dungeon "the figure of Christ" as no reader "can fail to see."

the device which characterizes the two grail romances which are the pre-eminent exemplars of the allegorical romance—interpreters within the work. One can sympathize with those who long for two or three *Queste*-like hermits who could be trusted to give us what the author thought he had signified in this or that character or revived myth. He has used various other devices, none foolproof. He names Despair—but names are to be mistrusted as being only the very grossest hint of what abstractions mean. This is shown in a small way in the Masque of Cupid, where the pleasure lies in the refinement of psychological definition, and thereupon in our elaborated understanding of what love is and includes a process in which the names assist but little. There seem to be many proofs that earlier eras were less convinced than ours that they knew what things were when they had ticketed them. Much more reliable than naming is the exhibited transformation of Malbecco into a universal. It is the story, not the final naming, which uncovers to us the radical nature of that perverted fury to possess and use and engulf, which must also be part of a presentation of love's works; Spenser had pointed to it time and again when he examined "chastity," and he is not afraid to introduce both ambiguities and humor into his portrayal of the condoned form of it in a Britomart, who has to learn what things are by experiencing them in many forms, as the other questers do. The use of myths or ancient images whose allegorical meanings had become like a known language of figures is not as reliable as the exegete-within-the-work, but it can be trusted if we attend to the same safeguards I have mentioned touching overreading of Christian significances. Classical images may not be trusted to "mean" whatever we find in Comes or Sandys unless Spenser indicates this, and the tone, feeling of scenes and decorum of the whole are the ways he takes to limit or steer our interpretations, while hot pursuit of equivalents leads to exactly the same errors.

One other safeguard, of which there is least awareness, is to watch the conventions of the romance genre he chose to write in. While these provide us with no laws, they do determine probabilities. We cannot read many romances without coming to expect that an author will not use deserted and wasted kingdoms, light, otherworld imagery, contrasts of black and white, certain animals, in entire innocence. But these meanings are not

stable, and we learn also that we may expect an author to confirm his double meanings if he has any. Perhaps most useful is
the sense we develop, through reading, of what does and does not
call for interpretation. We learn, as it were, not to erect theories
of deep Trinitarian meaning upon the fact that a concerto has three
movements not four.

The criteria for perceiving which details bear extraordinary
meaning are not those of nineteenth- or twentieth-century naturalistic fiction. Guyon faints in Bk. II.vii.66 as he comes into the
world of men again from his otherworld journey; if we are
to read this as a puzzle and erect interpretations upon it, Spenser
must indicate to us that he means it so. For faints are standard
behavior for heroes of romances. Lancelot faints of dismay when
he must keep his irrational vow to avenge the Wooded knight
by fighting his host (also a test, a crux, a hidden trial to face);
Agravain and Gawain both faint when they discover each other's
identity; King Ban faints at the realization of the loss of his son's
heritage as he looks back at his castle; Arthur faints in "triste apprehension" when the messenger comes to his court with news
of Gawain. Urban, in the Didot *Perceval*, faints when he hears
the warning voice of his damsel (clearly a fée and otherworld
lover), and Arthur, hearing of Gawain's death, faints more than
fifteen times with anger and sorrow.

On the other hand, by the repeated states of trance-like un-
consciousness, the nature of Lancelot's feeling for Guenevere is
tacitly identified for us. We should make very odd judgments
of Lancelot's character if we did not know that we're to expect
this special condition, as surely as we expect someone to faint who
has been in actual and continued contact with the supernatural
world; if evil is intimated, exhaustion and shock are the usual
reactions displayed to crossing that threshold. This safeguard
against overreading, of expecting the conventions of the genre,
is not the less important for being primarily preventive and
cautionary; but for example, given a romance name for a romance hero as common as Guyon (Guy of Warwick, an important tie for Spenser, Guiron le courtois, and the various Gaions,
Guidans, Guires, and Guionces of Arthurian tales), we might
be nearer the truth if we saw in St. Ambrose's river, Gihon,
not a reason for Spenser's calling his temperate knight Guyon,
and if we saw in the *Legenda Aurea*'s wrestler *geon* not an explanation

of a wrestling motif (if it be there)—but rather quite simply two additional associations which would surely have pleased Spenser.[50]

It seems probable that without the development of romances written to be read pleasurably, but nonetheless seriously as allegory, we should not have had the peculiar combination Spenser has contributed to English letters—readily as we admit that the *Faerie Queene* is far more properly described as "a Renaissance poem" than as "a belated mediaeval romance." The actual belated mediaeval romances, in the period just before Spenser, have some of the very faults we have chided critics for attributing to better pieces where they do not occur—the strings of rather thoughtless equivalents, the idea in a fiction which is imposed not inherent. We find Alain Chartier, good king René, Olivier de la Marche, allegorizing in this fashion, though such works luckily are not represented on the English scene by many besides Hawes. But it is difficult to imagine that Spenser's obvious return to the excellences of the tradition in its high days was based on these abuses. The point inclines us to think he must have read enough earlier mediaeval romance-allegories that "needes he mought be sunburnt" walking in the sun, in this as in his language. Somehow, at any rate, Spenser was able to make allegory function as it did in the days of it highest development, and to create almost the sole truly powerful secular allegorical work.

Thorough, sincere, and devoted Christian as he was, it is noteworthy that he did not choose to write Christological allegory into his romance; in this I think him firmly typical, for I do not believe Shakespeare or most contemporaries did either, modern interpreters to the contrary. It is all the more interesting that the one romance we possess which is a great artistic triumph, the *Queste*, is a strict allegory designed to convey Christian doctrine and Christian mysteries and a figure for Christ under cover of de-

---

[50] These situations may be found in Sommer, III, 198, 316, 13; Chrétien's (1530) *Perceval* (Hilka, p. 614); Didot *Perceval*, ed. Roach, pp. 199, 275. The extreme elaboration of Guyon's faint used to interpret Book II may be found in chs. 1 and 2, "The Hero Faints" and "Before and After the Faint," in Berger's *Allegorical Temper* (New Haven, 1957). The references to "The River Guyon" and to "Guyon the Wrestler" are respectively to A. D. S. Fowler in *MLN*, vol. 75 (1960), 289-92 and S. Snyder in *RN*, vol. 14 (1961), 249-52.

lightful fable. I believe Spenser to have read the *Queste*, and of course Malory's shorter version of it, but it would be treated here even if he had never seen it, for it is a great and beautiful example of an Arthurian romance allegorized, and teaches us more than any other work about allegory as a *literary* mode, insofar as romances could pass this down.[51]

I wish to make so serious an example of the *Queste* that I shall give first the data on its accessibility. "Tradition" is more frequently invoked of late years than one could have predicted in the days of revolt, but our faith in the power of traditions or in old mediaeval habits still obtaining must yet depend largely on whether or not there were means of carrying them down. But one work of genius outranks a dozen mediocre pieces. The originality and interest of the literary use of allegory by this author would not be seriously obscured by the aspect inimical to Protestant readers—the Cistercian monastic ideal of the hero's chaste devotion to God. The Eucharistic symbolism and the doctrine of grace were as good doctrine to Anglicans as to Romans, and Spenser in particular used Christian symbolism with respect for ritual and for the elaborations of mediaeval devotional literature.[52] One cannot believe that the beauty and interest of the

[51] After many years of silence, two books have appeared which consider the *Queste* as a work of literary art, and one (Arthos, *On the Poetry of Spenser and the Form of the Romances*; see above n. 1) treats of its structure and setting with Spenser in mind. But our differences are sufficient, and therefore I have left my text as it was. The other book is a study of the single romance, Frederick Locke, *The Quest for the Holy Grail*, Stanford Studies, in language and literature, 21 (1960). It perhaps overdoes the emphasis on "ritual pattern," Pentecost, liturgical connections, and at the beginning uses modern approaches which are of little relevance to our concerns, but it will be found informative touching the plot and management of the piece and touching Christian allegory generally. Much though not all of the first emphasis would be lost upon the sixteenth-century non-clerical reader. Cross references to the discussion here did not seem fruitful. I have simply taken the precaution of not reading remarks on symbolism in the *Queste* by my student and friend Helen Hennessy, "The Uniting of Romance and Allegory in *La Queste del Saint Graal*," Boston University Studies in English, vol. 4 (1961), 189-201. Since her introduction to the material was through my own Harvard seminar of 1956-57, we might overlap unavoidably.

[52] Though it may have gone too far, the re-capture of Spenser from the ranks of the Calvinists and his return to a more ordinary and unobtrusive place among the usual Anglicans of his decades, surely corrected errors. There is no

easily accessible *Queste* passed unnoted by those who were interested in successful use of the figure of allegory in romance.

The sixteenth-century man interested in romances of Arthur's
court could read the printed *Queste* in six places where I have
confirmed its fullness and its comparableness to our present text,
with a pretty certain seventh. He could also read in five editions an
English abridgment (Malory's) that would have taught him virtually the same lessons about reading a great allegory. He could
read two editions of a French abridgment that would deprive him
of many of these lessons and also of the extreme artistic pleasure of
watching the *Queste*'s author's handling of character in Lancelot
and in Perceval, though it would give him Galahad's story and the
scheme and great scenes of the allegory as it touches Galahad.

I dispose of the last-mentioned first and quickly: the strenuously
abridged *Queste* as it appears in the 1516 and 1523 editions of
Perlesvaus,[53] though interest-provoking comparisons were thus
made convenient, would only whet the appetite of an interested
reader and send him to the several accessible versions of the whole
romance. Although the beginning is similar (the perilous seat
at the Round Table, the sword-story, the tomb, Meliant and his
wrong path and his stolen crown), the virtual confining of the
story to Galahad's adventures means losing the richness and
variety of the allegorical pattern, for we lose the other questers
(Lancelot, Bohort, Perceval) with their different relation to the
central religious mystery, and problem (of grace). With the loss
of Lancelot, we lose our own allegorical appearance in the story;
at least the Everyman or Adam figura which is so powerfully
presented in Lancelot will seem to many a reader to cover his

---

cause at all for astonishment at the imagery of Bk. i.x. See ch. 2 above on some
of these matters and for citations, e.g. to the work of V. Whitaker which marks
the turn away from the pronounced stress on Calvinism led by Padelford (not
always with real evidence). The work of A. S. P. Woodhouse has emphasized
fundamental Christian doctrines more than sectarian differences.

[53] These are virtually the same text; see A. B. Swanson's *Study* cited in n. 40
above; the *Queste* text is not an important concern of Swanson's study, but
the similarity he notes obtains also for the *Queste* section of the two books. These
would still introduce a Renaissance reader to a revealing example of mediaeval
strict allegory used in reading secular romance materials, but the extent of the
abridgment may be loosely seen in the fact that it occupies only nineteen and
a half leaves, ff. 213-31, though largish and crowded (sgg. QQi to TTvi *in both*
editions).

case, though we have all known Percevals as well. But when
the seeming capacity of this allegory to cover all the varieties of
human response is lost by this attempt to isolate and present the
single unified story and significance of Galahad, the great scenes
too are bereft of their clear symbolic force. The incidents on the
ship or the final mystical triumph and death of Galahad lose
some of the power they had to carry timeless and universal religious meanings through a perfect knight who is a figure for
Christ.

Nothing could show more surely the value of the structural
device of entrelacement, for the presented parts, though scarcely
curtailed, do not read as they seemed to when we met them in
the uncut romance; they stagger under the weight of such powerful and important significances, making interpretations which
seemed natural and easy appear to be artificial or surprising
claims, or mere dead statements. The Christological allegory is
there to teach tact and reserve, the senefiance of major figures
is not omitted or changed—but the burden is heavy when we are
not slowly trained to expect these significances by the simpler
figurative action of less fully symbolical characters, other questers. There is at least a doubt whether this text of 1516 or 1523
would convey the meanings with conviction through the symbols;
a reader might emerge merely knowing what was represented,
whereas in the *Queste* proper he experiences the discovery of
something not represented but presented. This kind of possible
result shows the folly of our attention solely to plot.

The other appearances of the *Queste* are, of course, the important ones. Though not precisely the text as in manuscript, and
therefore not quite the *Queste* we all read either in Pauphilet's
edition or Sommer's Vulgate Cycle (vol. VI), they seem to me so
closely similar, and identical in such ways, that the same effects
we comment upon must have been felt. Specifically and most to
the point, the allegory would have been apprehended with the
excitement and tension we feel reading our better editions. There
were two chances to read the *Queste* in Vérard books of 1494, and
a third in 1504.[54] In each case the *Queste* appears as an ordinary

---

[54] The date is usually given: "1494"-[1504], 3 vols. It goes without saying that there are bibliographical complexities, which must here be deliberately
passed by, concerning almost every text I use. I ignore them with determination, except when the points at issue for us are affected. I generally cite refer-

continuation of the prose *Lancelot*—a "4th Part," or a portion sandwiched between the 3rd Part of the *Lancelot* and the *Mort Artu*, with rubrics continuing without break through the entire sandwich. It is not necessary to describe the varieties of separate title pages, etc.; but others will be saved from confusions if we merely note that the *Queste* appears in ff. 94v-165r of three editions: Vérard's of 30 April 1494; Vérard's of 1 July and n.d. 1494; Vérard's of 1504.[55] It had already appeared in the second volume (Dupré, 16 September 1488) of a Paris continuation of a Rouen edition of 1488. Sommer gives references to this edition (sgg. Q6-cc6).

These four editions are in handsome folio volumes, not too splendid for ordinary ownership but very far from the chapbooks we have come to think of as preserving the romances for later readers. The three smaller, neat volumes of 1513 have the *Queste* in vol. III, folios 81r-143r, and it appears on the same pages, same signatures, in an edition of 15 December 1520. Yet another edition, of 1533 (Le Noir Petit) shows the same rubrics and same divisions, familiar since 1494 at least, though it occupies different folios—65v to 115v. These last are the same folios as those cited in a 1526 edition noted by Sommer but which I have not seen.[56]

---

ences (if there are any) or identifications which will carry a student into the bibliographical problems which exist, but pass them by in silence unless they touch accessibility or would substantially affect the romance being read. Purely formal differences can of course *substantially* affect works of art. But some small differences are of crucial importance; a point may quite lose its validity if condensation between editions would concern it. On the other hand, I may speak of books which barely resemble each other bibliographically as "similar," if their presentation of a text would similarly affect readers. Fortunately, I think, differences in illustration—when there are any—would have next to no influence when it comes to our grasp of the allegory or of the story. Thus we are spared the careful description of those differentiations (even rather fully illuminated manuscripts do not assist our allegorical reading).

[55] These volumes are in each case vol. III (new signatures), generally called "vol. III of *Lancelot du Lac*," of a body of text occupying Sommer's edited vols. III-VI and called by him *Lancelot de Lac* (vols. III, IV, V), *Queste, Mort Artu* (both involve VI). They are generally therefore listed under *Lancelot*. I give the British Museum press numbers since there are difficulties of identification: of the "true April 1494," *G.10861*; of the second, July 1494, *IC 41161*; of the early sixteenth-century edition usually dated as in n. 54, *C.39.k.2*.

[56] See Sommer's Table of Manuscripts which gives folios occupied by the

It is apparent that there can have been little difficulty in coming upon the *Queste del saint Graal* in effective and moving form. Its excellence had something to do with its popularity; only the early part of the prose *Lancelot* equals it in either attribute. The two are printed together, with the addition of the *Mort Artu*, whose artistic value has always been acknowledged, in all these cited full forms, although on the face of it one would have thought this kind of allegory out of line with the taste of 1520 or 1533. Touching the tastes of English readers of the 1550's to '80's, we not only remember a characteristic time lag but a real revival of interest, as well as antiquarian and patriotic motives added to those of the anticipated French audience, for these many reprints. It would be impossible to believe that any educated Englishman of these dates would make an affair out of reading a French romance (and of course we know otherwise about Spenser from his youthful translations), but in this case we bring up the English translation because it was a great work of art in its own right. This is a judgment of Malory which Spenser could make as well as we, and we should never have had the insolence to suppose him incapable of it but for most narrow and unliterary conceptions of sources and influences.

I do not see how a man of Spenser's interests, with his particular plans for a long poem, could avoid reading a copy of Malory's *Morte D'arthur*, whether he picked up a recent one from 1557, or one that would be treasured, like the de Worde of 1529 (by patriots like Drayton who could put Wynkyn de Worde in an eclogue). Earlier editions, Caxton's of 1485, de Worde's of 1498,

---

Queste in a few of the printed versions, in his vol. I, p. xxxi. The Bodleian has the unfoliated 1488 edition but a more convenient 1533 edition; see under *Arthur*. I have checked samplings in all editions seen and have tried to check widely enough to avoid the insidious error of assuming Elizabethan familiarity with the materials and tools of present-day graduate schools. But obviously eight or ten rare texts could not be got at for comparison on each detail among many noted; though nothing is allowed to depend on such untested evidence, it must be noted that the state of our studies makes this task very difficult. I repeat this previously mentioned point because we are here thrust into investigations which could be better if the many dissertations, studies of changes in redactions, comparisons of texts, which ought to be done, existed at all. The problems are critical and aesthetic, but the close work involved apparently repels students. Meanwhile, the transition from manuscript to print is veiled in frustrating obscurity, even for well-edited mediaeval texts.

were read out of existence, though when East put out another in the early '80's (perhaps 1585), he used the two sixteenth-century ones.[57] When another was put on sale in 1634, a most agreeable volume, Stanby used East. I do not intend to enter the perhaps largely unnecessary arguments which have been raised by Vinaver's comparisons of the French and English *Queste* (Malory's Books XIII to XVII), since the high artistry of both is admitted, the power of the allegory is clear and astonishing in either, and I should find it hard to believe that Spenser did not know both. Since our fundamental purpose is to see what kind of allegorical reading one would give this work, and Malory requires much the same kind (though we are less subtly directed to it), we may as well use for exemplification here the completer form. This romance is the best school for allegorists (readers or writers) in secular letters, until the *Faerie Queene*; it can be more consistently successful because it can remain (unlike the *Faerie Queene*) within the purposes and themes of that strict religious allegory, developed in the Middle Ages, out of which the only great secular uses of allegory were born. The last work to show some traces of this unification is the *Faerie Queene*, and even if Spenser did not learn it from the *Queste*, we can learn from it how to read him.

It is such a romance as no sixteenth-century Englishman could have written. This is not because its basic doctrinal ideas were inimical to the later men, or rather, to those who were articulate as poets; the ideas about grace, about man's relation to the divine, about human sin and salvation, are those of general Christian doctrine. They are so wisely kept large in outline, or symbolic in representation, by the mediaeval author, that Elizabethan Christians like modern ones would believe in the poem's truth as they read without the constant intrusion of a sectarian reservation or an historical excuse to help along that needed state of belief which literature requires. It is typical that the work's greatest student—

[57] These are conveniently listed in Vinaver, *Works*, III, 1651. The dignified volume of 1634, or East's in the '80's, reminds us that these romances expected no audience of ignorant Rafes and scornful Aschams, much as does the equally well-mannered edition of Lord Berners' *Huon* that came out in 1601 ("the 3rd time imprinted"), with modernizations that change the effect very little; they are geared to the idealization of chivalry that marked the time.

Pauphilet—asks at length and does not answer in so many words the question "what is the Graal?"[58]

The great developing symbols, Arthurian quest-situation and Grail and Ship and Adam-figure, and land made waste through hybris, are all common inheritances elaborated; they are based on a common fund of scriptural and legendary materials, and all are so fully symbolic that their use in the work securely evades the deep differences between thirteenth-century Cistercian and sixteenth-century Anglican conceptions. The one idea operative as a plot motif which the later Christian would find unacceptable is the pronounced stress throughout on celibacy, on virginity in two questers and chastity in another (the distinction is made by the author). This stress does not tie the story irrevocably to its century and its author's monastic sympathies because chastity is conceived of as a choice of the highest love, here fidelity to God; even Lancelot's idolatrous love serves to speak against not only lust but all men's inveterate propensity to *all* kinds of sins. It rather symbolizes than reports what is fatally amiss. The inflexibility which would read the Bower of Bliss as solely about lechery has the same narrowing effect on the *Queste*; though its author's definitions are narrow, his allegorical method releases us from sharing them so literally, and to overstress the sexual morality is to miss this. Somewhere Spenser learned this power of the metaphorical dimension of allegory to give us this freedom—this sharing of beliefs about values and goods the while we quite differ as to the actual conduct used to exemplify them. We could no more agree with the Elizabethan Englishman than could he with the mediaeval Cistercian, but we agree with both poets.

An example of where Spenser fails is in the Anabaptist ("communist") giant of Book V; for here we are lashed to the particular. The furniture of hermitages and abbeys and taking oaths by the Virgin and confessionals and cross-signings would also not be the Elizabethans' choice, but that an educated one felt his own

[58] Not only Pauphilet's edition (Paris, 1923) is essential, but his *Études sur la Queste del saint graal* (Paris, 1921) is most valuable; citations of later work may be found in Frappier's article on the Vulgate Cycle in *Arthurian Literature in the Middle Ages*, ed. R. S. Loomis (Oxford, 1959); see Woledge, No. 96. W. W. Comfort, *The Quest of the Holy Grail* (Everyman, 1913), translates from Pauphilet. Sample comparisons of these two with the 1533 edition indicate that our present editions do not really mislead us as to the allegory a Renaissance reader would meet.

English history in these much as he felt it in fortified castles and armed knights seems true against what we know of the sixteenth-century revivals. Yet no Elizabethan we now know well could have written so sustained a piece of Christological allegory, with attention so fixed upon an order of reality to which the one we move in is subservient, and handling great mystical scenes and conceptions with so delicate a touch.

After all, few other mediaeval writers wrote such a work either. Its singularity, residing in the excellence with which it does what was common, makes it all the more valuable for teaching us through experience some of the habits of Christian allegory that have become alien to more and more people, and were already alien to some sixteenth-century persons. For the *Queste* seems to me the most imaginative single literary work compelling us to constant and profound allegorical reading. It cannot be read otherwise. Expositors within the work tell us the meanings of what we have seen, an incomparably trustworthy check upon our fancies and errors. But we do not wait for these assistances, to take in significances; we are able very soon to take what must have been the mediaeval reader's own pleasure in the hermits' expositions: corroboration of what we thought, a second and un-assailable confirmation of meanings, suggestions, connections, that we had felt and seen already through the action. The combination which effects this is the use of fully traditional Christian ideas and doctrines, added to the writer's skill in lighting up salient details which commonly hint at extra meaning—symbolic animals, morally weighted choices of paths to take or persons to rescue, actions famously proud, or humble, or concupiscent. But our obedience to indications of meaning would not be possible ex-cept for one extreme merit in the piece. Its author creates human characters which show such psychological niceties and depths that by leaps of sympathy we enter into the meanings of experience as they learned them through the action of their stories. These mean-ings are allegorically read, by us as by them. We merely follow.

The *Queste* author's fiction moves as easily among religious mysteries as among natural events; in fact, the second are the first. We are aware of this very early; at the latest, we realize it when the old man in white enters Arthur's court with a blessing, brings the nameless young man whom he refuses to identify, save that he is of the lineage of David and Joseph of Arimathea, and then is gone no man knows how. But even before this, a practiced eye detects hidden significances to come—in Lancelot's knowledge that he dares not touch the "best knight's" sword in the stone in the river, and that they will all be punished if they try to draw it, or in the clarity and irony with which Gawain's motive in trying to draw the sword (to please his uncle, Arthur) is shown to be that of the courtoisie terriene, which we sadly observe binding even this knight's admirable actions irrevocably to our blind, well-meaning mortal world. We are not told who the old man "is," and we are not supposed to scratch for something for him to equal or something for the sword to represent; at least this is not the mediaeval author's notion of what allegory requires, for he continually leaves certain kinds of purports unstated. We later perceive them to be unstatable. These meanings have a different kind of clarity which is progressive and retroactive. The sense of the significant informing the ordinary is common; what is unusual is the artistry with which the allegory grows, unified and single, as leaf is laid upon leaf in the mere telling of a tale not so different from others.

Despite this similarity to all quest-romances, the allegory is persistently that kind which fits the ancient definitions and uses guiding us in allegorical reading of scripture. We learn this slowly. Yet the *Queste* is not a treatise but a work of literary imagination and a fiction; though devout, it is secular as no doctrinal exposition or theological treatise is. This makes it helpful to us in our attempt to see whether strict allegory could ever be secularized, and whether depths and extensions of meaning in a truly secular work like the *Faerie Queene* bear some relation to the powers of strict allegory. For strict allegory functioned (and of course does in the *Queste*) to illumine questions that are basically of religious import. Perhaps such images always assume a substructure of religious belief, but they deal with such large simple profundities at so fundamental a level that they are not only in all religions but can make use of symbolisms that are not solely Christian or Jewish or Celtic or Greek. Only very slowly do we realize what these large meanings are. We turn and come at things from many sides before we see how the stories are opened to the light if we relate the Grail these men seek to ideas about God's grace. This is how we slowly begin, also, to think of Arthur's work as the work of grace.

A curious excitement and suspense is felt by a reader of the *Queste* which grows in tension so that the later huge images (of the Ship, with the Tree of three colors, and Solomon's Bed, or the final and fully mystical Grail appearances) are read with a breathless sense of anticipations about to be fulfilled. The revelatory character is proper to the mode and is not an uncommon experience with religious allegory or with typological significances where the burgeoning parallels sometimes seem to unveil the very singleness of truth itself. But it is extremely rare in secular pieces. It is felt most strongly in the *Queste* when the tree-image seems to give new insight into the nature of guilt, the relation to it of man's power to produce new living beings (for the Tree turned green when Abed was conceived beneath it) and the power at once of love and of sacrifice or death to erase guilt, though it supplants rather than restores purity. Not any of these concepts are even mentioned, as concepts; the imagery opens out and they lie within (much vulgarized here by the attempt to state them discursively). Or it is felt when the Church-ship is elaborated by all the Solomon-imagery, with its spouse-image in the lectulus Salomoni, its altar, its sudden surprises in the fitness of the Christ-figura for Galahad. This does have its counterpart in our conscious discovering as Spenser unfolds his large final or central images, first thus revealing the *connections* of narratives left behind, so that we read meanings in actions (quite wordlessly, in the best cases, as the Temple of Venus seems to flash light backward upon the meaning of the discords and concords of the previous part of Book IV). But chiefly it has its counterpart in the conviction we have, shared by so innumerable a crowd of readers, that we are in immediate contact with ideas of such importance (on love, on the nature of the divine, on man and nature) that they are usually part of metaphysics and religion but here are realized in images.

The strange first appearance of the Grail, filling all the court with the sweetness of grace, does differentiate this quest from others. Although Arthur's grieved foreboding, his sleepless night and his weeping colloquy at dawn as he foresees the end of his Round Table fellowship hint at something the knights are to learn about the vanity of earthly chivalry, we do not know it yet either; we think, as Arthur does, that he fears their deaths in the quest. The suggestions of hybris in presumptuous handling of what is holy are multiplied (as in the shield with the red cross[59] which Baudemagus is wounded for carrying); the motif begins early to carry those sad implications about the human condition which make Lancelot's innocently natural attempts to do the kind or right thing—and his failure because he is so humanly self-dependent—so poignantly ironic. The worst of these, much later, is Lancelot's instinctive attempt to help the priest, when the likeness of a man appeared at the elevation of the mass; his faint, and trance of twenty-four days, are just, but we mourn. By this time (Malory, Bk. XVII, ch. 15), we know what these things say about us and our pride, but earlier we learn only as the characters do.

Sometimes we are encouraged to read the tissue of events morally. We watch Melians taking the left-hand way despite the warning written on the cross by the parting, his concupiscent seizing of the crown in the forest, his almost fatal wounding. We grasp, before the old monk explains it, that his stubbornness came from the enemy's "dart of pride," which would court danger to display the valor befitting a new-made knight. But phrasings and language combine with old fragments of symbolic association, suggestions which cling to "those on the left hand and on the right," those which make words more important if they are upon a cross (Christ spoke before from one). We half know that the pride of young Melians is worse than some moral flaw since he takes the voie as pecheors by deserting la voie ihesu crist, and we are not really surprised when the interpreter at the abbey says, "li escris parloit de la chevalerie celestiene & tu entendis

---

[59] It is true that we become hypersensitive to this "Red Cross Knight's" shield when, reading some rather fully illustrated manuscript, we see it as the consistent way of identifying the Christian knight on his quest of holiness; picture succeeds picture, and there is no other way to distinguish Galahad from the other questers except by this outstanding scarlet cross. The notion, and the graphic form of it, are both so conventional that one is certain they are derivative, not invented, in Book 1 of the *Faerie Queene*. What seems so especially perceptive of Spenser is that his metaphor is equally hospitable to another reference—the ordinary soldier in Elizabeth's Protestant forces in Ireland who was commanded to sew a red cross upon his uniform for identification and never to appear without it. The unity of the ideas, historical and contemporary, is like Spenser and is precisely what the figure allegory does best; but we have to go back some years to find it as well done, with details falling into their places by congruity not by contrivance. The present reference is to Sommer, vi, p. 22; the Melian story following is pp. 30-33.

de la seculer" ("terrienne" in 1533). There are a very great many such small paths which we follow into the slow discovery of what the two chivalries mean in a human life.

The first aventure of Galahad only begins to open to us the mystery of what he will image. When he opens the tomb, recognizes the voice of the demon as that of "the enemy" (who recognizes and quails before him) and removes the usurping body, we see that his powers are Christ-like. But he is said by the holy man to be "like to" Christ, chosen above others to carry on the delivery of God's people, make truth manifest, keep men from false religion—"et *cele similitude* que li peres envoia a son fil en terre por delivrer son pueple est ore renovelee" (a form and an idea that are in the early editions, but cut by Malory [XIII.12], who withdraws from the typological, but whose reserve is nonetheless a more truly allegorical reading than the present-day careless equations with Christ). We might not have been conscious of a reference to the image of Old Law and New, in the body which has stolen into the place prepared for the body of the faithful. But once enlightened by the exegete in the story, the preudom who has entered religion, we become alert to it before it is explained—in the elder sister who usurps her younger sister's rights, vindicated by Bohort, in the complaint of the woman on the serpent who accuses Perceval of leaving his first allegiance and who will grant the younger woman on the lion no rights.

This is not to say that we learn a language of equivalences; we do not learn to recognize a lion as Christ, all younger sisters as Ecclesia. A lion can as well be pride. And later on, Lancelot again will fall pathetically into the sin of trusting his strong arm more than his Creator when he has lions to face; they are good guardian lions who know the true quester, but they are not Christ. On the other hand, four lions conduct the white cerf who shows himself in his true form as Christ during the mass, and we see them transformed into the four evangelists seen as their signs; then all vanish through the unbroken glass of the chapel. To speak of Christ's power requires one sort of image, and we see the church carried by the lion; another is required to speak of His relation to the evangelists, and of his transformation when He conquered death by His death on the cross "la ou il fu couvers de couverture terriene" (a phrase not in the 1533 edition, but related to the stag's reputed shedding).

I am not trying to show that symbolic meanings jerk about
and reverse themselves irresponsibly, but that the method of allegory forbids one to make rigid correspondences with objects;
the writer is making a web of his connected meanings, not setting
down notions in a picture-language of translatable signs. Similarly we do not say "Old Law" the moment we glimpse a
usurper; Gamelyn's older brother kept him out of his heritage,
but there is not the slightest warrant for seeing Christ's New Law
in the young man who became Rosader. The seven usurping
brothers, from whom Galahad delivered the Castle of Maidens,
do not direct us to look for some way in which Ecclesia established by Christ can be read in this castle on the Severn. The
injunction to avoid starting out from some equation to seek a
meaning is shown as necessary when we see the author himself
explain the seven brothers as the seven sins in one context, and
yet in another deplore Gawain's action in killing them, as a wicked
murder depriving them of their chance to repent. This is not
confusion; rather, it is allegory's way of experiencing meaning
through event; Galahad and Gawain had different meanings to
learn.[60]

Galahad is still appearing to us as one "compared to" Christ,
but the boldness of the hermit's interpretation of the Castle of
Maidens as a hell from which the innocent are delivered by a
saviour who harrows hell as Christ delivered the pre-Christian
faithful, looks forward to the gradual apotheosis of Galahad.
We watch the lines of difference fall between him and the other
questers who also seek and successfully find God's grace and
see the mysteries. Returning to him periodically, and for the last
climactic mystical events, we follow with mounting excitement
the author's daring design. The step he takes is the creation of
a true type of Christ; this is like an Old Testament type but in
Christianity's future time not its past, with an artist's imaginative
fiction furnishing the literal sense, instead of history as God wrote

[60] I do not try to refer to all these scattered bits of story in Pauphilet's
edition, for such a reading would destroy meaning, but for the reader who
wishes to check a detail, I give a few locations in Sommer. It is less pathless
than other texts because it has the annoying addition of English marginal
synopses. The early Galahad adventures are *ca.* p. 28, the *cerf* mystery at p.
167, the Castle of Maidens *ca.* pp. 35-40. In Malory's telling of Christ the
hart transformed (Vinaver, iii, 998ff.), the phrases are present which stress
Christ's double nature.

it and caused it to figure forth eternal truth. This relation of complete and pure truth seen in figura is the basis for typology, and we are reading an extremely bold example of allegory strictly understood. Though Galahad is the only type, the rest of the allegories show the same relation between what *happens* and how we *read* it, and only Christian allegory in its mediaeval development can show us how this complicated relation between events and meaning ever took shape. Although truncated in Malory, and not artistically so subtle and tense, the allegorical reading does not differ in character, and the mystical sense is clear and powerful. The romance is of course entirely devout and has "that which is to be believed" as its first concern. It is immediately discerned as figuratively different from moral allegory, in any of its translations or forms.

Naturally, therefore, the relations of the Old to the New Law, fundamental to strict allegory, are much more important to the total piece than is conveyed in the smaller incidents mentioned. The great image conveying these relations is the Ship of Solomon, with its Eve-and-Virgin-Mary paradox, its problem of how to pass on the truth to men in the distant time to come and Solomon's wife's device for it, Abel's death as Christ's, and the Tree as cross, the true tree of "life." The relations of the two Laws are far more varied and profound than the contrast and condemnation expressed in lesser uses like Perceval's dream or the familiar Synagoga images. But the great central figures are so climactic and clear when they occur, with their glancing light flashed upon deep and difficult ideas, that one finds oneself very unwilling to write descriptions of them. We have so consistently stressed here the uselessness of synopses of figures, equations that belie the relation, discursive language translating symbols, deceptive paraphrases, that it seems a simple folly to provide just those where the excitement of a literary *use* of a figure is at its height. This entire chapter has at heart not the conveying of some relations by one who has seen them to others who have not, but the urging of others to read certain pieces in which relations can be seen. I will therefore simply draw back from an attempt to describe the way mystical meanings arise from all the final events of the *Queste*. In part, images of ship, tree and journey are clear and profound because of the paths we have taken on our way to them, and we are similarly brought slowly to the final appearance of the Grail and to an understanding of how Galahad is a figure of Christ. I cannot reproduce that understanding here. It is in the romance, but even *that* author had to say it in a symbol.

Here the typical romance structure, the entrelacement of numerous threads which part and rejoin, is superbly suited to the nature and ends of the work. One notes again that this element of design is not simply the laying aside of one character's story while another is taken up, common enough in any novel and often annoying despite the excuse of suspense. We do follow Lancelot's quest, then Perceval's, then Bohort's; in between we meet Hector and Gawain engaged in acts which are yet to be told in separate quests, then go back to Lancelot and encounter Galahad as he joins with these others. But the time that is lived through with one is not then re-lived through with another; another kind of progression is taking place step by following step, for we are finding out the meanings which enable us to grasp what later events really mean when at last they happen, usually in large complexes of incident involving many questers. Or there are large knots of images where several characters and the basic ideas meet and enact some superlatively important figurative action (much as in the *Faerie Queene*).

As we travel away from Galahad and Perceval with Lancelot, we come to the cross he cannot read in the dark, go into the ruined chapel, see the vision of the knight healed by the Grail, share Lancelot's inability to move, his shame and repentance and grief when the voice says he is harder than stone, bitterer than the barren fig tree, and his desperate sense of alienation at dawn when the birds' singing seems only to confirm his different and forlorn and hostile condition, his failure both merited and unfathomable. Sidewise as it were, through Lancelot's pitiful re-trials and incapacities, the telling of which surrounds the tale of Perceval's adventures on both sides, we are drawn into perceiving the image of an Adam who cannot repair his frailties, a desperate suffering Lancelot who cannot even become a quester and who is yet the father of the perfect one. That these conceptions should be stirred to life, and fed by the hermit's bitter and loving analyses and warnings, is essential for our understanding the different way similar ideas arise as we read of Perceval.

"Man" as truly as Lancelot is "Man," and Perceval's naïveté and untaught grace are moving to us in a different way, as he

stumbles through his wild and deliberately comical mishaps—
his great black horse that vanishes from under him in mid-stream
as he crosses himself out of pure fright and habit, seeing the
black water shine in the moonlight (horses lent by the devil
vanish in this wet way); his hasty thought to help the lion
menaced by the serpent because it was the more natural beast of
the two; his irrational absurd trust as he sits till the hour of nones
with his lion on the high rock, watching till a ship shall loom up;
his guilt that he should all but put himself in the power of the
enchanting lady in the pavilion on her ship, never rationalized
away as by cleverer sinners on the ground that it was sent to him
for virtue when he gave similar friendly acceptance to the over-
tures of the man whose white ship came and went in the same
inexplicable way. The incident of the lady in the pavilion we
read with a consistent and clear doubleness, seeing the devil in
her, long before Perceval does; all the details of proud beauty
disinherited and scorned, of a war against the unfair lord, of uninterrupted enmity against Him and fear of His light and envy
of His creatures and all the rest are read both narratively and allegorically. What we do not anticipate, but understand the moment it happens, is Perceval's characteristic escape. He is walking straight for the noose opened by Lucifer to every sinner, but
he so habitually commends himself to God's care before he lies
down to rest that he picks up his sword with its red cross on the
pommel—then of course we do expect this offspring of the devil
to vanish in the usual black sulphurous cloud, as sons of the
devil will up through Sansjoy and Pigwiggen.

Our insight into the humble merits and the limits of Perceval's
unthinking but trustful grace, and our recognition of his enemies
before he does, are built partly upon what we have learned with
Lancelot, and we are slowly finding out what man is like and
what the quest is. It is not success in avoiding sin. The author
does not state these things and neither should we. But we are
not wrenched from Perceval's story when we find ourselves with
Gawain, whose worldliness will explicate the nature of Perceval's
unworldliness. Moreover, at no moment in any of these stories
have we left the allegory of grace and redemption and union.
The stories have not halted an instant or swerved an inch so
as to mean something. The fact that sometimes they mean what
their actors do not see, whereas we have been prepared to catch

these elusive significances, provides a current of irony in some portions. Nothing could outdo, for subtle restraint, the scene in which Gawain leaves the hermit who would show him the true frivolity of his self-centered courtesy; never was guest more emptily polite, "I should so like to have a talk, *a vous privee-ment*," never was man pressed more unfortunately by the fact that he must not keep Hector his companion waiting. Gawain bowing deep to the Lord God, à bientôt, monsieur, while no one suffers the discourtesy of waiting for anyone, is courtoisie ter-rienne incarnate, and we are simply trusted to pick up (and do) the wild gap shown between it and the chevalerie celestienne so variously entered upon by others.[61] Gawain and Hector start back to court in disgust *that they seem to find no adventures*. One of the amusements of this kind of writing is its sudden seeming fitness in modern contexts.

We are too well educated by the time we get to Bohort's ad-ventures to make the mistakes we might if ordinary psychological verisimilitude were the object. They are painfully true, and perhaps no reader can escape the sudden shaft of admiration and emulation, felt at that eye-opening revelation of unselfregarding love when Bohort comes back to consciousness, after the agoniz-ing decision to defend himself against Lionel's anger, with the words "biaus sire diex . . . benis soies . . . qui vous mavez mon frere sauve." But unalerted, we should take exception to Bohort's choice to ignore the utterly terrible tortures of his captive brother, and save instead a damsel flying from a knight who will ravish her. It bears remembering in Spenser that images of ravishment are closely associated with the sure damnation of being ravished *by our great enemy* (when we are by rights the espoused brides of God himself, a basic Old Testament image far too ingrained to explain or uproot). At any rate, we understand but do not share the fratricidal anger of Lionel that Bohort has not rescued him, follow the fight between the brothers with anguish almost

[61] Again, the whole web is what produces the effects claimed—in the best text, Pauphilet's. But it may be convenient to locate, in Sommer, VI, the Lance-lot early adventures around pp. 41-45, Perceval's journeys, pp. 66-76, the Gawain scene at p. 116. Bohort's terrible fight with Lionel is *ca.* pp. 136-38 (slight cuts in some early prints; the damsels, p. 130); and Lancelot's last pain-ful failure, p. 180, the Ship at pp. 152-61 (critical opinion no longer supports Sommer's claim there that the *Estoire* was prior and a source for this *Queste*-image).

as great as Bohort's (for fear the primal murder will be repeated), and welcome heaven's interposition. We are similarly too wary to be shocked by Bohort's allowing the supposed damsels to throw themselves from the roof for love of him, though I do not think those most plausible fakes, or the false hermit who gives the wrong exegesis, could have been allowed in the earlier pages of the story.

It should be emphasized that the *Queste* reads quite like an ordinary romance, not like some Sunday-school pious tale. There are the lectures of the hermits, but persons interested in the interpretation of figures would feel greatly deprived at their excision. It seems to me important that the two romances which are indubitably allegorical both take care to advertise the fact by furnishing exegesis from within the text. In case Chrétien dared depend on "tradition" to make his allegorical intents quite clear, it is interesting to note that in less than half a century this daring had quite vanished.

In fact, one of the lessons to be learned from romance literature was the sure, clear difference between fictions with double meaning and fictions without. I do not much care whether the reader thinks Spenser read earlier Arthurian romances or not, though I do not think he could produce so unselfconscious a romance without knowing some, nor such good allegory without having read mediaeval allegories (in romances or not). It seems to me questionless that he deliberately decided not to follow his predecessors in writing Christological allegory, and that one reason he had for excluding the Grail was that it was inextricably tied to Eucharistic symbolism by its literary history. He is more audacious. He turns to fundamentally Christian (but not ecclesiological) uses the symbolisms which he takes from materials not customarily religious. Perhaps the earlier Grail-romance writers had done this with *their* symbolism.

I mention this with diffidence. The origin of the Grail is matter for great controversy. But whatever the important differences, perhaps scholars no longer cling to the simple position of Bruce, that sees in it no hint of anything but the chalice of the mass, and the cup that held Christ's blood at the Crucifixion. It became a Christian symbol almost as soon as it was introduced into written European literature. But it was a *symbol* before that. Different readers take differently its manifest shreds of retained meaning as a vessel of plenty. But the cup of the Cena, like the Manna of the Old Testament, was symbolic of more abundant life, of supernatural benediction and nourishment, and communion. Perhaps the deepest religious allegory is possible when ancient symbols, religiously significant already, take on a new religious significance in a new ambience. If Spenser read the Grail romances and decided not to use their symbolism for grace and redemption and sacrifice, but instead to make new Christian symbols out of myths that were old when Christ was born, he did what the allegorists of the Grail had probably done. At any rate, he learned from someone how to make secular story carry without sentimental piety some of the deepest insights Christianity claims to have into the nature of love, of grace, of consecration, and of man's capacity to be an image of the divine.

LIST OF ILLUSTRATIONS
AND SOURCES

CHAPTER THREE

CHAPTER FOUR

APPENDIX
The Virtues and Vices

Gifts of the Holy Ghost	Vice	Virtue	Beatitude
1. timor domini (drede, peur)	superbia	humilitas	blessed are the poor in spirit
2. pietas (pitee, pitié)	invidia	mansuetudo (benignity, amitié)	blessed are the meek
3. scientia (cunning, science)	ira (wrath, felonie)	equité (temperance, discretion, measure)	blessed are they that mourn
4. fortitudo (strength, force)	accidia (paresse)	prowess	blessed are they that hunger and thirst
5. consilium (counsel)	avaritia (covetise)	misericorde (largesse, mercy)	blessed are the merciful
6. intellectus (understondyng, intelligence)	luxuria or gula	chastity	blessed are the clean of heart
7. sapientia (wisdom)	luxuria or gula	sobrietas	blessed are the peacemakers

CICERO	MACROBIUS	GUILLAUME DE CONCHES	ALANUS DE INSULIS

P R U D E N C E

(1)	(1)	(1)	(1)
memoria	ratio	providentia	intellectus
intelligentia	intellectus	circumspectio	ratio
providentia	circumspectio	cautio	providentia
	providentia	docilitas	circumspectio
	docilitas		docilitas
	cautio		cautio

T E M P E R A N T I A

(4)	(3)	(4)	(4)
continentia	modestia	modestia	continentia
clementia	verecundia	verecundia	castitas
modestia	abstinentia	abstinentia	pudicitia
	castitas	honestas	sobrietas
	honestas	moderantia	parcitas
	moderatio	parcitas	moderantia
	parcitas	sobrietas	honestas
	sobrietas	pudicitia	abstinentia
	pudicitia		verecundia
			modestia

F O R T I T U D E

(3)	(2)	(3)	(3)
magnificentia	magnanimitas	magnanimitas	magnanimitas
fidentia	fiducia	fiducia	fiducia
patientia	securitas	securitas	securitas
perseverantia	magnificentia	magnificentia	magnificentia
	constantia	constantia	constantia
	tolerantia	patientia	firmitas
	firmitas		patientia
			perseverantia
			longanimitas
			humilitas

J U S T I C E

(2)	(4)	(2)	(2)
religio	innocentia	severitas	religio
pietas	amicitia	liberalitas	pietas
gratia	concordia	religio	severitas
vindicatio	pietas	pietas	vindicta
observantia	religio	innocentia	innocentia
veritas	affectus	amicitia	gratia
	humanitas	reverentia	reverentia
		concordia	misericordia
		misericordia	concordia

INDEX

VIRTUES AND VICES, *cont.*

Idleness, 202

Impatience, 184

Innocentia, 68

Intemperance, 229

Ire (Ira), *see* VIRTUES AND VICES, Wrath

ius suum, 128

Justice (Justitia), 49, 66ff, 67n, 69, 74, 77, 78, 83, 116, 127, 128, 358, 364

Labor, 174. *See also* VIRTUES AND VICES, Fortitude

Largesse (Largitas), 67, 80, 125, 184

Lechery (Luxury, Luxuria), 119, 176, 183, 211, 368n

Liberality (Liberalitas), 67, 128, 184

Love, 184, 369

Luxury (Luxuria), *see* VIRTUES AND VICES, Lechery

Magnanimity (Magnanimitas), 60, 66, 74, 82, 83, 98

Magnificence (Magnificentia), 52, 57ff, 60, 77, 79, 82, 82n, 98, 99, 105, 107, 119, 132, 133, 143, 351, 352n, 358. *See also* VIRTUES AND VICES, Perseverance

Mansuetude, 184

Memory, 170

Mercy, 67n, 100, 101, 187n. *See also* Mercy, Seven Acts of

Misericordia, 67, 68, 128, 184, 187, 187n, 298

Moderation, 74

Nobility, 43-44, 49, 52

Obedience (Obedientia), 68, 196

Paresse, 174. *See also* VIRTUES AND VICES, Fortitude

Patience (Patientia), 59, 60, 74, 96, 166. *See also* VIRTUES AND VICES, Fortitude

Penance, 180, 188, 192, 196, 207

Perseverance (Perseverantia), 58, 59, 99, 166, 289. *See also* VIRTUES AND VICES, Fortitude

Peur, 323

Pietas, 68, 116, 128, 129, 182, 184. *See also* GIFTS, Pietas

Pité (Pitié), 298, 323

Poverty, 196, 197

Pride, 36, 38, 59, 106, 108n, 119, 121f, 175, 176, 179, 182, 183, 184, 188, 188n, 192, 195, 206, 229

Prowess (Prouesse), 42, 57. *See also* VIRTUES AND VICES, Fortitude

Prudence, 63ff, 69, 71, 74, 94, 127, 234

Ravin, 184

Reason, 49, 63

Religio, 67, 68

Reverentia, 68

righteousness, 77, 127

Sanctitas, 68

schema, 81

Securitas, 60, 69, 82, 82n, 98

Severitas, 67

Simony, 184

Sloth (Accidia, Tristess), 84, 97, 133, 190, 195, 206, 207, 209, 322

Sobrietas (Sobrieté), 101, 119, 131

Study, 196

Sufferance, 60. *See also* VIRTUES AND VICES, Fortitude

Temperance, 31, 33, 40, 49, 50n, 65ff, 69, 71, 77, 78, 78n, 94, 114n, 116, 127, 131, 133n, 140, 167, 183n, 287, 366, 367

Tolerantia, 60

Tribulation, 186, 187n

Tristess, *see* VIRTUES AND VICES, Sloth

Troth, 125

Truth, 67n, 120f, 127

untroth, 38, 123

Usury, 184

Vainglory, 59, 108n, 119n, 120. *See also* VIRTUES AND VICES, Pride

Veneratio, 68

Vilenie, 192

Virginity (Virginitas), 50n, 119, 184, 368n

Voluptas (Volupté), 33, 251

Wrath (Ire, Ira), 60, 69, 96, 106, 119, 140, 163n, 176, 183

Youth, 187n

virtues, classical vs. Christian, 76f

Virtues, four Cardinal, 57-69ff, 69, 81, 114, 116, 127. *See* individually under VIRTUES AND VICES

virtues, garden of, in heart, 102ff, 108ff

virtues, new iconography of, 63, 71, 114, 166